WISDEN ON
YORKSHIRE
AN ANTHOLOGY

WISDEN ON
YORKSHIRE
AN ANTHOLOGY

EDITED BY DUNCAN HAMILTON

Published in the UK in 2011 by
John Wisden & Co
An imprint of A&C Black Publishers Ltd
36 Soho Square, London W1D 3QY
www.wisden.com
www.acblack.com

ISBN 978 14081 24628

A CIP catalogue record for this book is available from the British Library.
Cover photograph © Press Association Images
Commissioned by Charlotte Atyeo
Edited by Rebecca Senior
Designed by Joc Lucas

This book is produced using paper that is made from wood grown in managed, sustainable
forests. It is natural, renewable and recyclable. The logging and manufacturing processes conform
to the environmental regulations of the country of origin.

Typeset in 10¼pt on 13 Minion by Saxon Graphics Ltd, Derby

Printed and bound in the UK by MPG Books

To Anthony George Nicholson,
1938–85.
With grateful thanks for a
memory of summer
from long ago.

Contents

List of Illustrations

Introduction:
Bloody good bowler,
bloody good man

I begin with a confession. I wasn't born in Yorkshire. I am an outsider, still to qualify for 'nationality' and 'passport' status. I grew up just south of Nottingham, a shilling bus ride from Trent Bridge.

My view of Yorkshire was shaped through J. M. Kilburn's *Thanks to Cricket* – time and again I took it out of the village library – and from watching Roses matches. These were shown live on Yorkshire Television, which our miniscule set could mysteriously pick up in dusty black and white from a nearby transmitter. Sometimes the players were just silvery pencil marks across the pale screen. By then the 1970s had dawned, and Yorkshire were coming to terms with the painful ordeal of reality. Their years of omnipotence – seven Championships and two Gillette Cups from 1959 to 1969 – were over. Winning no longer came as naturally as breathing to them, a purgatorial state that would cause tangled in-fighting of an Esher-like complexity and an oral riot almost every bleak mid-winter as private, ideological feuds became public. Sometimes it seemed like a non-stop concerto of indulgent and destructive whining. But the rows and recriminations also demonstrated – were it necessary – how much Yorkshire *cared*.

It seemed to me then that nowhere else was so absorbed in cricket or regarded it so earnestly; nowhere else studied it so thoughtfully or followed it with such obsessive passion, as if the scorecards were parchment scripture; and certainly nowhere else were the vagaries of the game so cherished, so understood or so utterly and deeply felt. In my eyes those who played or merely observed cricket in Yorkshire were sure of, and never lost, an appreciation of where they came from and the proud, firm sense of self it gave them. Being from, and belonging to, the geography of Yorkshire was fundamental to them.

To understand a river you must see it at source. To understand Yorkshire's preoccupation with cricket you must be aware of its past. In outlining it, as well as the county's tribal nature and guiding principles – a tireless, driven determination – Kilburn proved to be a good tutor. He came to know the make-up and motivation of both as correspondent of the *Yorkshire Post* for more than 40 years, which he christened his 'sweet summers'. As he rolled out its jewelled history and pinned it in front of me like a tapestry, I understood how much it mattered. In God's Own Country, God's game was indisputably cricket, and make no mistake about it. It was even spoken about in high-pulpit rhetoric.

Kilburn evoked names of which I was then only dimly aware: Herbert Sutcliffe, Maurice Leyland, Percy Holmes and Hedley Verity, and the benign ghosts of Bobby Peel, Major Booth and a cast of hundreds besides, who seemed to have the mists of history trailing behind them. Through Kilburn I came to know the importance of Yorkshire's neat, perfectly symmetrical progress: first match, against Norfolk in 1833 (Yorkshire won by 120 runs); first constitution (subscriptions from 10s/6d upwards) in 1863; and first official Championship in 1893 (George Hirst took 69 wickets). The bar for anyone following Hirst and his contemporaries was set at an onerous height and subsequent stumblings to vault it became hard to take as a consequence. They are *still* hard to take because the expectation of success – despite shifts in time, circumstances and custom – remains undiminished.

Kilburn made me conscious, too, of what it meant to play for Yorkshire – a privilege then exclusive to those born within its boundaries – and to wear the county cap. When the autocratic Lord Hawke once passed over Alonzo Drake for the honour, almost crushing his fragile spirit in the process, Drake's mother told him, 'Dunna fret about that cap, Lonza. If Lord Hawke won't give it to you, go and buy thysen one.' If only…

The value of those gathered quarters of dark-blue cloth is put into perspective by this: the swell of pride Len Hutton experienced after being awarded his own in 1936 was only ever equalled by his Knighthood, which came 20 years later. The cap was precious because the stitched White Rose represented acceptance, confirmation that the wearer had joined Yorkshire's aristocratic lineage, which stretched back to the mid-19th century, and because the competition to possess it was ferocious. Genius is never too strong a word to use about Hutton. But what strikes me most about him, especially at the beginning of his career, is his self-effacing response to his blessing of natural talent. After being told he'd make his first-class debut against Cambridge University, he was found 'enjoying a private joke'.

'What are you laughing at?' he was asked.

'Me, playing for Yorkshire,' he replied, properly understanding the full significance of it.

Hutton believed cricket constituted the core of Yorkshire. Economically, it turned on the sparks from steelmaking, the clang of the shipbuilder's hammer, the regular, rhythmic clack of the textile looms and the hacking out of coal from cavernous seams. Emotionally, it was defined and drew its sense of identity and swagger from the production of runs and the taking of wickets.

To begin anything with the phrase *legend has it* usually means that the facts don't fit whatever follows. But there are stories – perhaps ever so slightly embroidered or plainly apocryphal – that nonetheless emphasise it and convey the importance of cricket to Yorkshire. There was the tale of a man caught applauding with equal fervour both Yorkshire and Lancashire's efforts in a Roses game.

'Are you Lancashire?' demanded his neighbour.

'No,' he replied.

'Are you Yorkshire?'

'No,' he replied again.

2

'Then shut up and mind thi own business.'

From another, far older vintage, comes the story of a boy frantically forcing his way through the dense crowd until he finds his father near the boundary. 'Dad,' he said, 'I've summat to tell thee. Our house is on fire and mi mum can't find neither t' twins nor t' insurance policy.' The father is unimpressed. 'And I've got summat to tell thee,' he said, 'Sutcliffe's out.' As the writer A. A. Thomson made clear, 'The same tale was later told of Hutton ... and was, I have no doubt, told of all Yorkshire's men back to Louis Hall.'

Be that as it may, no illusion can be created except by reason, and even most myths contain a smidgen of truth. The glowing example of it is the now hoary, certainly stony, but absolutely sincere remark attributed to Wilfred Rhodes – his growl that, 'We don't play it for fun.' It is often re-quoted to satirise Yorkshire in the same way that James Gillray's drawings are re-hung to mock George III. Kilburn the craftsman expressed it more eloquently, 'In the Yorkshire philosophy of sport it is impossible to be too keen on winning a competitive engagement,' he wrote. Take your pick – the bluntness of Rhodes or the finesse of Kilburn. The difference between them lies only in the style of the message; for both sing from the same hymn sheet.

Alan Bennett put the contrary case in his first television play, *A Day Out*. It includes a cricket match set within the ruins of Fountains Abbey. The participants are members of a Yorkshire cycling club, who ride there in May 1911. The grey stone of one of the Abbey's inner walls becomes the wicket, which is haphazardly drawn with a stub of chalk. The bat is as dark as anthracite and bound near the toe with thin twine. The ball lacks a seam. The fielders scatter themselves haphazardly across an oblong of grass decorated with spots of wild flowers. Even someone with only an embryonic understanding of the history of Yorkshire cricket won't be surprised by what happens next. The friendly atmosphere immediately breaks apart under the competitive strain of the occasion. There is a disputed decision, which turns into a push-and-pull argument, and the game dissolves into controversy. Eventually the disgruntled batsman hurls down his bat and struts off in a huff. 'I don't know,' says the bowler, watching him stride away, 'It's nobbut a game.'

As with everything else he's ever written, Bennett not only captures the scene beautifully but also makes the viewer dwell on the nuances and layered meanings concealed within it. The skilful image he created stayed with me long after I'd first viewed it, as though the characters in waistcoats and braces, clomping boots and flat caps, were once as real as Tom Emmett, Ted Peate, Schofield Haigh or John Tunnicliffe. In particular, after turning the pages of the Wells-like time machine that is *Wisden*, the hissy fit over 'nobbut a game' made me curious. Was Bennett, born in Leeds, ever so gently satirising the Yorkshire devotion to, and obsession with, cricket and acting as the polar opposite to Rhodes and Kilburn? I wrote to him, and back came – almost instantly, in fact – a picture postcard depicting a spread of shadowed limestone pavement and a solitary, naked tree in the middle distance. Its branches resembled spindly brown bones. 'Below Ingleborough, Yorkshire Dales' read the caption beside Bennett's explanation in black ink. The line 'nobbut a game' originated from home and hearth. 'It was very much Dad's view of it,' he wrote. His father, Walter, was a butcher, who moved the family to Headingley in 1946. 'We lived for ten years or so around the corner from the cricket ground, but never went in,' he added. 'The only sport dad could tolerate was wrestling on TV on Saturday afternoon – partly because the wrestlers were "such bad 'uns". When there was too much sport on TV it would be referred to as "stinkin" sport. I think that would sum up his attitude to sport in general, "It's nobbut a game".'

Bennett's reply spring-boarded one thought and then another. Along with Rhodes' and Kilburn's assessments, it brought to mind C. L. R. James' pivotal tenant of faith – 'What do they know of cricket who only cricket know?' – and then John Arlott's stoic endorsement of it. 'I have enjoyed cricket more and served it better,' said Arlott, 'for realising it was never the be-all and end-all of everything as, alas, so many cricketers think it is.' Those separate quotations illuminate the same question: do we take cricket too seriously or not seriously enough? Any response can only ever elicit a point of view, rather than a definitive answer, because it hinges wholly on perception, prejudice and taste, which is always subjective. But – and I know this from trawling through 147 years' worth of *Wisden* – it is obvious in which ranking order Yorkshire places life, death and cricket. In a contest between them … well, let's just say, without too much exaggeration, that it's a close run thing. To a considerable extent, I came to admire Yorkshire for exactly that reason and because the past is always tangible in its present. But then, how could it not be?

Crowds of 8,000–10,000, fantasy figures for today's Championship, used to squeeze into Headingley or Bramall Lane, Scarborough or Bradford, Hull or Harrogate in anticipation of Verity tweaking the ball so it dipped unexpectedly late at the batsman; the bespectacled Bill Bowes twisting his lanky frame side-on beside the stumps; Rhodes and Hirst with stern, weathered faces and hooded, pebble-black eyes; Holmes and Sutcliffe striding out side-by-side with that edge of entitlement which distinguishes the genuine run-maker; and the quite extraordinary, multi-talented and uncommonly slender F. S. Jackson (*Spy* draws Jackson as if he's a heron holding a bat). Add Hutton and the aforementioned comprise the Yorkshiremen I'd most like to have actually seen play, rather than just half-glimpsed in snatches of scratchy film or framed in a monochrome pose behind glass. Imagine witnessing Verity's 10 for 10 against Nottinghamshire; Hirst's triple century at Aylestone Road; Holmes and Sutcliffe almost breaking the rattling scoreboard at Leyton; Hutton completing his hundredth hundred at The Oval.

A wonderful mythology is also heaped up alongside each of them too. Think of Hirst scoring a rapid half-century at Lord's, which was more agricultural than cultural. A top-hatted gent in the pavilion is supposed to have marked each shot with anguished disapproval, and the words 'disgraceful' and 'shocking'. Lastly, came his rebuke: 'Look at the fellow's feet?' he said, as though the innings was sacrilegious. 'Ay,' shouted back a Yorkshire voice, 'but look at t' scoreboard.'

Or think of Rhodes, already blind and in the glimmering evening of his life, travelling home by train from the Headingley Test against Australia in 1956. A stranger in the compartment asks his daughter, 'Is he your dad?'

'Yes,' she says.

'Blind, is he?'

'Yes.'

'I wonder if he knows anything about cricket.'

'A bit.'

'Fine. You ought to take him to a match or two and explain things to him. It would do him the world of good to have an interest.'

Rhodes used to quote that brief conversation to visitors, always ending with the casual, self-deprecating response, 'And there I was in my corner and I never cried squeak.'

And think of Jackson, who defies classification. He was the genuine all-rounder – batsman, bowler, MP, soldier, writer, Governor of Bengal, Knight and the survivor of an assassin's bullet. Some cricketer. Some life. Jackson once asked Hirst to speak on his behalf at a municipal election. Hirst's speech was short. 'Ladies and gentleman,' he said. 'Mr Jackson's a fine man and a grand cricketer. But if you get him on to this council, he'll play less cricket, and that'll be a bad thing for Yorkshire, England and everybody. So don't vote for him – any of you.' At Jackson's memorial service, the Bishop of Knaresborough recalled the scene at his funeral. 'There were hundreds of cricketers,' he said, 'and as I looked down on the rapt faces of that vast congregation I could see how their hearts went out to that great man, how they revered him as though he were the Almighty – only infinitely stronger on the leg side.' No novelist would dare to invent a character such as Jackson; his presence on the page would be just too implausible.

The purpose of this book is to celebrate Jackson, Hutton, Rhodes *et al.* With 30 Championships plus one shared, and 42 *Wisden Cricketers of the Year*, Yorkshire already has almost more history than it can consume. None of those honours could have been achieved without a necessarily hard, aggressive approach, which sometimes tipped into sheer bloody-mindedness. But it also took a consummate, adroit skill, which was sometimes overlooked or ignored, perhaps because of a touch of green-eyed jealousy elsewhere. The evidence of superior talent as well as toughness is found throughout *Wisden*. Contradictory as it seems, what follows both dispels and confirms the stereotypical classification of Yorkshire as attritional and austere, dour and dogmatic, win-at-all-costs and don't-let-the-buggers-grind-you-down.

From its contributors comes an amalgam of impeccable judgement and exceptional writing. Here is Neville Cardus on Holmes – 'volatile, unpredictable of mood, always alive by instinct, so to say, intent on enjoyment on the cricket field, or off it,' and, 'always first to admit that, like the rest of humans, he was fallible.' Here is R. C. Robertson-Glasgow on Verity's wily, biting spin, which he regarded as 'nature embellished by art'. Here is Bowes admiringly recalling Fred Trueman's 'sweet gathering of momentum' as he came 'hurtling to the bowling crease'. Here is Derek Hodgson explaining the painstaking preparation of Boycott, who 'knew most bowlers backwards, most pitches, even the direction of the prevailing wind.' Here is David Hopps on the 'broad-beamed, stomping gait' of Matthew Hoggard, which 'encouraged so much farming imagery it would have been no surprise had he stopped midway through his run to close a gate or chase a sheep.' Here is Mathew Engel on Darren Gough – 'an inspirational cricketer in an uninspiring era.' Finally, here is Cardus again on the beating heart and other pulses of Emmott Robinson. 'Few,' he said 'have absorbed the game, the Yorkshire game, into their systems, their minds, nerves and bloodstreams, as Emmott did … Yorkshire cricket was, for him, a way of living.' That last phrase defines Yorkshire cricket for me – a way of living, indeed.

I end with another confession. There is something uniquely personal about the bond I forged a long time ago with Yorkshire and its cricket. Odd, but there is a curious and arbitrary nature to the remembrance of things past; for often what is retained most vividly is the apparently minor, miniscule detail of seminal events. When, belatedly, I got to watch Yorkshire at Trent Bridge, I tucked myself, as I always did, on a rug beside the rope. The flow of the match was dull. It was rather like studying a pond in which there is barely a ripple to break the water. But, in yawning mid-afternoon, Tony Nicholson began patrolling the patch of outfield in front of where I was sitting. He began to speak to me. I remember what was said between us in vague generalities. How long had I been interested in cricket? How often did I go to Trent Bridge? Who were my favourite players? I could scarcely believe it. *A professional cricketer was talking to me!* Nicholson was compassionate enough to bother with a boy he'd never met before and would never see again.

The rest of that memory comes back to me as if it's just been freshly minted. The grassy stains streaked down his flannels, the tips of his huge fingers tinged with the red pigment of the ball and the sight of his spikes, small clumps of damp earth clinging to them, as he walked in before each delivery. From my crouched position I remember looking up at his blocky, rectangular frame, trunk-like legs and wide, square shoulders. To me, Nicholson looked nine feet tall. I remember, too, how unaccountably but ineffably sad I felt one morning in 1985 when I read that he'd died of cancer, aged 47. Preposterous as it sounds, it felt to me as if I'd lost someone with whom I'd once had a genuine rapport.

I was fortunate to catch the rump end of Trueman's career. I saw Boycott at his best; and Brian Close and Ray Illingworth too – albeit under the flag and colours of other counties. I've admired Michael Vaughan and especially the flashy, firecracker batting of Darren Lehmann. And I'd willingly pay to see Adil Rashid bowl anywhere – against that rough wall at Fountains Abbey, if necessary. I even feel a special affinity with Bowes because, after a few serendipitous twists, I now live beside the country lane where he used to walk his dog. From my kitchen window I can see the red-tiled roof of his former home in the middle-distance. Irrationally, I still hope one morning to catch sight of him in a contemplative stroll – leather lead wrapped in the hand that once bowled Bradman's first ball.

But no Yorkshire player will ever supersede Nicholson in my affections. Of course, he never knew it. I never told him how grateful I felt – and still feel – for his simple act of kindness. And I was never able to say to his face how often I thought about him afterwards.

At last I can record it publicly.

I once asked Geoffrey Boycott what he thought of Nicholson. 'Bloody good bowler,' he said – a compliment that I recognised as the equivalent of a gold star.

I nodded my head. 'Bloody good man too,' I replied.

Duncan Hamilton, Wharfedale, 2011

Chapter One:
The Greatest of the Great

He was only 13 years old, trudging off in the February snow of 1930 to his first net session at Headingley. In his pocket was the letter Yorkshire CCC had sent him. It was addressed to Mr Leonard Hutton. In his right hand was a kit bag containing his Harrow-sized, Herbert Sutcliffe bat. He said he felt very little – 'small in a sheepish sort of a way' – as he walked along the slushy streets of Leeds. 'They'll think me daft,' he said to himself, 'going to play cricket in winter.'

No one thought Hutton daft at the end of practice. Watching his new pupil's stylistic correctness, George Hirst said to whoever wanted to listen, 'There's nothing we can teach this lad.' Greatness knows itself, as Shakespeare said; but Hirst's instant appraisal of the boy, and his concrete certainty that he'd just met a genius, is proof of the beholder's almost supernatural talents too.

Hutton never let Hirst down, and his unfolding story was an authentic Ripping Yarn. Born into austerity and emotionally shaped by the mental discipline of a Moravian upbringing; run out for nought on his first-class debut ('Don't worry,' said a sympathetic Maurice Leyland, 'you've started at the bottom'); scoring that 13-hour, world-record 364 against the Australians at The Oval in 1939, aged only 22; injured so badly after a freakish fall that his left arm ended up two inches shorter than his right and required a bone graft from his leg, an operation regarded as pioneering in the early 1940s…

What came next is more dramatic still. Implausibly sacked in 1943 as captain of Bradford League Pudsey St Lawrence by a bone-headed committee for losing three successive matches; the first professional to take charge of England, despite loud harrumphing and surreptitious back-stabbing from the MCC's traditionalists; surviving (and prospering) in the West Indies during the most fractious and divisive tour since Bodyline; regaining the Ashes at home in 1953 and retaining them in Australia in 1954-55. Finally, a knighthood bestowed in 1956, an era of cavernous class division. For me, Hutton is the greatest of the greats in Yorkshire's history. He warrants the crown despite the cricketers who rival him.

This chapter celebrates Hutton alongside the many other extraordinary cricketers who make up that competition. Their inclusion – all except one – requires no elaboration.

True, the sunlit peaks of Ray Illingworth's career were reached only after he had left Yorkshire, but that doesn't matter. As Tony Lewis once said of Illingworth's capacity to register the smallest detail, 'On the field you sense that he knows every blade of grass by name. At Lord's, the Father Time weather vane turns by one degree behind his back and he will announce "wind's on the move".'

True, Michael Vaughan would have been here too – if the contract and commitments of the modern international cricketer had allowed him to play more matches for Yorkshire.

And true, F. S. Jackson could be considered a surprise pick.

Let me explain. In 2006 the Yorkshire Post ran a poll to determine Yorkshire's Greatest XI. Almost 5,500 entries arrived at the newspaper's offices. The team chosen was: Hutton, Sutcliffe, Leyland, Lehmann, Close, Hirst, Rhodes, Binks, Trueman, Bowes, Verity. The second XI wasn't bad either: Boycott, Holmes, Mitchell, Denton, Watson, Illingworth, Kilner, Bairstow, Haigh, Emmett, Appleyard.

Jackson didn't make either side. He nonetheless fascinates me as a person as much as a cricketer – a multi-skilled renaissance man. J. M. Kilburn even claimed on his behalf, 'No one ever came closer to the illustration of the complete player.'

The Yorkshire Post argued that the tireless, driven and determined Close ought to be put in charge of its team of all the talents. I know without doubt who should manage it: Colonel the Honourable Sir Stanley Francis Jackson PC, GCIE.

LEN HUTTON

Leonard Hutton was born in Pudsey in 1916. He made 19 Test centuries and scored 6,971 runs for England from 1937–55. He scored 129 hundreds (11 double centuries). He was Knighted in 1956, wrote about cricket for the Observer *and was serving a term as Yorkshire President when he died, aged 74, in 1990.*

The Master – by Neville Cardus, 1956

Len Hutton was the only batsman of his period to whom we could apply the term Old Master, referring in his case not to his number of years but to the style and vintage of his cricket. He followed in the succession of the classic professional batsmen who each went in first for his county and for England: Shrewsbury, Hayward, Hobbs and Sutcliffe – though Sutcliffe wore his classicism with a subtly Sutcliffian difference.

As Old Masters go, Hutton was young enough; the sadness is that physical disability put an end to his career in its prime. He had all the classic points of style when, not much more than 19, he came to Lord's in 1936 and scored 55. I then wrote of him in this strain of Cassandrian prophecy, 'Here is a young cricketer who is already old in the head and destined to enliven many a Lancashire and Yorkshire match of the future.'

If by means of some time machine capable of television we could today see a picture of Hutton batting 20 years ago, and one taken of him during his maturity, we would notice no fundamental difference in technique. We would see that his cricket had grown in experience and finish … that is all. Like the music of Bach, Hutton's batsmanship in its evolution from an early to a late period presented no marked divisions; it was never raw, unprincipled or embryonic. He batted grammatically from the start, choosing his strokes as carefully as a professor of logic his words.

Even when he first played for Yorkshire, beginning with 0, he seemed to begin an innings to a plan, building the shape and the duration of it to a blueprint in his mind, and to timetable. But once in the greenest of his salad days he fell into error. He opened a Yorkshire innings on Saturday at Bradford with Arthur Mitchell, dourest and most unsmiling of the clan. After a characteristically Yorkshire investigation of the state of the wicket, the state of the opposition bowling, the state of mind the umpires were in, the state of the weather and barometer, and probably the state of the Bank of England itself, Mitchell and Hutton began to score now and then.

Young Hutton was feeling in form, so after he had played himself in he decided to cut a rising ball outside the off-stump. Remember that he was fresh to the Yorkshire scene and policies. He actually lay back and cut hard and swiftly, with cavalier flourish. He cut under the ball by an inch, and it sped bang into the wicketkeeper's gloves. And Mitchell, from the other end of the pitch, looked hard at Hutton and said, 'That's no ******* use!' This was probably Hutton's true baptism, cleansing him of all vanity and lusts for insubstantial pageantry and temporal glory.

He observed the classical unities; that is to say, he did not venture beyond reliable and established limitations of batsmanship learned in the traditional school. Geometrical precision in the application of bat to ball, each movement of the feet considered until the right position was found almost instinctively, not bringing him merely to the ball and, as far as possible and if necessary over it, but also with body at the proper balance.

Never, or hardly ever, did Hutton play a thoughtless innings; his mind usually seemed to move a fraction of time in advance of his most rapid footwork and sudden tensions of limb, sinew and nerve. It is, of course, wrong to suppose that Hutton was at any time a batsman slow in his mental and physical reactions at the crease.

The scoreboard may have told us that he was not getting runs feverishly, but the vigilance of Hutton was eternal; the concentration in him was so intense that it frequently exhausted his not robust physique much sooner than did the more obvious toil and burden of the day. In the most austerely defensive Hutton innings we could feel a mental alertness; purpose in him suffered no weariness.

And whether or not he was putting into practice his wide repertoire of strokes, he was the stylist always; rarely was he discovered in an awkward position at the crease, rarely was he bustled or hurried. Once at Kennington Oval, Lindwall knocked Hutton's cap off in a Test match. Such an outrage could be equalled in a cricketer's imagination only by supposing that Alfred Mynn's tall hat was ever likewise rudely removed.

On a bowler's wicket, when the ball's spin was angular and waspish in turn, he could maintain his premeditated technical responses, often using a dead bat, the handle held so loosely that when the ball came into contact with the blade's middle it was as though against a drugged cushion: the spin was anaesthetised into harmlessness. But Hutton was, when grace descended upon him, a versatile and handsome stroke player. Old Trafford will remember that in 1948 he made a century of a brilliance that in the circumstances – Bank Holiday and a Lancashire v Yorkshire match – was almost pagan. He drove Lindwall with Spooneresque charm and panache at Brisbane in December 1950; at Lord's in the Test match of 1953, he played one of the most regal and most highly pedigreed innings ever seen in an England and Australia Test match on the hallowed ground. And he has contributed to a festival at Scarborough.

If Hutton had lived and played in the Lord Hawke epoch, when even Test cricketers in England had somehow to adapt themselves and their skill to matches limited to three days, he would have been a different batsman in his tempo and mental approach. But he could not possibly have been greater.

Any artist or master of craft is an organism in an environment; he is very much what circumstances and atmosphere make of him. His very greatness consists in how fully he can sum up the technique of his day as he finds it, and how representative he is of his day's spirit. MacLaren, lordly and opulent at the crease, was a representative man and cricketer in a lordly opulent period; Hutton's cricket has been as true as MacLaren's to the zeitgeist, to the feeling, temper and even to the economy of the age which shaped his character and his skill, both conceived as much in integrity as in joy.

As a captain he was shrewd but courteous; he knew the game's finest points, and though never likely to give anything away, was too proud to take anything not his due. Sometimes he may have allowed thoughtfulness to turn to worry; but this is a natural habit in the part of the world which Hutton comes from.

Hutton certainly showed that a professional cricketer could wear the robes of leadership in the field of play with dignity. At first, no doubt, he appeared at the head of his troops not wearing anything like a Caesarian toga, but rather the uniform of a sergeant major. But he moved up in rank and prestige until he became worthy of his command and defeated Australia twice in successive rubbers, wresting one from the enemy at the pinch and looting the other after a series of Tests which were, if I may be free with my allusions and metaphors, the Australians' Austerlitz.

One of Hutton's most winning characteristics – and his personality is extremely attractive – is his smile, a smile with a twinkle in it. He had many occasions in his distinguished career on which to indulge this smile, many provocations to it, and he never missed the joke. A Yorkshireman has his own idea of humour, and Hutton, as great or famous as any Yorkshireman contemporary with him, relished his laugh all the more because very often it came last.

A Cricketing Legend – by John Woodcock, 1991

Between the end of the First World War in 1918 and the start of the Second in 1939, English cricket produced three great batsmen – Walter Hammond, Leonard Hutton and Denis Compton. Each one was endowed with a wonderful talent, Hammond's enabling him to play with rare splendour, Compton's with an irresistible *joie de vivre* and Hutton's with a style that was all-embracing. Although Herbert Sutcliffe had a comparable record, compiled between the wars, he was not in the same way a product of the 1920s or 1930s, having been on the point of breaking through in 1914.

Len Hutton died on September 6, 1990, at the age of 74. He had slipped into Lord's only five days earlier to watch the final of the NatWest Bank Trophy from Paul Getty's box in the Mound Stand. He had been there, too, for the Test match against India in

July, and seen Graham Gooch get to within 31 runs of his own most famous record, the 364 with which he tormented Australia at The Oval in 1938.

Hutton retained until the end the unassuming manner that marked his apprenticeship. Sir Jack Hobbs had been the same; as disarmingly unboastful after being Knighted as before. There was also about Sir Len an apparent frailty at the crease, a characteristic that caused his son, Richard, who also played for Yorkshire and England, frequent anxiety until he was old and wise enough to recognise the artistry it disguised.

For the benefit of those who never saw Hutton bat, I have been trying to think of someone playing today who puts one in mind of him, and I am not sure that I can. This is surprising, for he was essentially orthodox and resolutely conventional. Except that he gives more of an impression of hitting the ball, and less of stroking it, than Hutton did, Stephen Waugh, the gifted Australian of similar build, probably comes as near to it as anyone. Mohammad Azharuddin is another who possesses that intuition which gives the great natural players such a start to life. There was something quite uncanny about the way, for example, in which Hutton coped with the mysteries of Sonny Ramadhin's spin while carrying his bat against West Indies at The Oval in 1950, just as there was in his handling of Jack Iverson's when doing the same against Australia at Adelaide only six months later. He was, hereabouts, at the meridian of his powers. So, besides Ramadhin and Iverson, were Keith Miller and Ray Lindwall. In fair weather and foul, at home and overseas, if Len failed, the chances were that England would.

Whether his character was influenced by being born at Fulneck, the village near Pudsey where there was an isolated Moravian community ('protestants of rare missionary zeal') is a matter for conjecture. To some extent it probably was, their significance being quite considerable. But cricket, too, was a family religion. Those who didn't take to it would have been put back if that had been possible, and being chosen for Yorkshire when still a month short of his 18th birthday – his first match was against Cambridge University at Fenner's in May 1934 – made Hutton the youngest player to appear for the county since George Hirst in 1889. He came into a side that had won the Championship for the previous three years – Yorkshire had not been out of the first four since 1911 – and, although they finished a disappointing fifth in 1934, to play regularly for them in those days gave a young man a distinct advantage. If the same applied today, Richard Blakey and Ashley Metcalfe would, I am sure, be nearer to playing for England than they probably are.

In Hutton's case, the transition from callow youth, cap steeply tilted, to one of the world's most accomplished batsmen was achieved in an extraordinarily short time. Yorkshire Colts getting a game for the county side in the middle 1930s were left in no doubt that they were there to be seen and not heard. It was an austere school, and Hutton was an astute observer. Within four years of joining it he had become a household name. Nothing was more remarkable about his tour de force at The Oval than that he was only just 22 at the time.

Then came the war, claiming several summers when Hutton's play would still have carried the bloom of youth, and leaving him, as the result of a training accident, with his left arm two inches shorter than the right. With the return of peace, the mantle that had been Hammond's passed to Hutton, whose batting, despite having been laid up for so long, had matured. Between 1934 and 1939 he had scored 11,658 runs at an average of 48.98. From 1945, when he played his next first-class innings, to his retirement in 1955 he made another 28,292 at 58.81. Although, hardly surprisingly, he himself felt handicapped by his disabled arm – its shortening was clearly visible – he made miraculously light of it. If Compton and Bill Edrich were the spirit of the immediate post-war years, Hutton was looked to in order to provide the stability. Between the three of them they did wonders for our rehabilitation.

That Compton rather than Hutton was made Freddie Brown's vice-captain in Australia in 1950-51 was for reasons of compatibility. When, in 1952, a more egalitarian age was dawning and a captain was being sought to succeed Brown, Len was the clear choice (although he had never led Yorkshire), and it fell to him to regain the Ashes in England in 1953 and then retain them in Australia two years later. In Australia he was quick to see the possibilities of a Statham-Tyson combination, despite Tyson's rather lumbering early efforts and although it meant leaving out Alec Bedser, which he did without the consideration due to so great a figure in the game.

Hutton was not, in fact, an easy communicator. It could be said that he distanced himself from his side when at times they needed a stronger lead. This was particularly so in the West Indies in 1953-54 on the first of his two tours as captain. On the other hand, they were in awe of him as a player, and that was a help. Just as Sir Henry Cotton dignified the status of the professional golfer, so Hutton did of the professional cricketer.

Still good enough to make 145 against Australia at Lord's in 1953 and to average an astonishing 96.71 against West Indies that winter, by the summer of 1954 Len was suddenly finding it much more of an effort to summon the skill, nerve and concentration needed both to captain England and to make runs. There were also suggestions that, although his side had staged an epic recovery in the West Indies, they had not covered themselves with glory in other respects. There were, accordingly, calls for a change of captain. These, happily, were resisted, and off to Australia he went in September 1954 for his third and last tour there as a player. In the event it took so much out of him, once England had been horribly beaten in the first Test – not least because Hutton had put Australia in – that, within a few months of his getting home in the spring of 1955, he put his bats away. His back was playing him up, and after the heat and burden of the last two years a quiet retirement in Surrey, with a golf course nearby, had an obvious appeal. Famous Yorkshireman that he was, the south, with its less competitive responses, suited him better than the north.

For a decade Len Hutton was the model for English batsmen. As a first movement he slid his right foot back and across towards the middle stump, from where, basically, he did what came naturally. He had a lovely stance, as still as it was relaxed. He would play right back but seldom right forward, preferring to let the ball come to him and playing it very late. Between bat and pad there was sometimes, dare I say it, a gap – the forward 'prop' had yet to come into fashion – and through it he was liable to be bowled by an off-break. Early in the season, undergraduates at Oxford and Cambridge were known to get him out this way.

> Yorkshire gave a trial to three young players, Lowson, an opening batsman, Close, an all-rounder, and Trueman, a spin bowler.
>
> **Cambridge University v Yorkshire, 1949**

There were occasions, too, when, because of his arm, he played his cover drive not leaning into the ball so much as reaching for it. But his timing and balance were such that it was still pleasing to the eye. He had all the strokes if he wanted them, though only when no risk was involved did he loft the ball. In his 19 Test hundreds he hit only two sixes, and one of those was to what was then the shortest straight boundary in Test cricket – Jamaica's Sabina Park. It was a drive off Gary Sobers, bowling orthodox left-arm spin.

Hutton never greatly cared for leaving his crease to the spinners, of whom there were vastly more then than there are now. Had he done so, the chances are that the generation that followed him, led by Peter May, Colin Cowdrey and Tom Graveney, would themselves have ventured forth rather more. Like all instinctively good judges of a run, he never looked to be in a hurry between the wickets. Studying under Sutcliffe in his early days for Yorkshire would have shown him the need for conviction in calling and let him into the secrets of the short single.

A broken nose gave Len a misleadingly rugged appearance. But to go with it he had a winning smile and blue eyes that regularly twinkled with his own brand of sometimes cryptic humour. He was full of paradoxes: self-contained yet vulnerable, reserved yet quizzical, shrewd yet enigmatic, gentle yet tenacious. He wanted to be judged as a person as much as in his role as a cricketer, and it may truthfully be said that, like Hobbs before him, he attracted widespread and genuine affection.

I see him on board ship in 1950 and again in 1954, bound for Australia and wrapped in contemplation. I see him working the ball around, seldom plundering the bowling, rather picking up runs as he went – a late cut here, a placed single there, and then, sometimes after a long wait, the cover drive that was his special glory. The modern game would have given us, inevitably, a different player: he would have had no chance to surpass himself, as he sometimes so memorably did, on drying pitches, and it is as dreadful to think of him in a helmet as it is to think of Compton, Hammond or W. G. in one.

I see him near the end of his tether, as a lot of us were, before the Ashes were safely in England's keeping in Australia in 1954-55. And I shall remember him at the Lord's Test against India last year, going quietly and a little wearily off into the twilight, content, I fancy, that his record score for England was still intact, though certain to have been just as affable had it not been. He was not one to shower compliments around, but by then he knew when they were due and duly paid them. A cricketing legend, he won as many hearts with his beguiling albeit watchful charm as with the mastery of his batting.

HEDLEY VERITY

Hedley Verity played in 40 Tests and took 144 wickets, including 8 for 43 at an average of 24.37. He took 1,956 first-class wickets at 14.90. His career began in 1930 and ran until the beginning of the Second World War. He was born in 1905 and died of wounds received in combat in July, 1943

By R. C. Robertson-Glasgow, 1944

Hedley Verity, Captain, The Green Howards, died of wounds a prisoner of war in Italy on July 31, 1943, some two months after his 38th birthday. He had been reported wounded and missing, and the news of his death came on September 1, exactly four years after he had played his last match for Yorkshire and, at Hove, taken seven Sussex wickets for nine runs in one innings, which finished County cricket before the war.

He received his wounds in the Eighth Army's first attack on the German positions at Catania, in Sicily. Eyewitnesses who were a few yards from Verity when he was hit, have told the story. The objective was a ridge with strong points and pillboxes. Behind a creeping barrage, Verity led his company forward 700 yards. When the barrage ceased, they went on another 300 yards and neared the ridge, in darkness. As the men advanced through corn two-feet high, tracer bullets swept into them. Then they wriggled through the corn, Verity encouraging them with 'Keep going, keep going'. The moon was at their back, and the enemy used mortar-fire, Very lights and firebombs, setting the corn alight. The strongest point appeared to be a farmhouse to the left of the ridge; so Verity sent one platoon round to take the farmhouse, while the other gave covering fire. The enemy fire increased, and, as they crept forward, Verity was hit in the chest. 'Keep going', he said, 'and get them out of that farmhouse'. When it was decided to withdraw, they last saw Verity lying on the ground, in front of the burning corn, his head supported by his batman, Pte Thomas Reynoldson of Bridlington. So, in the last grim game, Verity showed, as he was so sure to do, that rare courage which both calculates and inspires.

His Bowling Art

Judged by any standard, Verity was great bowler. Merely to watch him was to know that. The balance of the run up, the high ease of the left-handed action, the scrupulous length, the pensive variety, all proclaimed the master. He combined nature with art to a degree not equalled by any other English bowler of our time. He received a handsome legacy of skill and, by an application that verged on scientific research, turned it into a fortune. There have been bowlers who reached greatness without knowing, or, perhaps, caring to know just how or why; but Verity could analyse his own intentions without losing the joy of surprise and describe their effect without losing the company of a listener. He was the ever-learning professor, justly proud yet utterly humble. In the matter of plain arithmetic, so often torn from its context to the confusion of judgment, Verity, by taking 1,956 wickets at 14.87 runs each in ten years of first-class cricket, showed by far the best average during this century. In the recorded history of cricket the only bowlers of this class with lower averages are: Alfred Shaw, 2,072 wickets at 11.97 each; Tom Emmett, 1,595 wickets at 13.43 each; George Lohmann, 1,841 wickets at 13.73 each; James Southerton, 1,744 wickets at 14.30 each. It might be argued that during the period 1854 to 1898, covered by the careers of these cricketers, pitches tended to give more help to the bowler than they did during Verity's time. Verity, I know, for one, would not have pressed such a claim in his own favour. He never dwelt on decimals; and, while he enjoyed personal triumph as much as the next man, that which absorbed his deepest interest was the proper issue of a Test match with Australia or of an up-and-down bout with Lancashire; and if, in his country's or county's struggle towards victory, he brought off some recondite plot for the confounding of Bradman or McCabe or Ernest Tyldesley or Edward Paynter, well, then he was happy beyond computing.

Notable Feats

Yet his bowling achievements, pressed into but overflowing the ten years of his career, were so rich and various that they here demand some concentrated notice:

- He played in 40 Test matches, taking 144 wickets at 24.37 runs each. He took 100 wickets in Test cricket in a shorter period than any other English bowler.
- He is the only cricketer who has taken 14 wickets in a day in a Test match, this feat being performed against Australia at Lord's in the second Test, 1934. During this match, he took 15 wickets for 104 runs, thus sharing with Wilfred Rhodes, his Yorkshire predecessor, the honour of taking most wickets in an England v Australia match.
- Twice he took all 10 wickets in an innings: in 1931, against Warwickshire at Headingley, Leeds, for 36 runs in 18.4 (6-ball) overs, with 6 maidens; in 1932, on the same ground, against Nottinghamshire, for 10 runs in 19.4 (6-ball) overs, with 16 maidens – a world record in first-class cricket for the fewest number of runs conceded by a bowler taking all 10 wickets in an innings, and it included the hat-trick.
- Against Essex at Leyton, in 1933, he took 17 wickets in one day, a record shared only by C. Blythe and T. W. Goddard.
- In each of his nine full English seasons he took at least 150 wickets, and he averaged 185 wickets a season; he took over 200 wickets in three consecutive seasons (1935, '36 and '37). His average ranged from 12.42 to 17.63. He headed the first-class English bowling averages in his first season (1930) and in his last (1939), and never came out lower than fifth.

How He Began

Verity was born at Headingley, but passed his 25th birthday before he played for Yorkshire, in 1930, the year that W. Rhodes retired. Some of his earlier seasons were spent in playing as an amateur for Rawdon in the Yorkshire Council; for Accrington in the Lancashire League; and for Middleton in the Central League. He was then, as always afterwards when allowed, an all-rounder. As a batsman, his height, reach, concentration and knowledge of what to avoid raised him distinctly from the ruck of mediocrity; but, whereas his bowling included grace, his batting had only style. The former was nature embellished by art; the latter was art improved by imitation. As a bowler, Hedley Verity stands, and will stand, with his illustrious predecessors in the Yorkshire attack: Edmund Peate (1879–87), Robert Peel (1882–99), Wilfred Rhodes (1898–1930) – the dates indicate the time of their respective playing careers – but Verity was not a slow left-armer in the accepted sense, and he used to reject comparison with Rhodes so far as method was concerned, saying: both of us are left-handed and like taking wickets; let's leave it at that.

Verity's mean pace was what is called slow-medium; on fast pitches, often about medium; and he would send down an inswinging yorker of an abrupt virulence not unworthy of George Hirst. Naturally, on wet or crumbled or sticky pitches, he reduced pace and tossed the leg-spinner higher, but even here his variety of pace and of angle of delivery was remarkable. He was a born schemer; tireless, but never wild, in experiment; as sensitive in observation as a good host, or as an instrumentalist who spots a rival on the beat; the scholar who does not only dream, the inventor who can make it work.

Comparison of Giants

Just how good a bowler was he? In relation to rivals in his own craft but of an earlier day, such a question is useless except to amuse an idle hour or to excite an idle quarrel. We can only say that, in his own short time, he was the best of his kind. In England, day-in and day-out, he may never have quite touched the greatness of Robert Peel, Colin Blythe or Wilfred Rhodes. In Australia, neither in 1932-33 or 1936-37, did he perplex their batsmen quite as J. C. White perplexed them in 1928-29, but, as a workman-artist, he will take some beating. H. B. Cameron, that fine wicketkeeper-batsman of South Africa, playing against Yorkshire in 1935, hit him for three fours and three sixes in one over; but very rarely did a batsman survive a liberty taken with Verity. He had, besides, a wonderful skill in restoring the rabbits, early and with little inconvenience, to the hutch.

If a touchstone of Verity's greatness be needed, there is D. G. Bradman, the most inexorable scorer of runs that cricket has yet seen, whose Test match average against England stands at 91.42 in 46 innings. I think it was Verity who kept that average under 150. He was one of only three or four bowlers who came to the battle with Bradman on not unequal terms (*haud impar congressus!*); and Bradman was reported as saying, 'I think I know all about Clarrie [Grimmett], but with Hedley I am never sure. You see, there's no breaking point with him.'

Beating the Best

Verity timed his blows. In the fifth Test, at Sydney, early in 1933, Australia, 19 runs on the first innings, lost Victor Richardson for 0. Woodfull and Bradman added 115; Larwood, injured, had left the field – and that particular Larwood never came back – then Verity deceived Bradman in flight, bowled him for 71 and went on to take 5 for 33 in 19 overs and win the match. In the earlier Tests, amid the fast bowling and the clamour, not much had been heard of Verity, except as a rescuing batsman. But, when the last pinch came, there he was to relieve the weary line; very Yorkshire.

Verity never allowed the opinion that Bradman was less than a master on damaged pitches, refusing to stress the evidence of his own triumph at Lord's in 1934 (Bradman c and b Verity 36; c Ames b Verity 13) and referring to Bradman's two innings of 59 and 43 in 1938 against Yorkshire at Sheffield. It was a pig of a pitch, he said, and he played me in the middle of the bat right through. Maybe Verity's opinion of Bradman was heightened by a natural generosity in its giver, but on this matter I think that Verity had reason to know best.

As an all-round fielder, Verity was no more than sound, but to his own bowling, or at backward point, he sometimes touched brilliance; and there sticks in the memory the catch that he made at Lord's in 1938, when McCabe cut one from Farnes crack from the bat's middle.

Opened England Batting

As a batsman for Yorkshire, Verity was mostly kept close to the extras. His build and reach suggested power and freedom, but it remained a suggestion; and he was analogous to those burly golfers who prod the tee-shot down the middle to a prime 180 yards. A casual observer might have mistaken Verity for Sutcliffe a little out of form, for he seemed to have caught something of that master's style and gesture, and, like Sutcliffe, he could be clean bowled in a manner that somehow exonerated the batsman from all guilt. He never quite brought off the double, though in 1936 he took 216 wickets and scored 855 runs. But he had the sovereign gift of batting to an occasion. In the 1936-37 visit to Australia, G. O. Allen could find no opening pair to stay together, so he sent in Verity with C. J. Barnett in the fourth Test, at Adelaide, and they put up partnerships of 53 and 45. Not much, perhaps; but the best till then. In all Test matches, his batting average was close on 21; nearly 3 units higher than his average in all first-class cricket.

Verity had the look and carriage of a man likely to do supremely well something that would need time and trouble. His dignity was not assumed; it was the natural reflection of mind and body harmonised and controlled. He was solid, conscientious, disciplined; and something far more. In all that he did, till his most gallant end, he showed the vital fire, and warmed others in its flame. To the spectator in the field he may have seemed, perhaps, a little stiff and aloof; but among a known company he revealed geniality, wit, and an unaffected kindness that will not be forgotten.

There was no breaking point with Verity; and his last reported words: 'Keep going', were but a text on his short and splendid life.

An Australian Appreciation – by Don Bradman, 1944

The present war has already taken heavy toll of gallant men who, after faithfully serving their countries on the cricket field in peacetime, have laid down their lives for a greater cause. Of those who have fallen, Hedley Verity was perhaps the most illustrious and from the Dominion of Australia I feel it my sad duty to join with cricketers of the Motherland in expressing sorrow that we shall not again see him on our playing fields.

The anecdotes kept growing to the point where every cricket story ever told somehow attached itself to Fred. Some, at least, had the ring of truth. One, recalled by (Don) Mosey, fits with the scorecard of a game against Northampton in 1954. Johnny Wardle was bowled, horribly, by Tyson for nought. 'A bloody fine shot that were,' snorted Trueman, as he went out, just before meeting a similar fate. 'And a bloody fine shot that were, an' all,' was Wardle's greeting to Fred. But Trueman had a knack of getting in the last word, 'Aye, I slipped on that pile o' shit you left in the crease'.

Obituary – 2007

It could truthfully be claimed that Hedley Verity was one of the greatest, if not THE greatest left-hand bowler of all time. Most certainly he could lay just claim to that honour during the 1918–39 period. No doubt his Yorkshire environment was of great assistance, for left-hand bowling seems to be in the blood of Yorkshiremen. It is one of their traditions and inalienable rights to possess the secrets of the art. Although not a young man from a cricketing standpoint when the call came, Verity was little if any beyond the zenith of his powers. He was always such a keen student of the game, and his bowling was of such a type, that brains and experience played a greater part in his successes than natural genius. Although opposed to him in many Tests, I could never claim to have completely fathomed his strategy, for it was never static nor mechanical.

Naturally he achieved his most notable successes when wickets were damp. Nobody privileged to witness that famous Test at Lord's in 1934 (least of all the Australian batsmen) will forget a performance to which even the statistics could not do justice. But it would be ungenerous to suggest that he needed assistance from the wicket, as his successful Australian tours will confirm. The ordinary left-hander who lacks the vicious unorthodox finger-spin of the Fleetwood-Smith variety, needs uncommon ability to achieve even moderate success in Australia, yet Verity was the foundation stone of England's bowling in both countries during this era.

Apart from his special department of the game, Verity could also claim to be a remarkably efficient fieldsman close to the wicket where safe hands and courage are greater attributes than agility. Add this to the fact that once he opened a Test match innings for England, not without success, and we have a fairly general picture of a really fine player. Those of us who played against this swarthy, capless champion (I never remember having seen him wear a cap) probably appreciated his indomitable fighting spirit even more than his own colleagues. We knew, when war came, that he would plainly see his duty in the same way as he regarded it his duty to win cricket matches for Yorkshire no less than England.

During our association together I cannot recall having heard Verity utter a word of complaint or criticism. If reports of his final sacrifice be correct, and I believe they are, he maintained this example right to the end. His life, his skill, his service all merited the highest honour, and with great sorrow I unhesitatingly pay humble tribute to his memory.

BRIAN CLOSE

Brian Close was told by Yorkshire in 1970 to resign or be sacked. He went to Somerset and the move rejuvenated his new county. He returned to the England team in 1976 and had his flesh turned mauve and cadmium yellow by the West Indies pace bowlers. In 786 first-class matches, he scored 34,994 runs and took 1,171 wickets. He made 22 Test appearances (887 runs).

Cricketer of the Year 1964 – by W. E. Bowes

Because he was senior professional with the club, and the job was his by right, Yorkshire in 1963 offered the captaincy to their all-rounder Brian Close – left-handed batsman and right-arm utility bowler – who hitherto had never quite accomplished what was expected of him. It was a trial appointment. Nobody quite knew how it would work out.

The result was astonishing. Almost overnight it seemed that Brian Close matured. He showed a knowledge of his own team and the play of opponents that immediately stamped him as a thinker and tactician. His field placings were as intelligent and antagonistic as any seen in the county for 25 years and, like Brian Sellers before him, if a fieldsman was required in a suicide position the captain himself was first for the job. He kept the fiery and volatile Trueman happy, used him in effective short bursts, and balanced those occasions when he asked for long and sustained effort, with opportunities to bowl at tail-enders. Determination and purpose came into his own cricket. He regained his place in the England team and won national approval for the unflinching way he played the West Indies fast bowlers, Hall and Griffith. To his own great delight he saw Yorkshire, in their centenary year, to their 28th outright Championship success.

Dennis Brian Close, the second eldest in a family of four boys and one girl, was born at Rawdon, near Leeds, on February 24, 1931. His father, Harry Close, was a well-known wicketkeeper in the local leagues and it was understandable that the boys were taken down to the Rawdon ground by their father on practice nights and for the Saturday matches. Says Brian, 'We didn't interfere with the seniors. We played much more serious games with other boys behind the pavilion and, if we were beaten at cricket, we challenged our opponents to football.' It was soon obvious that he had above average ability. He was a natural ball player but, far more important in a working-class family, he was good at lessons, too. He passed his 11-plus exam when he was ten and went to Aireborough Grammar School, which Yorkshire and England left-arm bowler Hedley Verity had attended years earlier.

The possibilities of young Close were soon noted by the sports master. He was sent to receive coaching by the Yorkshire coach, George Hirst. Honours at both cricket and football came easily. He played in schoolboy representative matches at both sports. At soccer he was signed on amateur forms by Leeds United when he was 14 and, a year later, as an inside forward, toured Holland with the West Riding FA team. At cricket he played for the Yorkshire Federation against the Sussex Schoolboys when he was 15, and at 17 playing for Yeadon against Salts, in the Bradford League, he scored his first century – a success that brought him selection for the Yorkshire Colts against Sussex Second XI. As a scholar he was similarly outstanding and soon after his 17th birthday he had passed his Higher School Certificate and was all set for university. Unfortunately, however, the university would not take him until after he had completed his two years of National Service, which started at 18 and, in the meantime, Close decided to try his hand at being a professional sportsman. He signed professional forms with Leeds United and during the winter attended the Yorkshire nets for coaching at cricket. He was changed from being a seam bowler to being an off-spinner.

Brian was just 18 at the start of the 1949 cricket season when Yorkshire chose him for the two matches against the Universities. A splendid fieldsman, hard-hitting batsman and by now a very useful off-spin bowler he did so well that Yorkshire extended the trial into the County Championship matches. Against Worcestershire at Sheffield he claimed five wickets and against Essex at Headingley he scored 88 not out and took 5 for 58. Success followed success. He kept on playing for Yorkshire. He was chosen to play for England in the third Test against New Zealand at Old Trafford, the youngest player ever picked for England, and though he was dismissed for a duck and took only 1 for 85 young Close had every reason to be pleased with his start in professional sport. He proceeded to perform the double and was given his Yorkshire cap.

His call up for the Royal Signals came on October 6, 1949. He played soccer for the Services and for Leeds United reserves on occasion when leave could be arranged. During the summer of 1950 he did so well in cricket for the Army and Combined Services team that MCC asked for his release so that he could go with F. R. Brown's team to Australia. As sportsmen are considered ambassadors for their country the request was granted. In the first match of the tour against Western Australia he scored a century but then came failures. Lindwall and Miller soon found they could hurry him into mistakes by attacking the leg stump. He suffered a groin injury, too, and altogether he had a most unhappy tour.

Back in England in 1951 he scored a century for Combined Services against Cambridge, 96 not out against Oxford, 66 and 165 against South Africa and 100 for the Army against the Navy. It seemed he had recovered from his disappointments in Australia and, on leaving the Forces in October, he took on the other half of his professional hopes and signed with Arsenal. All went well until an FA Cup game at Highbury clashed with the opening fixture of the 1952 cricket season with the Yorkshire game at Lord's against MCC. Close tried to play in both matches but – because of a misunderstanding with the Yorkshire captain – he arrived half an hour late at Highbury and saw his team beaten 3-1. He was sacked.

With Yorkshire, however, he again performed the double, but instead of settling for professional cricket only Close had another try at football – this time with Bradford City – and he suffered a knee injury, which badly interfered with his cricket the next season and kept him out of football, too. Back in cricket again in 1954, Close scored his first century for Yorkshire, against Pakistan. In 1955 he was only three wickets short of his third double and MCC chose him for the tour of Pakistan. He was now established in the Yorkshire team and to the delight of many of his friends had given up all ideas of continuing as a professional footballer. Could he find a regular Test place?

In 1957 he played in two Tests against West Indies. In 1959, he appeared in one Test against India. Although he was a splendid all-rounder, England relied on a strong representation of specialist cricketers. In the Yorkshire side, Close was sharing the off-spin bowling with Illingworth. England had Laker. Close went back to his medium pace seam bowling and in 1960 as senior professional under Yorkshire's professional captain, Vic Wilson, he took 64 wickets and scored 1,699 runs with one really great innings of 198 against Surrey at The Oval. In 1962 his Yorkshire benefit realised £8,154 and once again he earned selection for England against Australia at Old Trafford. In the first innings he scored 33, but batting in the second innings at a vital stage of the match he lost his wicket with a cross bat sweep so incomprehensible that even his friends doubted whether he had the temperament for the big match occasion. It seemed he had had his last chance to prove himself. And that was the position until he became the Yorkshire captain. Responsibility seemed to bring out all the best in him. The England selectors were not long in recognising the change and Brian Close, playing in all five Tests against West Indies, finished third in the England Test averages with 315 runs in ten innings. In all cricket last year he scored 1,529 runs, average 32.53, and he took 43 wickets at 27.30 each.

His recreation is golf. It is interesting that from being a four handicap right-hand golfer he has turned left-handed. Within a month he was down to nine handicap and says, 'I could do a lot better with more practice.'

FRED TRUEMAN

Fred Trueman's final total of Test matches wickets was 307. He achieved them in 67 matches at an average of 21.57. He took 2,304 first class wickets at 18.29. He was born at Stainton in 1931 and died in 2006. He is buried at Bolton Abbey.

Fiery Fred: The Greatest fast bowler of all time? – by W. E. Bowes, 1970

Greatness is a relative term, but anyone making a study of the career figures of Fred Trueman could be forgiven if they claimed he was the greatest fast bowler of all time. He has more victims in Test cricket than any other bowler. In a career which began in 1949 and ended with his retirement at the end of the 1968 season, he took over 2,300 wickets at 18.3 each and, apart from obtaining all ten wickets in an innings, he claimed almost every honour in the game.

He performed the hat-trick on four occasions, claimed five wickets or more in an innings 126 times, and was credited with ten wickets or more in the match 25 times. As a hard-hitting batsman he hit three centuries. From the boundary edge he could throw low and accurately into the gloves of the wicketkeeper with either hand. He was a very good fieldsman at short-leg and, mainly in that position, he took 438 catches. An avid student of the record books and with a tremendous memory for facts and figures, Trueman could no doubt fill in most of the details of his performances and compare them with his contemporaries, but he would not lay claim to greatness. He would be happy to be classed with the other fast bowlers of his time and in particular with Brian Statham, of Lancashire, for whom he has a great admiration and with whom he opened the bowling for England so many times.

Most batsmen, especially those who played against Trueman during the years between 1959 and 1964, when I believe he had harnessed his great ability to a shrewd, calculating, assessment of the opposing players, say tersely, 'He was a great bowler.' He showed up mediocrity in an opponent in a manner no other bowler of his time could equal. He had a flair, as any cricketer of top rank must have, for being able to perform above expectations, above himself as it is generally put. In a couple of overs, Trueman could transform the whole outlook of a game. Sometimes it was a fluky shot through the slips, sometimes a stroke of copybook perfection that produced the spark that fired him. Sometimes it was for no other reason than that it was time somebody got somewhere.

A pitch, at one moment docile and easy paced, would suddenly become possessed of every kind of devil. Deliveries that had been reaching the wicketkeeper at ankle height would begin to crash into the gloves at chest height. Batsmen would play and miss in a manner that suggested movement from the seam and, if Trueman had the good fortune to get a wicket, no one could ride the crest of the wave better. He had the great asset, which the Australian fast bowler Ted Macdonald called giving the new batsman hell. It was rare for him not to leave a mark on any game with a vital wicket, a wonder catch, or a useful score of 20 or 30 runs.

The crowds loved Trueman. Not only had he an ability that they could enjoy; the newspapermen, television commentators and publicity men projected an image they liked. Freddie was a tremendous talker. In this department he was the greatest. He was never silent – except during his actual run-up to bowl and in the delivery action; it would have been a pity if anything had marred this beautiful, sometimes awe-inspiring, sight. He ran the length of another cricket pitch to bowl. Some critics said he ran much too far, but Trueman himself said he felt better that way.

This was the perfect answer and it meant much more than the opinion of Ranjitsinhji who thought all fast bowlers should take a long run because the longer periods of concentration required from the batsmen had a telling effect. There was a tendency for the concentration to wander.

With a sweet gathering of momentum Freddie, black hair waving, came hurtling to the bowling crease. With no change of rhythm there came the change from forward to sideways motion, the powerful gathering of muscles for the delivery itself, and then the explosive release. A perfect cartwheel action, with every spoke of arms and legs pointing where the ball was to go – the batsman seeing nothing but left shoulder prior to the moment of delivery – gave the ball its 90mph propulsion. There was the full-bodied follow-through to the action, a run through while he braked, which worried umpires if he got too near the line of the stumps and then, a hundred to one, more talk.

Sometimes it was to tell the batsman how lucky he had been. Sometimes it was to indicate to all and sundry how unlucky he, Trueman, had been; to congratulate a fieldsman on a good stop; to tell the skipper where he wanted the fieldsman to go; or to mutter darkly to himself under his breath. But he talked.

He talked in the field to anybody who would listen. He talked in the dressing room to such an extent that his Yorkshire teammates seldom answered back because this was encouragement, and as a result half an hour before the start of play in any match Trueman could invariably be found still talking in the dressing room of the opposing team where the audience was more polite.

He had a rich fund of stories, some of which could have been told in Sunday school. He had a knack of giving weight even to a triviality and no reporter ever went to him in vain for a story. There was a blunt directness about him and the interviewers successfully got this image over to the public. At times he revealed a sword-like wit but the punch line was often just as cutting. Fred's unhappiest moments on the cricket field were when his skipper, Brian Close, sent him down to the fine-leg boundary, twenty yards in from the spectators, where he could find no one to talk to.

One can only guess the innermost thoughts of opposing batsmen when Trueman, after holding court in their dressing room, got to his feet about 15 minutes before the start of play. 'So you're batting, eh? George,' (looking at the number one batsman), 'I shall get you wi't new ball. Charlie, I've no need to worry about you.' Then looking round the whole room he would add, 'I've got a few candidates today,' and his parting shot would be, 'I only want a bit of luck with you, skipper, and I've got another six or seven wickets.'

This was the Trueman known by the other players and most of them could add a little personal reminiscence. Ken Palmer, who began his career with Somerset in 1955, describes going in to bat against Yorkshire to join his captain, Harold Stephenson. 'Stevie hit Trueman for four, not a very good shot, and Trueman glared his disapproval. When he was walking back to his bowling mark, Stevie called up the pitch to me, "Ken, just tell Trueman to move that bit of paper that's blowing about at the back of him."

'I was a bit hesitant about doing it, but I'd been instructed and I was a new boy. I went up to him. I didn't know whether to call him Mr Trueman, Freddie, or what, and finally I said simply, "Skipper wants you to move that bit of paper before you bowl the next one."

'Freddie looked at me, then the skipper, and then at the bit of paper and said, "Well, just go and ask your skipper who the 'ell he thinks I am. Tell him I'm not the corporation dustman".'

In 1961, the Derbyshire wicketkeeper, Bob Taylor, played his first match against Yorkshire and pushing forward to Trueman scored a couple of runs straight back up the pitch. Trueman, trying to recover from his follow-through and field the ball, slipped and fell. He stayed on the ground until the batsmen had finished running and then glared at Taylor and asked, 'Can you hook 'em an' all?' 'I expected the next ball to be a bouncer,' said Bob, 'but instead he bowled me with one of the best yorkers I've ever had.'

And the story that many England players who were on the ship to Australia in 1961 love to tell is when Gordon Pirie was pressed into action to take the boys in PT and general fitness training. Said Gordon to Trueman one day, 'Freddie, it's your leg muscles that want strengthening…' Before he could go any further Freddie exploded, 'What? Well, let me tell you they've held me for 1,000 overs and more this year already.' He looked pointedly at Gordon and with the cutting-edge in full evidence continued, 'And they've never let me down when I've been performing for England.' It's more than a lot of sportsmen can say.

The conversation was at an end. There's no arguing with this kind of logic. Nevertheless, I think Freddie had my sympathy. If ever a fast bowler had a strong pair of legs that man was Trueman. Indeed, apart from a little stitch in his early years as a fast bowler Freddie kept amazingly clear of injuries. He made me green with envy when, after bowling eight overs flat out, he could field at short-leg crouching down on his haunches, sometimes sitting miner fashion on his heels, for a rest! Most fast bowlers doing that after eight overs would want a winch and not a helping hand to get them up again.

These three stories almost tell the career of Frederick Sewards Trueman, 5 foot 10½ inches, who was born at Stainton (near Doncaster) on February 6, 1931, and was one of a family of eight to a miner. His father, Allan Thomas, was a well-known local club cricketer, left-arm bowler and batsman, and fostered a liking for cricket throughout the family.

As a young fast bowler with his school team, Trueman was hit in the groin by the ball and for a couple of years was an invalid and in danger of losing his leg. Fortunately the doctors won. Freddie returned to his school team as a fast bowler, earned selection for the Federation team, joined the junior section at Sheffield United's ground in Bramall Lane, and from there was invited to attend the Yorkshire nets for special coaching. The coaches liked what they saw. Just after he was 18, without playing for the second team in any sort of game, F. S. Trueman was chosen to play for Yorkshire against Cambridge University.

They knew that with such a glorious action to work on Trueman must come good and, although he had not the full strength of manhood and was without the necessary control to be an immediate star, he was ripe for grooming. Yorkshire played Trueman in nine games, including one with the New Zealanders at Sheffield at the end of July, and altogether he took 31 wickets at a cost of 23 runs each. He was carefully nursed by his captain, Norman Yardley, who like every other player in the side could see the promise in this self-confident, almost arrogant young man who wore a yellow tie with a red dragon and thought he was the bee's whiskers playing for Yorkshire.

To Norman Yardley fell the job of encouraging, letting him get an easy wicket here and there against the tail-enders and fanning an enthusiasm and willingness to bowl that more often than not needed dampening. It was with a chuckle rather than an intentional compliment that Yardley would say, 'I think it's time for Fiery Fred to have a bowl now.' But Fred was not as good as he thought himself to be. Yorkshire turned to a schoolteacher, Bill Foord, to fill the bowling position because they thought the latter was a better prospect and, during the August holidays, was readily available.

Trueman, who strained a back muscle in the game against the New Zealanders, was not called upon again that season and the next he heard from Yorkshire was when he received his invitation to attend the nets during the winter once again for special coaching. Unintentionally, Yorkshire had given Trueman's pride a tremendous blow. Yorkshire did not give a damn about him. Well from now on he would not give a damn about them. He kept up this attitude to authority almost throughout his career, but with that greater characteristic that stamped all his cricket there came the determination to Bloody Well Show Them.

Yorkshire did not think he was good? He started talking in order to convince himself he was good and few people who knew Fiery Fred in later life realised his continual chatter stemmed from an inferiority complex. To try and convince opposing batsmen he was good, he overdid his use of the bouncer, which meant presenting runs on placid surfaces. This was the real purpose behind Somerset's skipper Stephenson asking for the bit of paper to be removed.

Throughout his career Trueman tended to overdo his use of the bouncer but, as he got stronger, it was something to be feared and watched for, even on the most placid surface. The visiting India side in 1952 first felt the impact of Trueman grown into the strength of manhood. He took 24 wickets in three Tests and in the match at Leeds, in front of his own spectators, I recall the excitement when India lost their first four wickets without a run scored, and (at Old Trafford) Trueman taking eight wickets for 31 runs put India out in 80 minutes for 58 runs. Riding on the crest Trueman seldom bowled faster and he admitted, 'I'd nothing else to do but bowl straight.'

The Cricket Writers' Club elected him the Best Young Cricketer of the Year. The success gave Freddie's talk more authority and as he found in later years there was a great deal of success from bowling straight – and very fast. At this time the former miner and now England cricketer, Freddie Trueman, was serving his first year of National Service in the RAF. He could seldom be given leave to play for Yorkshire, but in the national interest he could play for England. He claimed only 61 wickets in first-class cricket that season and in 1953, when the England selectors wanted him for only one Test against the Australians, he had only 44 victims.

It could be said that Trueman began his career as a cricketer during that winter of 1953-54 when, with his National Service completed, he was chosen to tour West Indies. And it was at this time his troubles began. The pressmen found plenty of sensational copy in his willingness to talk. His antagonism got him into trouble with umpires and at times the crowd, too. He had to be reminded that the England captain, Len Hutton, was now no longer a Yorkshire colleague but The Boss. If any cricketer did or said anything mean on this controversial tour Freddie got the blame. He was, to many people, a bother-causer.

The England captain and selectors somewhat understandably turned to Typhoon Tyson as their fast bowling partner for Statham. Despite 134 wickets in 1954, Trueman missed the tour to Australia and did not play in another Test match until Tyson blistered his heel and had to withdraw from the Lord's Test of 1955 against South Africa.

In 1956, Trueman was chosen for two Tests against Australia but this season was for him the worst experience of unfitness, sciatic nerve trouble, blisters and then a strained side – plus a very wet summer. His final return was only 59 wickets and he was omitted from the England team to tour South Africa. Newsmen, hoping for another sensational Trueman story, were assured by the chairman of selectors and the MCC secretary that there had been no victimisation and Freddie himself found consolation in these assurances. Once again came that determination to show 'em – and, of course, there was now considerable experience behind his efforts.

This was the start of the period mentioned earlier when Trueman, by general opinion, was a great bowler. And he was helped considerably by the Yorkshire captain, Ronnie Burnet, who took over the side in 1958. By consideration and encouragement, leading and never driving, he drew the best out of Trueman. Freddie now had the ability to suggest to a batsman that he was going to bowl a bouncer and send down a yorker and as he grew in confidence he began to feel he could answer back. Occasionally he guessed badly. He found the Yorkshire committee supported the captain Vic Wilson when Trueman arrived late for a game at Taunton. Fred later refused to subscribe to a retirement present for Wilson saying, 'What, show my appreciation for a chap who sent me home?' Again there was no refuting the logic but Mr Burnet wangled a compromise with Freddie's wife Enid.

All these things made Trueman a character the game and the public enjoyed, and yet, while giving this impression that he knew it all, there was that extreme and opposite side to him which responded to confidence, and was ready to listen to a helping voice. Then he could charm more than dominate. Towards the end of his career when seniority earned him the right to lead Yorkshire whenever D. B. Close was absent, he proved himself a capable and knowledgeable captain and had the high distinction of leading Yorkshire to victory over the touring Australian team. The honour put another yard of pace into his bowling. He wanted to prove he was still good.

He enjoyed being told he was good, too, and on these lines I cherish the story of Richard Hutton after Freddie had returned yet another of his many five-wicket performances. 'Well bowled, Fred,' he said. 'Outswingers, inswingers, bouncers, yorkers, you bowled the lot. Tell me, did you ever bowl a plain straight one?' Quick as a flash came the reply, 'Aye, one. But it was so fast it went through him like a dose a salts and knocked all three down.'

Fiery Fred held the stage for 20 seasons. In major or minor parts he commanded attention. He received a benefit of £9,331 in 1962 and bow(l)ed out in September 1968.

Bloody-minded, beautiful, t' best – by Michael Parkinson, 2007

In the late 1960s, I sat down with Fred Trueman to discuss working together on a book about his life. It soon became apparent we had different views on how this might be achieved. Fred thought the odd session with a tape recorder, a few jokes and a kick up the backside for the panjandrums of cricket would suffice. I thought differently. I saw him as a true working-class hero. Still do.

Fred didn't set out to change the world and would have dismissed any suggestion he was a revolutionary as nonsense. But there is little doubt that what his critics would term his boorish behaviour towards authority during the 1950s was part of the kindling for a drastic change in British society in the years that followed.

Certainly people of my background and generation saw Fred not simply as a great cricketer but as an emblematic figure: outspoken, bloody-minded, Jack-as-good-as-his-master. We sometimes forget how class-ridden Britain was 40 and more years ago and how cricket represented the status quo. The game was run by a private members' club. It was Gentlemen and Players, with the England team picked by the President of MCC and the cricket correspondent of the *Daily Telegraph*. Or so Fred believed. And he wasn't the only one.

But radical changes were afoot. The Butler Education Act had given bright working-class children the right to free education. A new generation began to question the old order. Fred – bolshie, outspoken and anti-authoritarian from the start – was a figurehead. I saw Fred in this context and wanted it to be a part of the book. Fred didn't, so our joint venture withered. In the end, John Arlott wrote it: *Fred, Portrait of a Fast Bowler*, a fitting testament written with a rare combination of insight and love. Shortly after publication, I called John to congratulate him. I told him of my failure to write the book and Fred's reluctance to be unduly introspective about his own life. I asked him how he had managed to persuade him.

'Oh, I didn't speak to him,' said John. 'Why?' I asked.

'Didn't need to,' said John. 'You see, I had seen him bowl.' The hack, elegantly and gently put in his place by the poet.

Out of our failed collaboration came the anecdote, repeated in many of the obituaries, about how Fred suggested his own grandiloquent title for his biography. It happened when I said we must think of a snappy title, one which would best sum up his life. Fred said, '*Fred: T' Best Fast Bowler that Ever Drew Breath.*' I said, sarcastically: 'Too short.' He came back, '*Fred: T' Definitive Volume on T' Best Fast Bowler that Ever Drew Breath.*' The title is now part of the Trueman mythology. It has been suggested it was intended to be self-mocking. I have to tell you I was there, and he was only half-joking.

I first met Fred Trueman early in his career when he was on leave from National Service and farmed out by Yorkshire into the leagues. My opening partner at the time was H. D. Bird, long before he found immortality as umpire, rain-maker and best-selling author. Trueman already possessed a daunting reputation as a fast bowler. He was quick and wayward, and must have licked his chops at the sight of two such pale and trembling victims. He hit Dickie under the heart midway through the first over, and a terrible moaning ensued. We gathered around the victim – in those days the opposition ministered to a stricken opponent – to check which parts might be damaged or missing. As we did so, I looked back to see the bowler squatting at the end of his follow-through, thoughtfully chewing a blade of grass. When eventually we had restored Dickie, I walked back past Fred. 'How's thi' mate?' he asked.

'He's on his hind legs, Mr Trueman. He'll live,' I said, with a fawning jocularity.

'That's all right then,' said Fred, and then, almost as an afterthought, added, 'But think on, you're next.'

When I reminded Fred of this story he said he must have apologised to Dickie because he always said sorry to people he hit but didn't bear a grudge against. This peculiar point of principle was substantiated by Trevor Bailey when recalling being felled by a Trueman bouncer at Leyton. Fred had been dropped by the England selectors and took his anger out on the Essex team. The previous batsman had lost most of his teeth trying to hook a Trueman bouncer and, as Bailey took guard, was on his way to hospital. Trueman, on the rampage, bowled short to Bailey who ducked and was hit on the head. As he lay on the ground assessing the damage, Trueman approached. He said, 'Sorry, Trev, old son, there are many more I'd rather hit than thee.'

Such anecdotes – and there are a thousand more where that came from – substantiate the image of Trueman as the plain-spoken, belligerent yet curiously honourable assassin of cricket. The guns linger with a conscience, Fred as Wyatt Earp. Lethal yet chivalrous. Except when confronted by the enemy, and then he was simply lethal. In Fred's case the enemy was the Establishment and all who wore its colours, such as a stripy cap or fancy cravat. Famously, faced with such an opponent, Trueman allegedly sent his middle stump flying, followed by the observation, 'It was hardly worth dressing up for, was it?'

You find yourself dwelling on the vaudeville persona of Fred Trueman at the expense of any proper analysis of what made him one of the greatest fast bowlers. In fact, the intertwining of the two, the combination of athlete and comedian, was what made him the most charismatic cricketer of his time. If Fred Trueman played today, Fred Flintoff would be a minor celebrity.

His first Test series established him as a fast bowler of rare venom. The Indians had seen nothing like him, and, when one or two of their batsmen sought refuge alongside the square-leg umpire, the legend was born…

Polly Umrigar, constantly stopping Trueman in his run-up to adjust the sightscreen. Umpire Chester, losing patience, 'Mr Umrigar, where ideally would you like the sightscreen?'

Umrigar: 'Ideally Mr Chester, between me and that mad devil Trueman.' In the end no one knew which bits of the narrative of his life were fact or fiction. Norman O'Neill told the story of sitting with Fred in the lounge of a Bombay hotel and saying to him, 'Fred, I believe those two Indians at the next table are talking about you.' To which Fred replied, 'Aye, Norman, they talk about me all over t' world.'

I once asked Fred how many of the stories told about him were true, and he said not many. On the other hand, he said he seemed to attract bizarre situations. He told me the story of touring India for the Bengal Cricket Association's silver jubilee celebrations. On a long and interminable rail journey, the train made an unscheduled stop in the middle of nowhere. Fred alighted and was greeted by the stationmaster. Fred asked for the whereabouts of a toilet, which seemed to fill the stationmaster with great excitement. He asked Fred to follow him, and led him to a room where he drew back a red velvet curtain to reveal a Victorian chamber pot on a plinth. What is more, the pot had the legend 'F. S. Trueman' painted on it. How it came to be there, what became of such an important piece of cricket memorabilia, how it was known that the Great Man would visit and, moreover, be in need of a pee, are important questions. Fred could offer no enlightenment except to say, 'How could I possibly make it up?' Nor could he have imagined that one day he'd be father-in-law to Raquel Welch's son; Fred's daughter married the film star's offspring. It was an intriguing, but unsuccessful, intermingling of cultures. 'My run-up lasted longer,' said Fred.

Trueman loved the adulation, fed it assiduously. Always a serious cricketer, he was also a gifted comedian and communicator. Yet the paradox of Fred Trueman was that the instinctive and charismatic entertainer on the field of play could be insecure and awkward off it. Sometimes he found it difficult to be a public figure, unable to understand that the blokey image he projected on the field might persuade his fans he was a laugh-a-minute in his private moments.

It is also important to remember that the cricket superstars of his day had no bodyguards, posh houses or cars with tinted windows to escape interference. What he developed was the ability George Best had (when sober) to be at the centre of attention and yet detached from it. Again, like Best, I suspect that for all he liked to be considered gregarious, Fred Trueman was, by nature, a loner.

Looking back over the 50 years I knew and observed him – trying to catch the flavour of the man, endeavouring to explain what I saw – I find myself prefacing every memory, good or bad, with the sight of him in full flow when he provided the most thrilling and beautiful spectacle not just in cricket, but in any sport I've ever seen. When I use the word 'beautiful', bear in mind I am talking about a man with a barrel chest, big backside and the kind of legs normally used to support billiard tables. It was a formidable physical presence, but far from graceful. When he turned at the start of his run-up, you would not have been surprised had he pawed the ground.

As it was, after the first few accelerating strides, he glided rather than ran to the wicket and with his final fulminating stride, left arm thrown high, the perfectly side-on arc of his body described the powerful bend of a bow. It was the action not simply of a great bowler but an artist with a proper reverence for the aesthetic possibilities of the loveliest of games. Technically speaking, his action defined Fred's belief that cricket is a side-on game. As a philosophical proposition, it offered a clue as to why the game attracts more poets, philosophers, writers and dreamers than any other.

For all that he projected the image of the fiery, confrontational Yorkshire fast bowler, he was a purist when it came to cricket. In conversation, the nearest he came to embracing poetry was when he described Hutton's technical perfection or the elegance of Tom Graveney's strokeplay.

I saw him in his hurtling youth destroy the Indians at Headingley. Sixteen years later, I saw his swansong at Bramall Lane when he captained Yorkshire to an innings victory over Australia. On that day, on the clay that shaped him, he came off his long run for the last time. The next time I saw that sublime action was in a nightclub, an image projected on to a screen through which he burst to meet his audience. He was making his debut as a stand-up comic. I could have done without that. So could Fred.

29

Yorkshire were playing Oxbridge. A wicket had fallen. Slowly, gracefully from the pavilion emerged a slim willowy figure most beautifully attired – the next man in. His flannels could only have been cut in Savile Row; his boots were new, his pads spotless. On his head set at a carefully cultivated devil-may-care Beatty angle was a multicoloured cap. Clipped round his neck to protect his throat from the rude winds of early May, which did not spare even university towns, was a silk scarf. On his way to the crease he played imaginary bowlers. With wristy cuts and flicks, perfectly timed drives and darting late glances and hooks he despatched the imaginary ball to all parts of the ground. The Yorkshire players watched his approach in silence. He eventually arrived at the wicket and looked all about him imperiously, like a king, come to his rightful throne. He took guard, and then spent a full minute making his block hole, shaping and patting it until it was to his satisfaction. Another look around the entire field – and he was ready to receive his first ball. Freddie Trueman bowled it and knocked two of the three stumps clean out of the ground. As our young exquisite turned languidly and began to walk away, Freddie called to him sympathetically, 'Bad luck, Sir, you were just getting settled in.'

Basil Easterbrook, 'The Dreaded Cypher', 1971

At about the same time he appeared as a front man for a television show called *Indoor League*, featuring pub games. For years, television executives have debated the host's first word in a programme. Should it be 'Hello'? Or is 'Hi' more friendly? Maybe it's 'Welcome', a cosy partnership of the two? Fred walked on and said 'Ayup', which didn't catch on but suited him to the marrow.

He found joy and satisfaction in his retirement on *Test Match Special*. He was a perceptive and demanding observer, but ripe for parody in his oft-explained view that the game was going to the dogs. He also invited scorn because of his support for Mrs Thatcher, whose virtues were rarely discussed in the coalfields of his youth. He failed to understand the discrepancy between the rebellious lad and the conforming adult, and the consequent dismay of those who had once imagined marching behind his broad shoulders. But then he never saw himself as anything other than a fast bowler and entertainer. The jibes hurt because he was a sensitive man with a long memory for insult, real or imagined.

He had reason to be disgruntled with Yorkshire when, after 20 years of service, he was handed a silver cruet as a departing gift. The cruet cost £220 but, because the committee had set a limit of £100, he was asked to pay the difference. What really upset him was when he arrived home; he found they hadn't bothered to inscribe the gift.

Sometimes we are careless with our heroes.

But his most heartfelt gripe was that he missed more than 30 Test matches because the selectors – dominated at the time by MCC – were set against him. He had a point. Particularly when you consider he was not chosen for the 1954-55 tour of Australia after a domestic season when he took 134 wickets at 16.

Fred mellowed in old age, but only in the sense that he was prepared to forgive and forget on a selective basis. Making it up with Geoffrey Boycott after both men fell out during one of Yorkshire's civil wars was well met. But on other deeper disputes he was implacable. He left the room and never returned. After he died, we expected a memorial service. It was not to be, and on his express orders. His final instructions were, 'When I'm gone I don't want any of these two-faced bastards who I didn't get on with standing up and saying nice things about me.'

He did not go gentle into that good night. He died as he had lived, chin up, bristling, glaring down the wicket at the enemy. A most singular man.

RAY ILLINGWORTH

Ray Illingworth led England on 21 occasions. He won 12 Tests, drew 14 and lost only 5. With Yorkshire, he won the Championship seven times and then won it again with Leicestershire (also taking them to two John Player Sunday League tiles and two Benson & Hedges Cups). He scored almost 25,000 runs in his first-class career and took more than 2,000 wickets. He returned to Yorkshire and captained them in 1982-83.

Keeper of the Ashes – by Trevor Bailey, 1973

From the moment Ray Illingworth established himself as a permanent and vital member of the Yorkshire XI there has never been the slightest doubt that he was a top class all-rounder, exactly the type of player any team would welcome. First, he was an off-break bowler with that natural mean streak which is second nature to any self-respecting Yorkshireman, an absolute detestation of presenting any runs to the opposition. His skill stemmed from those two basic essentials – length and line. To these he added the refinements of ability to spin the ball, and, as one would expect from someone who started life as a medium-paced seamer, to drift one away from the bat.

On good pitches he could be depended upon, while on a helpful wicket he was a match-winner, and it is noticeable how economic he still is in limited over cricket. In general, it would be true to say that he relies on beating the batsman off the pitch rather than in the air because his trajectory has always been rather flat and his arm relatively low. Another weapon he developed was a well disguised change of pace, and he also learned the virtue of bowling close to the stumps from over the wicket, but rather oddly he has always tended to go wide when bowling round the wicket which I fancy has reduced his effectiveness against left-handers.

Secondly, he has been an ideal middle-order batsman even though he started life higher up the order. If the early Yorkshire batting failed he was just the right person to restore normality to the situation because he enjoyed leading a recovery and possessed the attribute of a sound, correct defensive technique and the temperament for the job.

Thirdly, he was a most thoroughly reliable all-round fieldsman with a safe pair of hands, who was probably at his best in the gully. Although there has never been any question as to Ray's worth as an outstanding all-rounder in County cricket, some have reservations about his ability at international level and it must be admitted that until his recall to the Test scene several years after his career for England appeared to have ended, his Test record was unspectacular.

His bowling had always been tidy, but he had not proved as effective as either Freddie Titmus or David Allen in Test matches where the pitches, in general, are unsympathetic to off-spin. He had also failed to impress overmuch with the bat and he had at times suggested uncertainty against wrist spin, a not uncommon characteristic with Yorkshire players.

Ray became captain of England as a result of three different but related events, which had nothing to do with his performance as a player or skipper. First, after 17 years with Yorkshire he decided in the winter of 1968 to leave the club because he was dissatisfied with the length of the contract that had been offered him.

Secondly, Tony Lock, who had done so much to raise the morale of Leicestershire – he made them believe in themselves – failed to return from Australia, so that the county suddenly found themselves without a captain and spinner. To overcome this considerable loss Leicestershire sensibly turned to Ray Illingworth, who had both the skill as a player and the professional know-how to carry on the job begun by the former Surrey cricketer. The one thing they never considered was that they had engaged the future leader of England, and, in purely domestic terms, his selection proved something of a handicap to his new employers, because it meant him missing so many matches.

Thirdly, Colin Cowdrey, who had finally established himself as unchallenged captain of England, had the cruel misfortune to be seriously injured. The outcome was that the English selectors, who still seem to think that the England captaincy must go to a county skipper, despite Sir Leonard Hutton's record, turned to the newly appointed Leicestershire leader as a stop-gap measure.

Ray at that time had led Leicestershire on only a few occasions and he relied on the knowledge he had acquired during his long stay with Yorkshire. If he had remained with them; if Tony Lock had not stayed in Australia; and if Colin Cowdrey had not been incapacitated, he would almost certainly never have been appointed, which underlines that fate is responsible for more captains than anything else.

Ray Illingworth did so well for England, both as skipper and as player, that he turned a temporary job into a permanent one, going on to regain the Ashes and to retain the Ashes. And proving himself, in terms of results, one of the most successful of all the long line of England captains. His distinguished reign, which spanned 30 consecutive Tests and is presumably over, or nearing its end, has emphasised one fact.

The first requirement for a successful Test leader, apart from a good, well-balanced team, is a sound practical knowledge of the game and the ability of his players, plus personal skill to contribute as a player. At international level captains who are passengers are out and should never have been in. What is wanted is definitely not a dashing white charger, so beloved by all those who still believe that Waterloo was won on the playing fields of Eton.

Anybody who knew Ray Illingworth as a cricketer and had played with or against him should have expected him to captain England efficiently. He has always been a keen student and a real professional reared in the hardest of cricketing schools, Yorkshire. It followed that his approach was bound to be realistic rather than romantic. Just like his illustrious predecessor, Len Hutton, he only liked to gamble on certainties.

His first aim was to win, but when, in his opinion, the odds against appeared too great he would then fight for a draw. This was the outlook of a Roundhead, rather than a Cavalier, but who won the Civil War? He played cricket as he was brought up to play it, hard and seriously – giving nowt and expecting nowt in return – which is the best way to achieve results. What astounded the critics was not that Ray should handle his team most competently, but his own performances as a player, especially with the bat. In this connection I was less surprised than most because I had seen him bat well on so many occasions when I had been playing against him. It is an interesting fact that three of Ray's first four centuries were made against Essex and the other was during the Scarborough Festival when I was captaining the opposition. Each time our attack had made a substantial hole in the early Yorkshire batting and appeared to be very strongly placed until Illingworth's arrival. Then he proceeded systematically, with the aid of the straightest of bats, to rescue his side.

He frequently showed himself to be an especially fine player of seam bowling with plenty of determination and application. I believe he would have scored many more runs if he had gone in higher than number six for Yorkshire. His county possessed a strong batting line-up so that he often did not reach the crease, or arrived there with little time remaining. When he was promoted in 1959 he averaged over 40 with an aggregate of more than 1,700.

Ray has regularly proved himself to be a batsman for the occasion and he has plainly revelled in his new role as captain of England, responding with a number of valuable innings when most required. His greatest triumphs were against the powerful Rest of the World XI when in the five Tests he scored 476 runs. Since his appointment he has batted better than ever before, displaying greater confidence and freedom. In particular, he has improved his technique against the spinners.

One criticism that has been often levelled against him as captain is his reluctance to bowl himself as much as he might. There have been occasions when he has appeared to forget that he was the second spinner in his team and his own considerable ability as a bowler. He is a genuine craftsman who very rarely is off target. It might be argued that sometimes he does not give the ball sufficient air, preferring to tie down the batsman and hoping he will make a mistake rather than attempting to buy his wicket in a more subtle manner. This may well have been one of the reasons why he did not experience much joy in the Caribbean.

Although captaining England at home is very largely a tactical operation, taking the MCC abroad produces many other problems, many of which have no direct connection with the game itself, and it really needs another kind of leadership. It is true that MCC under his command regained the Ashes, but it was not a happy tour. My own impression was that it could have been a very different story if the management had been chosen with more foresight as to producing a harmonious atmosphere. In the circumstances Ray coped well with a job (a lonely one) that was made more difficult than it need have been for he enjoyed the support of his players and achieved the main purpose of the trip.

Last summer Ray led England against Australia in the best and most exciting series seen in this country for more than a decade. Although the rubber was tied, which was a fair reflection on the merits of the two teams, I felt that England would probably have just limped home at The Oval if Ray himself had not had to limp off with a damaged ankle at a crucial time when bowling well. Under his command Leicestershire won their first major award, the Benson & Hedges trophy, and would almost certainly have captured the John Player League as well if they had not experienced a whole spate of injuries to key members during the final run in.

There can be no denying that Raymond Illingworth has made his mark as a highly successful captain in various forms of the same. He has proved himself to be a serious, practical leader, lacking the panache of Brian Clough and close to Sir Alf Ramsey or Don Revie in his basic approach. He is a quiet thoughtful man, with a dry, somewhat sardonic, sense of humour who has forgotten more about cricket than most of his critics can ever hope to know. He also has a useful reply, 'Look in the record books.' He was one of *Wisden*'s Five Cricketers of the Year in 1959.

His accolade came in the New Year's Honours of 1973 when he was appointed CBE for his services to cricket.

GEOFFREY BOYCOTT

Geoffrey Boycott was born in Fitzwilliam in 1940. His first-class statistics were 48,426 runs from 609 matches (151 centuries). He made 108 Test appearances, which brought 8,114 runs (22 centuries). After his career ended he moved into the media, where his analysis is both cogent and treasurable.

The Centurions of 1977 – by Terry Brindle, 1978

Geoffrey Boycott's place in cricket folklore was assured long before that warm Headingley evening last summer when he succeeded where only would-be bombers and the infernal weather had succeeded before and stopped an English Test match in its tracks for almost ten minutes.

Boycott's hundredth century – in a Test match, before his Yorkshire public – was indeed the stuff that dreams are made of. There was hardly a dry contact lens in the house. But the abiding significance of his hundredth century was not simply statistical; Boycott himself conceded that one century on record was much the same as the one before or the one to follow. It was the realisation, vitally important to Boycott himself, that the public were prepared to accept his peace offering after a controversial absence from Test cricket.

Boycott and controversy have shared the longest opening partnership in the game. The owlish, introverted young man who broke into County cricket with Yorkshire in 1962 and who was regarded as a dedicated technician rather than a talented strokemaker, developed his skills to prove the unbelievers wrong and neglected his personality to convince his critics they were right. The trauma of Trent Bridge and the Headingley homecoming that followed combined, as never before, Boycott the public man with Boycott the private person. To his unconcealed delight, the public showed themselves ready to accept both.

Cricket tends to traditionalise its heroes, seeking to find in them all the qualities of unselfishness and character that lend an amateur's zeal to a highly professional game. Boycott, complex and warted, refused to fit the pattern and was not easily forgiven. Yet Boycott the technician has rarely been doubted. He is compact, beautifully balanced, professionally expert, arguably the most adroit player of the ball off the wicket in the modern game. The very soundness of his technique tends to detract from the drama of his innings, even of centuries carved with fastidious determination.

Others have created their own legends more extrovertly, more gloriously, more entertainingly. Boycott builds an innings brick by brick, cementing each stroke to the next with that extraordinary power of concentration that frustrates good bowling and intimidates poor. His centuries are an act of will. That single-mindedness has exposed Boycott to accusations of selfishness, which are bound to be levelled from a distance; easier to challenge with an insight into the man and the situation thrust on him as captain of a young and inexperienced Yorkshire side.

Boycott's responsibilities weigh heavily and the proven frailty of Yorkshire's batting has led him to believe he cannot, must not fail. The conviction that his runs are indispensable – and Yorkshire without them would have struggled fearfully in the recent past – feeds an already characteristic strain of stubbornness. Boycott in or out of form cannot contemplate giving his wicket away; the very idea is anathema, an admission of failure.

He is, consequently, a player less than ideally suited to limited-overs competition where the ability to improvise is ranked as important as ability itself. He has, consequently, an air of detachment during an innings that shuts out every consideration except the next ball, the requirements of the moment. His intensity is sometimes misdirected, often misinterpreted.

Taxed for playing a strangely hybrid innings against Glamorgan two seasons ago, when with excruciating slowness and devastating speed in turn he endangered victory and then clinched it, Boycott explained his approach. 'When you have played yourself in you have only three things to consider: how many deliveries will you face before the end of the match, which bowlers will you face those deliveries from and how many runs do you need from each ball to win. It is very simple; I knew we would do it,' he said. Victory that day was secured with 15 minutes to spare; Boycott scored 156 not out in a winning total of 320.

If his single-mindedness is a flaw, England were glad enough of it at Trent Bridge and again at Headingley. It is ironic and perhaps unfortunate that Boycott's moment of historic achievement should lend itself to discussion of his character, of his weaknesses as much as his strengths. Yet Boycott's character and performance are indivisible; more than any modern player he has been judged in terms of personality. Boycott, knowing it and sometimes wounded by it, withdrew into the security of the art he knew best and resolved that if he could not be the most popular of players, he would be the most effective. A century of centuries insists that he did not fail.

His welcome back into Test cricket and the warmth of his reception at Trent Bridge and Headingley tapped a fund of popular sympathy and admiration, which Boycott never knew existed. Rather like a clip from an old film in which a recluse Queen Victoria returns from a triumphal jubilee procession and confides with some surprise, 'Y' know, I really think they like me after all...' Corny, perhaps, but Boycott was never more sincere.

At 5.49 p.m. on August 11, Geoffrey Boycott reached one hundred hundreds and realised he could count on the support, understanding and even friendship of one thousand thousand. It would not be easy to decide which he values more. And he achieved the feat in his 645th first-class innings. Only Sir Don Bradman (295), Denis Compton (552) and Sir Leonard Hutton (619) did it more quickly.

The Master Craftsman – by Derek Hodgson, 1988

Geoffrey Boycott, an egocentric right-hand batsman of great defensive skills and an occasional in-swing bowler, will be remembered as much for his prodigious scoring record as for his impact, over 25 years, perhaps more, on the history of the Yorkshire county club. He has a facility for making enemies much faster than he made his runs, admits to very few friends, yet inspires a loyalty among his admirers that all politicians must envy.

As a cricketer, a batsman converted to opening in his early days with Yorkshire, he had no peers in England during his career. Abroad, only Sunil Gavaskar, the man who overtook Boycott's aggregate of Test match runs, could be compared in application, dedication, attention to detail, tactical acumen, patience and endurance. Even Boycott's critics would agree, too, that his runs were made often in far more difficult circumstances, in English conditions and on English pitches, than Gavaskar's. In batting on seaming or turning pitches, or when the ball cut or swung, Boycott for more than 20 years reigned supreme in the world.

This ability to score runs, albeit slowly, when all around him were grateful merely to survive, indicated that Boycott was far from limited in his strokeplay. All the shots were there, but only rarely was the full armoury uncovered; when he did settle upon an attacking innings, however, the ensuing firework display could be a brilliant memory. Three occasions come to mind, the first a brief burst at Bradford in 1977, when Yorkshire were chasing runs on the third afternoon against Northamptonshire and Boycott, astonishingly, was charging from his crease to lift the bowling straight. There was a humid Sunday afternoon at Worcester, where Boycott produced a dazzling 60 at a rate not even Milburn would have scorned.

But the outstanding recollection of Boycott in this mood must be of a World Series Cup match against Australia at Sydney during the 1979-80 tour under Mike Brearley. There had been speculation that Boycott might be dropped from the limited-overs side. Brearley, like every other captain, had his difficulties with Boycott, yet their relationship was only occasionally strained; and Brearley was able, as he was with most players, to inspire some remarkable performances. On December 11, Boycott walked out with Derek Randall and, against an attack featuring Lillee, Thomson and Walker, scored 105 off 124 balls, including seven fours. He reduced a rowdy Hill, primed to jeer him, to a respectful silence. Englishmen, by and large, are not disposed to embrace Geoffrey Boycott, but that was one time when he induced considerable emotion among the stiff upper lips.

The more customary Boycott, and the experience of batting with him, was summed up thus by a younger contemporary. You were always conscious that you were on your own, in that he was one partner unlikely to surrender his wicket to save you and that you were his partner on his terms. That accepted, there was a lot to learn because his mind, computer-like, was always working.

He would know who was to bowl and which end they would choose and why. He would anticipate bowling and fielding changes, calculating when and for what reason. He knew most bowlers backwards, most pitches, even the direction of the prevailing wind. You would always know when there was something he didn't like about one particular bowler when you found yourself with more of the strike than normal. Professionally he was a paragon, immaculate in his preparation and turnout, and for all the jokes it was an education to stand at the other end and watch him play.

Bradman apart, it is hard to imagine a stronger-minded cricketer in the history of the game. He entered the Yorkshire dressing room in 1962 and, with his short hair and rimless glasses, was regarded as a rather dull, painstaking young man from South Yorkshire who was unlikely to challenge the obvious rising stars, John Hampshire and Philip Sharpe among them. He was a mediocre fielder, and if anyone knew that he could bowl, his prowess remained a secret. Yet Boycott's will to succeed was so enormous that he swept into the Yorkshire and England teams with hardly a pause. He had achieved world class when political wrangling inside Yorkshire propelled him on to a larger stage.

By a process of mismanagement that would have brought courts-martial in another sphere, the Yorkshire committee allowed, from the sacking of Johnny Wardle in 1958 to the dismissal of Brian Close in 1970, almost a full Test match team to be dispersed. They preferred Boycott for the captaincy above two, possibly three, more experienced candidates; and then it was that the essential dichotomy in Boycott's character was fully revealed. How could a man so dedicated to personal accomplishment subordinate his own ambitions to the well-being of a team, and a young team at that, saddled with insecurities and the ever-present knowledge that they were forever being compared with their mighty predecessors? Other counties were opening their ranks to world-class players from overseas, making Yorkshire's task of competing doubly hard. Even the traditional reservoir of Yorkshire-born talent began to dry up as the leagues went over to limited-overs cricket. No Yorkshire captain, not Lord Hawke, nor Sellers nor Close, could have conjured up a Championship-winning team in those circumstances.

In a frustrating, difficult time, Boycott was the one link with a glorious past, the still unqualified success in an ever-gloomier world for the Yorkshire follower and member. Not surprisingly, he came to loom larger in the minds of the public, and of many Yorkshire members, than any officer of the club or any other player. Who were these little men who dared criticise the hero?

Boycott also found his international career in a cul-de-sac. What would have been a normal, acceptable and expected progress to the captaincy became complicated when he withdrew from consideration for selection in the mid-1970s mainly, it was alleged, because the England captaincy had not been offered when he expected it. When the crown became available, through Brearley's injury, in Pakistan and New Zealand in 1977-78, Boycott's leadership was not received well either by his hosts or his players.

His international career ended during the Calcutta Test of England's 1981-82 tour of India. He did not take the field on the final day of that match and returned home shortly afterwards on medical grounds. Memoirs published since, however, alleged that he was sent back as a disciplinary measure. He returned to domestic cricket, passing Yorkshire county records season by season until, in September 1986, the club brought his long career with them to an end by not offering a new contract. He remained, nevertheless, a member of the club's General Committee.

In 1987, Geoffrey Boycott published an autobiography, reviewers generally regarding it as a long, somewhat tedious attempt at self-justification. A sad book was an almost universal comment, a wry reflection on Boycott's own influence on the publication for his helper, Terry Brindle, is one of the most humorous of cricket writers. Nor is Boycott himself without humour, taking and giving the dressing room horseplay with some relish. But he could also, in his time as Yorkshire's captain, make the dressing room feared, almost hated, by young Yorkshire players.

So the paradox continues. Once asked to name his closest friend, he could not find one he was confident enough to nominate. Abominated by great Yorkshire contemporaries, he was found by many outside the game to be utterly charming.

Perhaps he was unfortunate to be born in an age when the public interest is served by a media intent upon prying and prising loose every single item, good but preferably bad. Had he lived in Victorian times he might have been regarded as one of the great eccentrics; an intensely private man is a phrase that might have been used. He would not have needed to appear continually before the cameras, the notebooks and the tape-recorders. Grace, MacLaren and Hawke never needed, nor were expected, to justify themselves. His resentment at the poking and probing into his manners, mores and style of life is understandable. A boy born into the South Yorkshire coalfield at any time in the last 50 years came into the world impressed with the need to retaliate first.

All over the world Boycott will be remembered for his batting: the ritual, almost fussy re-preparation before each ball, the tap of the bat, touch of the cap, reassurance that his pads were in place, and the relentless, straight-down-the-line forward push. Most of his runs came on the off side because that was where most bowlers bowled to him. The drive through cover, or extra cover, was minted silver. He was not less adept on the leg side, merely more circumspect, as if suspecting that the pull, hook or sweep all carried elements of risk. Such was his power and reputation at his peak that for him to be bowled was a major surprise. When an Oxford University bowler achieved that feat, the young man was a back-page sensation for a day.

Boycott's bowling was typical of the man, almost always of mean length and line with a huge in-swerve. He performed some notable little feats for Yorkshire on Sunday afternoons, but his captains knew they had to take him off the moment a batsman began to chance his arm. Boycott was deeply upset if he conceded many runs. He transformed himself from a poor fielder to an excellent boundary runner, with a strong, accurate arm, and from time to time he served his county well at slip. He might have been a great captain but for his notorious blind spots, for no one disparages his knowledge and understanding of the game.

Yet when his career is fully assessed and settled into the record, early next century, will all his foibles and prejudices matter that much? A batting record that stretches, vast and almost unsurpassable, like a distant view of the Himalayas, must put much pettiness into perspective, leaving all the discord in his wake no more than the odd trickle down a great stone face.

George Hirst

George Hirst was born in Kirkheaton in 1871 and died in Huddersfield in 1954. He scored 790 runs in 24 Tests and took 59 wickets. In his first-class career for Yorkshire, he scored 36,356 runs and took 2,742 wickets. The sum from his 1904 benefit is worth almost £500,000 at present rates.

Obituary – 1955

George Herbert Hirst was one of the most illustrious cricketers who graced the Golden Age. On the 24 occasions on which he played for England, Hirst achieved only a few noteworthy performances, but such was his prowess with bat and ball for Yorkshire in a career spanning 40 years that Lord Hawke described him as the greatest County cricketer of all time. Certainly this blunt, outspoken man of extreme buoyancy and cheerfulness brought such a tenacity to the game that no match in which he figured was won or lost till the last ball was bowled. Small wonder, therefore, that in Yorkshire he was an unchallenged hero, and throughout the length and breadth of England his popularity stood unrivalled.

Figures alone tell only part of the story of Hirst, but they show unmistakably his supreme prowess as an all-round cricketer in the fullest meaning of the phrase. Between his first county game for Yorkshire in 1889 and his last in 1929, Hirst scored 36,203 runs, average 34.05, and took 2,727 wickets, average 18.77. At his peak friends and opponents alike recognised him as the best mid-off in the country, with a pair of hands so sure that a considerable proportion of his 550 catches were made from scorching drives in a period when strong driving was an essential component in every batsman's game.

The measure of Hirst's ability is best reflected in that he accomplished the double feat of 1,000 runs and 100 wickets 14 times, a number surpassed only by his renowned contemporary, Wilfred Rhodes (16), and that he alone made 2,000 runs and took 200 wickets in a season, which he did in 1906. His figures were 2,385 runs and 208 wickets. Years afterwards, when asked if he thought his record might be broken, Hirst made an answer typifying his whole approach. With a twinkle in his eye, he replied, 'I don't know, but whoever does it will be very tired.' Yet, through the years, he himself showed little evidence of fatigue. Only a very fit man, such as he was, could have reached 1,000 runs in 19 seasons and taken 100 wickets in 15 different years.

The people of Kirkheaton and the surrounding areas almost lived for cricket and from an early age Hirst, born on September 7, 1871, showed that he would be a player of more than ordinary skill. He became associated with Huddersfield when 18 and before his 19th birthday his first ambition, that of playing for Yorkshire, was realised. Hirst was fond of recalling that in those days his equipment, which he carried to the ground in a canvas bag, was worth no more than ten shillings, that he wore a shilling cap, a sixpenny belt and brown boots. Success in County cricket came slowly, but after some seasons of quiet progress, he established himself in 1896 by scoring 1,122 runs and taking 104 wickets. Thenceforward he gathered strength as he went along.

Of his 60 first-class centuries, all but four were played for Yorkshire, his highest being 341 – still a county record – against Leicestershire in 1905. Leicestershire suffered particularly from his bowling as well as from his batting. Twice he did the hat-trick against them, once in a match in 1907 in which he took 15 wickets, his greatest success in one game. Five times Hirst bowled unchanged through a match, Rhodes being his partner on three occasions and Schofield Haigh on the other two, and twice he took three wickets in four balls.

The combination of Hirst and Rhodes was feared as much by batsmen as that of Peel and Briggs, Gregory and McDonald and, in later years, Grimmett and O'Reilly. In the 1902 Test match at Birmingham, Hirst and Rhodes bowled out Australia for 36 runs; their lowest total in any Test. Rhodes took 7 for 17, and Hirst 3 for 15. This was the most memorable joint feat of Hirst and Rhodes, but in the next match the Australians met Yorkshire, who put them out for 23 (Hirst 5 for 9 and F. S. Jackson 5 for 12). Another Yorkshire bowling triumph in which Hirst played a notable part occurred in 1908 when he and Schofield Haigh dismissed Northamptonshire for 27 and 15, Hirst taking 12 for 19 and Haigh 6 for 19.

On his two tours to Australia, with A. E. Stoddart's team in 1897-98, and P. F. Warner's side in 1903-04, Hirst did not realise English hopes but he played a conspicuous role in a dramatic victory over Australia at The Oval in 1902. When Hirst, who scored 58 not out in the final innings, was joined by the last man, his lifelong friend and colleague, Rhodes, England required 15 to win. The story has been passed on that, as

Rhodes met him on the way to the wicket, Hirst confidently murmured, 'We'll get 'em in singles, Wilfred,' which they proceeded to do. Whether true or not, that is the type of remark Hirst would have made. One last instance of his versatility: in 1906 he scored two centuries and took 11 wickets in the match against Somerset at Bath.

Essentially a self-taught batsman, Hirst frequently gave of his best when the pitch afforded help to bowlers. His remarkable quickness of eye and feet enabled him to develop the hook and pull strokes so well that some bowlers complained that they found exceeding difficulty in bowling to him anything except a yorker which he did not treat as a long-hop. His liking for the hook was costly only in Australia. By contrast to his right-handed batting, Hirst was a natural left-arm bowler, a shade faster than medium. After a long bounding run, he delivered with a free, easy action and he often made the new ball swerve and dip into the batsman so late that many of his victims confessed themselves as suspecting that they had been thrown out from cover. Hirst, in fact, has been described as the father of all modern seam and swing bowling. Before he showed its possibilities, bowlers rubbed the new ball in the dirt to take off the polish.

Hirst, short and thickset, found perpetual pleasure in every game he played and captains such as Sir Pelham Warner have testified that they could not have wished for a better man to be in their teams. Both as a player and as a personality, none could speak too highly of him. Sir Pelham has said that when things were going wrong on tour Hirst was first to come to the aid of everybody with his ready wit. When Hirst was given a benefit by Yorkshire in 1904 he received a sum of £3,703, a remarkable figure in those days. Seventeen years later a testimonial for him produced £700. Virtually that came at the finish of his active career, for he became coach at Eton College in 1921, but he played occasionally for Yorkshire for another eight years. During his 18 years at Eton, Hirst endeared himself to hundreds of young cricketers who benefited from his kindly guidance, and nothing was more fitting than that MCC should include him in the 26 professionals whom they honoured in 1949 with Honorary Life Membership.

Cricket was George Hirst's life and less than a year before his death he sat with Rhodes, now sightless, while England recovered from a seemingly hopeless position against Australia at the Leeds ground on which he himself so often stood in the breach.

WILFRED RHODES

Wilfred Rhodes scored 39,969 first class runs and took 4,204 wickets. He made 58 Test appearances (2,325 runs and 127 wickets). He was born at Kirkheaton in 1877 and died in Dorset in 1973. He had been blind since 1952.

Integral Part of the Game's History and Traditions – by Neville Cardus, 1974

Wilfred Rhodes was Yorkshire cricket personified in the great period of the county's domination, shrewd, dour, but quick to seize opportunity. For Yorkshire he scored more than 30,000 runs, averaging 30 an innings: for Yorkshire he took 3,608 wickets at

16 runs each. When he was not playing for Yorkshire, in his spare time, so to say, he played for England and amassed 2,000 runs, average 30, and took 127 wickets at the cost of 26.96 apiece. In his first Test match he was last in the batting order, and at Sydney in the 1903-04 rubber he took part in the most persistent and prolific Test match last-wicket partnership to this day; he helped R. E. Foster to add 130 for the tenth wicket, his share 40 not out. Eight years afterwards he went in first for England at Melbourne, and against Australia he was the partner of Hobbs in the record first-wicket stand of 323.

His career is already legendary; it does indeed read like a fairy tale. He was not 21 years old when he first bowled for Yorkshire in a match against MCC at Lord's. In the first innings he accounted for Trott and Chatteron; in the second for Trott, Chatteron, C. P. Foley, and the Hon. J. R. Tufton – a six wickets for 63, a modest beginning, true. But at the season's end he had established himself as the greatest slow left-hand bowler in England with 154 wickets, average 14.60.

During the period in which Rhodes and Hobbs opened every England innings by prescriptive right, Rhodes put aside his bowling. In the Australian rubber of 1911-12 he contributed only 18 overs. But then the war came, reducing the Yorkshire attack. In 1919 Yorkshire needed again the spin and flight of Rhodes, so he picked up his bowling arts exactly where years before he had laid them down; picked them up as though he had not lost touch for a moment. He headed the bowling averages of 1919 – 164 wickets, average 14.42 in 1,048 overs. He was nearly 42 by the calendar. In 1902 he had gone in last for England at Kennington Oval when 15 runs were wanted to beat Australia; George Hirst, with whom he always opened Yorkshire's attack, was holding the wicket at the other end. England won by one wicket.

Twenty-four years afterwards, Rhodes in his 49th year was recalled to the England XI and was one of the main causes of Australia's defeat and England's emergence from years in the wilderness. On this, his last appearance for England, Rhodes took the wickets of Woodfull, Ponsford, Richardson (twice), Collins, and Bardsley for 79 runs. He had probably lost by then much of his old quick vitally fingered spin: but as he explained to me, 'If batsmen thinks as I'm spinnin' them, then I am' – a remark metaphysical, maybe, but to the point. At Sydney, in December 1903, on the shirt-fronted polished Bulli soil pitches of that distant halcyon day for batsmen, Australia scored 485, and the might of Australia's champions commanded the crease – Trumper, Hill, Duff, Armstrong, Gregory. Rhodes bowled 48 overs for 94 runs, five wickets. It was on this occasion that Trumper, most brilliant of all batsmen, alive or dead, made his famous remark to Rhodes – 'for God's sake, Wilfred, give me a minute's rest.'

Rhodes could not turn the ball on the Australian grounds of half a century ago. He prevailed by length, variations of flight, but chiefly by unceasing accuracy of pitch, always demanding close attention from the batsman, the curving arc through the air, the ball dropping on the same spot over by over, yet not on quite the same spot, each over in collusion with the rest, every ball a decoy, some balls apparently guileless, some artfully masked – and one of them, sooner or later, the master ball. He was economical in action, a few short strides, then a beautifully balanced sideways swing of the body, the arm loose and making a lovely arch. He could go on for hours; the rhythm of his action was in its easy rotation, hypnotic, lulling his victims to the tranced state in which he could work his will, make them perform strokes contrary to their reason and intention. Batsmen of Rhodes's heyday frequently succumbed to his bait for a catch in the deep field. David Denton had safe hands at long-on; and the scoresheets of the period repeated day by day the rubric – c Denton b Rhodes. In rainy weather, c Tunnicliffe b Rhodes was familiar proof that Wilfred was at work on a sticky pitch, for Tunnicliffe was the best slip fielder of the century, a long giant with a reach into infinity.

Rhodes really was a slow bowler, not quick and low flight to the pitch, after Lock's manner. At the end of his career he proudly maintained that, 'Ah were never hooked and Ah were never cut,' a pardonable exaggeration considering the proportion of truth in it. Rhodes seldom pitched short. 'Best ball on a "sticky" pitch is a spinnin' half-volley,' such was his doctrine. And he bowled to his field with the precision of high mathematics. Ernest Tyldesley once told me that he often had no alternative but to play at least three balls an over, on a batsman's wicket, straight to mid-off, an inch off the spot where Rhodes had planted mid-off.

Rhodes made himself into a batsman by practice and hard thinking. He was one of the first batsmen to adopt the full-fronted stance, left shoulder pointing to forward leg. But it is a mistake to suppose that his batting was perpetually dour and parsimonious in strokeplay. In the Test match against the Australians at Lord's in 1912, England had first innings on a rain-damaged pitch. *Wisden* relates that Rhodes, with Hobbs as company, so monopolised the hitting that his share of 77 runs amounted to 52. On the whole and naturally enough, Rhodes distrusted the romantic gesture. One day in conversation with him, I deplored the absence in modern cricket of the cut. 'But it were never a business stroke,' he maintained.

While he was actively engaged in the game he was not a man given to affability. He was known as a natterer on the field; and to natter in the North of England means to talk naggingly, most to oneself, with the intention of being overheard. At Old Trafford in the 1930s Lancashire reached a total of 500 against Yorkshire. The Lancashire captain, Leonard Green, was about to take the bowling of Rhodes when the score was 499. Green was sure in his mind that a total of 500 would never again, or not for decades, be achieved by Lancashire against Yorkshire. He therefore determined that, come what may, he would himself score the 500th run. So he blocked a ball from Rhodes, then ran like the wind. The ball was picked up by Emmott Robinson at silly-point and hurled to the bowler's end, where it struck Rhodes on the wrist even as Green got home by the skin of his teeth. And in all the scurry and excitement Wilfred was heard to mutter, while he retrieved Robinson's violent throw, 'There's somebody runnin' up and down this wicket. Ah don't know who it is, but there's somebody runnin' up and down this wicket.'

He was a great player, one of the greatest of cricket's history, not only for his all-round performances denoted by the statisticians: nearly 40,000 runs scored in 37 seasons and 4,184 wickets taken. He was great because his cricket was redolent and representative of Yorkshire county. In his old age he lost his eyesight and found his tongue. He accepted his affliction philosophically, and consoled himself by a flow of genial chatter never before heard from him. He attended cricket as long as health would permit. With an acquired sense he was able to follow the play. 'He's middlin' the ball right'. But it was his delight in his last years to recall the old days. I asked him what he thought of Ranjitsinhji. 'He were a good bat were "Ranji". But I always fancied myself getting him leg before doin' that leg glance of his'. I tried again. What did you think of Trumper? 'E were a good bat were Victor'. There was no advance on a good bat in Wilfred's vocabulary of praise. Once, though, he let himself go. I asked him his opinion of Sidney Barnes as a bowler. 'The best of 'em today is half as good as Barnie'. He intended this as a compliment to the champions of today.

I last saw him as his daughter, Muriel, and her husband Tom Burnley, led him out of Trent Bridge at the close of play of a Test match. More than 50 years ago he had first played for England, on this same ground, in 1899, when he was 21. Now he was going home to Canford Cliffs, Bournemouth, white stick in hand, arm in arm with his son-in-law, his face ruddy after hours sitting and listening to cricket, and whether he knew it or not, himself a permanent part of the game's history and traditions.

HERBERT SUTCLIFFE

Herbert Sutcliffe was born at Summerbridge, near Harrogate in 1894 and died at Crosshills in 1978. He made 4,555 runs in 54 Test appearances, including 16 centuries. He scored 149 hundreds, which then became 151 when two innings were subsequently deemed to be first class.

One of the Greats – by J. M. Kilburn, 1979

Herbert Sutcliffe was one of the great cricketers and he brought to cricket as to all his undertakings an assurance and capacity for concentration that positively commanded success. His technical talent matched his character and his achievements were therefore on the highest plane.

In a career extending from 1919 to 1939 Herbert Sutcliffe scored more than 50,000 runs and averaged 52. He never knew a season of failure, except by the standard of his own astonishing peaks, and at the zenith of his career he scored 16,255 runs in five years as a measure of mastery in all conditions and over the world's best bowling of the time.

The First World War delayed his entry into County cricket until he was 24 years old when, after demobilisation from a commission in the Green Howards, he was given a place in the Yorkshire side. His quality was never in doubt and by the end of the 1919 season he had scored five centuries in an aggregate of 1,839 runs. He had also established a first-wicket partnership with Percy Holmes. For 14 years these two batsmen opened the innings for Yorkshire, representing a partnership of unparalleled success in which they put up the hundred on 74 occasions. Equally happy was Sutcliffe's Test-match association with J. B. Hobbs, for this became the most accomplished of all opening partnerships. Sutcliffe's good fortune, however, was only in the presentation of opportunity. Seizure of it was his own merit and with one partner or another he constructed 145 first-wicket century stands.

His artistry and efficiency in difficult conditions became legendary in his lifetime, with his centuries against Australia at The Oval in 1926 and at Melbourne in 1929 as historic examples. Matches against Lancashire stirred him to nine centuries. His defensive patience and skill became a byword, yet at need his hitting was brilliant in the extreme. Against Northamptonshire at Kettering he met spin on the sticky wicket with an innings of 113 which included ten sixes. At Scarborough against the fast bowling of Farnes and Nichols, Sutcliffe took his personal score from 100 to 194 in 40 minutes. His 100th first-class century was the 132 he hit in less than two hours at Bradford when Yorkshire were hurrying to defeat Gloucestershire.

Courage and concentration were his basic attributes. No prospect daunted him, no difficulty dismayed him, no crisis upset him. He was an artist of the dead bat and an uncompromising hooker of fast bowling. He sought solution to his batting problems by taking them as they came, one at a time. He never allowed the present to be influenced by the alarms of the past or fears for the future. In the means and manner of his performances he raised enormous prestige for himself throughout the cricketing world. He was admired and respected wherever he played and by his refusal to depreciate his own value he raised the status of his profession.

He took the supplementary rewards of his distinction with polished grace and unfailing consideration for colleagues. Herbert Sutcliffe the individual always made it clear that he was Herbert Sutcliffe inseparable from Yorkshire and England. He was as punctilious in acknowledgment of obligations as he was single-minded towards the immediate task in hand.

After the retirement of A. W. Lupton in 1927, Sutcliffe was offered the Yorkshire captaincy as a professional player. Although he was on tour in South Africa when the invitation came he appreciated the possibility of divided opinions and with characteristic diplomacy declined the appointment, giving an insurance of his willingness to play under any captain.

During his playing days he founded and developed a sports outfitting business, now directed by his elder son. After his retirement from the field he took a managerial appointment in the paper trade. He showed himself as successful in commerce as in cricket and for the same reasons of application and reliability. His repayment to the game that had given him so much was service on the Yorkshire committee, as an England selector, and as sponsor for many good causes in cricket.

Though he was born in Summerbridge, Sutcliffe was a Pudsey native in cricket association. There, as a schoolboy, he began league cricket and from there he advanced to the county, but neither Pudsey nor any other nursery could have claimed Herbert Sutcliffe as a typical product. He was a Yorkshireman in his loyalty and training, but he was cosmopolitan in approach and outlook. His manner fitted Lord's as expressively as it fitted Leeds.

Immaculate, alert, brisk of movement, serene in repose, he carried his character with a clear label wherever he appeared. His off-drive wore a silk hat and his hook was a ready response to the aggressive intent of any bumper. His defensive play was the reduction of risk to the minimum and his self-confidence was unshakable.

In his first-class career he scored 149 centuries. He shared with Holmes a partnership of 555 for Yorkshire, and with Hobbs a partnership of 283 for England against Australia.

Second in the nominal batting order, Herbert Sutcliffe was second to none in steadfastness on all occasions. He was esteemed for accomplishment; he was acclaimed for his unfailing resolution. His name will always stay in the headlines.

SIR STANLEY JACKSON

Sir Francis Stanley Jackson made 15,901 first-class runs and took 774 wickets. In 20 Tests he scored 1,415 runs and claimed 24 wickets.

By Hubert Preston, 1948

The passing of Colonel The Honourable Sir Francis Stanley Jackson, PC, GCIE, on March 9, in his 77th year, came as a shock, not only to all who knew him personally, but also to every lover of cricket who had watched and enjoyed his wonderful prowess on the field of play. From the time that F. S. Jackson at Lord's by his remarkable all-round success helped Harrow gain a victory over Eton by 156 runs in 1888, he went on from strength to strength, until he became one of the finest cricketers ever seen in England.

Unfortunately he could not go on any tour to Australia owing to business reasons, and the presence of Lord Hawke in command of Yorkshire until 1910 prevented him from ever being the county captain, though he was occasionally in charge of the side. He reached the zenith of fame in 1905 when captain of England against Australia. In all five Tests he won the toss; made 492 runs with an average of 70, among his scores being 144 not out at Leeds, 113 at Manchester, 82 not out at Nottingham, 76 and 31 at The Oval; took 13 wickets at 15.46 each, surpassing the efforts of all his colleagues and opponents. Of the five contests, England won that at Nottingham by 213 runs – after declaring with five men out – and that at Manchester by an innings and 80 runs, while they held much the stronger position in each of the three matches left unfinished. By a curious coincidence Stanley Jackson and Joseph Darling, then the Australian captain, were exactly the same age, both having been born on November 21, 1870. That was Darling's third visit as captain and his last tour in England. He died on January 2, 1946, and his obituary in last year's *Wisden* contains some of his experiences in opposition to Jackson.

Regarding his luck in winning the toss in those 1905 Tests and as captain of MCC, for whom he scored 85 in a rain-ruined match at Lord's, Jackson said that at Scarborough, when captain for the seventh time against the Australians, 'I found Darling stripped to the waist. He said, "Now we'll have a proper tossing, and he who gets on top wins the toss." So I said to George Hirst, "Georgie, you come and toss this time." Darling then said, "All right, we'll toss in the old-fashioned way!"' Again winning the toss, Jackson scored 123 and 31 not out, rain preventing a definite result.

Born at Chapel Allerton, near Leeds, Stanley Jackson showed remarkable batting ability when at a preparatory school before he went to Harrow, when he was in the XI for three years, being captain in 1889. He did little on the first occasion, and his father, then the Rt Hon. W. L. Jackson, a member of the Cabinet in Lord Salisbury's second government, promised Stanley a sovereign for each wicket he took and a shilling for each run he made. Stanley scored 21 and 59 and took 11 wickets for 68 runs; Harrow won by 156 runs. His father's generosity over cricket ceased with that match. Stanley's only comment was that he was glad he had come off, as it would do father so much good.

Next year, when captain, five wickets fell to him, and his vigorous 68, best score in the match, accounted largely for victory by nine wickets. Proceeding to Cambridge, Jackson gained his Blue as a Freshman, and in 1892 he headed both the batting and bowling averages, and in first-class matches came out third among the amateur bowlers with 80 wickets for less than 19 runs apiece. Re-elected captain, he led Cambridge to victory by 266 runs in 1893, showing such convincing form that he was given a place in the England team for the first Test at Lord's. He followed a splendid innings of 91 with 103 at The Oval, but when, late in August, the time came for the third Test – at Manchester – he and other Yorkshiremen who might have been included in the side turned out for their county against Sussex at Brighton. He was one of five all-rounders given prominence in the 1894 *Wisden*.

Describing his first Test innings of 91 in 1893 at Lord's, Sir Stanley smiled and then related that, in the second Test at The Oval, W. G. Grace, the England captain, said:

'With all these batsmen I don't know where to put you.'

'Anywhere will do.'

'Then number seven.'

'Thanks. That's my lucky number; I was the seventh child.'*

'And that match brought my first hundred for England. Mold came in last when I was 99. He nearly ran me out, so in desperation I jumped in and drove Giffen high to the seats, reaching 103. Then the bewildered Mold did run me out.'

Jackson figured in all the 1896 Test matches, also in the next visit of Australia when the rubber was extended to five fixtures, being credited with 118 at The Oval in 1899. In the great games of 1902 Jackson was England's best batsman. He did little at Sheffield, but at Birmingham, when three wickets fell for 35, he scored 53 and with J. T. Tyldesley saved England from collapse. At Lord's Fry and Ranjitsinhji were dismissed without a run, but Jackson and A. C. MacLaren, contemporaries at Harrow, raised the total to 102 without being separated before rain washed out the match. In the memorable Manchester struggle, which Australia won by three runs, five England wickets went down for 44 in reply to a total of 299, but Jackson and Braund pulled the game round with a partnership of 141, Jackson himself going on to make 128. At dinner in the evening of that great day a lady sitting next to him said, 'I was so disappointed that

---

* *There were five daughters besides the elder son, children of the first Lord Allerton. Stanley Jackson married in 1902 Julia, daughter of Henry Broadley Harrison-Broadley, then MP for Howdenshire. Their son, Henry Stanley Lawies, married in 1927 Grace Diana, daughter of Dr Arthur Phillip Beddard.*

Another story I associate with Jack Mercer involved Freddie Trueman on the 1953-54 tour of the West Indies. MCC were playing at Spanish Town, not far from Kingston, at a sugar plantation. Across the entrance was strung a banner exhorting the employees on the virtues of WORK, OBEDIENCE, DISCIPLINE. Trueman, who was sharing a car with Mercer and myself, looked with disgust at the banner and exploded, 'I bloody well wouldn't work here!'

Alex Bannister, *My Life Reporting Cricket,* **1980**

Ranjitsinhji failed' – and this remark was made to the man who had played the innings of his life. He was fond of telling this little yarn against himself. At The Oval Jackson scored 49, sharing in a partnership of 109 with G. L. Jessop, whose wonderful innings of 104 paved the way to England's one-wicket victory. Altogether Jackson scored 1,415 runs in Test matches against Australia – all in this country – with an average of nearly 49, and took 24 wickets at an average of 33.

Jackson played first for Yorkshire in 1890, and his last appearance for the side was in 1907. During that period he scored 10,405 runs for the county, averaging nearly 34 an innings, and dismissed 506 batsman for 19 runs apiece. In 1898, the only season when he appeared regularly for his county, he scored 1,566 runs and took 104 wickets. His highest scores for Yorkshire were 160 against Gloucestershire, 158 against Surrey and 155 against Middlesex. He appeared on many occasions for Gentlemen against Players, and in those games made 1,000 runs, average 31.50, and took 50 wickets. His aggregate for all first-class matches was 16,251 runs, average 33, and 834 wickets at 19 runs each. Among his bowling triumphs were eight Lancashire wickets at Sheffield in 1902 for 13 runs, and the last four Australian wickets in five balls at Leeds in the same year, his analysis being 5 for 12; he and George Hirst dismissed the Australians for 23. This happened directly after England in a drawn Test match had disposed of Australia for 36; Rhodes, who took 7 for 17, did not bowl in the more remarkable collapse of the Australians for the second lowest total ever recorded by an Australian side in England.

When in 1896 Harry Trott's team fell for 18 before MCC at Lord's, Jackson scored 51 on a treacherous pitch. In the Gentlemen and Players match at Lord's in 1894 he and S. M. J. Woods bowled unchanged. Jackson took 12 wickets for 77 and, in addition, made 63 – the highest score of the match, which the Gentlemen won by an innings and 37 runs before four o'clock on the second day.

Going to India with Lord Hawke's team in the winter of 1892-93, Jackson took 69 wickets at 10.27 runs apiece and tied for first place in the batting averages with A. J. L. Hill, a Cambridge contemporary. When again captain of the Light Blues in 1893, Jackson gave Ranjitsinhji his Blue. At Lord's he instructed C. M. Wells to bowl wides in order to prevent Oxford from getting a desired follow-on, and Cambridge won by 266 runs. This set an example followed by Frank Mitchell three years later, when Oxford won by four wickets, and so primarily led to an alteration in the laws, making the follow-on an optional choice for the side holding the upper hand.

President of the Marylebone Club in 1921, the highest honour that a cricketer can enjoy, Sir Stanley Jackson was chairman of the Test Match Selection Committee in 1934, and in 1943 presided over the special committee appointed by MCC to consider post-war cricket.

Well-built and standing nearly six feet high, Stanley Jackson was equipped with special physical advantages for cricket; to these were added fine judgment, perseverance, and, above all, exceptional courage which amounted to belief in his own abilities. Free and stylish in method, he drove splendidly on either side of the wicket and was perhaps the finest forcing on-side batsman of his time. While essentially a forward player on hard wickets, he had at his command on sticky wickets a strength and science of back play to which few men have attained. His great stroke sent a good-length ball through the covers; he cut square or late and turned the ball cleverly on the leg side with similar precision. Nothing was better than the way he jumped in and drove the ball over the bowler's head, as shown in the lifelike picture at Lord's, and as I saw at Bradford, where he sent the ball high over the football stand.

A right-handed rather fast-medium bowler with a nice easy action and plenty of spin, he kept a good length and often got on a sharp off-break. On a difficult wicket he was a bowler who might dispose of any side. While always a keen and smart field, especially at cover-point, he was not in his early days a sure catch, but steadily improved in this respect and made himself in every sense a great player. At Bradford on one occasion he was out to a brilliant catch in the long field, whereupon he tucked his bat under his arm and joined vigorously in the applause that greeted the fieldsman's splendid effort. On the same ground, where there is a stone wall in front of the pavilion, a ball bowled by Jackson was sent by a low skimming drive with such force that it rolled back from the wall into the middle of the field, coming to rest practically at the bowler's feet. Jackson, in appreciation of the remarkable occurrence, made the ball a dignified bow.

In the South African War Jackson served with the Royal Lancaster Regiment of Militia, and in the first Great War, 1914-18, he was Lieutenant-Colonel of a West Yorkshire Regiment battalion which he raised and commanded. He entered Parliament in 1915 and remained Unionist member for Howdenshire Division of Yorkshire until 1926. One day in the House of Commons dining room Mr Winston Churchill, who had been his fag at Harrow, said, 'Let me introduce you to Mr Lloyd George.' There came a quick exclamation. 'I have been looking all my life for the man who gave Winston Churchill a hiding at school.'

When he wanted to make his maiden speech the debate went unfavourably, and he received a note from the Speaker: 'I have dropped you in the batting order; it's a sticky wicket.' Then, at a better opportunity, he sent this hint, 'Get your pads on; you're next in.'

In 1922 he was appointed Financial Secretary to the War Office, and next year he succeeded Lord Younger as Chairman of the Unionist Party Organisation. In 1927 he went out to India as Governor of Bengal. There he proved equal to the most trying situation, behaving with splendid nerve and authority when he nearly fell a victim to attempted assassination by a Calcutta girl student who fired five shots at close range, narrowly missing Sir Stanley when presiding at a meeting. His London home was bombed in 1940, and in August 1946 he was run over by a taxi, receiving a severe injury to his right leg: a climax to unpleasant experiences which no doubt contributed to his last illness and hastened the end of this very distinguished Englishman.

Chapter Two:
We Don't Play It For Fun

In the introduction to his *History of Yorkshire County Cricket*, J. M. Kilburn offers a poised summation of the club he spent his lifetime covering. 'Yorkshire's story is more than a record of its most famous players,' he began:

> It is the story of many strivers, the 'bread and butter' cricketers who, day in and day out, made the basis of the county's cricket, welding themselves into the unit of a team, dissolving their individual talents in the essence of the whole and winning their renown *as much from what they represented as from what they were*. No county ever commanded a deeper loyalty from its players, or its officials, or its supporters. *Yorkshire cricket is a private enterprise with a public responsibility*, and the story of Yorkshire cricket is an account of the stewardship of that county concern.

This is a short extract from a book the size of a doorstep that long ago slipped out of print. But the core opinions Kilburn expressed – the italics are mine purely for the purpose of emphasis – strike me as still fresh and valid.

Yorkshire cricketers are made aware – especially by those who pay to watch them – that there is a tradition to be upheld, and that their cricket must be serious, appealing and successful as a consequence. Passing years have never diluted the strength of this belief. It often creates the feeling – albeit off the field – that Yorkshire regard themselves as aristocratic and think they ought to be treated as such, irrespective of what the Championship table says. Roy Hattersley's anecdote in his memorable piece 'To be disliked again' captures it perfectly:

> The chairman welcomed members to the 'AGM of the champion county' and added, 'We know which the champion county is, whichever team happens to be at the top of the table at the end of any one year.'

What he describes occurred at the end of the 1950s, after Yorkshire had failed to win the title.

This was not tongue-in-cheek, and something of the attitude continues to linger – perhaps because of Yorkshire's pride in its cricketing past, or its sheer bloody-mindedness. But without either of them, Yorkshire cricket just wouldn't be the same. And self-effacement isn't a Yorkshire trait anyway; there is truth contained within the hoary joke: 'You can always tell a Yorkshireman. But you can't tell him much.'

FIFTY YEARS OF YORKSHIRE

By Lord Hawke, 1932

There would seem to be little doubt that the origin of the Yorkshire County Cricket Club is to be found in the series of matches between Sheffield and Nottingham that began in 1771. Though there were only 26 of such games, the last one being played in 1860, the fact that leading players of both counties took part in them gave to Sheffield the sort of right that is due to custom of being regarded as the home of the game in Yorkshire.

They were, by the way, evidently keen enough on the game in my county in those days, as the first match, in 1771, began at 9 a.m.! And, in 1784, in the York rules I see that a fine of 3d was levied on any member who was not within sight of the wickets each morning before the Minster strikes five o'clock. Report has it that one of the Notts players was in the habit of rising before daybreak and riding on horseback all the way to Sheffield to play!

Nearly all these matches, however, were played for money – that of 1800, for example, for 200 guineas. In that year the second match took place on November 3, 4 and 5! These early games were played at Sheffield on Darnall Ground, the Hyde Park Ground, and at the present ground at Bramall Lane, where the first county match was Yorkshire v Sussex in 1855.

In the first Sheffield-Notts match at Bramall Lane there played for Sheffield (totals: Nottingham 130 and 93 against Sheffield 146 and 78 for 6, Sheffield winning by four wickets) M. J. Ellison, whom I succeeded in 1902 as President. Ellison held a record which must be very bad to beat, *viz*, that he shot grouse on the first day of the grouse-shooting season for 70 successive years. He was the second president of our county club, a post he occupied from 1863 to 1898. Mr T. R. Barker was the first president in 1863, though I understand he never attended a meeting.

Forming the County Club

A meeting at the Adelphi Hotel, Sheffield, on March 7, 1861, was the real beginning of the County Club. How soon they got busy is shown by the fact that the secretary at this meeting, Mr W. Whittles, was instructed to write to the players selected to play Surrey at The Oval to ask them their terms. Our out and home first two Surrey matches, in 1861, resulted in Surrey winning at The Oval and we at Bramall Lane. That, and the next year's efforts, ended on the resolution being carried on January 8, 1863:

'That a County Club be formed.'

Sheffield, however, did not have it all her own way, as in 1863 Bradford played Notts, and in 1864 Kent decided not to play Yorkshire owing to a Kentish doubt as to who were the proper parties to get up Yorkshire county matches. Mr George Padley was the first secretary but he resigned in 1864, when appointed borough accountant, and was succeeded by Mr J. B. Wostinholm, who served from 1864 to 1902. Mr Wostinholm was followed by F. C. Toone, of whom more anon. Thus, from 1863 to date the

Yorkshire CCC in 68 years has had only two presidents and four secretaries, including among the latter the present one, Mr Nash, who was appointed after Sir F. C. Toone died in 1930.

There followed in 1865 the strike of five of our professionals. The strike was not due to any friction with the county club, but was mainly on the ground of a supposed grievance against Surrey. The professionals suspected Surrey of having instructed John Lillywhite to no-ball Edgar Willsher, who was a member of the All England Eleven of which our George Anderson and others were members. One result of this strike was that Yorkshire did not win a game in 1865 and arranged no matches in 1866. Another result was that all five professionals took the proper course in 1867, and ever since then, 64 years ago, complete harmony has existed between the Club and her players.

Our professionals are handed a small printed brochure that gives in full all the facts of our Regulations relating to Players. In these the position with regard to match fees and talent money is plainly set forth, showing that professionals who have got their county cap get £2 more per match, away or in Yorkshire, than is paid to players who have not yet won their cap. The fee is at present £15 away and £11 at home for those with caps. For an Australian or South African match the professional receives £12, and in all cases £1 extra per won match. Twelfth man is paid the same, but no fee for a match won. It is a hard and fast rule with us that a professional on gaining his cap joins the Cricketers Friendly Society. A similarly definite rule is that professionals are not permitted to write to the press in any form whatsoever. We have made a solitary exception in the case of articles on hints how to play, etc., by Sutcliffe. But I think we are on sure ground in putting out of the way of our professionals the temptation to be paid for signing their names to articles which they do not always actually write.

In the matter of bonuses we have instituted in my time the system whereby players who have played regularly for five years get a bonus of £250 if their services are no longer required. If they have played for more than five but less than ten years, our committee guarantees them not less than £50 for each subsequent year above five.

Let me say that between 1870 and 1901 the sum of £13,298 was paid to 15 professionals as Benefits money, and between 1903 and 1923 a further sum of £15,483 was paid under the same heading to 12 professionals. Since George Hirst's £3,703 benefit in 1904, which was not a half-penny more than he deserved, for he was by far the greatest all-round county professional of all time, and Wilfred Rhodes' £2,202 in 1911, both records have been broken by the £4,016 benefit of the late Roy Kilner in 1925. In 1911 we resolved that the Committee guarantees £1,000 benefit to players of not less than ten consecutive years.

It is now 50 years last September since I played my first match for Yorkshire. It was in 1883 that I took over the captaincy from that genial old soul, Tom Emmett. Since 1886 I have been a Member of Committee, I was elected Vice-President in 1893, and I became President in 1902. Regarding developments in management, and referring to our great success on the field, I say unhesitatingly that the latter could never have been obtained without the keen interest of the committee and the *esprit de corps* of the team.

Leading Players

It is not possible to name even a quarter of those who have made Yorkshire history. Hirst, surely, must come first. What a hero! Two thousand runs and two hundred wickets in a season is surely a county record – not that I like records – I hate 'em! Yet the public always knows when a batsman has scored his one, two or even three thousand runs and applauds accordingly, forgetting all the time that a man may be playing for his own record and not for his side. Never in my long career would I give marks when I could see a man was playing for records which were detrimental to his side winning the match. I shall never forget when we had all agreed to get out in order to force a win – it was before the declaration rule came in – one batsman was determined to bat on. We were truly annoyed until old David Hunter said to me, 'Let me go in; I'll run him out!'

I have wandered away a bit from Georgie. Was ever anyone such a trier? Slack fielding he abhorred. Woe betide Scofie if he missed a catch, and wasn't Haigh himself frightened. However, with all his keenness Hirst was loved by the team and always had a good word for a youngster.

Ted Peate and Bobbie Peel, our great left-hand bowlers, had all too short careers before they made way for Wilfred. Peate's eight wickets for five runs against Surrey in 1883 at Holbeck, where we dressed in a tent in those days, is a County cricket record, and was about the greatest bowling feat I ever saw. Rhodes' numerous fine performances are too many to mention, but the manner in which he made himself from a last-wicket batsman to a number one with Hobbs will never be beaten. Georgie at Eton and now Wilfred at Harrow – lucky schools – ere long may they both produce some England players, is my heartiest wish.

What a bowler, too, was our Scofie Haigh. No one could spin the ball or nip in a real fast yorker better than he. Alas! I think he was a bit lazy about the latter, and many a time I had to remind him of it! Sure enough he produced it, and bang went the wicket. I had always a warm corner in my heart for John Tunnicliffe. He had not a great benefit and never got his deserts, but, as my right-hand man, he was charming to work with. His high moral character had a great deal to do with the success of the side. He was a good and ready speaker, and we always enjoyed listening to him at the annual Wighill outing.

Sutcliffe and Holmes

Sutcliffe and Holmes, the heroes of our first-wicket stands, and the former for years one of the mainstays of our England XI. Nobody I know trained, and trains, harder or more conscientiously than Sutcliffe. I ascribe much of his great success to that fact. Rhodes also deserves mention in the same category. It was told of him that once on the way back from India he took a glass of stout, but said he, 'it gave me rheumatism so I didn't have a second.' In the case of Holmes, we in Yorkshire shall always consider we had a few seasons back a little bone to pick with the Selectors for passing over such a brilliant field and resourceful batsman on any wicket. It was, perhaps, his misfortune to be generally regarded only as one of a first pair.

Macaulay, who has taken nearly 1,500 wickets in only 11 seasons, must not be forgotten. Verity, too, stepping into Rhodes' place, has already taken over 200 wickets in less than two seasons. There is also decided promise in the fast right-handed bowling of young Bowes. Last, but not least, I cannot forget our David Hunter. It was hard luck he never played for England, for he was one of the greatest keepers of the day. On one occasion at Leyton I had to leave early to catch a train and I told Georgie to take command. Poor old David, how hurt he was! I forgot he was senior player and never thought he wished to be troubled with the captaincy. Later, however, he had his chance and captained jolly well. His successor, Dolphin, was also a fine wicketkeeper.

Yorkshire's Amateurs

The above are some of our great Players, and I am the last to forget the help we received from Ernest Smith, Arthur Sellars, F. S. Jackson, F. W. Milligan, T. L. Taylor, Frank Mitchell and Rockley Wilson. We have often been accused of not playing Amateurs and that we are practically a Players side. My answer is that whenever we have an Amateur good enough he was always been asked to play. Did we not always welcome with open arms Smith and Rockley Wilson during August when, owing to scholastic duties, they could not play earlier? Our greatest amateur was undoubtedly Stanley Jackson, who was Jacker to everyone from his Harrow days. He was a great batsman, great bowler, fine fielder – a great cricketer to the core. He took 506 wickets for 19.18 runs for us and made 10,405 runs with an average of 33.78 during the 17 years he played for Yorkshire.

Few who remember him as a batsman, know that he was once number ten in the batting order for Yorkshire! This is how it happened. Though he had just taken 7 for 42 against Middlesex somebody had run him out for a song and he did not seem keen to play in the next match at Chesterfield. 'Why,' I argued with him, 'you've just got seven of 'em out at six apiece! You must come.' So he came all right. Next day, as I was writing out the order, I asked him where he'd like to go in, so he said, 'Oh! Don't know. Treat me as a bowler.' So I wrote him down as number ten. Brown and Tunnicliffe then proceeded to make 554 for the first wicket. I was number three that day in Jackson's place. As they walked out to bat I put on my pads. I took them off for the lunch interval; I put them on again and took them off again for the tea interval. Again I put them on, and sat another couple of hours. Such is cricket! I have never seen Jacker's equal at bowling for his field. I remember on one occasion when we were in the cart at Bradford against Surrey how precisely he bowled for his field, and how he apologised to me for having bowled a ball not intended. Though his grand batting for England is probably best remembered, he was a bowler of the very highest class, with a graceful, flowing delivery of a kind but rarely seen nowadays.

Since those happy days Jacker has passed through more serious times in Bengal. There, a couple of years ago, he and I were the guests of honour at the dinner to us of the Calcutta Cricket Club given at the Bengal Club. We both made speeches, and when he got up to speak first he said across the table to me, 'I've got first innings today, old man. You bossed me often enough in the past, but I'm boss here!' One of our greatest cricketers; what a pity Australia never saw him out there in his heyday.

Ernest Smith, really fast in his time, took 284 wickets for 23 runs each, and made 4,781 runs for 20.81 per innings often when badly wanted. One of his greatest innings was that at Leyton when, in saving the match, he batted an hour for 0. That was the innings in which our Georgie was in for five hours for 96 and then said he got out by accident! Rockley Wilson, of the perfect length, took 196 wickets for Yorkshire for 15.70 runs each, playing only in August, and the claims of business prevented T. L. Taylor playing for more than seven years, during which he made 3,951 runs for an average of 35.27. In conclusion I must not omit to mention, as an instance of the roughing that we old cricketers had to put up with, the reply given to me by the man responsible for the arrangements of the first county match ever played at Dewsbury, about the year 1882. On my hinting to him that the arrangements were somewhat primitive and that I saw no such thing as a bath, he appeared to have received the shock of his life as he replied, 'We old cricketers never had baths!'

An interesting fact concerning our XI is that since I retired from the captaincy in 1910 we have had eight captains, all but two of whom have been captain of the winning side in the Championship in their first year. I am aware that it is not good for a side to be always changing its captain, so I hope that now that we have a really good cricketer as captain in Greenwood he will lead us to victory on many more occasions as decisively as we won last year.

No other county can match this tale of success

By J. M. Kilburn, 1955

Yorkshire County cricket is not to be identified with any one Yorkshire centre. The administrative offices are in Leeds and only Headingley of the Yorkshire grounds is now granted a Test match, but there would be prompt and fierce protest from every Riding were any individual claims put forward for distinction as the home of Yorkshire cricket. The county club owns no ground, though it has financial interest in several. Home fixtures are spread as widely as circumstances and accommodation allow; playing resources are discovered and developed everywhere.

Sheffield Influence

This distribution of favour has its origins in the early history of the county's cricket when a narrow conception of resources and interests found little favour. The Kent secretary of 1864 remarked that it was difficult to know who were the proper parties to get up Yorkshire county matches, and some years passed after the formal foundation of the county club before its authority was accepted with much grace, or indeed accepted at all, outside the Sheffield area. Perhaps the difference of outlook was more an illustration of characteristic wariness than of protest against local leadership, because the original Sheffield resolution of formation did envisage an unlimited membership with subscriptions to provide funds for the playing of first-class matches in Sheffield and other centres. Moreover, when the first side was chosen it contained cricketers from Huddersfield, Bradford, Ripon and the North Riding as well as from Sheffield.

Storms soon blew into the life of the young Yorkshire club and in 1865 there was a secession by five of the leading players, less through any quarrel with their own management than because of personal ill feeling between players of the North and the South. Yorkshire, governed wholly from Sheffield, resolved to play and lose rather than abandon their venture, and determination preserved existence. Prodigals returned, new talent came forward and Yorkshire established themselves as a force in the cricketing land. In 1867 seven engagements were undertaken and in these matches 51 wickets went to George Freeman and 30 to Tom Emmett. The highest total of any opposing innings was Lancashire's 159. George Freeman was accounted the finest fast bowler of the day by his contemporaries, who included W. G. Grace and Richard Daft, and though his career was short he left an imperishable name. Tom Emmett lasted longer, playing from 1866 to 1888, carrying Yorkshire through the period of establishment of the County Championship and holding a principal part in a company that included Alan Hill as Freeman's successor in fast bowling; George Pinder, the wicketkeeper who was beyond compare in his time; Ephraim Lockwood, sturdiest of batsmen whose bucolic appearance belied his talent; George Ulyett, a bowler who fell in love with batting and was indulged in his fancy; and Peate and Peel, leaders of that long line of left-arm slow bowlers giving cause for so much Yorkshire gratitude.

The Disciplined Yorkshire

The potentialities in such a collection of players was beyond doubting. The results were wholly unworthy. The side remained a collection of individuals without common purpose or spur. In 1893 endurance reached its limit, and a complete re-organisation of the Committee was accepted. The change was wise and profitable, though its justice at the particular moment might be questioned. The new Yorkshire, the disciplined Yorkshire, began to satisfy themselves. There can be no doubt that much of the spirit inculcated into the Yorkshire side during the 1890s came directly from the leadership of Lord Hawke. It was his declared ambition to win for Yorkshire cricket not only admiration but respect, and he took some drastic steps to ensure that his teams became acceptable everywhere for their conduct both on the field and off. Lord Hawke could never be classed as an outstanding player. Experience gave him usefulness as a batsman in the lower half of the order and in his younger days he was certainly not a handicap to his team in the field, but other qualities than playing ability were needed to raise him to the eminence he attained on the fields and in the councils of cricket. Those qualities were an abiding affection for his cause, which was Yorkshire cricket, and a happy understanding of the men who played under his captaincy. As a captain Lord Hawke was a martinet; in course of time firmness could have been seen as obstinacy, depending upon the viewpoint, and his major interest tended to become paramount. Yet there can be no denying that in developing Yorkshire cricket Lord Hawke did rare service to cricket in its widest sphere. He set standards that have survived him and he took cricket to Australia, India, Canada, United States, South Africa, West Indies and the Argentine. He was captain of Yorkshire from 1883 to 1910 and President of the club from 1898 until his death in 1938.

By his influence alone Lord Hawke could have changed the character of the Yorkshire team, but he could not have achieved the historic results forever to be associated with his name without help from players of unimpeachable quality. Lord Hawke's time was the time of George Hirst and Wilfred Rhodes; of Tunnicliffe and Brown and David Denton; of Wainwright and Peel; of F. S. Jackson and T. L. Taylor and Ernest Smith; of Haigh and Hunter. He who gave such memorable service was himself well served.

Triple Champions

The peak of Yorkshire playing success under the captaincy of Lord Hawke came in the seasons of 1900–1902 when the Championship was won so comprehensively that the wonder of the time was not a Yorkshire victory but a Yorkshire failure to complete victory. In those three years only two championship matches were lost, both of them to Somerset, and some of the victories provided staggering figures. Nottinghamshire were dismissed for 13; against Worcestershire, Yorkshire were all out for 99 and still had margin to win by an innings. There seemed no end to the triumphs, and a new conception of cricketing power was created. Yorkshire have had benefit ever since. They have believed in themselves, and they have undoubtedly impressed that belief upon their opponents.

However great a part the determination to win and the strong team spirit may have played in Yorkshire's establishment as one of the most successful of all cricketing counties, the essential basis of rare technical quality must not be overlooked. Yorkshire have enjoyed the service of a succession of players to be ranked among the very highest, players as familiar by repute in Sydney as in Sheffield. There was never a more dominating cricketer than F. S. Jackson; never a cricketer more respected for his wisdom and skill than Wilfred Rhodes; never a cricketer to capture the heart and the imagination and the affections more firmly than George Herbert Hirst. Jackson was a player by the light of nature, gifted in the rhythm of movement, scarcely needing practice to attain perfection of form. He bowled with economy of effort and batted with graceful efficiency. He knew his own abilities and was surprised at personal failure because he counted it unreasonable. The more demanding the occasion the more likely his success, and his Test match record against Australia is incomparable.

Genius of Rhodes

Wilfred Rhodes has no parallel in cricket, in either the county or the international story. In his first season he established himself as one of the world's leading bowlers; 12 years later he was opening the innings for England; at the age of 48 he was playing again for England, an invaluable all-rounder. He was a cricketing genius; as a bowler with the genius that comes as a gift from the Gods, and as a batsman with the genius that is the infinite capacity for taking pains. He was born wise in cricketing ways. In more that 30 years on the first-class fields his principles of the game were never outmoded. Whilst Wilfred Rhodes was playing nobody ever ventured the opinion that Rhodes's type of bowling would not take wickets in current conditions. Results spoke only too clearly for themselves throughout a career that linked the batsmanship of Grace with that of Bradman.

Hirst the Warrior

George Hirst became the epitome of Yorkshire cricket, the happy warrior that every Yorkshire cricketing knight-at-arms would wish to be. It was part of Hirst's nature that the greater the need of the occasion the greater the response to be called from him. Often enough his innings was brief or his bowling comparatively unsuccessful when no particular demand was laid upon him, but in time of crisis he was the most trustworthy of all his contemporaries as either batsman or bowler. He seldom failed when a failure would have been fatal to his side, and this fighting spirit, presented always with the broad, bold facets of a noble character, brought him the affection and admiration of the whole county, and, indeed, of all the cricketing world. Yorkshire cricket will always accept George Hirst as its representative, anywhere in any age. His public esteem was reflected in his benefit match, which brought him, in 1904, the then enormous return of £3,700. His playing stature rests on the performances of perhaps the most amazing individual feat in cricket history; in 1906 he scored over 2,000 runs and took over 200 wickets in the first-class season. His batting average was 45.86 and his bowling average 16.50.

Hirst and Rhodes remained Yorkshire's leading players for many years after the disintegration of the great side of the early 1900s and they helped the county to Championship victories in 1905, 1908 and 1912. Hirst was still playing – and whenever he played he was a significant force – in the improvisation of 1919, but Rhodes went on alone into the second period of dominance, which began in 1922 and persisted for four seasons. In that era Yorkshire played 122 Championship matches, won 81 of them and lost only six. In general the performances were as remarkable as the figures, for Yorkshire were ruthless conquerors crushing their enemies so thoroughly that they came to regard the five-day week as an expectation rather than a privilege. In 1923 they won 25 of their 32 Championship matches, and 13 of the 25 were won with an innings to spare. Such achievements suggest, and rightly suggest, powerful batting resources, but it was the bowling strength in all conditions that made the side so formidable. Rhodes, after his period of concentration upon batsmanship, returned to full honour as a bowler; Waddington blazed across the cricketing sky; Macaulay and Emmott Robinson were surprised and disappointed if they did not take 100 wickets in a season; and Roy Kilner rapidly established himself, not as a rival to Rhodes, but complementary to him in the slow left-arm attack. As often as not Kilner bowled over the wicket, where Rhodes invariably bowled round in the classical tradition.

Success did not bring Yorkshire universal popularity. They were acknowledged cricketing masters of the counties, but they were not always on the happiest of terms with some of their rivals. The very fixity of their purpose, the grim determination of their methods cost them some affection, and there were one or two occasions when the pressure in the boiler of neighbourly goodwill ran dangerously high. Naturally enough, the bowling fires were the first to fade. When Lancashire took over the Championship in the late 1920s Yorkshire preserved their formidable batting, but awaited the arrival of new bowling of the necessary vitality. When they found it, the batting of Sutcliffe, Holmes, Oldroyd, Leyland, and their company guaranteed all the scope needed for the winning of more Championships.

The last day's play consisted of one ball. All the players changed into flannels for the rather farcical closing stage. Bainbridge bowled the only delivery needed and Bernard, whose name had been drawn out of a hat to accompany Nicholls to the wicket, off-drove to the boundary.

Gloucestershire v Yorkshire
Bristol, June 21, 22, 23, 1961

Holmes and Sutcliffe

Holmes and Sutcliffe developed the most successful of all opening partnerships in County cricket. They came together experimentally and began inauspiciously, for the first time they opened the innings together the scoreboard quickly showed 0 for 1, but their individual technical skill allied to the indefinable sympathy that grew between them soon made their association safe and their achievements historic. They put up a century partnership 69 times for Yorkshire and 74 times in all, and in 1932 they took the world's record opening partnership from their distinguished predecessors. Tunnicliffe and Brown made 554 against Derbyshire in 1898; Holmes and Sutcliffe made 555 against Essex. Curiously enough both these enormous stands were contrived with one of the batsmen under physical handicap. At Chesterfield, Tunnicliffe chose to sit up all night rather than risk unsatisfactory hotel accommodation, and he batted throughout the next day with a sandwich as his only sustenance because of catering confusion at the ground. At Leyton, Holmes was suffering from lumbago and in obvious pain throughout the long innings. Holmes played for Yorkshire from 1913 to 1933 and therefore saw the beginning but not the end of the wonders of the 1930s. Sutcliffe's career extended from War to War, and he was a member of the teams that won the Championship seven times in the nine seasons from 1931 to 1939. He was always an outstanding member because he scarcely ever knew a year of personal failure and because his was a personality that could never be overlooked.

Sutcliffe's batsmanship has been accounted of limited range, but no question of its efficiency has been raised. No question could be raised while memories last and scoreboards remain to be read. Sutcliffe's limitations were mainly self-imposed. He restricted himself because restriction best served his purpose. He batted in the light of circumstances. His problems were the problems of the moment, each to be treated as it arose and instantly dismissed upon solution. The sum of his achievements represents the adequacy of his exposition. For Yorkshire, and for England, he rendered imperishable service.

By 1930 Yorkshire had found the bowling they sought as the basis for a great team, and to Bowes and Verity, Wilfred Rhodes and Emmott Robinson hastened to pass on the legacy of accumulated wisdom and intensity of purpose. The training was invaluable, the material for instruction more than adequate. Bowes, Verity and Macaulay, with Smailes and Ellis Robinson in subsequent support, and Sutcliffe, Leyland, Mitchell, Barber and eventually Hutton, brought Yorkshire to glories as great as they had ever known. They became a living legend in all the cricketing lands. They toured Jamaica as a county side, and had Australian wish been granted they would have toured Australia, too.

The Sellers Era

It was not, of course, in the mere possession of individuals beyond the ordinary that Yorkshire found their strength. Great players do not necessarily establish great teams. Yorkshire had great players in the 1930s and they established a great team primarily because they were prepared to devote their special talents to a common cause. The character of the side became something more than the agglomerated characters of the members. Yorkshire cricket given to be the over-riding concern of every player and the personal achievement was the common satisfaction. The origin of this outlook lay far back in history but its development, or its renaissance, at least, was the contribution of A. B. Sellers, who took over the captaincy in 1933 and held office for 15 seasons. Perhaps Lord Hawke did more than Sellers in that there was more to do, but neither Lord Hawke nor any other Yorkshire leader brought greater devotion or persistent efficiency to the task in hand. Sellers drew loyalty because he gave loyalty. He maintained unswervingly the principle that team interests were paramount, and his principles were so clearly illustrated that they could not escape the notice of established player or newcomer. The Yorkshire of Brian Sellers' time would have been unmistakable in multicoloured caps and disguised by beards. They carried their character on to every field they visited.

Aggressive Fielding

Much was asked. Bowling had to be justifiable in cricket strategy; mere bowling and hoping for the best was not acceptable. Fielding had to be a positive ally to bowling. It was not enough to wait in likely places for catches to come; catches had to be created where none would have existed without courage, and confidence in the ability of colleagues. Yorkshire did not invent the aggressive field in the 1930s but they advanced its position in cricket. Their performances and their principles stood as the standard for the time and it is doubtful if the standard has ever been higher. In the nine seasons between 1931 and 1939 Yorkshire were County Champions seven times and there is no knowing how long their dominance would have continued but for the interruption of the Second World War. When cricket came again the greatness had gone. Sutcliffe and Wood passed into retirement; Bowes was no longer a fast bowler after four years in prison camps; Verity died of wounds in Italy. In 1946 the remainder of the old guard reassembled to win yet another Championship but their success contained the sunset gleam. Leyland and Turner brought their first-class careers to an end, Bowes and Smailes followed in the next season or two and Sellers himself handed on the torch of leadership in 1948, though he gave help when his appointed successor, Norman Yardley, was involved in Test match captaincy and selectorial duties.

Recent years have been spent in reconstruction; and in the inevitable experiment Yorkshire have missed both success and satisfaction. The Championship was shared with Middlesex in 1949 and second position has been attained three times in the past four seasons, but 1953 saw a humiliating descent into the bottom half of the table and the optimism of spring has rarely been matched in the reflections of autumn. Perhaps the essential lack has been a direct link between the old Yorkshire and the new. Players joining the side since 1946 could not acquire tradition by first-hand observation. They knew only their own way of playing cricket, the current way, and time was required for adjustment in a world inclined to be casual in reaction against the taut living of war.

Problems for Yardley

Yorkshire made mistakes in selectorial judgment as well as in playing technique and they had therefore to extend the period of experiment beyond the term expected. Yardley found himself with as difficult a task as any current county captain, for he had played long enough to appreciate needs and desires but could find no illustration of intentions for the newcomers. Young Yorkshiremen did not know quite what was expected of them and were short of a yardstick for comparison. Social circumstances were a handicap to every county and a particular trial to Yorkshire who have long expected their young players to fit into a given pattern, of proven worth. Yardley's success in captaincy has been limited by the lack of understanding and ambition in some of his players, but he has done invaluable work in keeping the good name of Yorkshire cricket at the highest level.

Another era of playing distinction comparable with those of the past still remains speculative. There are players of immense potentiality now wearing the Yorkshire cap and it is to be presumed that Appleyard, Close and Trueman among others have not yet reached the peak of their careers; but character has yet to be confirmed in the side as a whole, and there are obvious shortcomings to be eradicated before a good team can turn itself into a great one. The Yorkshire enthusiasm stands as high as ever; the Yorkshire ambition is in no way diminished. Cricket is an integral part of the Yorkshire scene and the club has never been in more flourishing financial condition. Len Hutton's genius in batsmanship remains a beacon to guide the struggling and a vicarious pride to every compatriot. Yorkshiremen need only be true to their inheritance to find the cricketing satisfactions they desire.

THE TOP COUNTY

By John Bapty, 1969

Yorkshire's 31st Championship* success in 1968 stands as their eighth since the war, their seventh in the last ten seasons and their fourth with D. B. Close as captain. Only Lord Hawke, eight in 28 seasons, and A. B. Sellers, six in eight seasons, achieved more than the man who in 1963 became the county's second professional captain. Whether

---

* Wisden *has since revised its policy regarding recognition of the Championship. See page 249 for clarification.*

Close's 1969 side can turn Yorkshire's fifth hat-trick of Championships into a run of four remains to be seen. The 1924 side completed four; so did Sellers and his second Championship hat-trick side when the 1946 title was put with those gained in 1937, 1938 and 1939. Now Close and the county Committee face a major reconstruction. Two men who have taken 3,135 wickets for Yorkshire have gone – F. S. Trueman into retirement with 1,745 wickets, R. Illingworth to Leicestershire with 1,390 – and with them K. Taylor, who, like Trueman and Illingworth, has been in the side in seven Championship seasons. Close, J. G. Binks, D. E. V. Padgett, P. J. Sharpe and D. Wilson, have been there as well, and with Trueman, Illingworth and Taylor, make eight of the 32 Yorkshire caps since the war.

The last cap went to R. A. Hutton in 1964. It followed those for G. Boycott, J. H. Hampshire and A. G. Nicholson in 1963. The next two caps must fit a paceman and an off-spinner if the traditional character of the Yorkshire attack is to be preserved. Close, capped in the fourth season after the war, spent ten seasons before he shared in an outright Championship; Trueman, capped in 1951, spent eight. Men such as W. Watson and J. H. Wardle, both capped in 1947, F. A. Lowson in 1949, and R. Appleyard, capped with Trueman in 1951, never enjoyed Championship success. Sir Leonard Hutton had only one post-war Championship, that of 1946, to put with four before the end of 1939.

Recollections of these men, their runs, their wickets and their ability in the field, make the failure of Yorkshire to do better than finish second between the end of 1949 – when they shared top with Middlesex – and 1959 – when J. R. Burnet began his second season – as remarkable as the command developed under Wilson and Close in the last nine seasons. Indeed, Yorkshire's work since the war may readily be divided into three parts – that of almost complete reconstruction immediately after the war, that of contrasting brilliance and frustration from 1950 to the end of 1958, and that which, furnished and maintained in the Yorkshire style, has produced what Yorkshire folk had for as long looked for in vain.

Beginning in the Championship year of 1946 without H. Sutcliffe, H. Verity, A. Mitchell and A. Wood, Yorkshire lost M. Leyland, W. Barber, C. Turner and P. A. Gibb before the next season and then W. E. Bowes (1947) and T. F. Smailes (1948). Sellers retired in 1947 but stood in for N. W. D. Yardley when there were Tests with Don Bradman's 1948 men. At that time about all that was left of the pre-war attack was found in E. P. Robinson's off-spin, Hutton's modest leg-breaks, and Yardley's ability to snatch a few wickets now and then. But, most important, Hutton's bat was there to ring truly as in the days before the war. He had the proper lead for the county's batting in 1949, the season of Championship division with Middlesex, when it seemed that all was right with Yorkshire again.

The happenings of 1947, when Yorkshire had finished as low as seventh were … well, just one of those unfortunate memories. Sellers in the 1948 *Wisden* told of Championship hopes for the early 1950s. The cricket of 1949 was confirmation. Big days were near again. Yorkshiremen all over the world believed in them. But expectation and realisation were not related. Yardley went through eight seasons as captain with nothing better than 1949's split title, and the thought of what might have been. More than once when Surrey were riding high, Yorkshire started as favourites without providing justification. Sometimes they failed when they should have been fighting; their slips were all the more marked because often they were not in the Yorkshire line. The team seemed to settle in the second position too readily. Yet in 1950 their two Championship defeats – by Lancashire at Sheffield, where they were beaten by 14 after Close had been run out, and Derbyshire at Bradford – were followed by 22 Championship games without defeat. And five years later, when Yorkshire had 21 wins and, for them, a record number of points, a run of three defeats in June, for which there was no adequate explanation, settled the argument. Surrey finished 16 points in front. Yorkshire were beaten by 21 runs at Hove where a third-day drizzle produced curious happenings; at The Oval there were 41 runs in it: at Bradford, Hampshire, with a total of 224, were allowed to win by an innings when Yorkshire followed-on.

To return to the start of the second part of Yorkshire's post-war adventures; a new opening attack had to be built for 1951. Ankle trouble had assailed R. Aspinall when the England selectors were becoming interested in him. A. Coxon had taken 100 Championship wickets in 1950, but it was his last season. By that time, of course, Yorkshire were being encouraged by the flashing promise of young Trueman and the way in which another youngster, the 18-year-old Close, had with seam and off-spin counted 100 wickets in his first season. Trueman, Close and Lowson played for the county for the first time at Fenner's in May 1949. Close and Lowson were in the Yorkshire coach from Leeds. Trueman, then 17, boarded it in Doncaster's main street which in those days was part of the A1 and that, looking back, seems to have been a very fair sort of tip. The idea was that the three lads should have a gentle breaking-in at Cambridge and Oxford; but, such was the form fired at once by Close and Lowson that each stayed with the side while Trueman returned to Yorkshire for the next stage of the development planned for his promise of rare pace which was to be so completely fulfilled. Never before can a county have taken into first-class cricket on the same day three youngsters destined to do so much.

That season Close became the youngest cricketer to play for England, against New Zealand at Old Trafford, and he scored 1,000 runs to go with his 100 wickets. He was the youngest all-rounder to complete the double and the youngest Yorkshireman to be awarded his county cap. Lowson stayed to partner Hutton for Yorkshire and for England, to make 13,897 runs and 30 centuries for his county, and to share 22 century stands with Hutton for the first-wicket. Trueman, in 1952, when India were here, followed Close and Lowson into the England side to make in the mighty years of his pace one part of the Test record book entirely his own. That May day in 1949 held even more than that, for in the Yorkshire team at Cambridge were three of the county's next four captains. No one could then have come anywhere near naming them, for the time had not come for even the thought of a professional captain for Yorkshire or, for that matter, for England. Yorkshire expectation, in fact, was that W. G. Keighley, the Oxford University batsman, would follow Yardley.

The county committee, by special resolution, had qualified the man born in France for the county with which his family had long-standing connections. But Keighley, like the man who was to have the honour and reward of Knighthood after his work as

England's first professional captain, was not to have the chance. He returned to his Australian home in 1951. Four years later back trouble put Hutton out of the game, the announcement of his retirement being delayed until the close season before W. H. H. Sutcliffe accepted the county captaincy to which his distinguished father had been so near a quarter of a century earlier. Young Sutcliffe was in that Yorkshire side at Fenner's in 1949, and so was J. V. Wilson, who in 1960 became Yorkshire's first professional captain since before Lord Hawke's time, and so, of course, was Close whose early climb in first-class cricket was so quick an affair that he was on the boat with the 1950 MCC team when they sailed for Australia. Yorkshire's fortune in finding the right men did not, however, extend to their immediate development. Close was not able to continue in County cricket; he had to complete his National Service when he returned from Australia. Trueman had to begin his when he left the pit, and so Yorkshire had to wait for the establishment of their second post-war attack.

There were difficulties all the way. Only Wardle was there all the time. Appleyard, brought in as an opening bowler when at the age of 26 he first played for the county, had a unique reward of 200 wickets for the thought, skill and variety which he gave to his accurate work in 1951, his first full season, and then, tragically illness took him away until 1954. Still, by 1951, Yorkshire had five men in Test action against South Africa – Wardle, Watson and D. V. Brennan, the wicketkeeper, as well as Hutton and Lowson – and there were six, Hutton, Watson, Lowson, E. Lester, Wilson and H. Halliday, with more than 1,000 Championship runs in 1952 when Wardle took 158 Championship wickets and Close 98. The one bowler on the 100-wicket mark in the Championship in that sad season of 1953 was Wardle. Hutton, Lowson, Watson, Lester, Wilson and Halliday were together again with more than 1,000 Championship runs, but only six games were won and Yorkshire counted few more than half Surrey's 184 Championship points. Hutton, Brennan (who retired at the end of 1953) and Sutcliffe had captained Yorkshire when Yardley was not there in that season in which there was drastic revision of the county's records. Glamorgan beat Yorkshire for the first time, and what was perhaps the most remarkable record of the lot went when Nottinghamshire beat Yorkshire for the first time at Trent Bridge since 1891. The margin was four wickets after an optimistic declaration had given Yorkshire's weak attack 70 minutes in which to get out a side needing 110. That was the season, too, in which Northamptonshire, often a two-day job in pre-war times, beat Yorkshire for the first time for 40 years.

In 1946 when Yorkshire's one defeat gave Hampshire at Bournemouth their first home win over Yorkshire since 1911, the feat – and it was regarded as a considerable feat – gained celebration speeches from the front of the pavilion. But, as it turned out, that was only the prelude to defeats each of which marked the end of a long period of Yorkshire domination. Counties whose men had suffered for years delightedly took plunder. The Middlesex 1947 win at Headingley was their first in Yorkshire for 27 years, Leicestershire's at Bramall Lane in 1948 was their first in Yorkshire for 38 years. Worcestershire's on the same ground in 1949 was their first in Yorkshire for 40 years, and Warwickshire's at Edgbaston in 1948 was their first at home against Yorkshire since 1893. There was no hint at what was to come in 1953, at the end of which the Yorkshire annual report had to regret the worst season from a playing point of view since 1892. Yorkshire, unbelievably, had dropped to the 13th position – and that in Hutton's second season as England's captain.

With Hutton in the England eleven which regained the Ashes at The Oval were Trueman, who then took his first four Australian wickets; Watson, who shared with Hutton the only two England Test centuries that summer, and Wardle. Besides giving those men to England, Yorkshire had Trueman for only a handful of games, when freed from the Royal Air Force. Close fell out after two games. An injury from the football season put him aside, with Appleyard who, happily, was making the recovery that enabled him to display his considerable skill to the game when he returned in 1954. A grim echo of it all was heard at Chesterfield in 1953 when the Yorkshiremen, having failed against Gladwin and Jackson, went down by ten wickets. It was Yorkshire's third defeat by Derbyshire in four seasons – their third, in fact, since 1905. A solitary spectator, just about the last to leave the ground, flung into the old press tent as he passed, 'They're not even common amusement now.' Only he knew whether he was an embittered Yorkshireman or a delighted Derbyshire supporter!

Wardle, Appleyard and Wilson went with Hutton's 1954-55 MCC team to Australia, where Wardle and Appleyard had their parts in keeping the Ashes. Wilson did not make the Test side, and it must be regarded as something of a curiosity that when 1959 came with, at last, a Championship for Yorkshire, he was the only one of the four in Australia five years earlier to be with Burnet's side. Hutton's victorious team returned to a summer of sunshine, and Yorkshire went into the 1955 campaign with reasonable hope that the bowling partnership of Trueman and M. J. Cowan, a left-hander who seemed to be built for the task, would lead powerfully the attack in which Appleyard, Wardle and Close each had a place of his own and in which young Illingworth, the off-spinner, was making progress. But the most important happening of Yardley's last season as captain was the end of the distinguished career of the great batsman who was soon to become Sir Leonard Hutton. Because of back troubles Hutton had been unable to keep the England captaincy after having been, for the first time, appointed for a complete home series. But at Trent Bridge he made his 85th century for Yorkshire – his 60th for the county in post-war cricket. In ten seasons after the war he had taken his Yorkshire total from 8,750 to 24,807, and 2,640 of those runs had been made in 1949 when his aggregate was 3,429, the highest by a Yorkshire player. He left a gap much too wide to be measured.

The victory which gave Yorkshire most satisfaction in 1955 was that over Surrey at Headingley where in the three days there were 60,000 people. Surrey, unbeaten since July 1954, led by 102 on the first innings, only to find the heat generated by Cowan and Trueman too much for them on the Monday evening. Cowan's 5 for 15 was a promise with a fine flourish, even if the light was such that when next Yorkshire passed through London a Surrey man saw to it that they had, with his compliments, a supply of night-lights! That was the fast attack for which the county had been waiting. Yorkshire, however, were not to have the full benefit of it, for Cowan hurt his back in Pakistan that winter and, though he returned to the side after a long absence to get a cap, his and the county's hopes were not completely fulfilled. Sutcliffe, who went to Pakistan that winter with the MCC team in which there was also a place for Close, returned to a two-year spell as captain. His hopes also were to be unfulfilled. At the end of 1956 the county's annual report talked of 'a difficult year for the new captain' before making plain the belief that the final position would have been above seventh had 'the men played in a more determined manner on all occasions'.

Appleyard, Trueman, Watson and Wardle had places against the 1956 Australians but Trueman had no more than 355 Championship overs for 33 wickets. Injury dogged him, Cowan and Appleyard. There were, however, occasions when the side did not look like a Yorkshire side, so far were the men in it short of their own potential and so far was the side short of the old spirit. Take the game at Bramall Lane, where Surrey, on their way to their fifth Championship in a row, were allowed to complete their first Yorkshire double for 36 years – and that without Laker's spin. Yorkshire, who had put Surrey in, began the last innings wanting 97. There was a possible 85 minutes left on that Monday. Next morning Yorkshire still wanted 67, and, after two and a quarter hours they needed 14 when Lock ended it. It was a game Yorkshire could have won on the Monday.

Sutcliffe's captaincy ended in 1957 with the side in third place. Illingworth, becoming more and more important, had 1,000 Championship runs. Watson and three other left-handers – W. B. Stott, Close and Wilson – were with him. No bowler had earned 100 wickets, and Yorkshire moved into the fateful season of 1958 with J. R. Burnet, a successful captain of the Colts, answering at the age of 39 a call he certainly had not expected at the beginning of 1957. Rain came – 17 of the county's 23 blank days were in Yorkshire – and Lowson and Appleyard, and then Wardle, left the side as Watson had done at the end of 1957 when he secured the release which enabled him to captain Leicestershire. Wardle, captain in eight of the first ten games when Burnet was injured, was last in the Yorkshire dressing room on the first morning of the August Bank Holiday game at Old Trafford. He did not unpack his bag. Two days earlier, during the Somerset game at Sheffield, he had been called to the Committee room and told that his services would not be required after the end of the season.

The sensation circled the cricket world, for, as things developed, with Wardle's Yorkshire place went his place in MCC's 1958 team for Australia. And, after the Committee's decisions, Burnet, at the beginning of the third part of Yorkshire's post-war story, found that his job had to do with the rebuilding of the attack. Trueman and Close, and J. V. Wilson, were there to link the first chapter with the third. Taylor, Padgett, Stott and Sharpe, young batsmen with so much to give in the field were there as well, eager and ready, and Binks, on his way to records of skill and stamina, was sure in his place with the other six – Pinder, the Hunters, Dolphin, Wood and Brennan – who have manned Yorkshire's wicketkeeping post for over 100 years.

D. Wilson moved into the place in which Wardle had taken, with his varied spin, 1,537 wickets, and, against all the odds, Yorkshire at once went to their first Championship for 13 hard years. Never had a side with more than five defeats finished at the top. But there were 14 victories and the vital one came at Hove, in the last match, a few days after Yorkshire had been put out for 35 at Bristol. There was no argument about the Hove affair. Two hundred and fifteen runs had to be made in a hundred minutes for the Championship. They were. Stott had 96 of them in 86 minutes. The youngsters had answered the call, with Trueman, R. K. Platt and Illingworth leading the bowlers – and they answered it again in 1960 when Burnet, his job done, retired and J. V. Wilson completed something started by T. F. Smailes in 1947.

Up to 1947 Yorkshire had always found an amateur when the need was there for a stand-in for the captain. Smailes captained the side occasionally in 1947 and 1948, and, the door having been opened, Hutton, Watson and Wardle in the following years filled the post which had never been occupied by Yorkshire's great professionals before the war. And when, at the end of 1962, Wilson retired with two Championships in three seasons, the authorities turned again to the senior professional, and Close had the satisfaction in his first season as captain of holding, in the county's centenary year, the Championship regained in 1962. The 1963 Centenary Banquet was taken (as had been that which in 1949 commemorated the centenary of Roses cricket) to Sheffield, and in that season Boycott, destined to step in England's batting where H. Sutcliffe and Sir Leonard Hutton had stepped, produced his first Championship 1,000 runs. By then Trueman had another opening partner – his last. A. G. Nicholson has settled where in turn there had been Appleyard, Cowan, Platt, Ryan, and, briefly, such as Whitehead, Holdsworth, Hodgson, Pickles and others. Two years went without the title; the Gillette Cup, superbly won, was taken in 1965, since when there have been Championships all the way for the side, at its best in the field where Close's close-in lead has never faltered.

Close became the third Yorkshireman to captain England in post-war cricket when in 1966 he took over against West Indies at The Oval. He left the post a year later, after the Edgbaston affair had produced the Advisory County Committee's condemnation of Yorkshire's time-wasting tactics against Warwickshire. To go with the 1968 Championship there is for the aggressive team moulded by Close, Trueman and Illingworth the warm memory of comprehensive victory over the Australians at Bramall Lane – something accomplished by no Yorkshire side since Sir Stanley Jackson and G. H. Hirst put out the 1902 Australians for 23 at Headingley. But there is a tale of changed times in the gate figures. Just over 14,500 paid at Sheffield for last summer's Australian game. In 1953, the season in which Yorkshire were 13th in the Championship, there was for Hassett's Australians an aggregate playing attendance of 42,670 on the same ground.

One other financial note – in the years since the war, benefits, testimonials and grants for men with a Yorkshire cap have produced over £95,000.

COUNTY OF THE CENTURY ... YORKSHIRE, BY A DISTANCE

By Philip Bailey, 2000

To prove that the methods of the hare occasionally prevail, Yorkshire have clearly emerged as the county side of the 20th century. They dominated the first seven decades, winning 26 Championships out of 60, and shared one of the others. Then they went to sleep, but still clearly emerged as the most successful county throughout.

Yorkshire achieved their 1,000th victory since 1900 at Trent Bridge in August 1999. No one else came close to reaching that target. They also lost almost 100 fewer matches than any of their rivals (excluding Durham). In many seasons, especially before the war, there were considerable disparities between the number of fixtures played by different counties. And since the points system has changed frequently, the percentage of wins was the fairest method to determine the century's champion county. But whichever criterion is used, the answer is the same.

Surrey had the second-highest number of wins overall and, on percentages, were just ahead of Kent and Middlesex. Further to the table of post-war success, published in *Wisden* 1996, Surrey have now climbed ahead of Middlesex as the most successful post-war team. Kent's record before then was exceptional. They and Yorkshire were the top two teams in each of the first four decades, even though Kent were not champions at all between the wars.

Over the course of the century, Somerset lost by far the most matches both numerically and (again excluding Durham) by percentage. On draws, the facts support the weather lore: Lancashire were the only county to draw more than 1,000 games. Their nearest rivals in percentage terms were Nottinghamshire (Trent Bridge pitches were once famously flat) and Glamorgan. Five of the top nine in the table will be in the second division in 2000.

County Championship 1900-1999		P	W	L	D	T	%W	%L	%D	Titles*
1	Yorkshire	2331	1,001	351	977	2	42.94	15.05	41.91	26
2	Surrey	2263	833	450	979	1	36.80	19.88	43.26	10
3	Kent	2235	819	603	808	5	36.64	26.97	36.15	6
4	Middlesex	2091	765	491	832	3	36.58	23.48	39.78	10
5	Lancashire	2315	789	451	1,073	2	34.08	19.48	46.34	6
6	Gloucestershire	2179	635	783	759	2	29.14	35.93	34.83	0
7	Essex	2169	613	631	920	5	28.26	29.09	42.41	6
8	Sussex	2303	646	715	936	6	28.05	31.04	40.64	0
9	Nottinghamshire	2151	593	585	972	1	27.56	27.19	45.18	4
10	Warwickshire	2141	589	618	933	1	27.51	28.86	43.57	5
11	Hampshire	2211	576	722	909	4	26.05	32.65	41.11	2
12	Derbyshire	2105	528	726	850	1	25.08	34.48	40.38	1
13	Worcestershire	2157	539	742	874	2	24.98	34.39	40.51	5
14	Northamptonshire	1983	484	688	808	3	24.40	34.69	40.74	0
15	Somerset	2091	492	812	784	3	23.52	38.83	37.49	0
16	Leicestershire	2143	493	755	894	1	23.00	35.23	41.71	3
17	Glamorgan	1781	388	604	789	0	21.78	33.91	44.30	3
18	Durham	141	23	79	39	0	16.31	56.02	27.65	0

* Denotes outright titles as Lancashire, Surrey, Middlesex (twice), Yorkshire and Kent have all shared the title. The list totals 87 outright titles, omitting ten cancelled because of wars and three shared.

County Champions, decade by decade		%W
1900–1909	Yorkshire	53.28
1910–1919	Kent	62.16
1920–1929	Yorkshire	51.68
1930–1939	Yorkshire	56.16
1946–1949	Middlesex	59.62
1950–1959	Surrey	56.07
1960–1969	Yorkshire	42.36
1970–1979	Kent	34.11
1980–1989	Essex	35.65
1990–1999	Warwickshire	42.70

TO BE DISLIKED AGAIN

By Roy Hattersley, 2002

On a warm afternoon in the late summer of 1946, my father – normally the most reticent of men – danced a little jig on the promenade in Morecambe. He had, as was his invariable summer habit, bought an evening paper to find out the cricket scores. To his delight he discovered that Yorkshire, already the County Champions, had lost to Hampshire. He addressed my mother and me in a voice of triumph, 'At least they haven't gone all season without being beaten.' It was then that I realised that the Yorkshire County Cricket Club attracted the animosity that goes with near invincibility. With any luck, we will soon begin to attract it again.

The complaint, in those days of constant Championships, was that the three Ridings were so big that the county club had a bottomless pool of talent from which to choose. Now, the contract system, which regrettably grows ever more like the football transfer racket, has ended all that. But when I first watched Yorkshire, there was an abundance, in a way an excess, of potential first-class players within the Broad Acres. In 1946, a 43-year-old spin bowler called Arthur Booth took a hundred wickets and topped the national averages. Before the war he had played only the occasional game when Hedley Verity was on Test match duty. But he had soldiered on in the Yorkshire Colts without a thought of playing for another county.

For years, Yorkshire ignored cricketers of the highest quality. Bob Appleyard took 200 wickets in his first full season with the county, 1951, and, as he was a 'mature' man at the time, John Arlott (commentating later on a Test in which Appleyard was playing) wondered aloud how he had spent his summers during his early twenties. Long after his retirement, I met the overnight sensation and asked him the same question. 'Bowling myself silly in the Bradford League,' he told me. Nobody has been able to explain why it took the Yorkshire committee so long to discover him.

League cricket – particularly the Bradford League – was half the secret of Yorkshire's success. Hundreds of tributaries flowed from the club grounds towards Headingley. The two Pudseys – one produced Sir Leonard Hutton, the other Raymond Illingworth – are the most famous examples of that secret strength. But there were dozens of other clubs that thought it their duty to prepare players for the county. In Sheffield, border country in the far south, we always suspected the northern leagues were as far as the county committee ever looked. The prejudice, if it ever existed, has clearly passed – though the young Darren Gough and Michael Vaughan were far too good to be ignored whatever part of the county they came from. What a pity that, now there are South Yorkshire players in the county team, the county team never plays in South Yorkshire.

Perhaps the idea that South Yorkshire got a raw deal was always a myth. But we certainly believed it. In the week that I was born, my father, a temporary Labour Exchange clerk after years of unemployment, was sent to work in Wath upon Dearne. Eating his midday sandwiches in the deserted cricket ground, he fell into conversation with the groundsman and naturally told him about the baby boy at home. 'He'll never play for Yorkshire,' the groundsman said. Thinking the dismissal of my cricketing ability a little premature, my father asked why he was so certain. The reply allowed no contradiction. 'Comes from South Yorkshire.' The pessimist's name was Turner, and his boy, Cyril, was finding it hard to break into the team. He became a regular member of the side that won the Championship four times before the war and once immediately afterwards.

Sixteen years on, when I was batting in the nets behind Spion Kop at Bramall Lane, the anti-Leeds feeling still persisted. There were rumours that a great fast bowler, a colliery electrician by profession, was about to emerge from Maltby and there were dark suspicions that 'the committee' would not do him justice. But nothing could hold Fred Trueman back. To the day of his death, my father (a Nottinghamshire man) argued that Harold Larwood was both more accurate and more aggressive. Filial piety requires me to conclude that Larwood and Trueman were the two greatest English fast bowlers of all time. Neither of them should be anything other than flattered by the comparison.

In the years that followed the war, we Yorkshire members grew used to success. Indeed, in the 1950s, when the team began to fail, we felt that the natural order of things had been disrupted. In 1958, when we came 11th in the Championship, Johnny Wardle, an ingenious spin bowler, prehensile close fielder and irresponsibly entertaining batsman, was sacked for defending himself from committee criticism in a newspaper. I attended the annual meeting with the intention of causing trouble about his treatment. The chairman welcomed members to the 'AGM of the champion county' and added, 'We know which the champion county is, whichever team happens to be at the top of the table at the end of any one year.' After that, no criticism was possible.

71

> Just before the end, a spectator wearing an Osama bin Laden mask and with a rucksack on his back ran on to the field; he was ejected from the ground.
>
> **Yorkshire v Warwickshire**
> **Scarborough, July 24, 2005**

After the 1950s the county recovered but continued in its profligate ways. Ray Illingworth left for Leicestershire – and became a highly successful England captain – following an argument about his contract. The accusation was that he was disloyal because he did not regard a year with Yorkshire as better than three with any other county. Brian Close, who led the last Championship-winning team, moved on to Somerset. Bill Athey went to Gloucestershire, and dozens of other players, less talented but highly able, drifted away. For a time it seemed that nothing could go right for Yorkshire. After the pride of a century was forgotten and an overseas player recruited, two of the world's greatest batsmen wore the White Rose for a single season. Neither Sachin Tendulkar nor Richie Richardson was a success. Yorkshire remained in the wilderness.

Perhaps, even in the early 1990s, Yorkshire were still suffering from the repercussions of 'the Boycott affair'. Whatever the merits of the argument – Boycott versus the committee – the damage that the conflict did to the county was immense. In 1978, members were asked to vote on what some thought were rival propositions: endorse sacking Boycott as captain or ask the committee to resign. I voted 'yes' to both, hoping that a clearout would put the damaging disputes behind us. It dragged on for year after year, making life impossible for some of the best Yorkshire cricketers of the age, John Hampshire, captain in impossible circumstances, amongst them.

It was all desperately different from 1938 when, as well as winning the Championship, Yorkshire provided five players for the final Test at The Oval. More than half of England's highest-ever total of 903 for 7 was made by Len Hutton, with his record-beating 364, and Maurice Leyland, whose century he overshadowed. Hutton, the greatest English batsman of his time, remains the example of what Yorkshire cricketers should be. Genius is not enough. Determination and dedication are equally essential. When I read of Yorkshire fast bowlers who worry about the strains of playing two Championship matches in a week, I wonder if they recall that Hutton lost two inches of bone from his arm in a wartime accident, came back to first-class cricket and almost immediately faced Ray Lindwall and Keith Miller.

Not all the Yorkshire fast bowlers whine about being overworked. Much to his credit, Matthew Hoggard, asked if he had fears about touring India, replied that he wanted to play for England and therefore had never considered refusing to go. Suddenly – partly owing to their academy and the new coaching regime – Yorkshire have a surfeit of fast bowlers and enough batting strength to make a second successive Championship a strong prospect. I still regret that Darren Lehmann, the star batsman of 2001's success, is Australian, and I wish that Michael Vaughan had been born in Yorkshire as well as being a clear candidate to succeed Nasser Hussain as England's captain. But the clock cannot be turned back – except in one particular. There is a real hope that Yorkshire will become so successful that we are really disliked again.

Chapter Three:
Follow the Leader

It is hardly classified information that the Yorkshire dressing room was not always a harmonious weave of personalities. The competing egos of players rub together like pieces of sharp struck flint. And sparks fly upwards.

From 1948 to 1955, however, the player in charge was said to be of 'sanguine temperament and modest assurance', a man who had 'ideas without being opinionated' (which hardly sounds like someone born in South Yorkshire). Len Hutton believed that 'a kinder and more considerate captain never walked on to a cricket field,' while the broadcaster Don Mosey went further: 'He had been schooled in that one-for-all and all-for-one tradition,' said Mosey, 'and any attitude in the side that showed itself as less than that was alien to him.'

Hutton and Mosey were referring to Norman Yardley. *Wisden* called him 'the finest Yorkshire amateur since F. S. Jackson,' yet he had the misfortune to run into the beginning of Surrey's sweeping dominance of the 1950s. When Yorkshire finished joint Champions with Middlesex in 1949, no one believed another ten years would pass before the title belonged to them again. Yardley's Yorkshire were four times runners-up to Surrey.

Michael Vaughan – who appears in this chapter because he is the most successful captain in England's history – claimed that, 'a lot of [it] is about acting . . . your job is to lead with a calm authority.' He added:

> I always tried to put myself in the position of the players and think about what they wanted to hear. Sometimes it has to be harsh words; sometimes you have to pick them up. But whatever it is, you have to speak naturally and be consistent.

Yardley evidently found it difficult. Brian Close remembers Yardley as 'soft spoken and gentle in his friendly encouragement.' Ray Illingworth counter-argued: 'His strength in this direction was his weakness in another . . . he was too nice a chap to stand up to the hard men.' What Illingworth summed up as the tragedy of Yardley demonstrates the dilemmas and the difficulties of captaincy; a job, in fact, which Illingworth himself would later describe as requiring, 'the patience of a saint, the diplomacy of an ambassador, the compassion of a social worker and the skin of a rhino.'

Alan Gibson focussed on Yardley's generosity: 'He could suffer fools gladly, and in one way or another, at one time or another, he has had to,' he wrote. But to suffer fools gladly isn't necessarily the prime qualification of a captain – particularly in a dressing room as combustible as nitro-glycerine. There were times when captaincy for Yardley was like toiling up a terrible gradient. Gibson thought he was nonetheless 'immensely liked and respected'. And while it hardly validates his appointment, it endorses his credentials as a patient and tolerant man.

NORMAN YARDLEY

Norman Yardley made 20 Test appearances and accumulated 812 runs. His highest score was 99 against South Africa at Trent Bridge in 1947. He made almost 19,000 first class runs.

Obituary – 1990

Norman Walter Dransfield Yardley, who died on 4 October 1989, aged 74, appeared in his first Test match for England at Johannesburg under W. R. Hammond, whom he was to succeed as captain after the Second World War. As a boy, Yardley enjoyed none of the advantages of coming from a cricketing family, but his great all-round promise was spotted as soon as he went to St Peter's, York. He was five years in the school XI, being captain in 1933 and 1934 and in the former year making more than 900 runs for an average of 88.43, including successive innings of 127, 171 and 167 not out.

He was also top of the bowling averages, his medium-pace in-swingers bringing him 40 wickets at just under 12 apiece. Such remarkable form brought selection for the Young Amateurs against the Young Professionals at Lord's, where he demonstrated his liking for the big occasion by hitting up 189. Denis Compton was on the fielding side. By the time Yardley established himself in Yorkshire's Championship-winning side in 1939, he had developed a fluent and attractive style as a batsman. He was on the tall side and strongly built, able to get out to the pitch of the ball and drive handsomely on both sides of the wicket. He was especially skilful at forcing the ball away off his legs in the arc wide of mid-on with shots demanding strength and flexibility of wrist. At school he had benefited from the coaching of the headmaster, S. M. Toyne, and Fred Roberts, the professional; as a Yorkshire Colt he came under the instruction of George Hirst at the county nets.

In 1934 he further enhanced his reputation by innings of 117 and 63 for the Public Schools against the Army at Lord's, Wisden describing him as 'the great batsman of the match'. He won his Blue as a Freshman at Cambridge in 1935; class rather than performance guaranteed his place. But the following year he showed himself to be fully

Parry, an umpire whose leg had been amputated below the knee, fell in getting out of the way of a ball, and fractured the maimed limb.

Gloucestershire v Yorkshire
Gloucestershire, May 7, 9, 10, 1927

attuned to the demands of the first-class game and topped the averages. In the University Match he played a fine innings of 90; and in 1937 he went one better with a high-class century. As captain in 1938, he made 61 in his customary elegant style. He played for The Rest in the Test Trial that season and spent the winter of 1938-39 with MCC in South Africa under W. R. Hammond. He was full of runs on this tour, but such was the strength of the England batting that he played in only one Test, making 7. This was not his first experience of touring, for he had been a member of Lionel Tennyson's team in India in 1937-38, when three unofficial Test matches were played. In 1939 he had his first full season with Yorkshire under A. B. Seller's dominating and forceful captaincy.

Within two days of demobilisation in 1946, after service with the 1st Battalion of the Green Howards, Yardley found himself at practice in the Yorkshire nets. The Yorkshire side had an unfamiliar look, with no fewer than six members of the 1939 team missing, yet they won the Championship in 1946 on the strength of their bowling. In 1947 it was a different story: a drop to eighth in the table was the lowest position Yorkshire had occupied since 1910, hardly an encouraging state of affairs for Yardley, who took over the captaincy from Sellers in 1948. However, he had earned the players' confidence and respect by making 1,906 runs in 1947 with five centuries to his name.

This was his highest aggregate in the eight seasons in which he passed 1,000 runs. Yardley's captaincy was shrewd and enterprising, but he allowed a much more relaxed dressing-room atmosphere than Sellers. The new players such as Trueman, Close and Wardle, especially Trueman, would have thrived under a sterner regime, and yet Yardley led them to a Championship shared with Middlesex in 1949 and to the runners-up position in four seasons.

All this time Yardley had other important commitments. Chosen as Hammond's vice-captain on the 1946-47 MCC tour of Australia, he was a distinct success, making useful middle-order runs and breaking partnerships. He claimed Bradman's wicket three times. When Hammond was laid low with fibrositis before the final Test at Sydney, Yardley led England courageously. In the best match of the series Australia squeezed home by five wickets. Hammond's retirement meant that Yardley was the automatic choice to captain England in the home series against South Africa in 1947.

At Trent Bridge in the First Test, when England were 170 for four in their second-innings and needed a further 155 to make South Africa bat again, he and Compton put on 237 for the fifth wicket, a record in England at the time, and averted seeming defeat. Yardley's 99 was his highest in Tests, and in the remaining matches he batted admirably in support of Compton and Edrich, who dominated the series. He took a rest that winter to be ready for the Australian challenge in 1948, which proved to be stronger than anyone could have imagined. Losing 4-0, Yardley would prefer to recall the memorable scene at The Oval when he called for three cheers as Bradman arrived at the crease, rather than the failure to prevent Australia from running away with the Fourth Test at Leeds.

In 1950 he led England against West Indies in the first three Tests, winning at Old Trafford but losing at Lord's and Trent Bridge. He then stood aside for F. R. Brown, as he could not be available for another tour of Australia. Yardley played in twenty Tests, in which he made 812 runs at 25.37 and took 21 wickets for an average of 33.66. In the fourteen in which he was captain, he won four and lost seven, not a bad record considering the strength of the opposition. In 446 first-class matches he made 18,173 runs at 31.17 and took 279 wickets at 30.48. Of his 27 centuries, the highest was an unbeaten 183 against Hampshire at Headingley in 1951. Six for 29 for MCC against Cambridge at Lord's in 1946 represented his best bowling.

Norman Yardley was a fine all-round athlete, winning Blues for hockey and squash as well as cricket. Indeed, he won the North of England Squash Championship in six consecutive years before the war. He served on the Test Selection Committee from 1951 to 1954 and was chairman in 1952. As Yorkshire's President from 1981 to 1984 he deplored the strife and bitterness of the Boycott affair, alike degrading and humiliating to his county, but could do little to heal the wounds. It was a far cry from the great days when he appeared on the scene, the finest Yorkshire amateur since F. S. Jackson.

BRIAN SELLERS

Brian Sellers captained Yorkshire to another Championship in 1946. He died in Bingley in 1981. He scored 9,270 runs in his first-class career. In his latter years he regretted not being able to watch matches at Headingley, blaming 'Sir Arthur Itis' for his absence.

Cricketer of the Year 1940

Arthur Brian Sellers stands out as the most successful county captain of all time. Elected second in command of the Yorkshire eleven in 1932 he soon found himself virtual leader, because F. E. Greenwood could play very seldom. The honour seemed to come naturally; he was in charge in 25 matches without knowing defeat. From that happy experience Brian Sellers went on from strength to strength; now he can look back and see his name fully described 'captain' with Championship honours rewarding Yorkshire five times in seven seasons. Nothing like such a run of success has come to any county and, therefore, never has a captain known reward like this.

Usually a captain, if figuring prominently in the public eye, has shown previous attractive powers with bat or ball, like W. R. Hammond, D. G. Bradman and S. M. J. Woods of high renown. Sellers may be overlooked in this class, but he holds records of his own. In 1934 he made the only century ever hit by an amateur for Yorkshire off Australian bowling, and his 204, two years later at Cambridge, stands as the only score of 200 by a Yorkshire amateur.

Content with a place in the lower half of the batting order, Brian Sellers can put up a dogged defence or force the game according to the needs of his side. In 1937 he played for the Gentlemen at Lord's; next season he scored 1,143 runs with an average of 27.41. These facts indicate that Sellers can bat; but fielding gives him chief claims to fame on the practical side of the game. Near the wicket he is without a superior, and, if fancying exercise, he can judge a catch or 'chase her' in the deep with certainty and vigour.

> Loye summed up the futility of the closing stages by fielding the final over in
> a black trilby lent by a spectator.
>
> **Lancashire v Yorkshire**
> **Old Trafford, August 8, 8, 8, 10, 11, 2006**

It is of interest here to trace the route traversed by Brian Sellers to his present exalted position. Born at Keighley on March 5, 1907, he is the younger son of Arthur Sellers, a batsman with beautiful style and effective methods who first played for Yorkshire in 1893 and retains a keen interest in the county club as a vice-president and chairman of the cricket committee. Inheriting the parental ability, Brian Sellers soon made a name at St Peter's School, York, where such a noted Yorkshireman as Frank Mitchell, a captain of Cambridge and South Africa, learned his cricket. When 16 Sellers captained the school eleven. This experience in boyhood was enlarged when in 1931 he led his town club in the Bradford League. So he entered the sterner fray of County cricket well versed in responsibility and knowledge of leadership.

Sellers has expressed the opinion that a clever bowler with ten good fieldsmen can 'shut up the game' except when such batsmen as Bradman, Woolley, Leyland or Hammond take command. His contention is that such a bowler, rather than the watchful batsman, causes slow cricket. About Yorkshire he has spoken candidly, 'We are out to win; if we cannot do so; good luck to our opponents, but we are not going to give them a chance if we can help it.' That is the determined tone required to merit victory, and his true English character made Brian Sellers a welcome addition to the Test Selection Committee in March 1938.

Vic Wilson

In his Wisden obituary – he died in 2008 – his colleague Ted Lester remembered Wilson as having 'the biggest hands you've ever seen'. Another teammate, Bob Appleyard, described him as 'straight down the middle... he had strong principles and in a quiet way he succeeded'. The obituary ended with the line, 'Abstemious and home loving, Wilson returned to the farm whenever he could, and spent the off-days during his career and the rest of his working life in the production of carrots'.

Cricketer of the Year 1961 – by W. E. Bowes

When in 1960 Yorkshire appointed John Victor Wilson, their 39-year-old left-handed batsman, to be professional captain – their first professional captain since Tom Emmett in 1882 – the attention of the whole cricket world was centred upon him and the doings of his team. Hitherto Wilson had never commanded the spotlight. A big, quietly spoken, typical Yorkshire farmer, he got on with his job to the best of his ability and allowed others to do the talking.

He had played with Yorkshire since 1946 and scored 18,302 runs in first-class cricket for an average of 33.03. A disappointing season in 1959, in which he had been dropped to the second team to try to find his form, had yielded him only 618 first-class runs and among these was a century in the last match, 105 against the Rest of England. This was the player Yorkshire chose to follow J. R. Burnet, the successful leader, who had seen Yorkshire end the seven-year run of Championship successes by Surrey. And how splendidly Wilson rose to the occasion. Authority fitted him well. Almost overnight a quiet firmness crept into his voice and there was purpose about his actions. The Yorkshire committee gave him 14 players (nine capped) from whom he had to find his best XI. Without fear or favouritism he set to work.

It was soon obvious that the new Yorkshire captain had assimilated a lot of knowledge during his time in the ranks. He knew the players in the opposition and the likely behaviour of the pitches. He chose the team accordingly. Being a brilliant close-in fieldsman he could always give the lead when occasion demanded a man in a suicide spot. Wilson caused a sensation in the first Championship match of the season against Sussex by declaring with all ten first-innings wickets intact and finally his side lost the game after he had instructed his players to go for runs. Yorkshire followed this defeat by beating Gloucestershire in the last over of the day at Bradford, vanquishing Somerset and Hampshire, and then, at Gravesend, Wilson completely out-pointed the Kent captain, Colin Cowdrey. Under Vic Wilson, Yorkshire went on to retain the Championship, and while he gave the reasons as Trueman's great bowling, the wicketkeeping of Binks, eight batsmen scoring 1,000 runs and more, and the efforts of the four Colts in his team, every player pointed first and foremost to the skipper. He never lost faith in himself or his team.

J. V. Wilson was born at Scampston, Yorkshire, on January 17, 1921. His father Herbert, a farmer, was a well-known East Riding cricketer – a right-arm bowler and left-hand batsman – and the boy always went with him to the matches. Occasionally he had to field substitute until a late player arrived. Sometimes he played the full match. When 11, Vic went to Norton Boys School where the sportsmaster, Mr Bruce Rolls, encouraged him at cricket. At 14 he was allowed to play for Malton for whom he made his first century, against Driffield in an East Yorkshire Cup game. When 16, another well-known local cricketer, Mr Tommy Hobson, took him to play for York where he won the league batting prize, and then, after leaving school, he moved to Scarborough. Working for his father, he had all the time off he needed for playing cricket. He went to the Yorkshire nets and had winter practice at Herbert Sutcliffe's school with Jim Laker and Harry Halliday. He played one friendly game with the Yorkshire Colts. War came. A nearby farmer and former Yorkshire fast bowler Sandy Jacques persuaded him to play in the Bradford League. He had four years with Undercliffe, two with Bingley and then one year with Pudsey St Lawrence.

Scoring three centuries in successive innings at Pudsey, he equalled a Bradford League record held by a present Yorkshire committeeman, Mr F. Popplewell. In the fourth game he made 75 against Queensbury and Vic smiled at the memory of the newspaper headline, 'Vic Wilson fails'. When war ended he began to play regularly with the Yorkshire Second XI and spasmodically with the senior side. That is, until 1948 when he made his first century against Surrey at The Oval. Later in the same season he was awarded his county cap. Loss of form in 1949 caused him to drop to the second team for a time but he returned to take 100 off Scotland at Hull. Not until 1951, when off-spinner Bob Appleyard took 200 wickets in the season, did he gain regular selection.

Wilson added another string to his bow. He was brought from the long field to the third short-leg position and he took 67 catches – the most in the country. In 1952 he made his top score, 230 against Derbyshire at Sheffield. He much preferred fast bowlers to slow twisters. Over six feet tall, he was able to get behind the short-pitched ball and kill it. This ability, and a century against Lancashire at Old Trafford, prompted the MCC to choose him for the 1954-55 tour of Australia. He did not play in a Test. He acted twelfth man in all five games, never grumbled, always tried his best, and came back with the reputation of being a splendid tourist. In 1958 his benefit realised £5,758.

His had been a satisfying if unspectacular career but his thoughts of retiring and taking a bigger farm were put aside with the offer of the Yorkshire captaincy. Wilson gave all he had to the job of leading a successful team and he proved an outstanding success. He also proved a professional could captain Yorkshire.

MICHAEL VAUGHAN

Michael Vaughan retired as the most successful captain in England's history – 26 wins from 51 Tests. In total he made 82 Test appearances and scored 5,719 runs (41.44).

Cricketer of the Year 2003 – by David Hopps

Michael Vaughan began 2002 keenly aware of the impatience for him to prove his worth as a Test batsman. If it emanated less from the England management than from the media, nonetheless the time was nigh for Vaughan to establish himself as a senior player and a worthy opening partner for Marcus Trescothick. Such was his response that, by the year's end, he was not just established, but had become England's most accomplished performer since the heydays of Gooch and Gower.

The transformation was striking enough in the scorebook. In 13 Tests up to the end of 2001, he had scored 679 runs at 33.95, respectable enough without being particularly eye-catching; in 2002, in one Test more, he stacked up 1,481 runs at 61.70, with six centuries – and another in 2003, in the final Ashes Test at Sydney, for good measure. He was Test cricket's leading run-getter in 2002, an impressive feat, if not the most meaningful one in England, where the cricketing year, like the financial, traditionally begins in April. Even more impressive was the style in which he made his runs. He had always been technically sound, but a reflective, somewhat pottering, even stressful air in his formative years encouraged some to harbour suspicions that he would be overpowered by attacks of the highest class. He answered that in wonderfully emphatic style. In 2002, cricket grounds in England and Australia resounded to a new Michael Vaughan, a batsman more confident in his method and much more forceful in his strokeplay. Deliveries that were once sneaked into the covers now pummelled the boundary boards. Short balls, and some not very short, were pulled and hooked in a manner that must have surprised even Vaughan himself. By the end of the year, his habit of touching the peak of his helmet, like a classical batsman of old respectfully touching the peak of his cap, had become a familiar sight. Throughout, he played with a dignity that signalled him a player of true worth.

Earlier in the year, Trescothick had been the England batsman attracting the plaudits. Vaughan remained on the fringe of the team after a lengthy apprenticeship in which he had always been thereabouts but not always there. Although he had made one Test century, against Pakistan in 2001, and had contributed crucial runs to two low-scoring victories over the West Indies in 2000, he had also attracted more than his share of injuries and other mishaps, culminating in being given out handled-the-ball in a Test match in India. Yet by the end of the English summer, Vaughan's four Test hundreds against Sri Lanka and India invited hopes that his opening partnership with Trescothick could be the springboard of a serious Ashes challenge. When an injury-ravaged England lost the Ashes series 4-1, Trescothick, who performed moderately, had been eclipsed; Vaughan was looking like the batsman around whom England could build for the next decade. Yorkshiremen were quick to hail Vaughan as one of their own, although had the ancient tradition of fielding only players born within the county boundary been maintained a few years longer, he might easily have been representing the old foe, Lancashire.

Michael Paul Vaughan was born at Salford's Hope Hospital on October 29, 1974, and lived in Manchester to the age of nine, when the family moved to Sheffield. Encouraged by his elder brother, he began netting at the Yorkshire League club Sheffield Collegiate, under the guidance of their junior coach, Jack Bethel, and Yorkshire age-group cricket quickly followed. It was while he was hitting a ball on the outfield at Abbeydale Park, during the interval of a county match, that Yorkshire's coach, the taciturn, gentle Doug Padgett, was stirred to put down his cup of tea on the pavilion balcony and wander on to the field to jot down his name. When Padgett heard that Vaughan had been born in Lancashire, he could barely conceal his dismay, but Yorkshire's

This match yielded 1,499 runs, the second largest aggregate for a three-day fixture. It was played in a light-hearted manner with no ducks because each batsman was given an easy ball to get off the mark and no lbw decisions because there was no appeal when the ball hit the pads.

T. N. Pearce's XI v Australians
Scarborough, September 6, 7, 8, 1961

junior ranks were relatively enlightened and Vaughan was repeatedly assured that the home-grown-only policy would soon be relaxed to encompass players raised within the county. So it did, although not before he had been invited to nets at both Lancashire and Northamptonshire (a perpetual scavenger of unwanted Yorkshire talent). Vaughan's presence in the Yorkshire side was never likely to bring protests. Polite and eager to learn, he won over even the crabbiest defenders of a faith that seemed even more outdated once Headingley's doors had been flung open to overseas players. He proved adept, as he remains to this day, at filtering advice from many sources. From Martyn Moxon he understood something of the opening batsman's art. From David Byas came the value of discipline. He watched Michael Bevan, who had two seasons with Yorkshire, and wondered at his ability to pace an innings with such calm.

An upbringing on Headingley's inconsistent pitches is not easy even for a batsman of high pedigree. Vaughan does not cavil at suggestions that it slowed his entry into the England side. But equally he credits life at Headingley with toughening him mentally, teaching him with every rogue ball and waspish comment from the crowd that cricket did not bestow its favours easily. That only made him work harder. He takes his profession seriously, if not himself. He respects the game, but he is a level-headed young man who keeps life in perspective and does not overreact to reward or failure. His head was not turned by winning the *Daily Telegraph* Under-15 Cricketer of the Year award in 1990, nor by becoming England Under-19 captain four years later, in preference to Trescothick. When he faced his first ball in Tests, at Johannesburg in 1999-2000, England were 2 for 4; Vaughan kept his cool and stayed in for two hours to make a composed 33.

He has always regarded his batting as a matter of trial and error, trying things to see if they work, discarding them quietly, without fuss, if they do not. By the end of the Ashes series even the Australians, not given to over-praising English cricketers, were speaking of him with undiluted respect. As the runs finally flowed, Vaughan kept telling the media, and himself, that the real test would come when they dried up. He will survive all this adulation without too much bother. His early England innings were introspective affairs. Another Yorkshire Australian, Darren Lehmann, advised him to quicken his running between the wickets, to run in Tests as he would in one-day cricket. Vaughan credits something so simple with perking up his entire game. He felt more confident, his feet moved faster, his mind was more aware of run-scoring possibilities.

Going into the England side at number four, and moving down the order before he went up it, he regards as beneficial, rather than adding to his uncertainty. He believes it made him a more adaptable player, as did his increasing opportunities in the one-day game. To Duncan Fletcher, whose stint as coach began with that same torrid Test in Johannesburg, he gives the warmest praise of all. 'He does not just grab your technique and try to change it. He will watch and watch and eventually volunteer something for you to consider. He might even spot a blemish in your game when you are about 120 not out. Not many coaches do that.' Not many batsmen give the coach five opportunities to do it in eight Tests.

Early in 2002, in New Zealand, Vaughan opened for England for the first time and unveiled his new liberated persona, twice racing into the 20s in as many balls. He felt he was playing well, but the ball zipped around on seaming pitches and the runs did not quite come. By the time Sri Lanka arrived at Lord's in May, Vaughan was not in great form. He was out hooking for a dogged 64 and guiltily apologised to his teammates as England followed on. But his first-innings graft had got him back into form and a hundred in the second saved the match, turned the series and began the sequence that changed his life. Lord's seemed to inspire him: another hundred followed against India. A duck in the first innings, when he was defeated by a big nip-backer from the left-armer Zaheer Khan, nudged him into a subtle shift in technique, to prevent his front foot getting too far across, and the rewards were gratifying. His 197 at Trent Bridge was celebratory: warm summer's day, flat pitch, large Saturday crowd and 'one of those days when everything was coming down like a beach ball.' He was in such command that he scored 99 between lunch and tea. The final Test of the summer, at The Oval, brought more sober satisfaction. England were weakening as the series went on and needed a draw to share the spoils. Vaughan steadied them by batting with great deliberation throughout a day's play – another ambition achieved, another hundred to add to the list. And the sobriety was relative: he made 182 in the day, scoring at a rate that only Trescothick could match, and dealt so commandingly with Anil Kumble's top-spinners and leg-breaks that Rahul Dravid, of all people, asked his advice on how to play spin.

A knee operation and a rest while England went to Sri Lanka for the ICC Champions Trophy ensured he was fitter than most for the start of the Ashes. He needed to be, as Glenn McGrath paid him the compliment of making him his number one target. The first impression Vaughan made on the series was to drop two catches at Brisbane, a persistent and puzzling frailty, but a breezy 33 off only 36 balls announced that he was not cowed by facing an Australian attack for the first time in Tests. Two weeks later at Adelaide, a resplendent hundred proved that unlike many good batsmen, including his predecessor Mike Atherton, Vaughan had it in him to see off McGrath and flourish against the rest of Australia's arsenal. To get out in the last over of the day frustrated him as much as it did England's travelling band of supporters, who knew in their hearts, as they applauded him into the pavilion, that another defeat was on the cards.

His run of injuries continued with a broken bone in his shoulder to go with the still-mending knee, but by now he was in good enough form to shrug them off. Back-to-back hundreds over Christmas and New Year, in Melbourne and Sydney, completed a wonderful series – 633 runs in five Tests, joining Brian Lara (546 in four) and V. V. S. Laxman (503 in three) as the only men to have taken 500 in a series off Australia in Steve Waugh's time as captain. To Vaughan, not one of the victors, went the spoils of the Player of the Series award, which prompted an Anglo-Aussie debate over whether he or Matthew Hayden should rightly be regarded as the number one opener in the world.

By the World Cup, he had joined England's management committee, alongside Hussain, Alec Stewart and Trescothick. He will probably captain England, although one hopes not too soon, because England's main requirement of Michael Vaughan at the moment is a mountain of runs. The responsibility is an onerous one, but he is equipped for the task.

PHIL CARRICK

Phil Carrick took 1,081 first-class wickets and scored 10,030 runs. He died of leukaemia in January 2000, aged 47.

By Graeme Wright, 2001

Phillip Carrick was captain of Yorkshire from 1987 to 1989. The highlight of his 24-year career with the club came when he led them to the Benson & Hedges Cup in 1987, perhaps Yorkshire's proudest day since they last won the County Championship 19 years earlier.

'Fergie' Carrick was a slow left-arm bowler, all too acutely aware that neither he nor his teammates could live up to the club's great traditions. In 1975, he took 79 wickets, including eight in an innings. But though he could turn the ball quite sharply then, he was forced to become more and more defensive in his bowling, and his arm got lower and lower. He was also a robust late-order hitter with a good eye, once smashing 105 on a terrible Headingley pitch in the 1978 Roses match. A man with a passion for cricket, and Yorkshire cricket in particular, he spent much of his time as captain frowning and doing the double teapot when things went wrong – but it was a mark of his commitment rather than of any ill-nature.

Even on the worst days, he was always ready to stay behind, chatting and theorising about the game and its strategies. In 1989, with the team struggling again, he wrote to the committee calling for the abolition of the policy of picking only Yorkshire-born players. He was turned down, and the affair was a factor in his loss of the captaincy, but his attempt helped pave the way for the end of the tradition three years later. Carrick played on until 1993, and was desperately keen to become the fifth player to reach 10,000 runs and 1,000 wickets for Yorkshire: he failed by just six runs. A Surrey player even dropped a catch to help him in the final match, but play had to be abandoned.

He went on to captain Pudsey Congs in the Bradford League and was still playing in August 1999 when he became ill. By this time, he had reached the first-class umpires' reserve list as a prelude to possible full-time umpiring, the perfect job for such an enthusiast. Carrick's premature death came only two years after that of his predecessor as Yorkshire captain, David Bairstow. His funeral, in a packed Bradford Cathedral, was attended by five England captains. One of them, Mike Gatting, said, 'There was never anywhere too far for Phil to go to see a friend, and we all felt the same about him.'

The coach, Ralph Middlebrook, said Carrick had helped hundreds of young players, 'He may not have been as good a bowler as Wilfred Rhodes, but in terms of acumen I would put him in the same bracket.'

Yorkshire hastily withdrew scorecards that billed it as England v West Indies.

England v South Africa, Headingley, 2008

DARREN GOUGH

Although he took 229 wickets in Tests, and finished with a first-class haul of 855 – as well as his 4,607 first-class runs – Darren Gough is also remembered for twice winning Strictly Come Dancing: the series and the Christmas Special of the BBC programme. He left Yorkshire for Essex in 2004, but returned and captained them in 2007 until his retirement the following summer.

Cricketer of the Year 1999 – by Matthew Engel

There are two different England teams these days. This is nothing to do with the increasingly disparate Test and one-day sides, because the difference affects them both. One lot is the downbeat, fatalistic crew who have become all too familiar: heads bowed, expecting the worst. The other is seen when Darren Gough is fit and firing.

At Old Trafford against New Zealand in 1994, Gough made one of the most sensational Test debuts of modern times. He took a wicket in his first over and had figures of 4 for 47. Earlier, he had gone out and hit a rousing 65, with ten fours. He was 23 years old. Everyone yelled 'New Botham', which was not a Yorkshire mining village but already a cliché, and later a rather sad joke. That winter, with England having been humiliated in the Melbourne Test, they went to Sydney looking hopeless. One young man took the game by the scruff. England 309 (Gough 51, and a thrilling 51 at that). Australia 116 all out (Gough 6 for 49). The Test was not quite won, but its hero was suddenly the hottest property in English sport. He was young, good-looking, an authentic Yorkshireman with that air of sleeves-up defiance which the nation adores. Vast wealth as well as glory looked a certainty.

But Gough had felt pain in his left foot even while the cheers were echoing. He ignored it. In a one-day international a few days later, he broke down and went home with his foot in plaster. It took four years to recapture that exuberance, in which time his career veered between wretched injuries and fated comebacks. His batting form went to pieces. And at the start of England's next Ashes tour, he became the sort of bowler everyone drops catches off, which was never Botham's fate. He was a star who twinkled rather than blazed. And yet the omens of 1994 have been proved right. And in 1998 he delivered. At Headingley, with his home crowd roaring him on, he ripped through South Africa's second innings to settle the series: 6 for 42 – three of them in a dramatic opening burst. Then he was at the heart of England's epic win in Melbourne before starting 1999 with a hat-trick in the Sydney Test. In any case, Gough's contribution to the team cannot merely be computed. He is an inspirational cricketer in an uninspiring era. And his successes make the Tests he has missed even more poignant.

Darren Gough was born at Barnsley on September 18, 1970. No town in cricket has such a rich tradition of character and characters: Geoffrey Boycott, Dickie Bird, Michael Parkinson. Gough was not born straight into the tradition. His father, a pest control officer, was a sports fan rather than a performer. But young Darren quickly established himself as a breathtakingly good sportsman and, at school, was captain of football, rugby and athletics as well as cricket. Football came first, and was the centre of Gough's early ambitions as he went through the Barnsley FC youth system and then became a government-funded trainee at Rotherham United. He was a midfielder – 'stylish' he insists – modelling himself on Glenn Hoddle, and dreaming of a transfer to Tottenham. It never happened. 'It was a time when football was all about quick runners, and I wasn't good enough'.

But then came another traineeship: this time with Yorkshire. And the club thought enough of him to give him a go in the first team right at the start of the 1989 season. The side travelled from Leeds to Lord's by train. Darren's dad took him to the station; David Bairstow, the captain, gave the lad, just 18, a big bear hug and promised Dad he would look after him. Pressure can override promises. Gough had to bowl 13 consecutive overs in the second innings. He ended up injured, and played only once more all season. As seems to be Gough's fate, fulfilment came slower than expected. He remained a member of the first-team squad, considered too valuable to be wasted much in the second eleven, but he was not getting enough chances to be kept happy. At the start of 1993, he thought he would give it one more season before thinking about another county. Then the opportunities came, and he grabbed them: 57 first-class wickets that season, followed by an A tour to South Africa, and his Test debut. But the glory was transient. He played again in 1995 when not quite ready. For a while, he ceased to be a certain choice, and was ignored (mysteriously) through the summer of 1996. In 1997, he began to feel pains in his left leg and was forced to pull out of the West Indies tour. When he reappeared, at Edgbaston, he broke a finger.

But the selectors knew now how much they wanted him: David Graveney, the chairman, called him the pulse of the team. And when Gough came back into the South Africa series, so did England. His bowling was highly skilled by now. Though he could not match Allan Donald on the speedometer, he was consistently quicker than anyone else, and was able to offer just about every other weapon in the fast bowling armoury as well – with the possible exception of really telling bounce. Pace bowlers like Gough who are not six-footers tend to produce deliveries that skid rather than leap.

Above all, though, in a team of brooders and worriers, he stood out for his bullish enthusiasm. England need Darren Gough, and not just for his wickets.

Above A Scarborough Festival of the 1950s, which to J. M. Kilburn was 'cricket on holiday' and a place that is 'always new but never changes.'

Below Bramall Lane, circa 1950, which was 'not among the loveliest of cricket grounds, but to many players and spectators down the years it was the one they loved most.'

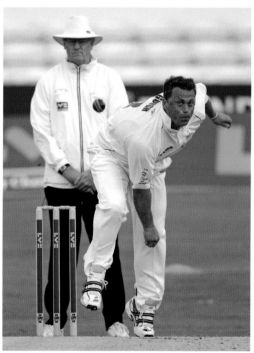

Above Fred Trueman, who Michael Parkinson described as a bowler with 'a barrel chest, big backside and the kind of legs normally used to support a billiard table,' but the sight of him in 'full flow' was still 'the most thrilling and beautiful spectacle.' Here is the proof of it – against Essex at Brentwood in 1951.

Left Darren Gough bowling for Yorkshire in 2007, having returned to the County as captain. In an England team of 'brooders and worriers' he 'stood out for his bullish enthusiasm.'

The 300th wicket. Trueman, sweater draped across his shoulder, is applauded in to The Oval pavilion after his landmark achievement. From the left are: Ted Dexter, John Price, Jim Parks, Ken Barrington, Tom Cartwright and Peter Parfitt.

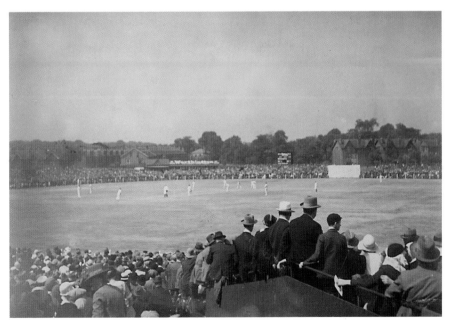

A land of lost content: a county match at Headingley in the 1920s – a period when Championship games there regularly attracted full houses.

Above The miracle of '81 and Ian Botham, who hit the ball 'into the confectionary stall and out again' and won England an Ashes Test in the most implausible circumstances.

Left Ray Illingworth at Scarborough in the 1950s. A real professional reared in the hardest of cricketing schools who forgot more about cricket than most others could ever hope to know.

Opposite Geoffrey Boycott. The date is August 11, 1977. The time is 5.49 p.m. The ground is Headingley. The on-drive – off Greg Chappell brings up the hundredth hundred of Boycott's career.

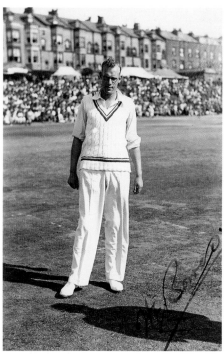

Above Brian Close, an inspirational captain who quickly established himself as a thinker and a tactician.

Left Bill Bowes at Scarborough in the 1950s, said to be the 'most difficult fast-medium bowler' in England and who later became a respected cricket writer.

Above left David Bairstow – loud, combative, combustible and whose captaincy of Yorkshire was described as 'a series of uphill cavalry charges.'

Above right Alonzo Drake, a difficult bowler on helpful wickets, who claimed all ten Somerset batsmen in an innings in 1914.

Right Lord Hawke, who 'never seemed to lose the joy of the game as played in the best sporting spirit.'

Len Hutton, a cricketing Knight who Neville Cardus thought had a mind which 'seemed to move a fraction of time in advance of his most rapid footwork.'

Chapter Four:
The History Boys

The saddest words of mouth or pen are simply these: *it might have been*. In Yorkshire cricket, the melancholic epigram is attached to the lives and careers of Alonzo Drake and Major Booth. More maudlin still is the team photograph of 1919, where those who remain after the Great War smile wanly into the camera as if flinching at the thought of absent friends.

Booth was named as one of *Wisden's* Cricketers of the Year in 1914. At the end of the summer, with war imminent, he'd claimed 157 wickets at 17.85 with swerve and swing and pace. He unhesitatingly enlisted in the Leeds Pals with the words, 'It is our duty . . . we cannot do anything else.' There is a poignant, final portrait of Booth gathered beside the other recruits. He is wearing civvies: grey suit, high white collar, slimly knotted dark tie. He looks like an off-duty bank clerk. In his cricketing whites, however, he was transformed, seeming taller, more agile and lithe.

Had war never come, Booth would have been bowling at Headingley or Hove, Old Trafford or The Oval in June 1916. But his field was no-man's land. He was struck in the heart and shoulder by shrapnel and died in the arms of Abe Waddington who himself returned from the war to play for Yorkshire; indeed, he stands in the back row of that distressed-looking photograph. Waddington nursed him in a shell hole choked with rats. Nine months later the remains of Booth's body were only identified because of an MCC cigarette case found in the pocket of the tunic. For the next 34 years his sister, refusing to believe Booth had died, kept a light burning in the window for him and left his room undisturbed until infirmity forced her to leave their cottage in 1950. Like so many others, the War dictated that Booth would be trapped forever in the summer before it began.

Drake, too, will always have the glint of promise about him. According to *Wisden*, he could, 'send down an unplayable ball that pitched on the leg stump and broke back nearly the width of the wicket.' In the penultimate match of 1914 – against Somerset at Weston-super-Mare – he took five wickets in the first innings and all ten in the second to finish with match figures of 15 for 51. Drake tried to enlist, found himself turned down on health reasons – a weak heart and an industrial smoking habit were to blame – and at the beginning of 1919 was openly predicting that he didn't have long to live. It was true. In February, he died, aged 34. 'In 1914 he seemed likely to have a big future,' said *Wisden's* obituary, and clearly meant it.

This chapter also contains accounts of five other cricketers who died relatively young. J. T. Brown was just 35, Ted Peate 45, George Ulyett 46, Schofield Haigh 49 and Edward Wainwright 54. They live on in the statistical and anecdotal records of the county.

ROBERT PEEL

Peel being 'sent off' was rather delicately put by Wisden. There are conflicting stories. One is that Hawke acted after Peel urinated on the pitch. Another is that George Hirst saw Peel in 'a proper condition' and put him to bed in the hotel, informing Hawke that his friend was 'taken queer in the night' and 'won't be able to turn out this morning'. Peel then made his own way to the ground and Yorkshire found themselves with 12 men on the field. Recognising his distressed state, Hirst heard Hawke say, 'Leave the field at once Peel.' Peel replied, 'Not at all, m'lord. I'm in fine form this morning.' According to Peel, 'Lord Hawke put his arm round me and helped me off the ground – and out of first-class cricket … What a gentleman!' Peel died at Morley in August 1941, aged 84.

Obituary – 1942

Robert Peel was one of the finest all-round cricketers of any time. Primarily he was a bowler, the second in the remarkable succession of slow left-handers – Edmund Peate, Peel, Wilfred Rhodes and Hedley Verity – who rendered such brilliant service to Yorkshire over a period of 60 years.

Born at Churwell, near Leeds, on February 12, 1857, Bobby Peel first played for his county in 1882, when Yorkshire were singularly rich in bowling talent, so that he had to wait several years before attaining real distinction. Still, being a capital fieldsman, especially at cover-point, and a punishing left-handed batsman, he kept his place in the team, and when Peate's connection with the county ceased in unhappy circumstances, Peel came to the fore. For nine seasons, with his fine length, easy action and splendid command of spin, this sturdily built left-hander regularly took over 100 wickets for Yorkshire, his county total amounting to 1,550 at an average cost of 15 runs each. He was often a match-winner. In 1887 he took five Kent wickets for 14 runs in an innings and, with 43 runs in a low-scoring match, helped largely in a victory by four wickets. In the same season 11 Leicestershire wickets fell to him for 51 runs at Dewsbury, five in the first innings for four runs. A year later he took eight Nottinghamshire wickets in an innings for 12 runs, while in 1892 five wickets for seven runs in an innings and 8 for 33 in the match against Derbyshire at Leeds was a startling performance. He did even better in 1895 against Somerset, 15 wickets falling to him in 36 overs for five runs, 9 for

Yorkshire's reply was delayed by a Ghurkha pipe band, who disregarded the end of the interval and continued marching at long-on, oblivious to the bewildered players and umpires.

Kent v Yorkshire
Canterbury, May 19, 2002

22 in one innings causing a sensation. At Halifax in 1897, a month before his county career ended, Peel dismissed eight Kent men in an innings for 53 runs, his match average showing 11 for 85; this performance gave Yorkshire an innings victory with 103 runs to spare in two days. Peel's full return in bowling in first-class cricket was 1,754 wickets at 16.21 runs apiece.

He did some remarkable things in Test matches with Australia, against whom he played for England 20 times. At Sydney in 1894, Australia set to get 177, hit off 113 of the runs for the loss of two wickets before stumps were drawn on the fifth day. The result then appeared a foregone conclusion, but strong sunshine followed heavy rain during the night. Peel slept through the storm.

Astounded when he saw the drying pitch, he said to the English captain, Mr Stoddart, 'gie me t' ball', and with Johnny Briggs, the Lancashire left-hander, also at his best, the remaining eight batsmen were disposed of for 53 runs. So England gained an extraordinary win by ten runs after facing a total of 586, then a record for these Tests, the previous being Australia's 551 at The Oval in 1884. Peel's analysis in the fourth innings was 6 for 67. Peel also enjoyed a large share in winning the rubber match of that tour. He took seven wickets, scored 73 in a stand for 152 with A. C. MacLaren, and following a grand partnership for 210 by Albert Ward, of Lancashire, and J. T. Brown, of Yorkshire, the two best scorers of England's first innings hit off the runs, the victorious total being 298 for 4 wickets. In 1896 at Kennington Oval, with conditions very difficult for batsmen, he and J. T. Hearne got rid of Australia for 44. Peel's share in the victory by 66 runs was eight wickets for 53 runs, and his last innings analysis six wickets in 12 overs for 23 runs – some revenge for getting a pair. Hearne's figures showed ten wickets for 60. That was the last match in which W. G. Grace led England to success over Australia.

Besides his great achievements as a bowler, Peel scored over 11,000 runs for Yorkshire, hitting two centuries. He obtained 210 not out in a Yorkshire score of 887 against Warwickshire at Edgbaston (1896), a total which remains a county match record. Peel and Lord Hawke, who added 292 for the eighth wicket, F. S. Jackson and E. Wainwright all reached three figures in that innings, then a record four centuries in an innings.

In 1889, the year in which the over was increased from four balls to five, Peel put together 158 in the Yorkshire second innings at Lord's, but yet was on the losing side, a brilliant 100 not out in 80 minutes by T. C. O'Brien taking Middlesex to victory by four wickets with ten minutes to spare. Yielding 1,295 runs for 36 wickets, the game produced a record aggregate for a match in England at the time.

Peel went four times to Australia, in 1884-85, 1887-88, 1891-92 and 1894-95, and in Test matches with Australia he took 102 wickets for less than 17 runs each. He also figured in Players teams against the Gentlemen from 1887 to 1897, taking in those games 48 wickets at a cost of 16 runs apiece.

He scored 1,206 runs and took 128 wickets in all matches in 1896, the year before his remarkable career came to an end. Sent off the field by Lord Hawke during a game at Bramall Lane and suspended for the remainder of the 1897 season, he was not seen

> The most notable event was the arrival of a member of the groundstaff with bucket, spade and besom to deal with some wasps that had congregated at the Vauxhall End.
>
> **Surrey v Yorkshire**
> **The Oval, September 16, 17, 18, 20, 1993**

again in the Yorkshire team. He did, however, appear for an England XI against Joe Darling's Australian side at Truro two years later, taking five wickets. His benefit match at Bradford in 1894 realised £2,000.

LOUIS HALL

Louis Hall was a non-smoker, a non-drinker and a Methodist preacher who later became chairman of the Cricketers' Benevolent Fund. He scored more than 12,000 first-class runs. He died, aged 63, in Morecambe in 1915.

Cricketer of the Year 1890

Louis Hall was born on November 1, 1852, and played his first match for Yorkshire at Prince's Ground in 1873. He did well on that occasion, but, failing to sustain his form, he dropped out of first-class cricket, and little more was heard of him till the season of 1878, when for Eighteen of Hunslet against the first Australian eleven, he created a genuine sensation by playing an innings of 79.

This performance against the bowling of Spofforth, Garrett, Boyle, and Frank Allan, none of whom he could ever have met before, at once reinstated him in the cricket world, and promptly regained him a place in the Yorkshire eleven. Since then he has been one of the most consistent of players, and has, year after year, been either at the top, or very near the top, of the Yorkshire averages, the county having certainly been able to boast no other batsman so safe, steady, and dependable. Having no grace of style to recommend him, his slow play is at times found very tedious by spectators, but a batsman is bound to adopt the game that suits him best, and as to Hall's immense value on a side there cannot be two opinions. To give an idea of what he has done for Yorkshire, we may mention that in the first-class county matches in 1886 he scored 811 runs, with an average of 30, and in 1887, 997 runs, with the magnificent average of 47.10. In 1888, the most wet and dismal of summers, he was at the top of his county's averages, but his aggregate declined to 473, and his average to 20.13. Hall is personally one of the most deservedly popular of cricketers, and his benefit match in 1890 – Yorkshire v Surrey at Sheffield – should bring him a very substantial reward for his many years of brilliant service to his county.

MAJOR WILLIAM BOOTH

Major Booth was born in Pudsey in 1886 and died in action with the West Yorkshire Regiment in July 1916 near La Cign. In 144 games for Yorkshire he scored 4,244 runs (22.65) and took 557 (18.89).

Cricketer of the Year 1914

Major William Booth, who took more wickets in first-class matches last season than any other bowler, was born at Pudsey on December 10, 1886. He began to play cricket when a boy at Fulneck School, and the first club he played for afterwards was Pudsey St Lawrence. He was a bowler at school, but for St Lawrence he gained his place as a batsman.

In 1907 he became a regular member of Yorkshire's second eleven, but there was nothing in his performances to suggest first-rate ability. He scored 242 runs with an average of 16, and took 23 wickets. Still, he must have shown a good deal of promise, as in the following year he was given a trial for Yorkshire against Somerset at Dewsbury, this being his first big match. It was not a very happy start as he was out leg-before-wicket for a single and only bowled half-a-dozen overs. Nothing was seen of him in first-class cricket in 1909, and for Yorkshire's second eleven his play, apart from an innings of 98, was quite ordinary. His real career as a County cricketer began in 1910, when he took part in 16 of Yorkshire's 28 county matches. Though he did nothing remarkable he got on well, scoring 326 runs with an average of 17, and taking 49 wickets for something over 21 runs apiece. At the end of the season Mr P. F. Warner wrote a short article for *Wisden*, dealing with the young cricketers of the year who struck him as having shown the greatest promise. He spoke favourably of Booth as a bowler, saying there was something puzzling about his flight, and that he made the ball swerve away at the last moment.

In the light of after events this criticism was significant, as qualities of flight and swerve have largely helped Booth to secure the position he now holds in the Yorkshire XI. In 1911 Booth was greatly handicapped by a strained side, and allowing for this disadvantage he did very well to take 74 wickets in county matches. Moreover he revealed himself as a brilliant batsman, playing a wonderful innings of 210 against Worcestershire, and scoring 1,125 runs. Sufficient that he has become one of the mainstays of the Yorkshire team.

With a free, natural action, he does a good deal at the end of his delivery, and makes the ball come very quickly off the pitch. His off-break, as the Middlesex batsmen found out in August, can be quite formidable, but he does not lean on it to any great extent. Swerve and pace off the ground are his strong points. If his bowling left him he could soon become a first-rate bat, but in Yorkshire's interests it is to be hoped that for the next few seasons he will not take his batting too seriously. His business is to get wickets, as he has not the physique, which has enabled George Hirst to be a crack bat and bowler at the same time.

ALONZO DRAKE

Alonzo Drake scored 4,789 runs and took nearly 500 wickets at 10.35. He died of a heart condition.

Obituary – 1920

Alonzo Drake. The death took place on February 14 of this well-known Yorkshire cricketer at his home at Westgate, Hanley, near Huddersfield. He was in his 35th year. Drake – left-handed both as batsman and bowler – first found a place in the Yorkshire team in 1909, having previously played for the second eleven. Tried in five matches, he showed distinct promise, but in the following season he fell below expectation, and it was not until 1911 that he firmly established himself in the side. In that season he had a batting average of 35 in county matches, and took 61 wickets. Thenceforward, until the outbreak of the war put a stop to first-class cricket, he was one of the best men in the Yorkshire eleven. In 1913 he came right to the front as a bowler, taking 102 wickets and heading the Yorkshire averages with the late M. W. Booth next to him. Finally, in 1914, he bowled better than ever, taking 135 wickets and being again practically at the head of the averages. Eclipsing everything he had previously done, he took all ten Somerset wickets in one innings at Weston-super-Mare, his analysis for the full match being 15 wickets for 51 runs. For some little time before his death he was in a bad state of health. On a wicket that helped him he was a very difficult bowler, and in 1914 he seemed likely to have a big future. He was born at Parkgate, near Rotherham, April 16, 1884.

LORD HAWKE

Martin Bladen Hawke was born in Gainsborough in 1860 and died in Edinburgh in 1938, aged 78. He scored 16,749 first-class runs and made five Test appearances.

By Hubert Preston, 1939

When first a Cambridge light blue cap caught my eye it was worn by the Hon. M. B. Hawke fielding for Yorkshire in front of The Oval pavilion. A prominent figure then, with his speed and sure picking-up, he became the dominant personality during many years to those who made frequent journeys to report matches in which Yorkshire were engaged. That was my good fortune when Lord Hawke captained the team which, under his firm, friendly leadership, had already become the strongest of the counties – a position retained with him as president.

Personally, throughout his active career, he experienced all the vicissitudes inseparable from cricket and never seemed to lose the joy of the game as played in the best sporting spirit. Some occurrences come to mind with the vivid memory of a close watcher and reporter of all that happened. One of the strangest was in August 1898 when at Chesterfield, John Brown, of Driffield, and John Tunnicliffe, of Pudsey, scored over 500 on the first day. For some reason Lord Hawke put himself down 'number three', the place usually given to F. S. Jackson; the captain wore his pads from 12 o'clock until the drawing of stumps and again on the Friday morning until the opening stand ended for 554. Sir Stanley will remember the occasion – not without a chuckle – a reference to the score shows him the best Yorkshire bowler with 7 for 78 in the two Derbyshire innings.

During the impregnable period from August 1899 to July 1901, when Yorkshire went unbeaten, Hirst, Rhodes and Haigh made a bowling combination perhaps never surpassed on all kinds of pitches. After seeing them supreme very often, it came as an astonishing change to find Hirst toiling in the deep at Headingley, while Somerset ran up a score of 630, and then gain an amazing victory by 279 runs after being 238 behind on the first innings. Lord Hawke was powerless; not one of his bowlers could stop the flow of runs that came from the bats of Lionel Palairet, Len Braund, F. A. Phillips and S. M. J. Woods, whose cogent word 'Magnum' expressed the delighted feelings of Somerset on returning to their hotel victorious over the Champions.

With so many superb players under his command, Lord Hawke could afford to take a risk though this was seldom necessary. The opposition so often fell easy victims that, no doubt, he considered the position quite safe when he declared at Bradford in August 1908 and sent Middlesex in after lunch, wanting 269 to win with two hours forty minutes left. To everyone's surprise Middlesex went for the runs. James Douglas stood away from the stumps and used the cut or drive in grand style when Hirst bowled inswingers to a packed leg-side field. F. A. Tarrant often ran down the pitch and got the bowlers off their length so that he could drive, pull or cut with impunity. The task was reduced to 51 wanted with 20 minutes remaining. Albert Trott, another Australian of exceptional ability, was the man to do this, but, attempting a run for a stroke to the unguarded offside, he collided with Newstead, also a heavyweight, dashing across the pitch from short leg. Both men fell; Hirst returned the ball and Trott, to his disgust, was given 'run out' – a doubtful decision after an absolute accident when the batsman was obstructed! Lord Hawke's judgment in the powers of his side at least to avoid defeat proved sound, for Middlesex finished 36 behind with two wickets in hand. Such an afternoon makes the game great.

In 1896 Lord Hawke scored 166 towards the 887 made by Yorkshire at Edgbaston against Warwickshire, the record total for any first-class match in England until the 903 for 7 in The Oval Test last August. He and Robert Peel put on 292 – still the highest eighth-wicket partnership by English batsmen. The best last wicket stand for Yorkshire was by Lord Hawke and David Hunter, 148 against Kent in 1898.

In another record of a very different kind, Lord Hawke was concerned closely, for he chose F. S. Jackson to open the bowling with George Hirst in the second innings against the Australians at Leeds in 1902 and the total – 23 – remains the smallest by an Australian side apart from the 18 for which Harry Trott's eleven were sent back by the MCC at Lord's in 1896. The preference for Jackson to start the bowling was the more noteworthy because that distinction usually belonged to Wilfred Rhodes who, four days before, when sharing England's attack with Hirst at Birmingham, had taken seven Australian wickets for 17 runs. Jackson dismissed the last four batsmen in five balls – his match record was nine wickets for 42 runs.

Thoughtful interest for the general welfare of his players was apparent even in the stern measures which Lord Hawke found necessary to take when he turned out of the side one of the best all-round cricketers of the time. Such strong discipline, exercised for the second time by Lord Hawke, sufficed to cure any player's possible lack of self-control in the future. While Lord Hawke, from 1883 until the time of his passing, became more famous as captain and president than he ever was as a batsman, he played many a fine innings and, late in the batting order, he frequently turned the scale in favour of his side by sound defence and hard clean hitting – notably the powerful off-drive for which his height and robust figure were well suited.

For many years Lord Hawke's speeches at the annual general meeting of the Yorkshire County Club contained outspoken comments on current cricket which always commanded attention. At other times his caustic remarks were wrongly construed in some quarters; notably when he expressed the fervent hope that England would never be captained by a professional. This was not derogatory of the players for whom he had done so much and always held in high esteem, but expressed his strong desire that there would always be a Gentleman good enough a cricketer for the high position as leader of our eleven. No one knew better than did Lord Hawke the heavy responsibilities of captaining a cricket eleven.

J. T. BROWN

In his eight Tests J. T. Brown made 470 runs. In total, he scored 17,920 runs in first-class matches. He died in London in 1904.

Cricketer of the Year 1895

J. T. Brown, who comes from the small town of Driffield in Yorkshire, was born on August 20, 1869, and is thus at the present time in his 26th year.

He first played for Yorkshire in 1889, appearing in seven of the 25 matches in which the county eleven took part, but his reputation has been made in the last two seasons. In 1893, when Yorkshire carried off the Championship, there was a close race for first place in the averages in the county matches between Brown, Tunnicliffe and Mr Sellers, but Brown just won with 712 runs in 16 fixtures and an average of 28.12. In all matches for Yorkshire that year he was third with an aggregate of 1,141 runs, and an average of 23.14, while in first-class matches he was ninth among the professional batsmen, obtaining 889 runs, and averaging 23.15. Writing of his performances for his county we said in *Wisden* that he gained the place of honour, and thoroughly deserved it. Indeed, it was the general opinion when the season of 1893 ended that Yorkshire had found a batsman of first-class powers, and that, well as he had already done, Brown was likely to do still better in the future.

These expectations were abundantly borne out last season, when Brown won an unquestioned position among the best professional batsmen of the day. In all matches for Yorkshire he had far and away the highest aggregate, and was only fractionally behind F. S. Jackson in the averages, while in the general first-class averages he came out ninth on the list, scoring 1,397 runs with an average of 30.17. On three occasions he obtained a hundred or more, scoring 141 for Yorkshire v Liverpool and District, 101 for the North against the South and 100 for Yorkshire against Gloucestershire.

Brown is a batsman of great resources and though, like everyone else, he is seen at his best on a firm lively pitch, he has over and over again proved his ability to get runs under difficult conditions. A fine illustration of his power to force the game on a wet ground was afforded in the Yorkshire and Kent match during Canterbury Week. Nature has not been over liberal to him in the matter of height, but he makes up by skill for lack of inches, the way in which he can master a quick-rising ball being remarkable. He has a strong and watchful defence, and many ways of getting runs. Up to the end of 1893 he had been regarded as an outfield, but last season, owing to some affection of the feet, he was placed at point, in which position he was most successful, repeatedly stopping the hardest hits, and bringing off some brilliant catches. Indeed it is doubtful if last summer there was a better point in England.

Brown was the last choice for Mr Stoddart's team for Australia, only being asked when Abel had declined an invitation.

TOM EMMETT

Tom Emmett was known for his sense of humour. Sailing through the Bay of Biscay he responded to the particularly rough seas with the observation that someone had forgotten the heavy roller. He took 1,216 wickets (12.71) and scored 6,315 runs (15.10).

Obituary – 1905

Tom Emmett died suddenly on June 30, in his 63rd year. He had long ago dropped out of the public gaze, his connection with the Yorkshire eleven ending in 1888, but he had assuredly not been forgotten. There was never a more popular professional, his cheery nature, and the inexhaustible energy with which he played the game, making him a prime favourite wherever he went.

His closing days were, unhappily, rather clouded, but on this point there is no need to dwell. He was, perhaps, the only instance of a great fast bowler who was skilful enough to remain effective after he had lost his pace. Those who only saw him bowl in the latter part of his career, when his main object was to get catches on the off side, can have no idea of what he was like when he first won fame in the cricket field. His speed for five or six years was tremendous, and every now and then he would send down an unplayable ball that pitched on the leg stump and broke back nearly the width of the wicket.

Born in September 1841, he was rather late in coming forward, being a man of nearly 25 when he first found a place in the Yorkshire team. Once discovered, however, he jumped almost immediately to the top of the tree, playing for England against Surrey and Sussex in Tom Lockyer's benefit match at The Oval in 1867 – his second season. A still greater bowler – the late George Freeman – was getting to his best at the same time, and from 1867 to 1871 inclusive, the two men did wonderful things together. How they would have fared on the more carefully prepared wickets of these days is a question difficult to answer. The important point is that under the conditions prevailing in their own time they were irresistible. It is quite safe to say that a more deadly pair of purely fast bowlers never played on the same side.

After 1871 business took Freeman away from first-class cricket, but Emmett found another excellent colleague in Allen Hill, and in later years he shared Yorkshire's bowling with Ulyett, Bates, Peate, and Peel. As time went on his pace left him, and he became the clever, dodgy bowler – full of devices and untiring in effort –whom men still young well remember. The charm of Emmett as a cricketer lay in his keen and obvious enjoyment of the game. No day was too long for him, and up to the end he played with the eagerness of a schoolboy. He was full of humour, and numberless good stories are told about him. He went to Australia three times, and was the mainstay in bowling for Lord Harris's team in 1878-79. During the first of his three visits he took part at Melbourne, in March 1877, in the first match in which the Australians ever met an English eleven on even terms. Charles Bannerman scored 165, and the Australians won by 45 runs.

No one in this country had any idea in those days of what Australian cricket would become, but Emmett, on his return home, spoke very highly of the colonial bowling.

EDWARD WAINWRIGHT

Edward Wainwright bowled with the ball between his thumb and first finger and put so much into each delivery that the flesh was bleeding by the end of a day's play. He scored almost 13,000 runs and took 1,173 wickets. Wainwright was the first Yorkshire bowler to take all ten wickets in a match – against Staffordshire at Sheffield in 1890.

Cricketer of the Year 1894

Edward Wainwright, a native of Tinsley, near Sheffield, was born on April 8, 1865, and first found a place in the Yorkshire eleven in the season of 1888. His reputation, therefore, has reached its present point in half a dozen summers. He did not score very heavily in his first year, but an innings of 105 against the Australians at Bradford showed that he had plenty of batting in him, and as a bowler he had the satisfaction of standing second for Yorkshire in the first-class county matches.

In the following year he improved as a batsman, but went back as a bowler, and it cannot be said that, speaking generally, he much advanced his position. In 1890, curiously enough, his cricket was of a diametrically opposite character. As a batsman he did so little for his county that in 28 matches he only scored 514 runs, but as a bowler he took 97 wickets at an average cost of 13.71. In 1891, a season of great disaster for Yorkshire, he made a still further improvement as a bowler, taking 67 wickets in the first-class county matches, and in all engagements for the county obtaining the fine record of 107 wickets with an average of 13.20.

His batting, however, was still ineffective, and in the course of 25 matches for Yorkshire his highest score was only 68. So far he had proved himself a useful member of a county team, but had not been thought of in connection with representative elevens. Promotion, however, came in 1892, when he fairly established his position among the leading professionals of the day.

His advance upon anything he had ever done before was, indeed, remarkable. In Yorkshire's first-class county matches he stood second in batting and first in bowling, while in the first-class averages for the year he could point to the splendid record of 890 runs with an average of 25.15, and 104 wickets at a cost of 16.31.

He was chosen for the Players against the Gentlemen both at Lord's and The Oval, and at the former ground met with remarkable success, scoring 56 not out, and taking, in the Gentlemen's second innings, five wickets for 37 runs. He did not, last season, prove so successful in batting, but as a bowler he did great things, taking in first-class matches 119 wickets for something over 14 runs each. He had the honour of playing for England against Australia at Lord's, and would also have played at The Oval if the Yorkshire Committee had been willing to let him off from a county match. Wainwright is emphatically an all-round cricketer, his fielding being quite as good as his batting and bowling. As a bowler he only misses greatness by reason of the fact that his accuracy of pitch is not commensurate with his break and spin.

SCHOFIELD HAIGH

Schofield Haigh made 11 Test appearances and finished his career with 2,012 first class wickets. He died in Huddersfield in 1921.

Cricketer of the Year 1901

Schofield Haigh was born on March 19, 1871, at Berry Brow – a suburb of Huddersfield, situated about two miles outside the town. After taking part in some school cricket, he threw in his lot, at the age of 18, with Armitage Bridge-Moorhouse's old club. At that time a medium-pace bowler, Haigh did well, and before very long came under the notice of Louis Hall. That veteran batsman was then in the habit of taking teams up to Scotland at the close of each summer and on his recommendation, Haigh was engaged by the Aberdeen Club, with which body he remained for three seasons. He then went to

Perth, and it was during his engagement there – which lasted two years – that the Yorkshire authorities first found out what an extremely promising bowler he was.

He played for a Scotland team against the Lancashire eleven and the match, as it happened, proved the turning point of his career. The first time he went on to bowl in the game, 63 runs were scored off him before he took a wicket, but after that he carried all before him and finished up with a record of 8 for 78. He settled down at Leeds in 1896 and, while engaged on the Headingley Ground, commenced the connection with the Yorkshire eleven that has since brought him such fame in the cricket field.

In a match against Durham, at Barnsley in 1896, he took 14 wickets for 50 runs, and at the beginning of the following week he was included in the team that met the Australians at Bradford. This was his first opportunity in important cricket and he made the most of it, obtaining in the Australian second innings eight wickets – five of them bowled down – at a cost of 78 runs. Yorkshire lost the match by 140 runs, but Haigh's position as one of the best young bowlers of the day was firmly established. For the rest of the season he was a regular member of the Yorkshire team and for a few weeks he bowled with conspicuous success, taking 12 wickets against Derbyshire at Sheffield, 11 against Warwickshire at Harrogate and doing good work in several other matches. Towards the close of the summer the strain of three-day matches told on him, but for all that he came out first in the Yorkshire bowling for the season with 84 wickets for little more than 15 runs apiece.

From 1896 to the present time he has, as everyone knows, been one of the mainstays of the Yorkshire eleven, but his career as a bowler has not been one of unmixed success. Indeed, in 1897, 1898, and 1899 he scarcely fulfilled the hopes formed of him in his first season, and, though doing good work, seemed to be going back rather than forward. In the three years he took in county matches alone 70, 88 and 79 wickets, but his average was never so good as it had been in 1896. Last season, however, he jumped to the top of the tree and among the county bowlers of the year had, on results, no superior except his colleague Wilfred Rhodes. The two bowlers worked splendidly together and did more than anyone else to carry off the Championship for Yorkshire.

His improvement was probably due in some measure to the fact that he modified the tremendous plunge with which he used to finish his delivery. Be this as it may, he certainly seemed to bowl with greater comfort to himself than in previous seasons. Technically a medium-pace to fast bowler, Haigh commands a good variety of speed,

---

Yorkshire won with 18.1 overs to spare. They did so in dark blue kit, after Wood went out to toss in their intended yellow away shirt and was attacked by a swarm of insects.

Sussex v Yorkshire
Arundel, June 27, 2004

and when the ground helps him his off-break is, in the opinion of a good many batsmen, almost unplayable, the ball pitching outside the off stump and often hitting the leg stump, this doing more than the width of the wicket. Those who were behind his arm in the pavilion at The Oval in August during Surrey's sensational second innings saw him at his deadliest. Haigh as a cricketer is far more than a mere bowler, being a capital hard-working field and a resolute bat with a happy knack of making runs when the position is critical. This faculty was never more strongly revealed than in Yorkshire's match last July, at Worcester, when he helped to save Yorkshire from what had looked like an impending defeat.

JOHN TUNNICLIFFE

Lord Hawke described him as the 'loyal of the loyal'. As well scoring more than 20,000 runs he also took 691 catches. Only Wilfred Rhodes (704) took more.

Cricketer of the Year 1901

John Tunnicliffe was born on August 26, 1866, at Pudsey, the day happening to be Feast Sunday in the little Yorkshire town. He played all his early cricket in connection with the Pudsey Britannia Club of which he became a member when he was about 16 years old. He is not absolutely certain on the point, but he believes as that he played for the first eleven before he was 17. Of these youthful doings he cannot recall many particulars, but he remembers that he made his first hundred against Armley on his 18th birthday. Two years afterwards he played for the Colts of Yorkshire against the County eleven at Sheffield, scoring 11 and not out two and – being something of a bowler in those days – taking two wickets.

Albert Ward came out the same year and but for the circumstance of his qualifying for Lancashire and playing for that county in 1889, after having had three trials for Yorkshire in 1886, might for the last dozen seasons have been a colleague of Tunnicliffe's on the Yorkshire eleven. In 1887 Tunnicliffe played for the Yorkshire Colts against the Notts Colts but his day had not yet arrived and he heard nothing from the Yorkshire authorities as to making an appearance in the county eleven. He had to wait a considerable time longer for his chance and it was not until the season of 1891 that he gained a place in the Yorkshire team. As he was then 25 years old be must be regarded as very late in coming forward. At the same age many famous batsmen, both professional and amateur, had already had a distinguished career to look back upon.

Tunnicliffe's first season for Yorkshire was in no way sensational. Everyone realised that with his enormous advantages of height and reach he had possibilities, but he did nothing out of the common, only scoring in all matches for the county 374 runs with the modest average of 13. Tunnicliffe thinks that he first impressed the Yorkshire Committee in this same season of 1891 in a match at Sheffield between the Notts Colts and the Yorkshire Colts. Little Bobby Bagguley – one of the smallest men that ever appeared in first-class cricket – was just coming out for Notts, being then a lad of 18, and was looked upon as a bowler of more than ordinary promise. It had been raining hard the day before the match and the wicket was very soft indeed. Tunnicliffe thought the only chance of getting runs on such a pitch was to have a dash and he did, sending Bagguley twice in succession into the little refreshment stand at the left-hand side of the pavilion and twice hitting him on to the seats. This little innings of 27 was the first revelation of the great hitting power that Tunnicliffe possesses – a power that he always has in reserve no matter how long he may at times repress it.

Since the season of 1891 he has never looked back and has been a regular member of the team which, though of course with varying fortune, has so splendidly upheld the fame of Yorkshire cricket. There is no need here to go into statistics. All Tunnicliffe's performances – and they have been many and brilliant – are accessible to those who wish to study them. If asked to describe in a phrase Tunnicliffe's chief peculiarity as a batsman we should say that, like the great Australian left-hander Darling, he is by nature a big hitter, but has rigidly schooled himself to play a steady game. In his early days he was decidedly rash and hit up so many catches in the long field that his brother professionals had more than once to remind him that Bramall Lane was rather bigger than the cricket ground at Pudsey.

Last season he was at his very best as a batsman, perhaps combining hitting and defence in better proportion than ever before. The innings that saved the match at Worcester showed his stubborn qualities at their highest development, just as his big score on a soft wicket at Trent Bridge showed to the fullest extent what he could do when a forcing game was demanded. Even if he had not been quite such a good bat, Tunnicliffe would have lived in cricket history as the very best short slip of his day. Perhaps no cricketer has in the same position brought off so many wonderful catches. Time stands still for no man, however, and now at the age of 34 he does not find it quite so easy as he did to fling himself down at full length and bring off a one-handed catch six inches from the ground. Still, if he cannot stand comparison with himself, he is vastly better at slip than most men who field there.

GEORGE ULYETT

At Bramall Lane – in June 1898 – Ulyett came across George Hirst on the pavilion steps. 'I'm finished, young 'un,' he said. 'Nay, niver in this world,' Hirst is said to have replied. Ulyett died less than a week later.

Obituary – 1899

George Ulyett died in only in his 47th year, his last season in the Yorkshire eleven being 1893. His health had been failing for some time, but the immediate cause of death was an acute attack of pneumonia, contracted at Bramall Lane during the Yorkshire and Kent match. Yorkshire has always been rich in first-rate cricketers, but a finer player than Ulyett the county has never produced. He was for years the best bat in the team, and even if he had not been able to get a run he would have been worth his place for his bowling and fielding.

His career for the county extended over a period of 20 years, his first appearance in the eleven dating back to July 1873. It was seen at once that a player of remarkable gifts had been discovered, and before very long he was at the top of the tree. To begin with, he was played as much for his fast bowling as for his batting. One talent, however, developed to a much greater extent than the other, and in two or three seasons he was quite as good a bat as Ephraim Lockwood, who, when Ulyett came out, was the bright particular star of the Yorkshire eleven. Once having established his position Ulyett never looked back. There was no doubting his class as a batsman after his first visit to Australia with James Lillywhite's team in the winter of 1876-77, and from that time till 1891 he was always in the front rank. Of course, like other great batsmen, he did much better in some seasons than others, but he never lost his place as a representative cricketer. A peculiar interest attaches to the tour of James Lillywhite's team – not, in some respects, very brilliant – as it was then that the Australians first ventured to play an English eleven on even terms. Thanks to a wonderful innings of 165 by Charles Bannerman, Australia won the first match, but in the return the Englishmen had their revenge, Ulyett's batting deciding the fortunes of the game. It was the fine play they showed that season that led the Australians to pay their first visit to England, a momentous chapter in the history of modern cricket being thus opened.

At home Ulyett, of course, played many times for England against Australia, and in two memorable encounters at Lord's he contributed in a very marked degree to England's success. The first of the two matches was in 1884, when A. G. Steel scored 148 – the innings of his life. On the Tuesday afternoon the Australians, with a balance of 150 runs against them, went in for the second time. The wicket had not worn well, and Peate, bowling from the Nursery End, had the batsmen from the first in obvious difficulties. After a little time, however, to everyone's surprise, Lord Harris took him off and gave Ulyett the ball. Never was a captain better justified by results. The broken places on the pitch which had made Peate difficult rendered Ulyett well-nigh irresistible. Bowling his fastest, and repeatedly breaking back several inches, he had one of the strongest of all Australian teams at his mercy. At the drawing of stumps that evening four men were out for 73, and the next morning the Australians were all out for 143, England winning the match by an innings and five runs. Ulyett took seven wickets in 39 overs and a ball, and had only 36 runs hit from him.

It was on that eventful Tuesday afternoon that Ulyett caught and bowled Bonnor in a way that no one who was present will ever forget. Bonnor's mission was to knock the fast bowler off, and he did his best. He drove a half-volley with all his force, but the ball – travelling faster than an express train – went into Ulyett's right hand instead of to the boundary. Bonnor wandered disconsolately back to the pavilion, and the England players gathered round Ulyett, curious, perhaps, to know what manner of man he was, and anxious to congratulate him on his escape from imminent danger. One can remember, even now, the look of wonder on the faces of A. G. Steel and Alfred Lyttelton.

Ulyett himself was very modest about the matter. Complimented on the catch, when the day's play was over, he said simply that if the ball had hit his fingers instead of going into his hand he should have played no more cricket that season.

The other England match was in 1890. England had much the stronger side, and won in the end by seven wickets, but on the first day there was a period of great anxiety. The ground had suffered a good deal from rain, and after the Australians had been put out for 132, England lost W. G. Grace, Shrewsbury, W. W. Read and Gunn – the four best bats on the side – for 20 runs. Turner and Ferris were bowling their best, and the outlook was, to say the least, cheerless. However, Maurice Read and Ulyett saved the side from collapse. They put on 72 runs in an hour and a half, and next morning Ulyett carried his own score to 74. That was the highest innings he ever played for England against Australia in this country, and, curiously enough, he never appeared for England again. The Yorkshire authorities would not let him off for The Oval match in 1890, and when the Australians paid us their next visit, in 1893, his star had waned.

Of Ulyett's doings for Yorkshire and in the Gentlemen and Players matches a column could easily be written. He was at his very best for this county in the season of 1887, when he and Louis Hall did great things. The one brilliancy itself, the other a miracle of patience, they were an ideal pair to start an innings. It is a moot point whether bowlers were the more disturbed by Ulyett's hitting or by Hall's unwearying defence. Some preferred to bowl at Ulyett because he hit at so many balls that there was always a chance of getting him out. Alfred Shaw for one never despaired of seeing him caught if the ground was large enough to allow of the outfields being placed very deep. To say that Ulyett was the greatest batsman Yorkshire ever possessed would scarcely be exceeding the truth, but Lockwood in the past and F. S. Jackson in the present must in fairness be classed with him.

TED PEATE

Ted Peate lies in an unmarked grave in Yeadon Cemetery near Leeds.

Obituary – 1891

Edmund Peate, the most famous slow bowler of his day, died on March 11, at Newlay, near Leeds. Though he had long since ceased to take part in first-class cricket – dropping out of the Yorkshire eleven at the beginning of the season of 1887 – he was quite a young man. He was born at Holbeck on March 2, 1856. His career was exceptionally brilliant while it lasted, but very short. Earning a place in the Yorkshire team in 1879 he rose in the following season to the top of the tree, and there he remained till the end of 1884, succeeding Alfred Shaw as the representative slow-bowler of England. There ought to have been many more years of good work before him, but he put on weight to a great extent, and in the summer of 1886 it became evident that his day was over.

Without using a harsh word, it may fairly be said that he would have lasted longer if he had ordered his life more carefully.

He never entirely lost his skill as a bowler, and even up to the last year or two he was successful in club cricket in and around Leeds. At his best he was a great bowler. As to that there cannot be two opinions, though it is true that he was fortunate at the outset of his career in playing in very wet seasons. He did not set store on a big break, but on most wickets he could make the ball do enough to beat the bat, and his pitch was a marvel of accuracy. He has had brilliant successors in the Yorkshire eleven in Peel and Rhodes, but many batsmen – W. L. Murdoch among the number – who met him in his prime are of opinion that as a left-handed slow bowler he has never been equalled. The immediate cause of his death was pneumonia, but his health had been in a bad state for some time.

Some of his best performances with the ball were:

6 wickets for 14 runs	Yorkshire v Middlesex	at Huddersfield	1879
5 wickets for 11 runs	Yorkshire v Derbyshire	at Derby	1880
14 wickets for 130 runs	Yorkshire v Sussex	at Brighton	1881
14 wickets for 77 runs	Yorkshire v Surrey	at Huddersfield	1881
8 wickets for 71 runs	England v Australia	at The Oval	1882
8 wickets for 57 runs	Shaw and Shrewsbury's XI	at Sydney	1882
6 wickets for 12 runs	Yorkshire v Derbyshire	at Derby	1882
8 wickets for 32 runs	Yorkshire v. Middlesex	at Sheffield	1882
8 wickets for 5 runs	Yorkshire v Surrey	at Holbeck	1883
5 wickets for 17 runs	Yorkshire v Notts	at Sheffield	1883
6 wickets for 13 runs	Yorkshire v Gloucestershire	at Moreton-in-Marsh	1884
10 wickets for 51 runs	North of England v the Australians	at Manchester	1884
10 wickets for 45 runs	Yorkshire v Derbyshire	at Huddersfield	1885
6 wickets for 17 runs	England v Shaw's Australian XI	at Lord's	1885
9 wickets for 21 runs	Yorkshire v Sussex	at Huddersfield	1886

In all first-class matches in 1882 he obtained 214 wickets at a cost of 2,466 runs. He first represented the Players against the Gentlemen in 1881, and took part in the matches for six years, bowling in 11 matches (21 innings), 3,227 balls for 996 runs, and 39 wickets, average 25.53.

He took more than 1,000 career wickets for Yorkshire and England and twice claimed 14 in Championships matches. Against Australia at The Oval in 1882, England needed 85 runs to win a low scoring Test. With just ten required, Peate tried a haymaking slog and was clean bowled. Four days later *The Sporting Times* published its mock obituary

Yorkshire were unable to muster enough second-innings runs to set a challenging target. They might have put more pressure on Surrey had it not been for a bizarre interlude when Blakey swept a four into the press tent. After the ball was fetched, Hollioake noticed some tooth marks; the culprit, it transpired, was Bumper, a Labrador who belonged to Geoffrey Dean from *The Times*. The damage prompted Hollioake to take the new ball – 21 overs after it had become available – and Surrey's seamers quickly despatched the Yorkshire tail.

Surrey v Yorkshire
Guildford, July 24, 25, 26, 27, 2002

of English cricket – the body to be cremated and the Ashes taken to Australia. But another, more obscure lamentation on the defeat appeared in *C. W. Alcock's Cricket: A Weekly Report of The Game* on the morning after Peate's stumps were uprooted. It read:

> Sacred to the memory of England supremacy
> in the cricket field which expired on the
> 29th day of August, at The Oval:
> 'Its End was Peate'.

Chapter Five:
Big Hearts of the Broad Acres

Whenever I hear the phrase *Yorkshire grit*, I think of the one man who embodies it for me. It isn't Len Hutton, despite the physical and psychological obstacles he had to overcome, and my profound admiration for him (even though I never saw him play). It isn't Wilfred Rhodes or George Hirst, who often won matches through the force of bruising will. Nor is it any of the more recent characters whose spikes touched Headingley's pavilion steps, admirable though they may be.

Bob Appleyard inspired this chapter.

Bill Bowes' piece, written on Appleyard's becoming one of *Wisden's* Cricketers of the Year in 1952, doesn't contain half of his extraordinary story for the straightforward reason that the intensely moving and headline-making part of it was still to come. Bowes described Appleyard's taking of 200 wickets in his first full season – aged 27 – as a 'fairytale', and said of him, 'His accuracy, change of pace and mixing of spin and swing put even the best batsmen in difficulties.' But it was the difficulties that Appleyard himself faced which were to set him apart – as a man as much as a cricketer.

In the spring of 1952, as the final pages of that year's *Wisden* were being set in cold type, he was diagnosed with tuberculosis. His surgeon warned that a 'little surgery' would be necessary. The operation lasted six and a half hours and led to the removal of half of his left lung. The resulting scar stretched from his armpit to his waist. He spent the next eleven months convalescing in bed. To bowl again he had first to learn how to walk again. He did it with dignity and a level of courage that, no matter how many times I dwell on it, still leaves me in silent awe of him. The progress medical science makes allows every generation to receive better medical care than the one before it. The treatment Appleyard received was the finest any British hospital could provide at the time. To us, however, an amalgam of hindsight and surgical advancement makes it seem rough and almost prehistoric, a knowledge which accentuates the skill of the surgeon's scalpel and the stoic faith of the patient.

Appleyard, glad merely to be alive, didn't play for two years. In his improbable comeback summer of 1954, he took 154 wickets, won a place on the tour to Australia and went on to claim match figures of six for 71 (three for 13 in the second innings) in the fourth Test at Adelaide, where England won in oven-heat to retain the Ashes. Nothing more needs to be said except the obvious: the biggest heart in the broad acres belongs to Bob Appleyard.

CHRIS OLD

Chris Old made 46 Test appearances, taking 143 wickets and scoring 865 runs. He played a significant role in the Miracle of Headingley – England's 1981 Ashes win over Australia. In first-class cricket, he took more than 1,000 wickets (average 23.48) and scored over 7,500 runs.

Cricketer of the Year 1979 – by Terry Brindle

The now-indisputable talents that lifted Chris Old to a distinguished career with Yorkshire and England might never have been allowed to develop had two older Olds had their way. The youngest Old was an impressionable four years of age when he was allowed to take part in his first cricket match, and older brother Alan and eldest brother Malcolm nominated him as wicketkeeper, declaring sternly that he was not allowed to bat or bowl.

Happily, Christopher Middleton Old outgrew his penance as wicketkeeper and his awe of older brothers, but he never outgrew his love of cricket. The 1978 season, which he regards as the most satisfying of his career to date, revealed him at 29 as a mature bowler, a model of accuracy and control. Brother Alan, perhaps as a result of so much early batting and bowling practice, has played for Durham and has won greater honours as an England and British Lions rugby union fly half. Indeed, Chris and Alan provide the only instance, it is thought, of brothers playing for England at different sports on the same days. It happened while Chris Old was with England in the West Indies in 1974. On February 2, Chris played in the first Test at Port-of-Spain and Alan appeared for England against Ireland at Twickenham; on February 16, when Chris played in the second Test at Kingston, Alan played against Scotland at Murrayfield.

Born at Middlesbrough on December 22, 1948, Old made his mark in schoolboy cricket as a left-handed batsman, playing for Durham, North of England, and then England Schools before graduating to the Yorkshire nets and into the county second eleven. He was 13 when the Middlesbrough club recommended him to Yorkshire – as they had Alan and Malcolm before him – and he arrived at the nets as a batsman who bowled right-arm a bit at medium pace. Arthur Mitchell, a stern taskmaster with that typically abrasive coaching technique that few outside Yorkshire seem to understand, encouraged him not to ignore his bowling, but it was as a batsman that Old first played for the second eleven. His only concession to the role of all-rounder, which he was to develop with distinction, was to bowl one over in the match. He made his Yorkshire debut at Portsmouth in 1966 and the composition of that side – Taylor, Sharpe, Padgett, Close, Hampshire, Illingworth, Binks, Wilson, Nicholson and Trueman (with Boycott away playing in a Test match) – was enough to suggest he might have more opportunities as a bowler than as a batsman. His chief rivals for a bowling place then were Waring and Stringer. In Trueman and Nicholson, Old found two willing advisers very different in emphasis. Trueman preached fire and brimstone, 'Even now he is always ready to tell me what I am doing right and wrong'; Nicholson taught him how to shine and swing the ball. 'One of the finest swing bowlers the game has ever seen,' says Old. Such an apprenticeship was not wasted.

Old's action has much of Trueman's natural grace and rhythm, little of his elemental speed or hostility. In philosophy and function, he is much more reminiscent of Statham. 'People always expected me to be Fred's natural successor, to bowl as nastily as him. It's only in the last four or five seasons that I have outgrown the comparison,' he says. Nevertheless, by 1969 he had assumed the responsibility for opening the Yorkshire attack after Trueman's retirement, and within four seasons he had become an ever-present in England's Test match squad. Only injuries have threatened his career with England, but that threat alone has been real and insistent. Operations on both knees in 1970 and 1971 were followed in 1976 by the possibility of major surgery, which might have finished him as a player. There was no guarantee of success and a real possibility that knee operations might leave him badly incapacitated. 'I might have still been in a wheelchair,' he recalls. But Old was determined to take the risk; indeed, was already booked in for surgery when it was suggested that special remedial treatment might stimulate dormant thigh muscles. A severe course of weight training and electric impulse treatment produced amazing if painful results.

He is still dogged by shoulder trouble, which makes throwing from the outfield uncomfortable without seriously impairing his bowling action. Yet that did not prevent him from making 1978 a year to remember. After bowling well on England's tour of Pakistan and New Zealand, Old demoralised the Pakistanis with 6 for 36 for MCC at Lord's and then decimated them in the Edgbaston Test match, where he took 7 for 50, including four wickets in five balls. 'Bob Willis and I switched ends at lunch and I was just plugging away trying to keep the runs down,' he says disarmingly. His fine form for Yorkshire reached a pinnacle at Old Trafford, where he took nine wickets and scored 100 not out against Lancashire, statistically the best all-round performance of his career. On other occasions Old has revealed his power of stroke with the bat. Indeed, he is credited with the second-fastest century in first-class cricket – 37 minutes with six 6s and thirteen 4s, his second fifty coming in only nine minutes. That was against Warwickshire at Edgbaston in 1977 at the expense of some very ordinary bowling.

It was suggested that Old's bowling success last year was attributable to a shortened run-up, but he still bowls off his normal length of about 20 yards. 'The difference was

In his highest Test innings against Australia, Sutcliffe batted seven hours and a quarter, but he hit only 13 fours. He had one great piece of luck when he was 43, playing a ball on to his wicket without, however, removing the bails.

Australia v England
Sydney, December 2, 3, 5, 6, 7, 1932

probably that I stopped trying to bowl really quick. My run-up has always been the same but I feel now that my mental attitude is a lot better'.

MARTYN MOXON

Martyn Moxon scored nearly 19,000 runs for Yorkshire and made ten Test appearances. He was unbelievably unlucky against New Zealand in Auckland when he was out for 99 – shortly after a shot he clearly struck from the middle of the bat was mistakenly given as leg byes. In the next Test at Wellington he was on 81 not out when rain washed out the match.

Cricketer of the Year 1993 – by Michael Henderson

Some cricketers are born great, others achieve greatness and an unfortunate few have greatness thrust upon them. Len Hutton obviously belongs in the first category, Geoffrey Boycott in the second. Any heir to county cricket's burnish'd throne, the Yorkshire opener's spot, must bear the weight of tradition that comes with the last curse.

Although he has come closer than a good many predecessors to realising a youthful potential that brought unwarranted comparisons with the rich lineage of Yorkshire batsmanship, no one could say Martyn Moxon is a great player. However, the county's captaincy is an office great enough to snap the resolve of anyone ill-prepared for the club's frequent outbreaks of self-flagellation; in that respect he has done the state some service. If he was not fully versed in the committee-room squabbles that make a Sicilian village resemble a model of harmony, he is now. The three seasons of his captaincy, unsuccessful in terms of winning trophies, have nevertheless steeled him for the years ahead and strengthened his position. Without an obvious challenger in the dressing room, he will preside over the short to medium-term future of the world's most celebrated competitive cricket club. Detractors have suggested it is a club with a glorious future behind it, but Yorkshire have learned to live with such jibes. Craig McDermott, had he been available as expected, might have made a big difference to their bowling last season. When the Cricket Academy at Bradford gets into a full, productive swing, the committee should have more encouraging matters to discuss.

Despite the arrival of Sachin Tendulkar, in McDermott's stead, the sans-culottes proved reluctant to storm Headingley's ramparts. Only a few Yorkshiremen, of the public variety, ripped up their membership cards in protest against the inclusion of an outsider, and flounced off to watch Durham. In common with many more significant amendments of law and common law, Yorkshire's repeal of their non-native policy met with general acquiescence. That self-erected barrier, and the financial crisis that threatened to engulf the club, provided the backdrop to the situation Moxon inherited. Stripped of their exclusive birthright, the modern Yorkshire side is much like Essex or Northamptonshire, only less successful. The longed-for revival has yet to take shape.

Martyn Douglas Moxon was born in Barnsley on May 4, 1960, two years before Boycott took his first steps as a Yorkshire cricketer. He joined the ranks in June 1981 as

Two men dressed in a pantomime-cow costume cavorted round the boundary, and were crash-tackled by officials after play: the man playing the rear end, Branco Risek, needed treatment in hospital. Brian Cheeseman, a university lecturer dressed as a carrot, was frogmarched from the ground for 'drunken and disorderly behaviour'. He vehemently denied the allegations. Mr Cheeseman has been attending Headingley Tests in fancy dress since 1982.

England v Australia
Headingley, July 24, 25, 26, 27, 1997

Boycott's locum, making 116 on his first-class debut against Essex at Headingley (the first Yorkshire batsman for 60 years to do so). Batsmen often have difficulty finding their range and repertoire. This is particularly true of opening batsmen, who must always remember Picasso's maxim, liberty within order. It took Glenn Turner the better part of his career to throw off the shackles and, although Moxon's flowering has been less obvious, he is certainly a freer player now than he was five years ago, even if he gets bowled too often, front leg buckled. In 1992 he stood apart from his teammates, as a serious captain should. The dropping of Ashley Metcalfe, his regular opening partner for five years, showed that reputations would no longer take precedence over the team's better interests. After missing four Championship matches with a broken finger, Moxon himself returned to make the business runs that betokened a batsman at the flood of his talent, and he ended the season with 1,385 at 53.26. He made them attractively, excelling in the drives through cover and mid-wicket, but when the call came for an opener to accompany Graham Gooch, it went to Michael Atherton. In every era there are batsmen whose ability is more commonly recognised by their peers than by the selectors: in the 1970s it was Trevor Jesty of Hampshire. It must now be uncertain whether anyone, including Moxon himself, will ever know his true measure. In Yorkshire they have watched in stupor as others, less gifted and less constant, have got the nod: at almost 33 he is not ideally placed to resume a Test career that brought ten caps between 1986 and 1989.

Injuries may have played too prominent a part. In 1984 a cracked rib deprived him of an appearance against West Indies at Lord's, delaying his debut for two years. In 1991-92 he was due to lead the England A team but broke a thumb in a beer match in Bermuda on the first day of the tour. Even when he seemed well set for a century at Auckland in 1987-88 he joined the 99 Club instead. Overlooked for the senior team the past two winters, despite convincing claims on paper, he faces opposition from younger, more favoured players when Gooch retires from Test cricket. Two of the favoured share the same dressing room. Moxon, to his great credit, greeted Richard Blakey's promotion to the England one-day side, and subsequently to the touring party for India, with kind words, while he had to make do with taking the A team to Australia. It must have been harder to accept the call-up for Paul Jarvis graciously, given the bowler's record of injuries, moods and rebellion. Moxon was eight when Yorkshire won their last Championship. Since then a generation has grown up more familiar with discord than the club's glorious pageant. Whether he likes it or not, the honour invested in his job obliges him, as the club's figurehead, to remind the next generation of that tradition.

WILLIE WATSON

As well as his cricket prowess, Willie Watson was a wing half for Huddersfield, Sunderland and Halifax. He later managed Bradford. He made more than 25,000 first-class runs. He died in 2004.

Cricketer of the Year 1954 – by W.E. Bowes

In all things except his batting Willie Watson, of Yorkshire, is a right-hander. Yet in his stance at the crease and his movements to the ball there is nothing strained in this unnatural type of play. He is a stylist. The pendulum-like movement of bat to ball following a straight back-lift stamps him as a player hard to get out.

Unfortunately, a quiet modesty – perhaps until recently an inferiority complex – prevented him making full use of his ability He thought the opponent always better than himself and as a result Watson concentrated on defence. Only occasionally did he exhibit the powerful pull or the stroke to cover as smoothly perfect as any by Frank Woolley, the ball either bruising the fencing or causing the fielders to rub their tingling fingers. From choice, Watson's cricket has been of the unspectacular, plodding type, and not until the second Test match against Australia at Lord's in 1953 did his patience, and endurance, fire the imagination. Then his match-saving 109 – his maiden Test century on his first appearance against Australia – brought him headlines in every newspaper in the country.

Perhaps, too, it convinced the player that he was as good as the next man. Slowly a more positive approach became evident in his batting, and, though it is saying much about a player who in Test matches – always going to the crease at a vital time in the England innings – has averaged 35.5 runs per innings in ten games, there is great hope of better things to come. Already Watson has gained in confidence.

Willie Watson was born at Bolton-on-Dearne, March 7, 1920. He was the second son to a Willie Watson who had made fame as a left-half with Huddersfield Town FC, and, like his brother Albert, young Willie promised to have the family flair for sport. He was sent to the Paddock Council School, and before he left at 14 to become apprentice upholsterer he had earned representation with Huddersfield Boys at soccer and had played for the Yorkshire Boys as a number five batsman. He continued to play cricket with the Paddock Club in the Huddersfield League and football with Outlane FC in the Red Triangle League. At 16 he signed amateur forms with Huddersfield Town at soccer, and a year later became a full-time professional. In 1946 he joined Sunderland FC.

A not out 120 in a Sykes Cup match brought him to the notice of the Yorkshire county officials, and Mr Herbert Robinson, the dynamic president of the Huddersfield League, never missed an opportunity of furthering the claims of this young cricketer. Watson was invited to the Yorkshire nets and soon gained selection for the Second XI. He began with three ducks in succession, a pair of them against Lancashire seconds. Says Willie, 'The only man who seemed to have faith in me still was Mr Robinson; I had little myself.' But the Yorkshire selectors, too, had faith. They picked him for the very next match against Staffordshire, and Watson scored 63. Before war came in the autumn of 1939 he had been selected for the Yorkshire first team, but his first appearance, against Essex, brought him yet another duck and four in the second innings, a game in which Yorkshire received their fourth defeat of the season. During the war, when he was stationed at Rhyl as a physical training instructor, Watson marked time with his cricket but forged ahead at football. He played for Western Command, the Army and the FA, and toured Italy with a representative side. But it was at Colwyn Bay at the end of the 1945 summer that Watson did himself the most good. Playing cricket for the local club against a strong Yorkshire and International side, he scored a century. The Yorkshire players, and particularly the captain, Brian Sellers, were most impressed.

In June 1946, as soon as he was released from the forces, Watson was chosen to play for Yorkshire against Derbyshire at Chesterfield, and the same weekend – no doubt through Brian Sellers, who was a Test selector – he was chosen for a Test Trial at Canterbury. Watson was, so to speak, singled out for honours even before he had played one Championship game for his county. He scored 61 in the second innings of the trial, but he did not continue with scores sufficient to bring him international honours. He had to wait until 1951 before he was selected for England against South Africa. He made his mark by steady, painstaking scores of 30s and 40s and brought a steadying influence to England's middle batting which too often had crumbled. He was chosen for all five Tests. Watson played in one Test against India during 1952, a season in which he finished fifth in the all-England averages, and against Australia in 1953 he played the innings of his life to force a drawn game (with Trevor Bailey) in the second Test at Lord's. Watson at long last, just as Brian Sellers knew he would in 1946, had made his mark. The player was convinced he could play cricket well. When he received an invitation to tour West Indies with Len Hutton's team, he readily accepted.

Now 33, he was easily persuaded to bring a football career that had brought him four caps for England and selection for the Rio World Cup side (in 1950) to a close. In his new-found confidence and full-time attention to cricket, Watson is one of our great hopes for the team that will visit Australia next winter with the intention of keeping the Ashes in England. A most pleasing feature of Willie Watson's cricket is his chasing of a ball in the outfield. He is a beautiful runner who, like all good fieldsmen, is moving to the ball before it is hit towards him. He has a safe pair of hands and his judgment of the high catch or the point where a ground hit can be intercepted while on the full burst is superb.

Unfortunately, like many outfielders of long service, his throwing arm is not good. That important muscle on the point of the right shoulder went in that very first game he played for Yorkshire at Chesterfield in 1946, and since then Watson has sought to perfect a low trajectory throw employing, in the main, forearm and wrist. His fleetness of foot, on that account, is only of service in the saving of runs. The satisfaction of run-out victims by the dozen is denied him.

J. H. WARDLE

Johnny Wardle's county career ended when he was sacked by Yorkshire in 1958 and then withdrawn from the MCC touring party (see page OOO). He later played for Nelson and Rishton and Cambridgeshire. He took almost 18,500 wickets. He died in 1985.

Cricketer of the Year 1954

To laugh at the hard knocks of life is a characteristic of the North Country miner, and John Henry Wardle, the Yorkshire left-arm slow bowler, born at Ardsley, January 8, 1923, is typical of a calling which would have claimed him had it not been for a great natural aptitude at cricket. His father was a miner.

Humour on the cricket field, especially in a Test match between England and Australia, is rare. The seriousness of the occasion precludes funniness unless the antics of a number eleven batsman trying to put his bat to a top-class bowler are considered funny. Yet who could do anything except chuckle – at Lord's of all places – when Johnnie Wardle was hit on the thigh by a Lindwall express and he immediately began to rub his elbow? Or, when the attempted cover-drive soared over the slips, this same player took an imaginary bit of chalk and rubbed his bat, and, on another occasion for the same type of miscued stroke, he seriously applauded himself for the four runs that resulted. Most humour comes at the predicament or the expense of a third party. The best humour comes from the man making fun of himself.

As a youngster at the Brampton-Ellis Senior School, Wardle revealed that first essential in all sportsmen. He was the first boy at the school who managed to hit a six on their spacious playing fields. When hitting, kicking, throwing and bowling, it was apparent that he had a highly developed ball sense. Mad keen on cricket and all ball games, young Wardle moved to the Wath-on-Dearne Grammar School when he was 11. The seniors at school failed to realise the urge and latent possibilities in the boy who frequented the nets whenever they were at practice. In that hard, practical way of senior boys they kicked him out unceremoniously.

At 14 he was still considered one of the juniors in the school at Wath, but in the neighbouring village of Brampton, where they had a club playing in the Southern Yorkshire league, there was encouragement and frequent inclusions in the side. By dashing home from school and hurrying to the cricket ground he managed to be on hand whenever the side playing in the Mexborough league were a player short. His lively enthusiasm brought him many games with the men. It was in one of these games that boy John Wardle had his sweetest moment. The school captain came to play for an opposing team and Wardle bowled him for a duck.

His inclusion in the school team came automatically, and at the end of his first season he had scored more runs, taken more wickets and was credited with more catches than any other player in the side. He won a 'Herbert Sutcliffe bat' with a bowling performance of 8 for 4. At the school prize distribution there were five school crickets caps on the headmasters desk for presentation. Says Johnnie, 'I expected my name to be called. After four had been given away I was out of my seat and moving along the row to get the fifth, but it wasn't for me.' With that capacity to laugh at the knocks, Wardle chuckles, 'I did feel a fool, and I never got a school cap.'

He left school at 15 to become an apprentice fitter at the Hickleton Main Collery, and it is worthy of note in his next five seasons – playing for Hickleton, Brampton and Denaby – he won the League Junior Bowling Prize four times. In the 1940 season he made his first century, 104 not out against Mexborough, and a few weeks later he took all ten wickets for 36 runs against Rockingham. It is worth reporting too, that when he was only 17, Major Frank Buckley gave him trials as an inside forward with the famous Wolverhampton Wanderers football club and desired to sign him. But Wardle decided otherwise because so many of his local cricket clubs were wanting him to turn professional that, what with his job and being paid for cricket, he was better off staying in Yorkshire.

In 1943-44, when playing for Denaby in the Yorkshire Council League, Wardle established a record by taking 113 wickets in the season. He was known throughout Yorkshire as one of the most promising left-handers in the country and when, after the war, Yorkshire played their first friendly fixture with Lancashire in 1945, Wardle was included in the team for Old Trafford. He did little except note the virtues of length and direction as demonstrated by the veteran left-handed Arthur Booth, who took eight wickets for 54 runs in the second innings. Booth was chosen as the bowler best suited to fill the gap in the Yorkshire team caused by the loss of Hedley Verity, but two swashbuckling innings of 64 and 48 for Yorkshire against Derbyshire at Sheffield a fortnight later served to keep Wardle's name to the fore. He played regularly for the Yorkshire Second XI in 1946, and when Booth fell ill, in the first match of the 1947 season, Wardle was the natural replacement. In all matches he took 86 wickets for 25.64 apiece and averaged 18.18 with the bat. Among his performances were 6 for 28 against Surrey at Bradford and 7 for 66 in W. E. Bowes' benefit against Middlesex at Leeds. He was chosen to go to the West Indies with G. O. Allen's side.

One of the disappointments of the tour, Wardle says, 'I was far too inexperienced. I believe that a player should be sent on tour to get added experience. He needs to have plenty before he goes.' However, in the long run the experience was good. From the 1948 season onward Wardle has taken his hundred wickets a season easily. There is no doubt that the weak state of Yorkshire's attack in recent years has meant that Wardle has been over-bowled. With much truth the players named him 'perpetual motion Wardle'. Originality and experiment in his bowling had, of necessity, to be replaced by steady negative attack. Against Middlesex at Lord's in 1951, he was called upon to bowl from 11 a.m. until 4.15 p.m., and the scorers returned an analysis of 53 overs with five wickets for 66 runs. Yet there is no reason to believe that Wardle has stopped spinning the ball.

Returns of 6 for 12 and 6 for 18 against Gloucestershire, 6 for 20 and 6 for 19 against Kent, and 7 for 49 against Middlesex are performances in recent years that give the lie to such a suggestion.

Against Australia at Lord's last season he bowled – in his capacity of stock bowler – 75 overs and took 5 wickets for 188 runs. On a turning pitch in the last Test match in Manchester when Australia lost eight wickets for 35 runs, Wardle took four victims at a cost of only 7 runs.

Alert and reliable in the field, a hard-hitting batsman who violated Roses match tradition by hitting five sixes in an innings of 79 against Lancashire, Wardle in one way or another is always a useful member of a side.

ROY KILNER

Roy Kilner scored nearly 15,000 first class runs and took 1,003 wickets, chiefly after the war when he proved his all-round credentials. He made nine Test appearances.

Obituary – 1929

Roy Kilner, born at Low Valley, Wombwell, near Barnsley, on October 17, 1890, died of enteric in the Barnsley Fever Hospital on April 5, aged 37. By his early death English cricket lost, not only a notable exponent of the game, but also a man of rare charm. Few modern professionals commanded such a measure of esteem and kindly regard from his own immediate colleagues and his opponents in the cricket-field, as did Roy Kilner. He was modest to a degree concerning his own abilities, and generous in his estimate of those he played with and against.

Kilner's cricketing life consisted of two separate and distinct periods. Before the war he was essentially a batsman, Yorkshire having such a wealth of bowling talent that the need for him to exploit this part of the game did not really arise. The death of M. W. Booth – killed at the Battle of Lens, just before which Kilner himself was wounded in the right wrist – followed, after hostilities had ceased, by that of A. Drake, and the retirement of George Hirst, brought about a considerable change in Yorkshire's strength in attack.

Without neglecting his batting, Kilner turned his serious attention to bowling, but the season of 1922 had dawned before he became one of the leading left-handed bowlers in the country and an all-round player of marked ability. His powers as a batsman were a little slow to ripen, for, although he gained a place in the Yorkshire eleven in 1911, not until two years later did he firmly establish himself. Left-handed, as in bowling, Kilner could, if necessary, play a dogged game, but that was foreign to his temperament, and he will always be remembered by his rather aggressive methods. He drove with considerable power on the offside and pulled very hard. For Yorkshire he put together 15 hundreds, and in all matches for his county scored 13,014 runs with an average of 29.91. Four times in his career he accomplished the double feat of making 1,000 runs and taking 100 wickets in a season.

In 1927, although he scored 1,004 runs with an average of over 33, his bowling seemed to have lost some of its former deadliness, even in favourable conditions. At his best, however, he was a fine slow bowler, spin and accuracy of length making him at times almost unplayable. To a close student of the game he afforded the greatest interest. His admirable length enabled him to keep on for long spells without undue punishment, and he never ceased during these to try all sorts of experiments in the way of variation of flight and pace. In his hands the spinning ball, just a trifle faster than usual with no apparent change of action, proved most effective. He took part in seven Test matches against Australia, three when a member of the MCC team under Mr A. E. R. Gilligan in the winter of 1924-25, and four in England in 1926. He achieved little of consequence in the latter matches and did not appear in The Oval match when England regained the Ashes, but he accomplished useful work in Australia, where in all games he had a batting average of 31 and obtained 57 wickets for less than 20 runs apiece. At Adelaide, on a treacherous pitch, he and Woolley finished Australia's second innings by getting down the last seven wickets in an hour for 39 runs, Kilner taking 4 for 14. But Australia, after a great struggle, won the match by 11 runs. Kilner's benefit – against Middlesex at Leeds in 1925 – realised £4,016 – a record. The play was watched by 71,000 persons.

In the winter of 1924-25, he went to Australia, where he scored 448 runs, average 24.88, and took 40 wickets for 25 runs each, and in the West Indies in 1925-26 he averaged 22.63 for 249 runs, with 34 wickets at a cost of less than 30 each.

The highest of his 15 three-figure innings for Yorkshire was 206 not out v Derbyshire at Sheffield in 1920. He also made 113 in the Gentlemen v Players match at Lord's in 1920 and 103 for England v West Australia at Perth in 1924-25. In other matches he took 5 for 11 for North v South at Eastbourne, in 1922, and 6 for 16 in first innings and 8 for 23 in second for Europeans v Hindus at Lahore in 1922-23. For the Players at Lord's, in 1924, besides scoring 113, he took 6 for 20 in the second innings (not bowling in the first), 5 of these being obtained in the course of 5 overs for 2 runs. During the last winter in which he accepted an engagement in India, he played an innings of 283 not out for

A very disagreeable incident marred the pleasure of a game that presented few features of interest. Owing to the state of the ground a start could not be made at the ordinary time on the first day, and a section of the crowd indulged in a most unseemly demonstration, such insulting remarks being addressed to Mr H. T. Hewett that that gentleman – who was to have captained the England team – retired from the match after fielding till the luncheon interval. We think he acted unwisely, but he was much provoked.

Yorkshire v An England Eleven
Scarborough, September 5, 6, 1895

Rajendra Gymkhana v Gurgaon at Delhi, in November 1927, hitting six 6s and forty 4s. He was nephew of the late Irving Washington, of Yorkshire, and brother of Norman Kilner, of Warwickshire. His portrait appeared in *Wisden's Almanack* of 1924.

ARTHUR WOOD

Arthur Wood was born in 1898 and died in 1973. He kept wicket for 222 consecutive county games until, at Brighton in 1935, captain Brian Sellers heard him boast of his record (since beaten by Jimmy Binks) and said, 'If that's the case, Arthur, you deserve a rest.' He gave the job to Paul Gibb. Bill Bowes said of him, 'At rhyming slang, so popular in the thirties, he was an expert. He never asked a groundsman if there had been any rain. "Had any France and Spain?" he asked. He raised his "titfa" (tit-for-tat, hat) to acknowledge the applause of the crowd. Sometimes he called it "talk and chat".' Bowes concluded, 'He had a heart as big as mountain.'

By E. Eden, 1972

Arthur Wood played for Yorkshire from 1927 till 1946 and was first choice as wicketkeeper between 1927 and 1939. He helped in the dismissal of 848 batsmen – 603 caught and 245 stumped – and scored 8,579 runs for the county at an average of 21.13. His best season as a run-getter was that of 1935 when he hit 1,087, average 36.23, and put together the only century of his career, 123 not out off the Worcestershire bowling at Bramall Lane. He gained his first Test cap a few days before his 40th birthday and I had something to do with him receiving the honour. While reporting a match at Lord's, I was sent a message in the press box from Sir Pelham Warner, then chairman of the England Selectors, asking me to go to the pavilion to see him. This I did and Sir Pelham told me that he was worried because Leslie Ames was indisposed and unable to play at The Oval. He asked me if I could recommend a wicketkeeper-batsman as replacement. At once I suggested Wood and, sure enough, he got the place. That was the match against Australia in which Len Hutton hit his record-breaking 364. Wood got 53, but the score had exceeded 500 by the time he went in. Noted for his sense of humour, he said when congratulated upon his batting success, 'I was always good in a crisis.'

It was a strange game ... sea mist and a distant foghorn provided an eerie atmosphere at the start, and a bizarre fault on the PA system meant spectators were given commentary on a nearby bowls match.

Yorkshire v Warwickshire
Scarborough, July 18, 20, 21, 2006

JIMMY BINKS

In a 14-year career Jimmy Binks missed only one match of the 492 played over that period. He took 895 first-class catches and 176 stumpings.

Cricketer of the Year 1969 – by W. E. Bowes

In June 1955 a slightly built, fresh-faced 19-year-old wicketkeeper, Jimmy Binks, arrived at a Nottingham hotel to take part in his first game for Yorkshire. He was playing for the Colts eleven at Jesmond when he received the instruction to join the senior side.

He knew nothing of Yorkshire's idea to play him for the rest of the season after trying Roy Booth for the first half of the season. They planned to give each player an extended trial before deciding who was the better. His memories of the game are still fresh. 'It was the best batting surface I ever saw. Hutton and Hardstaff scored centuries and the leg-break bowlers, Leadbeater and Dooland, each had more than 100 runs hit off them.' The young Binks collected his first three victims behind the stumps and was delighted when he was told he was wanted for the next fixture. He played to the end of the season, found no joy in the winter news that Roy Booth asked Yorkshire if he could have permission to join Worcestershire, and felt no rancour when Yorkshire played him completely through the 1956 season on a match-to-match basis. The committee wanted to be certain that Binks was the man for the job and they did not decide this until the 1957 season was four weeks old. He had a long apprenticeship.

Facts have since demonstrated how right the committee were. On August 18, 1968 against Derbyshire at Bradford, Binks caught Hall from the slow bowling of Wilson to obtain his 1,000th scalp. At the end of the 1968 season, after playing 13 and a half years of almost uninterrupted cricket with Yorkshire he had claimed 1,008 victims. In the whole of that time he missed only one match for Yorkshire when, at the start of the 1964 season, MCC invited him to play at Lord's against Surrey instead of playing for his county against Oxford University. At the end of the 1968 season he had played in 388 consecutive Championship matches – a wonderful record for a wicketkeeper. There is every indication of Binks being the fourth great and long serving 'keeper for Yorkshire, following David Hunter 1888–1909, Arthur Dolphin 1905–1927, Arthur Wood 1927–1946.

James Graham Binks was born at Hull on October 5, 1935. His father, Jim, was a keen cricketer and kept wicket for the GPO and Hull second eleven. His fingers were gnarled and misshapen. He stood up to the stumps for every bowler, suffered many injuries, and for this reason wanted his son to be a bowler. But the son wanted to be like father. He played for Maybury High School as an opening batsman and wicketkeeper. It was the same at Riley High School and at Hull Technical College where he studied engineering. He was chosen as a wicketkeeper for the Hull second eleven. Binks left college at 18 and was immediately called for National Service, only to be discharged after ten days with suspected lung trouble. In the meantime, as the result of his father writing to the Yorkshire club, Jimmy at 17 had played as deputy for the Yorkshire stumper, Don Brennan, in a pre-season practice fixture against Hull University. He did so well that J.S. Rhodes offered him the position of wicketkeeper in the Leeds League side and after one season the Leeds club offered him a similar opportunity with their Yorkshire Council side at Headingley. Following two months in bed and three months in a rehabilitation centre, the tuberculosis cleared. Binks began the 1955 season playing with Leeds. His steady reliable performances brought selection with the Yorkshire Colts and this led to the Yorkshire committee's decision to give him an extended trial.

S. Hainsworth, a keen Yorkshire cricket supporter and head of the firm of Fenner's in Hull, offered him a winter post in the Time study and Production Control department. He still works with this firm and, of course, there was no difficulty when in 1962 MCC asked Binks to fly to Pakistan as a replacement for the injured Murray, nor in 1964 when he was invited to tour India. On this tour he played in his only two Tests to date. In the first at Bombay he opened the second-innings with his former Yorkshire colleague, Brian Bolus, and in a stay of three and a half hours scored 55 in a first-wicket stand of 125 – the first such partnership of the tour. 'But,' says Jimmy frankly 'I kept wicket worse than at any time in my life. In the first Test I missed stumping Borde and in the second Test, although I took five catches, I missed several chances I should have taken.' In his quiet, pleasingly modest way, as he puts it, 'I had my chance and did not grasp it.'

Cricketers generally are surprised that Binks has not again found favour with the selectors and this, allowing for the fact that they gave preference to the batsman-wicketkeeper. The majority of the 6,385 runs scored by Binks have been made when Yorkshire badly needed them. When the pressure has been on, when a nightwatchman has been required or a batsman needed to shut up an end, few tail-enders have proved more reliable. His highest score is 95 against Middlesex at Lord's in 1964.

In 1960, Binks established a new record for Yorkshire with 108 victims in the season, 97 caught, 11 stumped. As a wicketkeeper Binks would undoubtedly have played in more representative games had he been more noisy and flamboyant, more of a showman. The Yorkshire public in 1967 rewarded his reliable efficiency with a benefit of £5,351. The compliment about being little noticed is that there can be no mistakes.

TONY NICHOLSON

Tony Nicholson was born in 1938 and died in 1985, aged 47. He took 879 first-class wickets from 283 matches (19.76) and 173 A-list wickets (17.05) from 120 games.

Obituary – 1986

Anthony George Nicholson was a medium-paced bowler who played a big part in Yorkshire's five Championship-winning seasons in the 1960s. When they won in 1962, Nicholson played in only five matches, but a year later he took 65 wickets, and when they became champions again, in 1966, at the start of a three-year run, he took 113 wickets at 15.50 apiece. This was his best season. He swung the ball, had excellent control and was often found to be sharper in pace than the batsman expected. He played for Yorkshire from 1962 to 1975, having previously been a policeman in Rhodesia, and took 876 first-class wickets at 19.74 each.

More than once Nicholson was close to playing for England. He was picked for the 1964-65 tour of South Africa but had to drop out through injury. Later, when he was a still better bowler, there were more good bowlers of his type available, and being a modest batsman with a build that made him less than agile in the field he did not have the all-round qualifications of others. After retiring from first-class cricket he became a brewery representative. He played league cricket for some years and at the time of his death was the captain of the Ripon City Golf Club.

BOB APPLEYARD

Bob Appleyard contracted tuberculosis in 1952, which threatened his life. But he returned to cricket in 1954, took 154 wickets and won an England cap. In all, he made nine Test appearances and took 31 wickets (708 in first-class matches), including 3 for 58 and then 3 for 13 in the Adelaide Test, which clinched the Ashes for Len Hutton's 1954-55 tourists.

Cricketer of the Year 1952 – by W. E. Bowes

In a younger man the magnificent performance of Robert Appleyard of taking 200 wickets in his first full season of county cricket would have provided the perfect fairy story. Nevertheless, it was amazing that a 27-year-old bowler, comparatively unknown, should begin a first-class cricket career with such unprecedented success.

Appleyard bowled Yorkshire to second position in the Championship table. With his last ball of the season he took his 200th wicket at an average cost of only 14.14 runs each and, if a solitary bowling performance of Sonny Ramadhin in an end of the season festival game is discounted, was easily top of the England bowling averages. Appleyard confounded the critics.

When the 1951 season began and it was known that Yorkshire would be without opening bowler Coxon, who had moved to league cricket, and off-spin bowler Close, still in the Army, forecasts were made that Yorkshire would have a very ordinary season. Little thought was then given to Appleyard, born at Wibsey, Bradford, June 27, 1924. He had given notice of his approach the previous season when, playing for the Yorkshire second eleven against Staffordshire, he returned a match analysis of 41.2 overs, 13 maidens, 63 runs, 15 wickets and topped the second team averages with 29 wickets at 7.89 apiece. Who was to know his successes would continue with the first eleven?

Appleyard was selected to play in the second match of the season against Oxford University – after the other Yorkshire bowlers had received a trouncing from MCC – and his four for 26 runs started a season without parallel in Yorkshire records. With a smooth, high action, using all his 6ft 1½in, Appleyard opened the bowling with fast-medium inswingers. As the ball lost its shine and newness he intermingled slower off-spinners. His accuracy, change of pace and mixing of spin and swing put even the best batsmen in difficulties. In one man Yorkshire had found a substitute for both Coxon and Close. Appleyard took 99 wickets by the end of June and, had it not been for an attack of pleurisy that kept him out of two matches, he almost certainly would have been the first bowler to take 100 wickets last summer. As it was, another Yorkshireman, Laker of Surrey, beat him.

Called upon to use all his energy for bowling, to become a match-winning bowler on both hard and soft pitches, Appleyard was understandably nursed in other branches of the game. In the field he proved a good catcher and stopper and, though not professing to be a batsman, he showed promise of developing into a useful tail-ender.

In his early days Bob Appleyard was a batsman. He played with St Matthew's School, Bankfoot, until his father refused to let him take part in a school play. The sports master, who was also in charge of the Dramatic Society, retaliated by not selecting him for the cricket team. However, at 11, Appleyard went to Wibsey Modern School and, unusual in that he was competing with boys of 14, was chosen as number seven batsman for Bradford Boys. At 12 he moved to Priestman Central School, Bradford, where, encouraged by two masters, Mr Cedall and Mr G. L. Cottam – the former a Bradford League cricketer – he began to take bowling seriously. He became captain of the Bradford Boys and in the final of the Yorkshire Elementary Schools Competition against Sheffield Boys took 5 for 5 in a total of 22. Occasionally, while still at school, he played for Bradford Park Avenue third eleven and was shown how to bowl the off-spinner by Stanley Douglas, a Bradford and former Yorkshire cricketer.

Appleyard left school at 15, in the year war was declared, and was apprenticed to engineering. He is now representative for a firm of lift makers. His cricket continued with Manningham Mills in the Bradford Central League and in turn with Bowling Old Lane with whom, apart from one season at Undercliffe, he played until his selection for Yorkshire. Mr Ernest Holdsworth, President of Bowling Old Lane and Yorkshire Chairman, introduced him to the county winter nets for coaching by Arthur Mitchell and Bill Bowes. With his ideal physique, smooth action and quiet thoughtful manner, Appleyard immediately impressed. He mastered control of spin and swing bowled at different paces, and next season, 1950, was chosen for the Yorkshire second eleven. He also played two matches for the first eleven against Scotland and Surrey. In The Oval game he bowled Fletcher for eight, P. B. H. May for a duck and finished with 4 for 47 runs.

In 1951 Appleyard was the most successful bowler of the year and his own application to bowling was shown by the fact that he changed to bowling the off-spinner from the second finger of his right hand instead of from the first. After only half a dozen matches Appleyard noticed that Len Hutton, fielding at slip, always went deeper when he ran up to bowl his faster ball. 'How do you know when to go deeper?' he asked. Said Len, 'I can tell from the way you hold the ball.' Appleyard immediately set about developing a grip suitable for both the spinner and the swinger, and Hutton now says, 'He is a very difficult man to detect.'

With such a fine utility bowler in the side, Yorkshire need to be careful they do not give him too much work to do. At times last season he was over-bowled. Some Yorkshire officials say, 'We hope he never takes 200 wickets again'. By that they mean that with adequate bowling support such a feat will not be necessary but, when a man can be so valuable as to be opening bowler, spin bowler and stock bowler combined, the temptation to use him to the full is hard to resist.

BILL BOWES

In his first-class career of 372 games, Bowes took 1,639 wickets at 16.76: as he made only 1,530 runs, his wickets outnumber his runs. In 15 Tests, his figures were 68 wickets at 22.33.

By R. L. Arrowsmith, 1988

William Eric Bowes (Bill), who died in hospital on September 5, 1987, aged 79, was one of the great bowlers of his day. He is often, for convenience, loosely classed as fast, but Robertson-Glasgow, writing in the early days of the war, described him, correctly, as the most difficult fast-medium bowler in England. It was, no doubt, partly because he never tried to acquire the extra yard or two of pace which would have put him indisputably in the ranks of the fast that he was such a fine bowler. And like most of the great, he came off the pitch faster than the batsman expected.

No man has ever worked harder at his art. He was constantly practising, constantly experimenting, but throughout he remained content with the ten yards to which that great coach, Walter Brearley, had cut his run when he first went to Lord's. He concentrated on control of length and direction and on moving the ball. He could always bowl a late inswinger, but Brearley told him that he would never reach the top class unless he could make the ball run away as well. This it would occasionally do by a fluke, as at the Scarborough Festival in 1929, for example. George Hirst was persuaded to play and Bowes bowled him with one that pitched on the leg stump and took the off bail. Hirst, typically, said, 'Well bowled. That would have been too good for me when I was good.'

Yet by the middle of 1931, after three years of trying, Bowes was no nearer to discovering how to produce this ball. Meanwhile he was already on the fringe of the England side. Most men in this position would have been satisfied, and concluded that away-swingers were not for them. Not so Bowes; he went on trying and finally found the required hint in an obscure coaching manual, which told him it was all in the position of the feet at the moment of delivery. Within a week or two he was bowling away-swingers as easily as inswingers, with a barely perceptible change of action. Thenceforward the batsman who had successfully cut two or three inswingers, and tried to repeat the stroke, was liable to find that he had picked the wrong ball and to chop it into his stumps. That season his wickets cost him four runs apiece fewer than in 1930.

Yorkshire had in those days no nursery; players were picked from the nets and graduated through the second eleven. Bowes, wanting a secure tenure, applied with typical enterprise, and with the approval of the county authorities, for a place on the groundstaff at Lord's. He was taken on for 1928, and in his first first-class match for MCC he took 5 for 69 against Wales; in his second, against Cambridge, he did the hat-trick. Naturally Yorkshire became interested, and after some complex negotiations it was agreed that, while his contract with MCC should stand, he should be released to play for Yorkshire unless MCC required him for a first-class match. As a result he played a few times for the county in 1929 and did enough to show his possibilities, his figures for all first-class matches being 65 wickets at 19 each. In 1930, after several successful matches for Yorkshire, culminating in 8 for 69 against Middlesex at Sheffield, he received his county cap. From then on, though his contract with MCC did not end till 1937, they claimed his services only on special occasions and he was a regular member of the county side.

There can be no doubt that his engagement at Lord's had been an advantage to him. Not only had he received much admirable advice and coaching, but he had been carefully nursed and saved from the grind of bowling six days a week in County cricket before he was strong enough, something which has ruined so many promising bowlers. Now that he was a recognised member of the Yorkshire side, he was taken in hand by the senior professionals and taught his trade with a thoroughness that does much to explain why for so many years the county was by and large the most formidable in the Championship. Night after night he and Verity, who started at the same time, were taken up to a hotel bedroom and the day's cricket was discussed, the field set out on the bed with toothbrushes, shaving tackle and the like, and praise and blame administered impartially as required. At one of the first of these sessions Verity, who had accomplished his biggest performance to date, 7 for 26 against Hampshire, was greeted with, 'Seven for 26 and it ought to have been 7 for 22! I never saw such bowling. Whatever wast thou doing to give A. K. Judd that four?' There is precedent for this attitude. In 1918 Eton dismissed Charterhouse for 13. That great man, C. M. Wells, for many years in charge of Eton cricket, entered the dressing room with the words: 'Should have been nine'. But, however outspoken the Yorkshire professionals were about anything of which they disapproved, there was no lack of praise either. Who could fail to learn in such an atmosphere? There can never have been a greater cricket school than the Yorkshire sides between the wars or two apter pupils than Bowes and Verity. And strong though Yorkshire were in every department, it was the bowling of these two more than anything else that won them their Championships in the 1930s.

There has probably never been a great cricketer who looked less like one than Bowes. Standing 6ft 4in, he was clumsily built and a poor mover. Wearing strong spectacles, he looked far more like a university professor, and indeed batted and fielded like one. However, no side has been so closely welded as Yorkshire in the 1920s and 1930s: every man knew just what he was expected to do and did it without being told. When Bowes suggested that it might be a good thing if he were taught the rudiments of batting, he was told firmly that his job was to take wickets; he was not to waste his valuable strength on making runs. If he ever showed signs of forgetting this, his partners were expected to run him out. Similarly in the field. He was stationed at mid-on and, if the ball came to him, he was to catch it or stop it as the case might be. But if it passed him, he was not to move; it was someone else's duty to chase it and throw it in. This was fully understood on the Yorkshire side. After all, Bowes was their great opener and they had no alternative to him.

But England had Larwood (and later Farnes), Voce and Allen, all faster than Bowes and all but Farnes far better bats and fields. Besides them there was always Hammond, a much better bowler than was generally realised, to open if required. In those days three quick bowlers were usually regarded as ample; a place had to be kept for a slow left-arm bowler and a leg-spinner, if a good enough one could be found. So it is not surprising that selectors often passed Bowes over. Tests against Australia then stood on a footing of their own. Between 1932 and 1939, England played 20 Tests against Australia and Bowes was picked for six only; but as in these he took, in an era of mammoth scoring, 30 wickets at 24.70, it was clear that he was in no way out of his class. Yet even for the 1932-33 tour of Australia, his one tour abroad, he received his invitation only three days before the team sailed, having forced himself into the side by some superb bowling in the last weeks of the season.

One wicket on that tour in particular is remembered and deserves description. At Melbourne in the second Test, Bradman, who had missed the first Test, came in to such tumultuous applause that Bowes had to stop in the middle of his run for it to subside, and 'to fill in time' he moved mid-on to silly mid-on. Again he started, again he had to stop, and this time he moved his deep fine leg. He noticed that Bradman followed these moves with grave attention, and he felt sure that he expected a bouncer. So he ran up with his most threatening expression, but instead of digging the ball in he deliberately bowled one little more than stump high. Bradman, already halfway in position to hook, had suddenly to alter his stroke and in so doing pulled the ball into his wicket. In other words, a great piece of bowling.

In fact, although with his height Bowes naturally had a steeper rise than most bowlers, and was always prepared to bowl a bouncer, he did not rely on it as a regular form of attack and, as he gained in experience, used it less and less. His use of the bouncer has probably been exaggerated by a famous incident at The Oval is 1932, a month or so before the start of this tour, when he bounced some at Hobbs. On that occasion, as far as the two protagonists were concerned there was no lasting ill feeling, though Hobbs never approved of the Bodyline tactics.

Getting a commission in the war, Bowes was captured at Tobruk in 1942 and spent three years as a prisoner. By the time he returned home, he had lost four and a half stone and was not really fit to stand the rigours of first-class cricket. Moreover, at 38 he had reached an age at which a bowler of his type is sure to have lost some of his fire. His troubles were compounded by a severe strain to the muscles of his side and back. Nonetheless, bowling at a reduced pace, he struggled bravely through two seasons, still taking wickets cheaply for the county and even playing against India at Lord's. In 1947 his benefit brought him £8,000, at that time a record, and he decided to retire, though Yorkshire were anxious to retain him even if he could bowl only off-spinners. Fortunately he had still 40 years of service to cricket in front of him. To the day of his death he wrote regularly on cricket for the papers, and with his profound knowledge of the game every word he wrote was worth reading. His autobiography, *Express Deliveries*, published in 1949, is probably the best book on cricket ever written by a professional; certainly the best since Albert Knight's *The Complete Cricketer* 80 years ago.

Chapter Six:
God's Own Country

J.M. Kilburn believed the pleasure of watching a game is accentuated or diminished by the scene around it, and claimed that 'the cricket counties reflect something of their environment in their play.' Middlesex, he said, carried 'a metropolitan flavour'; Hampshire and Sussex 'the salt of the sea and the wind of the Downs'; Kent was 'lawns and parks and strawberries for tea'; Essex had 'an air of improvised day-to-day existence through its admirable underlying organisation.' Gloucestershire, Somerset and Worcester were imbued with 'soft air and orchards' and 'the essential jollity of West Country cricket.'

What of Yorkshire and the drably functional Headingley? Kilburn regarded them as 'hard-headed, reluctant to concede a point' and 'tenacious of grip'.

Kilburn called his argument a 'pleasant fancy', and was sufficiently level headed to appreciate that personal preference and perceptions dictate an emotional response to the architecture and ambiance of a county ground. Still, a sage observer, he had identified the important of place in cricket.

For reasons both practical and financial, the days are long gone (and will not come again) when Yorkshire toured like a theatrical repertory company, toting bag, baggage and props across the county: Hull, Harrogate, Middlesbrough, Bradford and Sheffield as well as Scarborough and Leeds. Those who followed them still feel a nostalgic tug for the rooflines of Bradford, the prim trimness of Harrogate and the landscape of the Humber. Keith Farnsworth articulates it wonderfully well in the opening paragraph of his lament for Sheffield: 'Bramall Lane was not among the loveliest of cricket grounds, but to many players and spectators down the years it was the one they loved most,' he writes. That line emphasises how the charm – or otherwise – of a place lies, precisely like beauty, in the eye of the beholder. It underscores something else too: Kilburn was right. Surroundings do shape the cricket played within them and, more significantly, the way we feel about it.

In particular Kilburn adored Scarborough – a romance that his prose, and Yorkshire's annual journeys there, continue to foster. He distilled its attraction in three frequently quoted words: 'cricket on holiday'. In his era, the town dressed up for the annual festival with banners and bunting and a brass band. The shop windows were decked in Yorkshire's colours and filled with accoutrements of the game.

Not any longer. Yet the atmosphere at North Marine Road is nevertheless exactly as Kilburn left it. The ground, it has to be said, is almost the same too, with its closeness to the sea bringing a sense of blissful escape.

I am as sure as I can ever be that Kilburn formed his theory about 'environment and play' from the Press Box at North Marine Road.

FAREWELL BRAMALL LANE

By Keith Farnsworth, 1974

Bramall Lane was not among the loveliest of cricket grounds, but to many players and spectators down the years it was the one they loved most. Countless cricketers, and not all of them Yorkshiremen, will remember it with genuine and lasting affection, just as they viewed with sadness the steps that saw the Sheffield ground close its doors on the summer game at the end of the 1973 season.

Sheffield United's shareholders, in a referendum only three or four years ago, voted for the retention of cricket at the ground. A more recent public debate in the city saw a motion passed calling for cricket to stay. But all the words which emphasised Sheffield's traditionally strong feeling for the sport fell on deaf ears: United's chairman, Richard Wragg, successfully urged the club's board to put all their eggs into the soccer basket and embark on a £1 million venture to make the ground a four-sided football stadium.

So, after the Roses match with Lancashire, Yorkshire CCC closed the book on an era which had spanned 118 years. Perhaps it was mere symbolism, or maybe it was a telling reflection on the state of the game in modern times: but, anyway, the last day of a rain-hit match produced nothing by which the small crowd could remember the occasion.

Bramall Lane is assured of a lasting place in the annals of cricket. Other grounds have, perhaps, a more illustrious history, but the Lane (or t'Lane as it is known locally) was famed as the place where the spectators knew their cricket from A to Z, where wit and humour lent colour to the greyest day, and where the crowd and the play invariably epitomised the Yorkshire tradition and spirit.

Sheffield for a long time had the image of a dark city, full of smoke and grime, and they used to say that when Lancashire or the Australians were batting the local workshops deliberately stoked up their chimneys to assist Yorkshire's cause! The tales were untrue, but the darkness of the old town was a fact of life.

When Bramall Lane was opened as a cricket ground in 1855 it had been chosen because the site was removed from the industry of the town and thus was free of smoke. In the second half of the 19th century, and well into the 20th, the ground was one of the best-equipped sports centres in the provinces. Only one Test match was staged – England lost to Australia in 1902 – but several soccer internationals, an FA Cup final, and a string of semi-finals have been played there. But it was a home of cricket long before Sheffield United chose, in 1889, to form a football section; and the Lane was one of the reasons why Sheffield was the birthplace (and for many years the headquarters) of Yorkshire cricket.

When a lot of other things about Bramall Lane cricket have been forgotten, the crowd, especially those spectators who sat in the Grinders' Stand, will be remembered.

Those men, who worked hard and believed in getting value for their money, won the respect of the cricket world because of their remarkable knowledge, not only of the game's finer points but of an individual player's career. Many are the stories of a burst of applause at an unexpected moment during a match: it usually transpired that the batsman had just reached a personal milestone and didn't know it himself until the crowd told him.

Back in the 19th century the bowling action of Tom Richardson of Surrey was an issue of controversy, but it was said that if his action was at all faulty the Sheffield crowd would be quick to point it out. When Surrey visited Bramall Lane the crowd saw Richardson claim nine wickets without a whimper: it was almost akin to official clearance, and the controversy was quickly forgotten.

Surrey were involved in several notable moments in the history of the ground. In 1861 William Caffyn and his men were making their way to the station after rain had caused abandonment; but a group of ruffians forced them to return and finish the match playing with water up to their ankles. 'We've paid threepence to watch cricket, and we want cricket for our money,' argued the chief ruffian.

In 1933, following the notorious Bodyline tour during which England had regained the Ashes, the Sheffield crowd gave Douglas Jardine an unforgettable and immensely moving reception as he went out to bat for Surrey. The England captain had taken a tremendous battering from his critics because of the tactics his team had employed in Australia; but the Bramall Lane spectators made it clear that they were behind him to a man. Bill Bowes swears he saw a tear in the eyes of the Iron Man.

Two of the most remarkable finishes in Sheffield matches involved Surrey. In 1923, thanks to Roy Kilner's brilliant 5-for-15 spell, Yorkshire won by 25 runs after staring defeat in the face; and in 1956, Surrey enjoyed their revenge, succeeding against all the odds by 14 runs. In the latter case Lock and Loader took the honours, but Yorkshire's batsmen, needing only 67 with eight wickets left, were heavily criticised for spineless batsmanship.

Three matches in which Yorkshire clashed with the Australians have become a part of White Rose folklore, even though in one of them, in 1886, Yorkshire were humbled by the tourists. In fact, it was the feat of the Australia captain H. J. H. Scott in hitting 22 runs off the last of the four-ball overs that clinched victory and a place in the records. Saul Wade was the unfortunate bowler. In 1938 Yorkshire were all set to inflict the first defeat of the tour on Bradman and Co, but the rains came to break the hearts of all those Tykes on the Grinders' stand. In 1968 the White Rose bloomed, and Freddie Trueman captained the side that thrashed the Australians by an innings and 69 runs.

The legendary Tom Emmett is said to have stopped batting in one match in order to lecture the wits and critics on the Grinders' Stand. George Pope tells how a grinder lectured a member sitting on the pavilion balcony, 'The member held up play by standing up behind the bowler's arm, and, amid a deathly silence, the grinder said, "Aye, plenty of ruddy money, but no ruddy sense!"'

A famous story is told of the day South Africa's H. B. Cameron hit 30 runs off an over from Hedley Verity. Yorkshire wicketkeeper Arthur Wood cried down the wicket,

'Hey up, Hedley, tha's got 'im in two minds – he doesn't know whether to hit thee for a four or a six!' In hitting one of his sixes, incidentally, Cameron put the ball on to the pavilion roof: it was reported lost, and didn't turn up until some workmen were called in to investigate a blocked drainpipe the following winter.

The highest individual score made at Sheffield was 311 by J. T. Brown against Sussex in 1897. Len Hutton hit an undefeated 280 against Hampshire in 1939 and 271 not out against Derbyshire in 1937. When Brown made his 311, he and John Tunnicliffe shared an opening stand of 378, the best by a Yorkshire pair at the ground.

In first-class matches at Sheffield the feat of ten wickets in an innings was achieved by Australia's Clarrie Grimmett in 1930 and Wootton, playing for an All-England XI in 1865, also performed the feat. Grimmett's analysis read 22.3-8-37-10, while Smailes returned 10 for 47 in 17.1 overs to complete a match analysis that read 21.4-5-58-14. (Five of Derbyshire's wickets in that match, incidentally, were claimed by a Colt called Smurthwaite at a cost of only seven runs.)

Bobby Peel once claimed eight wickets for 12 runs before lunch against Notts in 1888; the Notts bowler Wass (7-28) helped shoot out Yorkshire for 61 before lunch in 1905; and in 1910 George Hirst bagged 8 for 80 on the first morning of the Somerset match. But the bowling performance that stands supreme in Bramall Lane records was achieved in 1936 by the same Hedley Verity so cruelly punished by Cameron. It was against Kent that Verity claimed 6 for 26 in the first innings and followed it by taking nine wickets in 39 balls in the second, at a cost of a mere 12 runs! He finished with a match analysis of 19.3-8-38-15. Perhaps Verity was avenging Yorkshire's fall of 1865, when Willsher of Kent bagged 12 wickets for only 28 runs.

One could recall hundreds more memories and incidents that make up the Bramall Lane story. For t'Lane was more than a cricket ground: it was a centre for the summer game. Yorkshire cricket is much the poorer for its loss.

OVER 100 YEARS OF SCARBOROUGH FESTIVAL

By J. M. Kilburn, 1977

Like so many institutions of sturdy growth and long life, the Scarborough Cricket Festival derived from seed casually scattered on fertile ground. In the mid-19th century Scarborough found fashion in its spa waters, attracting visitors not only from the Yorkshire hinterland but also from London and its expanding environs. Some of the younger members of the holiday families were cricketers and sought scope for their interest by improvising teams to play against local clubs. They discovered a ready response and enjoyable cricket.

In 1871 a special occasion was designed. The Visitors arranged a two-day match against a team raised by the first Earl of Londesborough. The moving spirit among the Visitors was Charles Inglis Thornton, a London timber merchant renowned in cricket as a powerful batsman for Cambridge University, Kent, Middlesex and MCC. Lord

> Yorkshire suffered their third successive Championship defeat. David Bairstow, an 18-year-old schoolboy, on the second day of his Championship debut, took his A-level examinations at 7 a.m. by special arrangement and later held four catches at the wicket in an innings, but there was little other satisfaction for Yorkshire.
>
> **Yorkshire v Gloucestershire**
> **Bradford, June 3, 4, 5, 1970**

Londesborough was an eager patron of sport, with a particular devotion to cricket, and his estates included a Scarborough residence.

Lord Londesborough undertook the presentation of the match. He staged it in the recreation field on Castle Hill, inviting public attendance without charge and providing marquees and enclosures for his personal guests. For his team he engaged leading Yorkshire professionals. Thornton captained the Visitors, who included two of the famous Walkers of Southgate. The game was played in showery weather on September 11 and 12 and was left drawn, but with every indication of public appeal. It stirred fires of ambition in Robert Baker, secretary of the young Scarborough Cricket Club and himself a player of first-class standard and experience. In 1875 he persuaded Lord Londesborough and Thornton to promote another match, Yorkshire v MCC, on Castle Hill and in the following year the same organisers presented nine days of September cricket to found the Festival.

After two years the Festival – or Carnival as it was commonly called – was brought down from the windswept and inconvenient Castle Hill to the transformed ground of the Scarborough club, adjoining North Marine Road. There, Baker's resolution and energy had turned a meadow into a comparative magnificence. From a rough, steeply sloping field, Scarborough constructed a splendid setting for cricket. An enclosing wall was built, the playing area was levelled to leave a terraced embankment on the seaward side, a wooden pavilion was put up and tenancy was exchanged for freehold ownership. These undertakings involved heavy expenditure, but the cricket club found accommodating supporters. Patrons and donors carried the Festival first to possibility and then through years of establishment to an independent prosperity. Help given was in finance, hospitality and influence. Lord Londesborough opened his house to playing guests; Thornton assured prominent cricketers that the Scarborough experience was not to be missed, administrative enterprise created attractive fixtures including Australian representation. Private patronage nurtured the Festival but the ultimate development depended on public favour. The Festival grew in strength and reputation because it was wanted by cricketers and cricket followers. It gave good value for gate money.

All the great players appeared in their turn and most of them left a memory of characteristic achievement. Thornton, the mighty hitter, hit the mightiest of sixes over bordering four-storey houses. W. G. Grace made centuries for the Gentlemen against the Players and for South v North. Bannerman and Spofforth illustrated Australian power in batting and bowling. In the Golden Age the Festival knew golden hours in innings by Ranjitsinhji, Jessop and Jackson, and in 1899 a young bowler named Wilfred Rhodes took nine wickets for 24 runs against the Australians. Festival prestige grew with the passing years and Festival structure was strengthened when W. W. Leadbeater became the Scarborough secretary and a Festival character. Leadbeater was a cripple, who struggled through a lifetime of disability that creased deep lines into his face and made him sometimes sharp of tongue, but he was a man of careful judgment, high principle and firm friendships. He held office from 1898 to 1930 and raised the Festival to self-sufficiency, though the background of willing patronage remained available. He instituted the 'London Committee' which, through Lord Harris, Lord Hawke and H. D. G. Leveson Gower, ensured the assembly of players when Thornton grew old. Leadbeater's management brought pitch-covering into Festival custom and innumerable ground improvements were initiated and supervised by him. His efficient organisation gave the Festival first place in its sphere of cricket.

The Great War broke the sequence of Festivals, but revival was immediate in 1919 and from then until the second interruption Scarborough was at its most profitable and prestigious. Players, professional and amateur, welcomed invitations; spectators from all parts of the country arranged co-incidental holidays; an express train, the Scarborough Flier, ran with crowded carriages from King's Cross. The match programme was not sacrosanct but it had a prevailing pattern of Yorkshire v MCC, Gentlemen v Players and the touring team of the season against a side under the banner of Lord Londesborough, C. I. Thornton or H. D. G. Leveson Gower. The cricket was recognised as first-class, it was undertaken seriously and specific contrivance was acceptable only if it would give general benefit. A follow-on, for example, would not be enforced at the risk of an early third-day ending, but the element of contest had to be preserved. An individual requiring a few runs or a few wickets for some personal record would be

---

About one thousand people assembled to witness the match, which was played on the understanding that when a man had made 25 runs he was to retire. The Sheffield men had much the best of the battle when 'time' was called; but as William Mycroft, H. Charlwood, J. Rowbotham and other celebrated cricketers played, it will be more satisfactory to give the score; here it is.

Chesterfield: 113 *(H. R. Charlwood 25, C. H. Trown 25, J. Rowbotham 4 wks)*; **Sheffield:** 125-7 *(S. Blyde 25, R. Gillott 25, W. Shearstone 25, J. Rowbotham 25).*

Chesterfield v Sheffield
Played on the ice on a dam near Brampton, January 22, 1879

offered opportunity but not a manifest gift of the wanted wickets or runs. Play could be relaxed but it had to preserve reality. In the phrase of a Festival historian of the period, Scarborough offered 'first-class cricket on holiday'. The holiday atmosphere was created in the background of luncheon tents and fluttering flags and a brass band.

The Festival gained repute not only through its customs but also through association with players who served long and well. In the early 1920s A. P. F. Chapman won high regard for wonderful fielding in the covers, J. B. Hobbs for unselfish displays of his own batting at its best and J. W. H. T. Douglas became 'popularly unpopular' for dour batting that reflected his cricketing character in seeking to save losing causes. The 1930s were the decade of R. E. S. Wyatt, who was willing to bat or bowl all day and every day if necessary, and of Patsy Hendren who came to Festival after Festival with a smile and a practical joke and played some magnificent innings.

After the Second World War the Festival hurried back into activity and announced return with one spectacular hit for six. C. G. Pepper, playing for the Australian Services, matched Thornton's huge straight drive of 59 years earlier over the Trafalgar Square housetops. For a few seasons of nostalgia the Festival thrived on trappings and beliefs of an era departed, but it could not evade a changing outlook on cricket and on social pattern. There were misconceptions of Festival purpose on the field. Paying spectators were subjected to the spectacle of a fast bowler presenting slow leg-breaks. The desirable element of challenge was conspicuously absent in some of the bowling, fielding and captaincy. In one unworthy year batsmen were given their first run by connivance and legitimate appeals were forsworn. Batting and bowling figures lost meaning in a context of the first-class. A few spectators were perhaps amused, but the majority were not and cricket writers with the Festival future at heart composed firm reproof. The lesson was quickly learned. The Festival pulled itself away from the brink of the farcical, but an older following had been disturbed and a new one was not easily promoted in changing circumstances. The family seaside holiday was giving way to the lure of the motor car and of continental expedition. Playing resources diminished as amateurs disappeared and professionals were committed elsewhere. Australian touring teams shortened their programme in England and left before September. T. N. Pearce, who succeeded Leveson Gower in management responsibilities, found a harassing task in trying to present attractive players and fixtures. The Festival began to lose both glamour and practicality.

The chosen road to survival involved a change of format and of financial foundation. Commercial sponsorship was accepted, one-day matches were introduced and a week was substituted for nine days. Whether or not future prosperity has been assured remains for decision, but crowds have certainly been attracted to the Fenner Trophy tournament, the band still plays, the flags still fly and September cricket at Scarborough is still an enviable experience. The Festival goes optimistically into a second century of existence.

Chapter Seven:
Character and Class

Whenever he arrived first at the hotel on away trips, Percy Holmes would tell the receptionist: 'Register us as Percy Holmes and his circus.' The brief story matches the face: wide, jovial features with dark eyes that hint at a benign streak of mischief, he might have been a stage comedian about to break into his patter. He was well liked, specifically because he possessed what Neville Cardus defined as an 'infectious, though not demonstrative, Yorkshire nature.' Of course, in his partnership with Herbert Sutcliffe – 74 stands of 100 or more – it was always Holmes *and* Sutcliffe; and yet the imperious and meticulous batting of Sutcliffe constantly nudged Holmes into the background. As a consequence, he hasn't always been given sufficient credit for the impeccable straightness of his bat or his dashing, fast feet. The pragmatic Bill Bowes thought Holmes light, quick and supple enough on his toes to be 'a ballet dancer'.

He was a generous man too. Among the possessions of his friends, who – unlike him – went on the 1932-3 Bodyline tour of Australia, is a small silver watch and chain. Holmes bought and had inscribed one for each of them, to commemorate the successful series. He did it without fuss or fanfare. Nor was it done in expectation of gaining a solitary thing in return.

As well as his unquestionable class, Holmes epitomises for me the principles of cricket, which were perfectly evident in his character – so too do the other men who share this chapter with him. Among them are David Bairstow, who Matthew Engel argued was 'perhaps the only unequivocally popular man in Yorkshire'; Maurice Leyland, a man who *Wisden* editor Norman Preston declared 'breathed the true spirit of cricket and companionship'; and Dickie Bird, encapsulated in a memorable description by Tony Lewis: 'Everything he said was in the manner of the lugubrious northern over-the-garden-wall comedian.'

Mr Alexander Merlin Corbett appeared for Yorkshire v Gloucestershire at Bramall Lane, Sheffield, in 1881 when, in his one match for the county, he was dismissed twice without scoring. In the first innings he had an unusual experience, for he played forward to a ball which got up, went off his bat to his forehead and straight into the hands of W. G. Grace; the bowler was W. Midwinter.

'A bit of a blow', 1935

The perceptive Cardus said of Emmott Robinson, 'No statistics can get to the value of him … The score-board cannot reflect human nature, Yorkshire human nature, in action.' This is a valid point about all the cricketers in this chapter. And it applies to Darren Lehmann too, though born in south Australia rather than South Yorkshire. But then, Australians are merely Yorkshiremen in disguise…

PERCY HOLMES

Percy Holmes made more than 35,000 first-class runs with a highest score of 315 not out. He was born at Oakes, Huddersfield in 1887 and died there in 1971.

A true Yorkshireman and a whole volume of Yorkshire's cricket history – by Sir Neville Cardus, 1972

Over decades a Yorkshire batsman has been one of the two opening an England innings in Test matches, Rhodes with Hobbs, Sutcliffe with Hobbs, Hutton with Washbrook; now Boycott sustains the great tradition. But one of Yorkshire's most accomplished number one (or number two) batsmen only once raised the curtain of an England innings v Australia; his name Percy Holmes, a name as famous in Yorkshire during the 1920s and early 1930s, as Brown or Tunnicliffe, or Sutcliffe or Rhodes, or Boycott.

Holmes opened for England at Trent Bridge against Gregory and McDonald, the fearsome bowlers of Warwick Armstrong's rough-riding team, which arrived in England in 1921, having defeated J. W. H. T. Douglas's hapless England contingent five times in five Test matches in Australia, each played to a finish. And in 1921, blessed by a glorious English summer, Armstrong's conquerors proceeded to annihilate England in the first three Test matches, three-day engagements. And the victories were settled well within the allotted time span.

Percy Holmes walked jauntily to the wicket at Trent Bridge on May 28, 1921, accompanied by D. J. Knight. England were all out for 112 and Holmes defended stoutly for 90 minutes, making top score, 30. Next innings he made no more than 8. The match was all over on the second afternoon. And this was the end of his Test match appearances until the South African season of 1927-28. He then went in first with Sutcliffe in five consecutive Test matches, at Johannesburg, Cape Town, and Durban; his scores were 0 and 15 not out; 9 and 88; 70 and 56; 1 and 63; and in the fifth game of this rubber 0 and 0.

In 1932, ten days after Holmes and Sutcliffe had made 555 together at Leyton, Holmes once again, and for the last time, received recognition from the English Selection Committee; he went in first with Sutcliffe at Lord's v India, scoring only 6 and 11. So, altogether this superb batsman played for England on seven occasions, and his modest record of 14 innings, 357 runs, average 27.46, is a complete falsification of what manner of cricketer and what manner of Yorkshire character Percy Holmes was, season after season.

His name was household in Yorkshire, as closely and proudly linked with Sutcliffe's as Tunnicliffe's with Brown's. As everybody knows – or should know – Holmes and Sutcliffe surpassed the first-wicket stand and aggregate of 554, incredibly achieved by Brown and Tunnicliffe v Derbyshire, at Chesterfield in 1898. Holmes was 44 years and troubled with lumbago in 1932, when he and Sutcliffe belaboured the Essex attack and after what the politicians call a recount, went beyond the Brown-Tunnicliffe scoreboard marathon.

Holmes, seven years to the day older than Sutcliffe, technically was perhaps Sutcliffe's better. His range of strokes was wider; he was the more versatile and impulsive batsman of the two. But Sutcliffe knew that very rare secret, which is revealed to few men, whatever their vocation. Mastery comes to him who knows his technical limitations. Again, Holmes, as a temperament, was at Sutcliffe's extreme; he was volatile, unpredictable of mood, always alive by instinct, so to say, intent on enjoyment on the cricket field, or off it. He was always first to admit that, like the rest of humans, he was fallible.

Sutcliffe seldom, if ever, admitted, as batsman, to ordinary mortal frailty. In other words, Sutcliffe found it hard to imagine that any bowler could get him out, whatever the state of the game or the cricket. One day, I saw Maurice Tate clean bowl Sutcliffe, at a game's outset – Yorkshire v Sussex. The ball was good enough to overwhelm Bradman. As Sutcliffe returned to the pavilion, I commiserated with him. 'Unlucky, Herbert, to get such a ball at the beginning of the morning'. But Sutcliffe reacted to my sympathy in high dudgeon. 'I could have played it,' he asserted, 'but a man moved in the stand, unsighting me. I could have played it,' he repeated. I felt that I had offended Sutcliffe family pride.

Holmes, as I say, was different. At Lord's, in 1925, he actually accumulated 315 v Middlesex, in ten minutes under seven hours, with 38 boundaries, as comprehensive an exhibition of strokeplay as well could be imagined, all round the wicket, brilliant with late cuts and enchanting flicks to leg. Yet, when later he talked of this innings – it broke a century-old record at Lord's – and a year afterwards it was beaten by the Master Batsman of All (Sir Jack Hobbs) – Holmes could not account for it, at least not for the first half hour of it. He exaggerated by reckoning he was morally out half-a-dozen times in the first few overs. One of the Middlesex bowlers who had to cope with Holmes in these first few overs, confessed to me that he hadn't so and so noticed Holmes's insecurity. He never missed a ball he intended to play.

Holmes was a great Yorkshire cricketer in one of the most historical periods of the country's many triumphant summers. From 1919, his real baptism to top-class cricket, till his last year of 1933, Yorkshire won the County championship eight times. And in his prime, Yorkshire were more or less invulnerable – 1922 to 1925.

These were the halcyon years, when Old Trafford, Leeds, Bradford and Sheffield would close gates at noon for a Yorkshire v Lancashire match. Nearly 80,000 people watched Lancashire v Yorkshire at Old Trafford, in 1926.

Holmes was one of the characters, identifiable as soon as he took guard, twiddling his bat. Robertson-Glasgow, brilliant as observer as with his wit, rightly discerned in Holmes a certain aspect of an ostler inspired to cricket. There was a curious horsey stable-boy air about him; he seemed to brush an innings, comb it, making the appropriate whistling sounds. He was not of the broadly soily nature of Emmott Robinson and Rhodes. I doubt if Rhodes, in his heart of hearts, really approved of Holmes's delight in a late-cut. Cuts were never business strokes, quoth Wilfred. Roy Kilner, lovable as Maurice Leyland, would describe Percy as a bobby-dazzler. (By nature's law of compensation, there are usually one or two rich genial spirits in the Yorkshire XI, to allow cheerfulness occasionally to creep in.)

Holmes really played cricket for fun. In a word, he was an artist, revelling in his batsmanship for its own sake. If he was furthering The Cause – the Yorkshire will-to-win, all very well. But he set himself to drink deeply from the sparkling wine distilled in most innings he played. In his career he scored 30,574 runs, average 42.11, including 67 centuries; and I'm pretty certain that the bulk of them, the ripe bin of them, were vintage stuff.

Holmes and Sutcliffe made a most fascinating conjunction and contrast of character and technical method: Holmes was as spruce and eager to begin a Yorkshire innings as a jockey to mount his horse, using his bat as a sort of pliant persuasive whip to urge his innings along the course to the winning-post of a first-wicket century partnership.

Sutcliffe was all relaxed as he took guard. Then, very likely, he would wave, with his bat, some obtrusive member in the pavilion, even at Lord's, out of his way, wave him into crawling oblivion – and the poor exposed movable spectator could easily have been our Lord Chancellor. But, as soon as the bowler began his attacking run, Sutcliffe became almost stiff and angular with concentration. He scored with the air of a man keeping an appointment with a century, and must not be late.

Holmes often appeared to improvise; he could change stroke whenever his first glance at a ball's length had deceived him. He might move forward anticipating a half-volley; if the ball dropped shorter than its first flight advertised, he would, on swift feet, move back and cut late exquisitely. There was a certain light-footedness in his batsmanship; he could defend as obstinately as most Yorkshiremen, but even then, he gave the impression that he was defending by choice, by compulsion. He was an artist, as I say, expressing himself through cricket.

Sutcliffe, of course, was also an artist expressing himself in a different temperamental way. Never let it be thought that Sutcliffe was a tedious batsman; whether or not he was moving the score ahead, he remained an individual, lord of all that he surveyed. He was the image of supreme confidence, basking in it.

Holmes was prepared to risk the mercy and indulgence of fortune. Sutcliffe was not only surprised but scandalised if he was bowled; Holmes accepted such a downfall as part of the common lot of cricketers and of human nature in general.

Some 69 times Holmes and Sutcliffe rounded the hundred mark for Yorkshire's first wicket. Undoubtedly Holmes would, but for the omniscient presence of Hobbs, have opened for England with Sutcliffe against Australia, not once but perennially. Most of the achievements batsmen dream about came to Holmes – a century in each innings v Lancashire at Old Trafford in 1920; 1,000 runs in a single month, June 1925, average 102.10; 2,000 runs in a season seven times, over 30,000 runs in his career.

But the scoreboard could not tell of his personal presence and animation. He seldom seemed static; he was always in the game. Between overs, and in the field, he was, as they say, eye-catching; but not self-consciously 'producing' himself. He was as natural as could be, not aware that, as Percy Holmes, he signed everything he did.

His end as a cricketer arrived with an abruptness which, I am sure, tickled his mellow sense of humour. In 1932, he took part in the gigantic 555 first-wicket stand. The summer following, in 1933, he batted for Yorkshire 50 innings, scoring only 929 runs, average 19.25. This was the fall of the curtain for him. True, he was in his 46th year; but somehow none of us suspected that age was on his heels and shoulders. He is a permanent chapter, not to say a whole volume of Yorkshire's cricket history.

He had the talent – not always nurtured in the North country – to play hard for Yorkshire and, at the same time to spread over our cricket fields flashes of pleasure by his batsmanship, his nimble fielding and – best of all – by his infectious, though not demonstrative, Yorkshire nature.

EMMOTT ROBINSON

Emmott Robinson was born in 1883 and died in 1969, played for Yorkshire from 1919 to 1931 and afterwards became a first-class umpire. He scored 9,774 first-class runs and took 902 wickets.

The personification of Yorkshire cricket – by Neville Cardus, 1970

Emmott Robinson was as Yorkshire as Ilkley Moor or Pudsey. He was the personification of Yorkshire cricket in one of its greatest periods, the 1920s, when the county appeared to look forward towards winning the Championship by a sort of divine right. He came to first-class cricket in his late 30s – and thrive he did, though bandy.

Statistics tell us little of his essential self; in 12 seasons he scored 9,444 runs and took 892 wickets. Many cricketers have surpassed these figures; few have absorbed the game, the Yorkshire game, into their systems, their minds, nerves and bloodstreams, as Emmott did. Yorkshire cricket was, for him, a way of living, as important as stocks and shares.

With Rhodes he established the unwritten Constitution of Yorkshire cricket, the skipper content to serve in a consultative capacity. Nowadays we hear much of the supposition to the effect that first-class cricket in recent years has become more scientific than of yore. To speak the truth, there are few players of our latest modern times who would not seem to be as innocent as babes talking tactics and know-how in the company of Rhodes and Emmott.

It was these two shrewd men who evolved – with rival competition from Makepeace and Co. in Lancashire – the protective philosophy: how to close a game up, how to open it out, how to stifle the spin on a sticky wicket with the dead bat. 'Loose grip on top of 'andle,' said Emmott. The shrewdness, humour, and uninhibited character of North of

England life was marvellously revealed and fulfilled in Yorkshire v Lancashire matches of the 1920s. Gates closed at noon; 30,000, even 40,000, partisan spectators watching. Watching for what? Bright cricket? Not on your life. 'We've won the toss,' Harry Makepeace would announce in the Lancashire professionals' dressing room. 'Now lads, no fours before lunch.' And Emmott Robinson was already polishing the new ball, holding it up to the light of day, as though investigating an egg. He bowled outswingers; for in his heyday the lbw rule rendered inswing more or less harmless. He swung the ball from middle and leg, compelling a stroke of some sort.

He was shocked if anybody wasted the new ball. After he had bowled the first over, he would personally carry the new ball, in cupped hands, to the bowler at the other end. At Bradford in 1920, he took nine wickets in an innings against Lancashire. At a crisis for Yorkshire too! Lancashire needed only 52 to win, six wickets in hand. Then Emmott turned the game round violently. For some reason or other, I did not, in my report of the match, praise Emmott in generous enough language. I was not a convert to seam bowling in those days; and am not a bigoted convert yet. When Emmott next met me he said, 'Ah suppose if Ah'd tekken all ten Lanky's wickets, tha'd have noticed me.'

As a batsman he exploited pad-play to perfection. Remember that the lbw law of Emmott's halcyon years permitted a batsman to defend with his pads a ball pitching outside the off stump. If any young greenhorn, batting for Yorkshire or Lancashire, were to be bowled by an off-break, he received severe verbal chastisement. 'What dos't think thi pads are for?' was Emmott's outraged inquiry.

Emmott was one of the pioneer students of the green wicket and its habits. One day, at Headingley, rain soaked the field, then the sun shone formidably. After lunch Emmott and Rhodes walked out to inspect the pitch. Arrived there, Rhodes pressed the turf with a forefinger and said, 'It'll be sticky at four o'clock, Emmott.' Whereat Emmott bent down and also pressed the turf with a forefinger. 'No, Wilfred,' he said, 'half-past.'

These grand Yorkshiremen in general, and Robinson in particular, never were consciously humorous. Emmott was a terribly serious man. He could not, as Freddie Trueman did, play for a laugh. One summer at Lord's, Yorkshire got into dire trouble against Middlesex. During a tea interval I ran into Emmott. 'Hey dear,' he growled, 'fancy, just fancy Yorkshire getting beat by Middlesex. And wheer *is* Middlesex? Is it in Lundin?' A far reaching question; because London swamps county boundaries and identities. We know what county means in Yorkshire and Lancashire.

Stevenson, in his delivery stride, caught umpire Bird a painful blow in the face causing a hold-up for a few moments. On the resumption, Bird awarded the bowler an lbw decision from his next ball!

Derbyshire v Gloucestershire
Ilkeston, June 1, 2, 1978

Emmott merged his ability as a cricketer into the Yorkshire XI entirely; by sheer power of will he added a technical stature which, elsewhere, might not have amounted to much. A celebrated Indian batsman, introduced to Rhodes in Rhodes's wonderfully blind old age, said he was honoured to meet so great a cricketer. 'Nay,' said Wilfred, 'Ah never considered myself a star. I were just a good utility man.'

Thus might Emmott have spoken; no part, no individual, was greater than the part of any Yorkshire team. 'Aye,' Emmott once reminded me, 'and we are all born and bred Yorksheer. And in thy county, tha's tekken in Ted McDonald. A TASMANIAN, mind you,' as though a Tasmanian was beyond the pale. He maintained an average of round about 24 while compiling more than 9,000 runs in his years of active service. The point about his use of the bat, aided and abetted by the broadest pads procurable, is that every stroke he ventured to make was part of a plan, designed to win the match for Yorkshire or save it.

I imagine that in all his days in the sun and rain, his keen eyes were as constantly on the clock as on the scoreboard. But, in the field, crouching close to the bat, he missed nothing. A lordly batsman who could hit, asked Emmott to move away a little, for the sake of self-preservation. 'Thee get on with thi laikin', and ah'll get on with mine,' retorted Emmott – and for the benefit of the uninitiated I herewith translate: laikin' means playing; get on with thy playing.

As I write this tribute to Emmott Robinson, with as much affection as admiration, I am bound in fairness to the memory of him, to recount an incident at Old Trafford in 1927. The wicket prepared in those days, for the Lancashire and Yorkshire match, was a batsman's sleeping bed stuffed with runs. Match after match was unfinished – nonetheless, a grim fight for first-innings points (78,617 rabid Lancastrians and Yorkshiremen paid to watch the Lancashire v Yorkshire match at Old Trafford in 1926, fours before lunch or no fours).

Over after over did Emmott resist on this occasion in time and space, when he was, with Rhodes, salvaging his county. Suddenly, for no reason, in fact, as he later admitted, against all reason, he indulged in a most elegant late-cut towards third man. So transfixed was he by this stroke that he stood there contemplating it. And when he emerged from the realm of aesthetic contemplation to the world of inescapable reality, Wilfred Rhodes was on his doorstep and was run out. Consequently Yorkshire lost. 'Fancy,' he said sorrowfully to me (years after), 'fancy. What could Ah'ave been thinkin' about? Me and mi cuts! But, mind you, Wilfred should never'ave come runnin' down the pitch. Runs didn't matter with game in that sta-ate. They counted for nowt.' He was an economist. 'Must not waste new ball.'

One Saturday Yorkshire batted all day at Lord's, scoring 350 or thereabouts. Sunday morning was drenching, a thunderstorm cleared up by noon, followed by dazzling sun. In Hyde Park near four o'clock I came upon Robinson and Rhodes. 'A lovely afternoon,' I said to them, in greeting. 'Aye,' snapped Emmott, 'and a sticky wicket wa-astin' at Lord's.'

He was richly endowed by native qualities of character, and gave himself, heart and soul and with shrewd intelligence, to Yorkshire cricket. That's why he is remembered yet; that's why no statistics can get to the value of him. The scoreboard cannot reflect human nature, Yorkshire human nature, in action. He was not named Emmott Robinson for nothing.

DAVID BAIRSTOW

David Bairstow's son Jonathan was named Wisden *Schools Cricketer of the Year in 2008 and made his Yorkshire debut in 2009.*

By Matthew Engel, 1988

David Leslie Bairstow was found hanged at his home on January 5, 1998. He was 46. Reports said he had been suffering from depression: his wife was ill, he had financial troubles, he faced a drink-driving charge and was in pain from his own injuries. The news stunned cricket, especially as Bairstow had always seemed the most indomitable and least introspective of men, and led to much comment on the problems faced by retired sportsmen.

David 'Bluey' Bairstow was not merely the Yorkshire wicketkeeper but almost the embodiment of the country's cricket throughout the 1970s and 1980s. He arrived in county cricket amid a blaze of publicity when he was drafted from grammar school in Bradford into the Yorkshire side as an 18-year-old on the day he sat an English Literature A-level. He was allowed to sit the exam at 7 a.m., then went out and caught five Gloucestershire batsmen over the next three days. From then on, he was a regular, and while Yorkshire's affairs swirled turbulently around him, Bairstow was always there: loud, combative, combustible. 'He wasn't a great wicketkeeper and he wasn't a great batsman,' said his team-mate Phil Carrick, 'but he was a great cricketer.' His fighting qualities overrode any technical deficiencies, and he did equal a world record by taking 11 catches against Derbyshire at Scarborough in 1981. But he was at his best when batting in one-day games when victory was improbable but just short of impossible: in the Benson & Hedges Cup at Derby in 1981, he was joined by Mark Johnson, the number 11 and a debutant, with Yorkshire 80 short of victory. Bairstow hit nine sixes in an innings that left everyone on the ground aghast; Yorkshire won with Bairstow on 103, and Johnson four. He was picked for The Oval Test against India in 1979, made a brisk 59 in the second innings, and went to Australia for the post-Packer tour that winter. Though Bob Taylor played in the Tests, Bairstow was a regular in the one-day games, and played a succession of small but vital innings. Most famously, Graham Stevenson walked out to join him at the SCG with 35 wanted from six overs. 'Evening, lad,' said Bairstow. 'We can piss this'. Which they duly did.

He played two more Tests the following summer, and one on the 1980-81 tour of the West Indies, but he could not force his way into the team again. In 1984, he became captain of Yorkshire, after Geoff Boycott's supporters had seized control of the club. With the rest of Yorkshire torn asunder, depending on whether they worshipped Boycott or loathed him, Bairstow seemed the last man to believe he was still leading a normal cricket team. His three years of captaincy were, in Derek Hodgson's words, 'a series of uphill cavalry charges'. The attack was appallingly weak – his main tactic was to shout 'C'mon Arn' at his weary spearhead Sidebottom – but Bairstow's sheer willpower saved Yorkshire from utter collapse; indeed, having been bottom of the Championship the year before he took over, they improved slightly in each of his seasons in charge.

He was perhaps the only unequivocally popular man in Yorkshire. Bairstow believed he could intimidate the bowling simply by announcing that he was going to whack the ball back over the bowler's head, and often enough he kept his promise. His wicketkeeping, never beautiful but usually efficient, seemed to deteriorate at the same time, possibly because his insecurity kept him playing through injuries that should have been rested. When he was appointed, the committee had wanted him to play only as a batsman. But he refused, causing Steve Rhodes to move to Worcestershire.

Both the captaincy and, in 1990, his place in the Yorkshire team had to be prised from him, but Bairstow had a last hurrah in the Caribbean in March 1990 when he was on a pre-season tour with Yorkshire, and an injury-hit England team stretched the Laws by calling him in to keep wicket as a substitute against Barbados. His 961 career catches have been bettered by only six wicketkeepers in history, though he had only 138 stumpings, putting him 14th in the list of all-time dismissals. His son Andrew played briefly for Derbyshire. His thoughts never seemed private, and he was a firm believer that there was no dispute that could not be settled by a shouting-match over a pint or six. Even after he died, people wrote of David Bairstow's 'unquenchable spirit'. But in the end, the stress of life outside cricket meant his spirit was quenched, and crushed.

MAURICE LEYLAND

Maurice Leyland died after a long illness, aged 66. He scored 33,660 first-class runs and took 466 wickets. He played in 41 Tests and averaged 46.06. In his Wisden *obituary – from a story attributed to Bill Bowes – Leyland claimed he was responsible for the term 'Chinaman'. Because his chances of bowling were few, he began bowling the occasional left-hander's off-break instead of the normal and natural leg-break. Whenever two batsmen were difficult to shift or something different was wanted someone in the Yorkshire team would say: 'Put on Maurice to bowl some of those Chinese things.' Roy Kilner explained, 'It's foreign stuff and you can't call it anything else.' He became Yorkshire coach from 1951 until 1963. Wisden editor Norman Preston said he 'breathed the true spirit of cricket and companionship.'*

By R. C. Robertson-Glasgow, 1943

In his early days Maurice Leyland played cricket for the Harrogate Club. There, too, he played Association Football; and I can imagine that his more delicate and tactful opponents were apt to pass the ball on before they met that square, resilient, and muscular frame. 'They shall not pass' must be the text for any sketch of Leyland, and he would have been a fit companion for Horatio on the bridge. He has taken the view that to every bowler, every pitch, every occasion, there is the more than equal answer; and, before that Fifth Test at The Oval in 1938, when Hutton and he together scored 382 for the second wicket against Australia, Leyland remarked quietly, 'I think I've got Bill O'Reilly taped.' Of the other bowlers he said nothing. He had his eye on one only, the greatest of his kind in the world. They had fought often before, and there had been little enough between them, and now the batsman had measured and weighed the whole armoury of skill, and was calmly sure that the last victory would not go to the other.

Yet, for all his genius of opposition, there is nothing merely stubborn about this great left-hander. His bowling, which consists mainly in enormous left-handed off-breaks, amuses him as much as it puzzles the batsmen. A less humorous man would doubtless have been content with the orthodoxy of a slight and continuous bias from leg. This was good enough for the great Wilfred Rhodes, who would no more have bowled an off-twiddle and laughed at it than Mr Gladstone would have contributed a risky paragraph to the 'Pink 'Un'. In later days, too, there was the studious Verity to take on the mantle of respectability. So Leyland provided the speciality. It has brought him 447 wickets at 30 each.

Leyland, as a batsman, cannot claim the beauty of Frank Woolley or the consistency of Philip Mead, and he has had more bad times than either; but for England against Australia, when the gong goes, as they say, he is with the greatest. In 34 of these innings he has scored 1,715 runs, seven centuries; average 57.16, 15.69 more than his average in all first-class cricket. Mediocre bowling has seldom brought the best out of him, and he is apt to bat like any ordinary county player in a match without high issues. In a sense, the very strength of Yorkshire has weighed against him. So often Sutcliffe and Holmes laid a foundation that was too easy for others to build on.

Leyland does not thrive on comfort, ease, and harmony, but on rescue, storm, and violent enemies. He is the salvage-expert among batsmen. In Tests his great innings have been played when something has gone wrong with the others. At Lord's, against Australia in the second Test of 1934, our first five batsmen scored respectively 82, 20, 2, 13, 33; Leyland followed with 109. In the Fifth Test, at The Oval, when the ordinary man's hope had gone and five of England were out for 138 runs from the bat, he played an innings of 110 which was plainly framed in a spirit of victory, without an eye to the scoreboard. In 1936, at Brisbane, his 126 came after scores of 0, 69, 4, 0; at Melbourne he made 111 not out when the first three had contributed 90 – scarcely a start in a timeless Test; and, at The Oval in 1938, when O'Reilly had got Edrich caught for 12 and was properly glorying in his 100th wicket in Tests against England, W. R. Hammond judged nicely to send in Leyland at number three to join his young fellow Yorkshireman, Hutton. For six hours and a half the Australians bowled at them, till Leyland was run out, narrowly, by a wonderful piece of anticipation on the part of Bradman. Nothing, I think, but run out or carried out could have parted them.

Born on July 20, 1900, Leyland first played for Yorkshire in 1920. He appeared in one match, had but one innings, and scored 10, out. What the committee thought about it is not recorded. In 1921 he was allowed seven innings, and made 115 runs, his highest score being 52 not out against Leicestershire at Leeds. He also took one wicket for 43 runs. There was a fine future for a young man, as English cricket was slow to recover after the war of 1914-18. England had lost five Tests in a row in Australia during 1920-21, when in each Test, after Hobbs was out, we sat, in the phrase of a Yorkshire bowler, 'like a row of birds with pads on at a funeral.' Three more Tests were then lost to W. W. Armstrong's team in England. But Leyland's time was not yet. He was given his Yorkshire cap in 1922, though his batting average sank to 13.75 for an aggregate of 220 in 17 innings, once not out; and, in bowling, he did not repeat his one wicket of the year before. Humble enough beginnings of greatness; but even then he looked a cricketer, especially in the outfield, where his short legs carried him nimbly round the boundaries, and with his left hand he threw far and straight. He had a steady gaze; square, strong, and calm.

In 1923 he played right through the season, having 50 innings, a number that he never later exceeded. There was no century among them, but he made 1,088 runs at an average of 27.89, his highest innings being 89 against Gloucestershire at Bristol, where Hammond, just 20 years old, was beginning to surprise critics and bowlers by the power of his driving. Once more Leyland took his one wicket, at the decreased cost of 32.00. In 1924 he made his first century in first-class cricket, 133 not out against Lancashire at Old Trafford. In Yorkshire at least he was made. There was another century, 100 not out against Hampshire on his home field at Harrogate, and in all he scored 1,259 runs at 30.70 an innings. But he had to wait two years for another wicket. Next season he scored 1,572 runs at 40.30 an innings, with centuries against Worcestershire, Gloucestershire and Middlesex.

For the fourth year running Yorkshire were champions, and, for all their more recent triumphs, I doubt if any of their later teams have quite equalled the combination of skill and stark efficiency that made them almost invincible in the years from 1922 to 1926. Sutcliffe, Holmes (P.), Oldroyd, Leyland, Kilner (R.), Rhodes, Robinson (E.) – that was an awkward list for a bowler to read at breakfast. Robinson, Waddington, Macaulay, right-hand, Rhodes and Kilner, left, provided an attack of both severity and subtlety; and the fielding was Yorkshire's own. There was, perhaps, a spirit of keenness that sometimes turned rather grim and sour, a failing that the present captain, A. B. Sellers, has never allowed. It was a hard school for a young cricketer, but Leyland thrived on such discipline, and he has never lost his laugh.

As yet the path to the England side was stiff with obstruction. At number four, Leyland's usual place, Hendren, of Middlesex, made over 2,000 runs every season from 1920 to 1929, only varying it with 3,000 in 1923 and 1928. There was also Philip Mead, to say nothing of such men as Frank Woolley, Ernest Tyldesley, Jack Hearne and Andrew Ducat, who could fill any of the higher batting positions with distinction. So Leyland went on steadily for Yorkshire. In 1926 he scored 1,561 runs at an average of 39.02, with five centuries; but, with one wicket at 101.00, he showed a decline in his bowling, not enough to stir the critics, but perceptible to his admirers. In the autumn he went out to India, to coach for the Maharaja of Patiala. In 1927 he advanced a little more, averaging

41.66, and scoring his first double century, 204 not out against Middlesex; and, with four wickets at 33.00, he could dream of the day when he would be a change bowler. In this year, too, he played for the Rest v England at Lord's, and, like a true Yorkshireman, took his chance with an innings of 102. In 1928 he averaged over 50 (54.03) for the first time, scored five centuries for Yorkshire – top score 247 against Worcestershire – and was picked for England against the West Indies at The Oval. He failed to score. But the selectors included him in the side to go to Australia under A. P. F. Chapman, and he celebrated the honour by scoring 56 and 76 against C. I. Thornton's XI at Scarborough, at one point hitting Wilfred Rhodes for three sixes and a four in one over.

Fame did not hurry to meet Leyland. Here he was, at the age of 28, going on that visit which is the dream of all cricketers; but with him were such batsmen as Hobbs, Sutcliffe, Hammond, Jardine, Hendren, Tyldesley (E.), and two left-handers, Mead and Chapman himself. With Larwood, Tate, Geary and J. C. White waiting to bowl, Duckworth to keep wicket, two batsmen must be omitted. So Leyland remained in reserve till the Fifth Test, at Melbourne, where Chapman was unable to play and White was captain. The match was lost, but Leyland was not likely to fail; in his first innings against Australia he made 137, in the second 53 not out. In all matches on the tour he scored 614, average 43.85, and, besides the innings at Melbourne, made centuries against South Australia and Queensland. His four wickets cost 89.25 runs each.

Leyland's selection for that tour raised something of a storm in Kent, for the great Woolley had been passed over. Sir Pelham Warner, in his *Cricket Between Two Wars*, recalls the difficulty that confronted the selectors. England's three best left-handers, Woolley, Mead, and Leyland, had all done remarkably well in the English season of 1928. They had returned, respectively, aggregates of 3,352, 3,027, and 1,783, for averages of 61.03, 75.67, and 54.03. 'After much cut and thrust in debate … the choice fell on Mead and Leyland, whereupon a wail went up from Gravesend to Dover.' But, whatever might be the rights of the matter between Woolley and Mead, Leyland was surely a man to take, for his outfielding was of the highest class and he had the youth, speed, and strength so necessary for what J. C. White has described as 'an endless fight in an oven'. In the controversy one Kent supporter and whilom player even referred to Leyland as 'a cross-bat village-greener'. In this hyperbole lay a certain truth. Cross-bat Leyland was not; but his springy and muscular physique told of generations of health and sense and open air. Of such a type had been the men who drew bows at Crecy and sailed with Drake to singe the beards of kings. Leyland has always stood very still at the crease, whether waiting for the bowler or watching the striker; there is no fuss, no fidget, there is no nervous adjusting of pads or gloves, no jerky talk with umpire or fieldsman. He has a task and its answer, and he addresses himself to it, broad-bottomed, straight-eyed, with the forearms of a blacksmith, yet nimble, strangely nimble of foot.

His fame was now fixed, and for the next ten years England could rarely do without him. In 1929 he scored 1,931 runs, average 42.91. His Test aggregate was 294, average 42. For the first time he ran the risk of being called an all-rounder, taking 50 wickets at 30.26 each. In 1930 W. M. Woodfull brought young Bradman and ageless Grimmett to rob us of the Ashes. For once Leyland's part in the Tests was undistinguished. He did not play in the first two, and in the last three made only 103, average 25.75. For Yorkshire he batted finely, making five centuries, average 66.95. For the first time he passed an aggregate of 2,000, and took three more wickets than in 1929 at an average of three less. Chosen to go to South Africa under A. P. F. Chapman that winter, he made 300 runs in the Tests, average 42.85, highest score 91.

In 1931 he seemed stale. His aggregate dropped to 1,228 in 41 innings, average 38.37. The first three months of season 1932 brought him little good. Then he shook himself. In the whole season he scored 1,980 runs at an average of 52.10, with six centuries; and his 23 wickets cost him only 20.83 runs each, his lowest average up till then. In that earlier lean period Leyland, to all outward appearance, remained unmoved. I happened to be sitting by him one day during the middle of his failure. He was next in to bat. He talked with the calm confidence and untroubled wit of a man expecting to add yet another century to those he had not so far scored. Then, as at many another time, I understood the source of Leyland's strength and success. He gave fate thumping kicks from behind.

So, in the autumn, he set out under D. R. Jardine on that celebrated, if somewhat weight-reducing, trip in Australia. His figures in those Tests are not startling: nine innings, 306 runs, highest score 86, average 34.00. But he was not found wanting in crisis. His 86 was played in the second innings of the Fourth and deciding Test at Brisbane, a match famous for Paynter's 'sick-bed' 83 in the first innings. England needed only 160 to win. But the heat was intense, climatic and temperamental. Leyland was the man for all that. In the Third Test, when the Rubber stood at one match each, his innings of 83 helped Wyatt to add 146 for the fifth wicket, after four good men had gone for only 30. In the Fifth Test he was run out, through his partner's error, when well set at 42. In each match against South Australia he made a century. He had at least maintained his now high reputation. Returned to the calm of England, he topped the 2,000 for the second time in his career, and scored seven centuries, including 210 not out for Yorkshire against Kent at Dover. He played, but failed, in the first Test, at Lord's, against the West Indies. Perhaps he missed Brisbane and the shouting. But his bowling, which increasingly interested and amused him, gave him 37 wickets at 28.13 each.

In 1934 Leyland reached the height of his powers. Ripe in technique, rich in experience, like granite in battle, he was in this season England's greatest batsman. In all matches he totalled 2,142 runs, with an average of 53.55, and made seven centuries. Of these, three were taken off the Australians in the Tests.

In 1935 Leyland's batting average, which had exceeded 50 in five of the last seven years, dropped to 38.61. In 1936 he scored seven centuries and averaged 45.89. MCC picked G. O. Allen, who had enjoyed a most successful season, to captain the English team in Australia, and Leyland was an early choice. Indeed, apart from him and Walter Hammond, the batting looked somewhat brittle. The team sailed with many good wishes but little expectation. Some prophesied that Bradman would never get out at all and that we would be lucky to reach a total of 300 against O'Reilly. Yet England won the first two Tests, and, if Voce had not strained himself and Allen could have won the toss at Melbourne, the Ashes would probably have come home.

In 1937 Leyland was kept from cricket by a broken finger for several weeks, and he played in none of the three Tests against the visiting New Zealand team. His aggregate and average, modest for him, were respectively 1,306 and 36.27 with three centuries. In 1938 the Australians came here under D. G. Bradman. Leyland, now at an age when injuries are not so easily thrown off, suffered from a severe strain in the shoulder, and he did not find his form till June was out. A week before the Fourth Test at Leeds, for which he was almost certain to be chosen, a disastrous match was played at Lord's between Yorkshire and Middlesex. Hutton's finger was broken, Gibb had a nasty crack on the head, and Leyland had a fracture of the left thumb. Australia won the Test, one of the very finest matches ever played between the two countries, largely owing to the great bowling of O'Reilly – 10 for 122 – and yet another wonderful innings by Bradman, who scored 103 in a total of 242. But a month later Leyland and Hutton went, fit, to The Oval to be joined in that second-wicket partnership of 382, the highest stand ever made by two England batsmen against Australia – a grand day for Yorkshire.

Young Hutton, with his Test record of 364, took the limelight and the printer's ink; but Leyland, in his quiet old way, must have been a happy man as, from the other end, he watched in Hutton the fulfilment and operation of those same qualities that had brought fame to himself, the steadfast purpose, the invincible will, the skill that grows greater with the need. One more season of solid achievement lay before Leyland; but that match at The Oval was his climax – the reward of service and the triumph of character.

DARREN LEHMANN

Darren Lehmann scored more than 25,000 first class runs at an average of 57.83 and made 27 Test appearances (1,798 runs at 44.95).

Cricketer of the Year 2001 – by David Warner

Domestic first-class cricket in the first year of the new millennium was dominated both in Australia and England by Darren Lehmann, who transferred his phenomenal form in the 1999-2000 Pura Milk Cup to the County Championship with sublime ease. In doing so, he confirmed his peerless ability to adapt to different weather conditions and pitches.

Lehmann returned to Yorkshire for a third season after a break in 1999 because of the World Cup and now felt an even closer part of the family, having married Craig White's sister, Emma, at Christmas. He turned up at Headingley for a practice match in mid-April, after a few days' belated honeymoon in Paris, and the weather could not have been less welcoming for a batsman who, in recent months, had plundered seven centuries in ten first-class matches for South Australia. Yet the shivering rain held off just long enough for Lehmann to stroll out, strike three fours and a six, and play one or two cheeky reverse sweeps. It was, said one teammate, as if he'd never been away. And that is how it continued throughout the summer, by the end of which Lehmann emerged as the country's leading run-scorer in first-class matches with 1,477 runs at an average of 67.13. Such was the solidly built left-hander's consistency that he weighed in with four centuries and nine half-centuries in his 23 innings; at one stage he had consecutive scores of 77, 83, 56, 115, 66 and 116 – and this after starting out with knocks of 95, 85 and 133. Without his contribution, Yorkshire would not have finished third in Division One of the Championship or second in Division One of the National League. The rest of their batting was too brittle by far. As ever, Lehmann was a delight to watch. If sometimes he failed to convert fifties into centuries, owing to a moment's carelessness, that is the price he has to pay for being a Compton or a Miller, rather than a Boycott or a Lawry. He hit it off with players and officials immediately he joined Yorkshire in 1997, and proof that his popularity was not on the wane came late last season when his contract was extended to 2003 and he was appointed vice-captain to David Byas.

Darren Scott Lehmann was born in Gawler, South Australia, on February 5, 1970, and went on to represent South Australia at all age groups before making his Sheffield Shield debut for them in 1987-88 as a precocious 17-year-old. Two seasons later, at 20 years 32 days, he became the youngest Australian to score 1,000 first-class runs in a domestic season, and has since been in Sheffield Shield-winning sides for both Victoria and South Australia. After three seasons with Victoria in the early 1990s, he returned home to establish himself as one of the most successful Shield batsmen of all time. Having taken over the captaincy of South Australia from Jamie Siddons in 1998-99, he entered the 2000-01 season with a career record of 9,519 Sheffield Shield/ Pura Cup runs, a figure exceeded only by Siddons himself with 10,643 and Dean Jones with 9,622. His reward for his phenomenal 1999-2000 season was to be chosen as Pura Milk Cup Player of the Year, and he rounded off his English season with the Walter Lawrence Trophy for the fastest first-class hundred, made off 89 balls against Kent at Canterbury.

Astonishing, therefore, that despite such mastery with the bat, Lehmann should by that time have played only five Tests for Australia, and 60 one-day internationals. Indeed, he holds the dubious distinction of scoring more runs than any other Australian before making his Test debut, and the frequent snubs suggest his face does not quite fit. Perhaps it all dates back to his teens, when he rejected an invitation to join the Australian Cricket Academy because he was already scoring heavily for South Australia. He felt – as did his captain, David Hookes, and others – that he had reached a standard where playing for his state was more beneficial than being at the Academy.

Although not bitter, Lehmann was undoubtedly conscious, when he returned to England for the 2000 season, that a lengthy and distinguished Test career was slipping him by. 'If I don't make the Ashes party in 2001, then I'm unlikely to play for Australia again and my future will be in the Sheffield Shield and County Championship.' Not that Yorkshire will complain if they have his uninterrupted company over the coming three summers. It is hard to imagine that he was their third choice in 1997 when their previous overseas player, Michael Bevan, was included in Australia's squad for the tour of England, along with Michael Slater. Now, they simply wouldn't dream of being without him.

PHIL SHARPE

Phil Sharpe took 618 first-class catches and 17 in 12 Tests. He scored more than 22,500 first-class runs and finished with a Test average of 46.23. He retired in 1976.

Cricketer of the Year 1963 – by W. E. Bowes

To the casual observer Philip Sharpe, the Yorkshire number three batsman, could be anything except a professional sportsman. He has one of those skins that does not redden or tan in the summer sun and there is more of a suggestion of the bowler hat and rolled umbrella than a cricket bat or hockey stick.

He is only five feet seven inches, but he has a pair of broad shoulders. He is stocky and compact, but he gives the impression of being dumpy because he wears trousers with plenty of room in the beam. He is probably the best slip fieldsman in the country today and he says, 'I like room to move and bend in comfort.'

Last season, suddenly fulfilling the promise he showed as a schoolboy, he scored 2,352 runs, average 40.94. He finished top of the Yorkshire averages, established a new county fielding record with 71 catches – beating John Tunnicliffe's 70 – and became third to W. R. Hammond and M. J. Stewart for the most catches taken in a season. The Cricket Writers' Club voted him the Best Cricketer of 1962.

At hockey, which is his winter game, he plays for the Ben Rhydding Sports Club; he has appeared regularly for Yorkshire since 1958 and in 1960, as a left half, he was chosen for two England trials. He is a sportsman far above average ability.

Philip John Sharpe was born on December 27, 1936, at Shipley in Yorkshire. He went to Bradford Grammar School and at 12 to Worksop College. His father, Mr F. G. Sharpe, a Bradford mill executive, had a deep love of cricket although he did not play himself. During the school holidays he sent the boy for coaching under the former Yorkshire cricketers, Arthur Mitchell and Wilfred Barber. Says Phil, 'They taught me to stop the ball reasonably correctly. I was less than five feet tall then and I could not hit it. While the other boys batted I bowled very high and very slow off-spinners.'

This ability to bowl got him a place in the Colts XI when he was 14, and then, playing against St Peter's, York, for the first XI he played a long not-out innings of 20 as a number eight batsman. The school captain was most impressed and gave his opinion that Sharpe might make a batsman. The headmaster, Canon Maloney, gave his opinion, 'The boy will never play cricket, he is too small.' Young Sharpe, however, began to grow. In the next year or so, as he puts it, 'I shot up to five feet seven.' He played for his college at cricket, hockey, rugby, squash and tennis. At 17 he scored 499 runs in the season with 90 against Old Worksopians and 91 not out against Craven Gentlemen.

He was made school captain at 18 and, with success that brought him mention in almost every newspaper in the country, totalled 1,251 runs for an average of 113. He made 240 against Wrekin, 216 against Cryptics, and, chosen to play for the Yorkshire Cricket Federation XI against Notts, he scored 200. 'I thought cricket was an easy game and an ideal way of earning a living. I talked over the idea of being a professional cricketer with my father, and after a time, he agreed I should have a try.'

He left school in September 1955, but as Craftsman Sharpe he had to do two years of National Service in REME. Playing for the Combined Services he scored half-centuries against Warwickshire, Worcestershire and Surrey, and in one game for the Yorkshire Colts made 67 against Lancashire second XI. His father gave him a job learning wool sorting, alongside another Yorkshire batsman, D. E. V. Padgett, to occupy his time in the winter and then in 1958 came the serious effort of trying to prove himself a cricketer.

With the Yorkshire Colts he began with six or seven consecutive scores of over 40 and he was chosen for a four-match trial with the County XI. He was twelfth man for the first game against Surrey, scored 7 and 56 not out against Sussex at Worthing, failed against Kent at Maidstone but scored 141 against Somerset at Sheffield. He kept with the side to the end of the season. Sharpe's main weakness in those early days was a tendency to turn chest on to the bowler when playing defensively. It caused the bat to travel across the line of flight of the ball instead of moving like a pendulum down the line of flight.

In 12 innings at the start of the 1959 season he made only 90 runs and a score of 202 against the touring India side for the Minor Counties did not change his luck. He finished the season deputising for the Yorkshire scorer who had been taken ill. The fault in technique persisted. He scored a double century for Yorkshire against Cambridge University at the start of the 1960 season but this failed to impress. Sharpe was more often twelfth man than player and he had just over 1,000 runs to his credit at the end of the season. Yorkshire, nevertheless, encouraged him by giving him his county cap.

In 43 innings for the county in 1961 he scored only 1,000 runs with a highest score of 87 and an average of 27.02. Although Yorkshire had 14 capped players to choose from they persisted with Sharpe because the bowlers liked to have him at slip. He was alert and had a good pair of hands. He had a subtle, almost impish sense of humour, and he was good to have about the dressing room.

Says Sharpe, 'On the experience gained I suddenly realised that my real mistake was that I had been playing at cricket rather than playing cricket. I needed to concentrate ... and a funny thing, in coming to this conclusion I found a confidence I had only experienced in my last year at Worksop.'

Almost immediately his cricket took on a new character. He contributed over 50 runs in six out of the first seven games. He scored centuries against Lancashire, Pakistan, Surrey, Nottinghamshire, Northamptonshire and Lancashire again. The tendency to turn chest on went. Batting or fielding he had a contribution to make to every game and in 64 innings during the season he averaged over 40.

He became a strong candidate for a place in Dexter's MCC side for Australia and probably only missed because the selectors wanted all-rounders, batsmen who could bowl off-spin. Yorkshire's faith in him has been fully justified and he is confidently expected to join the county's long list of successful Test players.

Matthew Hoggard

Matthew Hoggard's Yorkshire career ended in 2009 when, after taking 43 wickets to finish as the county's leading strike bowler, he was not offered a revised contract. He moved to Leicestershire and became the county's captain in 2010.

Cricketer of the Year 2006 – by David Hopps

Of England's fast-bowling quartet in the Ashes series, Andrew Flintoff was the Herculean all-rounder who became a nation's favourite; Simon Jones cut a dash with his mastery of reverse swing (the summer's most sought-after style accessory); and Steve Harmison, however patchy his form, had the automatic appeal of an out-and-out fast bowler.

Hoggard? He was the other one. The one with the lank fair hair that, allied to a broad-beamed, stomping gait, encouraged so much farming imagery it would have been no surprise had he stopped midway through his run to close a gate or chase a sheep. The one with a mildly deranged sense of humour that proved solid Yorkshire virtues do not have to come hand in hand with dourness. The one, more to the point, whose captain, Michael Vaughan, a county team-mate aware of his strengths and his weaknesses, used only sporadically for more than half the Ashes series. But if Matthew James Hoggard, born in Leeds on New Year's Eve, 1976, was 'the other one', what an other one! On the last day of the Ashes series, Simon Hughes, in *The Daily Telegraph*, uncovered a remarkable statistic. In 2005, Hoggard had unobtrusively assembled the best strike-rate among the year's main Test wicket-takers, with a wicket every 38 balls. This faded a little during the autumn in Pakistan, as much else did for England – but only to 42, far better than any of the world's gaudier fast bowlers.

Hoggard's greatest success of the year came early, when he bowled England to a gloriously improbable victory at Johannesburg by taking the first six wickets, and seven in all. For a while, it seemed as if he might take all ten. Yet this was the bowler, a few months later, who many outside the England 'bubble' feared might not last the Ashes summer. He was their leading wicket-taker in the two Tests against Bangladesh, but he is a man with a sound perspective on life and pronounced that he had 'bowled like a trollop'. He was not in England's one-day side and his county figures were unexceptional. There was talk that Australia intended to target him. If it didn't swing, they planned literally to drive him to distraction. When he disappeared for 65 runs in four overs in a Twenty20 Cup tie against Lancashire at Headingley, a month before the First Test, the omens did not seem promising. Only by the end of the summer did Hoggard's assessment of that performance seem fitting. 'Daft cricket,' he said. 'They slog your good balls and get out to your bad ones'.

That Hoggard was deemed so vulnerable owes everything to the vagaries of swing bowling. It can be a mocking, unpredictable gift, sometimes refusing to appear, on other occasions appearing so lavishly that it can lead to wild inaccuracies. He had naturally swung the ball as a junior at Pudsey Congs, where he learned good attitudes from the former Yorkshire captain, Phil Carrick. But as late as 2001 – the year after he had made his Test debut against West Indies at Lord's – Yorkshire's array of fast bowlers still left him insecure enough to toy with joining Worcestershire.

For the first three Ashes Tests in 2005, he bowled only 56 overs and, recognising that his loosener had brought a wicket on three occasions, suggested ruefully that Vaughan might soon start bowling him in one-ball spells. He seemed fated to be remembered largely for the remark on the eve of the series that Australia's attack was getting on a bit, a playful suggestion predictably misinterpreted by the more po-faced representatives of the media. But Trent Bridge, the fourth venue, favoured his traditional out-swing, rather than fashionable reverse swing. (Hoggard can reverse the ball modestly at times but, as they say in his neck of the woods, 'tha's only sum as catch on'). If he was under pressure in Nottingham, he shrugged it off, grateful that this time he would at least have the chance to bed in. Eleven overs with the new ball brought 3 for 28 – Hayden, Martyn and Langer. And two more second-innings wickets included an inswinger for an lbw decision against Adam Gilchrist – a collector's item, that one, as Gilchrist had never before been dismissed lbw in a Test by a fast bowler.

But it was his match-winning eighth-wicket partnership of 13 with Ashley Giles on the fourth afternoon that will remain etched on the memory. Hoggy shambled out as if it was an Evening Cup tie at Farsley, but he had long taken pride in a stubborn defence, and the very occasional stroke of genius. The 90mph-plus full toss from Brett Lee that he somehow drove through extra cover he later deemed the greatest shot he had ever played with his eyes closed.

After a tense Sunday morning at The Oval, with Australia threatening to square the series and retain the Ashes, he again answered England's call, taking four wickets for four runs as England obtained the unlikeliest of first innings leads. It was as satisfying for him as striding across Ilkley Moor with his dogs. And that can never be suggested lightly: this was a man who, on an England tour of India, once claimed to have kept himself sane in uncomfortable Ahmedabad by taking an imaginary dog for an imaginary walk. In 2005, when it mattered most, he did everything for real.

DICKIE BIRD

As well as an MBE and an autobiography, which sold more than a million copies, Dickie Bird was given the Freedom of Barsnley and the honour of unveiling a statue there in his honour.

The man who stole the show – by Tony Lewis, 1997

Harold Dennis Bird known to the cricket world as 'Dickie', retired from Test match umpiring in 1996, aged 63. He had completed 23 years at the top and his 66 Tests were a record; he stood in three World Cup finals and 68 one-day internationals. His career coincided with the advent of television coverage of cricket by satellite to many parts of the world; consequently his fame was global. Frank Chester, who umpired in England between 1924 and 1955, was once described as 'the most famous of all umpires'. There is no doubt that this accolade now belongs to Dickie Bird.

Personal celebrity, however, was never thought to sit easily alongside excellence in a professional cricket umpire, and so Bird's retirement provoked debate. Was he television-made? Was he better known for his eccentric, theatrical behaviour than for his wise judgments? Administrators of the British game used to throw their hands to their faces, hoping to mask the sight of Dickie running to the boundary behind the bowler's arm to deliver loud Yorkshire strictures to someone disturbing the batsman's concentration. Hands on hips, he would address a hospitality box three floors above, informing them that their open glass door was reflecting sunshine into a player's eyes. Everything he said was in the manner of the lugubrious northern over-the-garden-wall comedian. 'Shut that door. Shut it. Where d'yer think you are?'

Sometimes he himself seemed to be the interruption. When he prepared to umpire in Sharjah, in the Gulf, for the first time, he was advised not to subject his eyes to the dazzle of the sun which bounced up off the shiny pitch. Instead he was told to look away from the playing surface between balls, and to divert his eyes to the grassy surrounds. So after the first ball from his end, he set off on a crouching, circular walk, like someone searching for a lost contact lens within a 15-yard radius of the stumps, and kept that up all day. Afterwards, he thanked his adviser, 'Me eyes were great, they were. Great they were, me eyes.' The conclusion was that he was not performing theatricals but that it was 'just Dickie'.

In Frank Chester's day, umpires were seen but rarely heard. They had been brought up as players on ground staffs in counties captained by amateurs but heavily influenced by the senior professional. There was hierarchy and discipline, and so the control they exerted as umpires was by the odd word to the captain or senior pro – and perhaps only a whisper, 'Have a word with your fast bowler. He's pushing his luck with that appealing.'

Chester virtually created the modern profession of umpiring by his serious approach to the smallest detail. After him, Syd Buller was outstanding: massively unobtrusive, entirely dependable. His decisions were quick and clean. Players were happy with his judgments; even if they had not been, no one would have dared leave the field with a shaking head. Charlie Elliott, another protector of the spirit of cricket, was often Buller's companion in Tests, and also operated without fuss or palaver. And so it must have been a fascinating umpires' room at Headingley in England's Third Test against New Zealand in 1973 when Elliott, of the old school, welcomed Dickie Bird to Test cricket.

'I have never seen anyone so nervous in my life,' Elliott recalled. 'I thought he would never make it to the middle let alone give good decisions. Then I saw something which was a clue to his future reputation. He gave Ray Illingworth out lbw. The bowler was the New Zealand seamer Bruce Taylor and he was bowling round the wicket. I thought from square leg, "How can that be out? A seamer bowling right-arm round the wicket?" But I saw it later on television and I liked what I saw. Dickie was absolutely correct: the ball had moved back into Illingworth from the line of off stump. It was a top-class instant decision.'

There are not many secret corners to Dickie Bird's life; he has written autobiographies and has been the subject of many written and broadcast profiles. Son of a Barnsley miner, still cared for by his sister; nervous, dithery off the field, highly strung. A former Leicestershire teammate of his, Ray Julian, remembers how Bird needed help to strap on his pads and put his sausage-fingered gloves on the right hands before walking out to bat. And not a lot has changed when we share an umpires' dressing room now. Julian, like Charlie Elliot, talks of a different Dickie once he is crouched behind the stumps.

There is no doubt that his failure to become an established county cricketer heightened his appreciation of being an umpire. But it was the cricket he did play – from 1956 to 1959 with Yorkshire, from 1960 to 1964 with Leicestershire – that helped him become such an outstanding umpire. So has it been with most first-class umpires in England. Bird carried over from his playing days a strong sympathy for the legion of cricketers who plied their daily trade. He cared for professional standards.

Everyone agrees that he has been a very good umpire for a long time. It is the other little choices he has always found so difficult. But there is a special relationship between Bird and other umpires. His colleagues have been willing to take over when Bird's nerves are twanging at the thought of making tricky decisions about bad light or resuming play after rain. Where Dickie has been unique is in his rapport with players, and with the crowds watching at the ground or on television. The message emanating from Bird's whole being is his complete understanding of the spirit of the game, and his ability to preserve sporting play. Charlie Elliot agrees that international umpiring is more difficult these days. There is far more shouting, far more concerted appealing; as fielders, protected by helmets and padding, have moved in closer to the bat, the appeals for catches off bat and pad are now acted out in order to deceive the umpire. This is cheating.

If there was similar trouble in the old days, Buller or Elliot or Harry Baldwin would simply address the captain and tell him to control his players; the captain, after all, is responsible for preserving the spirit of the game. Bird, however, was able to chide individuals who specialised in sledging opponents and cursing umpires. He had their respect. Merv Hughes, Dennis Lillee and Javed Miandad, who were all verbally bellicose, accepted that he could laugh with them and yet caution them. They knew Dickie Bird put cricket above his own life.

As he leaves the Test match scene, the job has become more and more burdensome. Decisions made by humans in white coats are checked endlessly against technology on television and they are sometimes proved wrong. The use of a third umpire to pass judgment may bring about correct decisions but it undermines the authority of the umpire in the middle and erodes his confidence.

We are left looking back at the Dickie Bird phenomenon. His huge appeal was based on his personal vulnerability. He was a magnet for minor disasters. But the watching world was affectionate; old ladies wanted to mother him. Here was a real character, fun to observe in days when the cricketers themselves had become anonymous under helmets and behind visors. In a busy main street in Colombo he once got out of a car on the wrong side and found himself in the middle of hooting Ambassador cars, fast bicycles, slow ox-carts, and listing Leyland buses, all bearing down on him. Suddenly everyone stopped. They began pointing and shouting, 'Mr Dickie Bird'. He played to the crowd and gave them his funny hunched run to safety, repeating louder than any of them, 'Mr Dickie Bird. Mr Dickie Bird'.

His final exit at Lord's, 1996, was incredible. He was given a Hollywood-style reception which has never been afforded to any player, let alone an umpire. Don Bradman and Viv Richards were applauded to the crease when they played their last innings in England, and The Don was given three cheers. Umpire Bird walked out of the Long Room and the whole of Lord's stood and applauded. Even more, the players of the England and India sides were out on the grass to form a corridor of appreciation. Frank Chester would not have recognised the scene nor, I guess, would he and his contemporaries have approved the elevation of an umpire so far above the real craftsmen who bat, bowl and field.

But if you wanted the essence of Dickie Bird encapsulated in a few minutes, you could have seen it that day. One moment he was dabbing at his tears with a handkerchief; then at the fifth ball of the match he gave a rock-solid decision for lbw against Mike Atherton, the England captain. It is probably true that Dickie was a natural character who became a conscious character. But he never allowed anything to stand in the way of the fair conduct of the game. This is why he retained the trust of the players and stayed at the top so long.

Chapter Eight:
Honorary Yorkshiremen:
Bradman, Botham and the Ashes

At the end of his valedictory 'Invincibles' tour of England in 1948, Yorkshire awarded Donald Bradman its equivalent of the Order of Merit. It gave him honorary life membership of the club, which was tantamount to making him an honorary Yorkshireman too. The newly christened Tyke responded politely, 'I shall never cherish any memory more than the reception in Leeds,' he said. 'Not only was it the greatest I have ever received in this country, but also the greatest I have ever received from any public anywhere in the world.' Bradman was talking about his final appearance at Headingley. The cheering for him lasted almost as long as some of his finest innings. Romantics still hear the echo on summer days.

Bradman belonged to Headingley. A part of that 'foreign field' was forever his own. He scored a record 963 runs in six innings there – 334, 304, 103, 16, 33 and an unbeaten 173 – at an average of 192.60. His star never glimmered out.

The sweetest Bradman vintage came in 1930 – an unbeaten 309 in a day, which comprised: 105 before lunch; 115 between lunch and tea; a mere 89 between tea and the close. He struggled to get off the field, a uniformed policeman cutting a narrow path for him through awed middle-aged men in dark suits and trilbies, who later peered at him through the dressing-room windows. The Australians taped sheets of brown paper to the glass to protect his privacy.

His brief diary entry that night is dead-pan to the point of parody, and yet it explains everything about his character: glacial determination and the capacity to separate himself from his own genius. 'Beautiful day with just a nip in the air,' wrote Bradman. 'We won the toss and batted. Archie [Jackson] out for one. I followed, and at stumps was 309 not out.' He went on to a world-record 334.

When Bradman was dismissed for 78 in the tour match, a voice was heard to yell out in dismay: 'We do not come to see the Australians play, we joost come to see Bradman baht.' But for all his undoubted greatness, even Bradman was upstaged in 1981 in what is frequently described as the 'Greatest Test of all Time', the 'Miracle at Headingley' or, in even simpler terms, as 'Botham's Test'. Ian Botham belting the ball in to the 'confectionery stall' and then out again, plus Bob Willis bowling like a blasting wind to take 8-43, devastated the Australians and mesmerised anyone who saw it or read about it since.

As Fred Trueman used to say: 'You're always guaranteed a headline from a Test in Yorkshire.'

Third Ashes Test, 1902
Sheffield, July 2, 4, 5

The third of the Test Matches was brought to a definite conclusion and resulted in a severe disaster for England, the Australians winning at a quarter past one on the Saturday, by 143 runs. They played the finer all-round cricket, and fully deserved their victory, but it is no more than the truth to say that all the luck of the game went their way. Bad light towards the close of the first day and a pitch damaged by rain the following morning told against the Englishmen, and in the closing stage of the match the wicket showed unmistakable signs of wear. An appeal against the light might well have been made earlier than it was on Thursday, and the saving of two wickets thereby involved would possibly have put the elevens on equal terms on the first innings. The match – the first of its kind ever decided at Bramall Lane – naturally proved a strong attraction, but a mistake was made in fixing it for the latter part of the week, Monday being always the best day for public cricket at Sheffield.

The Australians played the same eleven that afterwards represented them in the Test games at Manchester and the Oval, the three men left out being Jones, Howell and Carter. The presence of Hugh Trumble in itself made them stronger than they had been either at Birmingham or at Lord's. As regards the England team, Lockwood and Haigh were among the twelve players selected but they were both left out, the final place being given at almost the last moment to Barnes. As the Lancashire bowler took six wickets on the first day at a cost of only 49 runs criticism was disarmed, but in the light of subsequent events there can be no question that a grave mistake was committed in not playing Lockwood. It was not originally intended to play C. B. Fry, who on the day before the match had to take the place of Ranjitsinhji – disabled by a strained leg.

At one point on the first day the Englishmen had much the best of the match as, after getting rid of the Australians for 194, they had 60 on the board when their first wicket went down. When, however, a quarter of an hour before the time for drawing stumps the bad light was successfully appealed against, five wickets had fallen for 102. The cause of this startling change in the game was the bowling of Noble and Saunders, Noble, who had previously shown the best batting for his side, being in wonderful form. Sufficient rain fell in the night to affect the wicket for a time, and the Englishmen on resuming their innings cut such an inglorious figure that by a quarter to twelve the innings was all over for 145, the last seven wickets having actually gone down for 44 runs.

The batsmen on the second morning were quite at fault in dealing with Saunders' breakbacks. Holding a useful lead of 49 the Australians went in for the second time, and in the course of the three hours and fifty minutes they ran up a total of 289. This was quite enough to make them pretty sure of the match, but at one time they seemed likely to do a great deal better, their score when the fourth wicket fell standing at 187. Rhodes finished off the innings with a wonderful piece of bowling, taking four wickets in 19 balls. At the start of the innings MacLaren made a mistake in not putting him on at the end from which Saunders had been so successful. Trumper in the course of the season

In 1939 when war with Germany was obviously drawing nearer the second National Government invited various people to speak around the country to set up recruiting. I was invited to address the City of Bradford with Herbert Sutcliffe as my partner. I had been warned by Auckland Geddes that Bradford could be difficult an audience as Manchester had been for him the previous week when it kept chanting 'Tripe! Tripe!' When I stepped forward on to the platform at the Alhambra on that Saturday evening I said I hoped the citizens of the Bradford would not suppose I was a representative of the National Government. 'What I think of the National Government could not be said on any platform or any pulpit on a Sunday evening.' When I sat down Herbert Sutcliffe turned to me and said:

'Oh my, how I wish I could speak like you.'

'You don't wish nearly as much that you could speak like me as I wish I could bat like you,' I replied.

Sir Compton Mackenzie, 'Shillings for W. G.', 1973

made many bigger scores than his 62 but on no occasion did he play a more marvellous innings. He obtained his runs out of a total of 80 in fifty minutes, doing just what he liked with the English bowling. Hill, who went in first wicket down at 20 and was out at 225 to a wonderful catch – high up at cover slip with one hand – played a great innings on a wicket that was never easy. His cricket was not entirely free from fault as when his score stood between 70 and 80 he might have been caught at slip, and gave a very difficult chance in the long-field, but these were small blemishes in a most brilliant display. He was batting for rather less than two hours and a half. Darling, it should be mentioned, had a very unhappy experience in the match, being in each innings caught at slip off Barnes, without getting a run.

England wanted 339 to win, and it was felt that the task would prove too heavy. However, a good start was made, the experiment of sending Jessop in first with Abel proving a great success. Without being in any way reckless the famous hitter played a brilliant game and, when just before six o'clock, bad light stopped cricket for the day, he was not out 53, the total being 73 for one wicket. Any hopes that the Englishmen might have had were soon destroyed on Saturday morning, Jessop, Tyldesley and Fry being all dismissed in the first half hour for an addition of 25 runs. MacLaren made a great effort to save a lost game, and for nearly an hour found a valuable partner in Jackson, but it was all to no purpose. After Jackson's dismissal at 162 the end soon came, the last five wickets falling for 33 runs. In this closing part of the match Noble bowled magnificently, breaking back again and again in an unplayable way. His average from the time he went on for Saunders on Saturday morning came out at five wickets in twelve overs for 22 runs, and in the whole match he took eleven wickets for 103 runs. Trumble who, owing to a blow on his thumb, did not bowl on Friday afternoon, did admirable work at the finish.

AUSTRALIA	First Innings		Second Innings	
V. T. Trumper b Braund	1	– c Lilley b Jackson		62
R. A. Duff c Lilley b Barnes	25	– c Hirst b Rhodes		1
C. Hill c Rhodes b Barnes	18	– c MacLaren b Jackson		119
*J. Darling c Braund b Barnes	0	– c Braund b Barnes		0
S. E. Gregory c Abel b Barnes	11	– run out		29
M. A. Noble c Braund b Rhodes	47	– b Jackson		8
A. J. Y. Hopkins c Braund b Barnes	27	– not out		40
W. W. Armstrong c and b Braund	25	– b Rhodes		26
†J. J. Kelly b Barnes	0	– c Hirst b Rhodes		0
H. Trumble c and b Jackson	32	– b Rhodes		0
J. V. Saunders not out	0	– b Rhodes		1
B 3, l-b 5	8	L-b 3		3
1-3 2-39 3-39 4-52 5-73 6-127	194	1-20 2-80 3-80 4-187 5-214 6-225		289
7-137 8-137 9-194 10-194		7-277 8-287 9-287 10-289		

First innings – Hirst 15–1–59–0; Braund 13–4–34–2; Barnes 20–9–49–6; Jackson 5.1–1–11–1; Rhodes 13–3–33–1.
Second innings – Hirst 10–1–40–0; Rhodes 17.1–3–63–5; Barnes 12–4–50–1; Jackson 17–2–60–3; Braund 12–0–58–0; Jessop 4–0–15–0.

ENGLAND	First Innings		Second Innings	
*A. C. MacLaren b Noble	31	– (4) c Trumper b Noble		63
R. Abel b Noble	38	– c Hill b Noble		8
J. T. Tyldesley c Armstrong b Noble	22	– b Trumble		14
F. S. Jackson c Gregory b Saunders	3	– (6) b Noble		14
C. B. Fry st Kelly b Saunders	1	– lbw b Trumble		4
†A. F. A. Lilley b Noble	8	– (7) b Noble		9
L. C. Braund st Kelly b Saunders	0	– (8) c Armstrong b Noble		9
G. H. Hirst c Trumble b Saunders	8	– (9) b Noble		0
G. L. Jessop c Saunders b Noble	12	– (1) lbw b Trumble		55
W. Rhodes not out	7	– not out		7
S. F. Barnes c Darling b Saunders	7	– b Trumble		5
B 4, l-b 3, n-b 1	8	B 4, l-b 1, w 1, n-b 1		7
1-61 2-86 3-101 4-101 5-102 6-106	145	1-14 2-75 3-84 4-98 5-162 6-165		195
7-110 8-130 9-131 10-145		7-174 8-174 9-186 10-195		

First innings – Trumble 18–10–21–0; Saunders 15.3–4–50–5; Trumper 4–1–8–0; Noble 19–6–51–5; Armstrong 5–2–7–0.
Second innings – Noble 21–4–52–6; Saunders 12–0–68–0; Trumper 6–0–19–0; Trumble 21.5–3–49–4.

Toss won by Australia   UMPIRES J. Phillips and W. Richards
Close of Play First day: England (1) 102-5 (Lilley 0, Braund 0);
Second day: England (2) 73-1 (Jessop 53, Tyldesley 11).

Third Ashes Test, 1930
Leeds, July 11, 12, 14, 15

The Third Test match, while it afforded that remarkable young batsman, Bradman, the opportunity of leaving all individual batting records in representative matches far behind, was in many respects an unsatisfactory affair. England had the worst of it from start to finish but escaped with a draw, a heavy storm on Sunday night, followed by further rain on the Monday restricting the third day's play to forty-five minutes while, on the Tuesday, further delay occurred owing to defective light.

The game will go down to history on account of the wonderful batting performance accomplished by Bradman who, with an innings of 334, beat the previous highest – 287 by R. E. Foster for England at Sydney – which had stood since December, 1903. In the course of this, Bradman achieved fame in other directions. Like C. G. Macartney on the same ground four years previously, he reached three-figures before lunchtime on the first day. Not out 309 at the close he had then exceeded a total of a thousand runs in Test cricket and reached an aggregate of exactly 2,000 runs for the season. In playing two consecutive innings of over 200 in Test matches he equalled the performance of Hammond during the previous tour in Australia. He also equalled Macartney's performance of 1926 in scoring three separate hundreds in successive Test matches. Truly could it be called Bradman's Match. Bigger though it was and characterised by splendid stroke play, Bradman's innings did not quite approach his 254 at Lord's in freedom from fault, but as to its extraordinary merit there could be no two opinions. As usual, he rarely lifted the ball and when making two or more consecutive scoring strokes seldom sent it in the same direction. His footwork was admirable as was the manner in which he played his defensive strokes to balls just short of a length.

Australia, who had played the same eleven in the previous two games, had to make two changes. Suffering from gastritis, Ponsford stood down and Fairfax had not completely recovered from an operation he had had to undergo at Nottingham. Jackson and a'Beckett, therefore, played in their first Test match in England. England also had alterations. Woolley, Hendren, Allen, Robins and White were all dropped, Sutcliffe, Larwood and Richard Tyldesley coming back and Leyland and Geary being included. As events proved, some of these changes might just as well have not been made. For one thing, the English fielding compared most unfavourably with that in the earlier matches. Tyldesley, avowedly brought in with the idea of keeping the Australian batsmen quiet, again failed in his mission, Geary's bowling had no terrors at all while Larwood, still looking very drawn as the result of his illness, had not the stamina to bowl at his full pace and was terribly expensive. Tate, as usual, bore the brunt of the attack and bowled as pluckily as ever but, taken all round, the Englishmen lacked the attributes of a great side and Hammond alone made over fifty runs.

This time, Woodfull won the toss and Australia led off so brilliantly that, when the first day's play ended, they had 458 runs on the board with only three wickets down.

The pitch, like those at Nottingham and Lord's, was, on the first day at any rate, lacking in life and pace and all in favour of batsmen. Opening the innings with Woodfull, Jackson off the fifth ball of the second over was caught at forward-short-leg but England had to wait until five minutes past three before they took another wicket, Woodfull and Bradman, in the meantime, putting on 192 runs in two hours and thirty-five minutes. This was very largely the work of Bradman who, quick to settle down, completed 102 out of the first 127 in ninety-five minutes. All the same, Woodfull, by another great display of defensive cricket, rendered his side invaluable assistance. After Woodfull left, bowled in trying to hook a shortish ball, Bradman found another admirable partner in Kippax, who if overshadowed by his colleague, played uncommonly well in helping to add 229 in rather less than two and three-quarter hours. The next day McCabe, who had batted twenty minutes overnight, stayed until 63 runs had been put on but nothing of any consequence was accomplished by the rest, the last seven wickets falling in a hundred minutes for 108 runs. Bradman, sixth out at 508, obtained his 334 in six hours and a quarter, his score being made up of 46 fours, 6 threes, 26 twos and 80 singles. When he had made 141 he put up a ball towards mid-wicket and at 202 he skied a ball over Tate's head at mid-on. Indeed, a man a little quicker on his feet than Tate might have made a catch of it. Actually, Bradman gave only one chance, being missed at the wicket off Geary at 273 when the total was 385. He hit very hard in front of the wicket, scored splendidly on the leg side and very often cut in dazzling fashion. Nobody could have had a better reception than that accorded to Bradman on his return to the pavilion.

Before lunch Hobbs and Sutcliffe scored 17 runs for England but the total was only 53 when Hobbs was out in a manner which provoked considerable discussion. A' Beckett, fielding very close in on the on-side to Grimmett's bowling, took the ball from a gentle stroke very low down, turning a complete somersault but retaining possession. Hobbs was about to walk away but stepped back into his crease on overhearing a remark by Oldfield and an appeal from other members of the side. An appeal having been made, Hobbs was perfectly justified in waiting for the decision. Oates, the umpire at the bowler's end, was unable to give one, a' Beckett in falling over obscuring his view, so he referred to Bestwick standing at square-leg. Unhappily, Bestwick hesitated before holding up his finger, and the great majority of the crowd took the view that a' Beckett had not properly made the catch.

Soon afterwards Sutcliffe was out but Hammond and Duleepsinhji added 59 and then Leyland helped to put on 83, Hammond, when 52, having just previously been missed by Oldfield standing back to Wall. Geary was run out at 206 and England at the close of play, with five wickets down for 212, found themselves 354 behind and requiring 205 to save the follow-on. On the Monday the weather following a storm in the night, which resulted in water lying in patches on the ground, was very bad. So long a delay occurred that not until half past five was play proceeded with. From the manner in which the pitch rolled out it was quite obvious that cricket would have been possible at least an hour earlier. Thirty runs were scored before an appeal against the light at a quarter past six was upheld.

On Tuesday morning Duckworth, who had gone in for ten minutes on Saturday evening, batted so well that the score was up to 289 before he was caught at the wicket, 83 runs having been added in rather more than two hours. Hammond stayed until the score was 319 after resisting the bowling for five hours and twenty minutes. He hit only 14 fours but gave a splendid display of skilful batting, neglecting very few opportunities of scoring off anything in the nature of a punishable ball. Chapman, hitting hard, put on 51 runs with Tate but England were all out at a quarter to three for 391, their innings lasting nearly eight hours. The last three wickets fell in half an hour for 36 runs.

England followed on 179 behind and, as over three hours remained for cricket, there was always a possibility of them losing. Hobbs and Sutcliffe opened the innings in a very poor light. After a quarter of an hour, they appealed against it and the players went in. For some extraordinary reason the crowd took this in very bad part, booing the batsmen and cheering the Australians, while on the game being resumed there was a continuance of this unseemly behaviour. With 24 scored, Hobbs was brilliantly thrown out by Bradman from deep-mid-off but Sutcliffe and Hammond stayed nearly an hour to add 50. After Duleepsinhji had been caught at point off a ball which he afterwards confessed he did not see, another appeal against the light was made at ten minutes to six and no further cricket took place. The total attendance reached 77,500, and the gate receipts £8,597.

AUSTRALIA	*First Innings*	
*W. M. Woodfull b Hammond	. . . .	50
A. Jackson c Larwood b Tate	. . . .	1
D. G. Bradman c Duckworth b Tate	. . . .	334
A. F. Kippax c Chapman b Tate	. . . .	77
S. J. McCabe b Larwood	. . . .	30
V. Y. Richardson c Larwood b Tate	. . . .	1
E. L. a'Beckett c Chapman b Geary	. . . .	29
†W. A. S. Oldfield c Hobbs b Tate	. . . .	2
C. V. Grimmett c Duckworth b Tyldesley	. . . . .	24
T. W. Wall b Tyldesley	. . . .	3
P. M. Hornibrook not out	. . . .	1
B 5, l-b 8, w 1	. . . .	14
1-2 2-194 3-423 4-486 5-491 6-508		566
7-519 8-544 9-565 10-566		

First innings – Larwood 33–3–139–1; Tate 39–9–124–5; Geary 35–10–95–1; Tyldesley 33–5–104–2; Hammond 17–3–46–1; Leyland 11–0–44–0.

ENGLAND	*First Innings*		*Second Innings*
J. B. Hobbs c a'Beckett b Grimmett	29	– run out	13
H. Sutcliffe c Hornibrook b Grimmett	32	– not out	28
W. R. Hammond c Oldfield b McCabe	113	– c Oldfield b Grimmett	35
K. S. Duleepsinhji b Hornibrook	35	– c Grimmett b Hornibrook	10
M. Leyland c Kippax b Wall	44	– not out	1
G. Geary run out	0		
†G. Duckworth c Oldfield b a'Beckett	33		
*A. P. F. Chapman b Grimmett	45		
M. W. Tate c Jackson b Grimmett	22		
H. Larwood not out	10		
R. K. Tyldesley c Hornibrook b Grimmett	6		
B 9, l-b 10, n-b 3	22	L-b 8	8

1-53 2-64 3-123 4-206 5-206 6-289   391   1-24 2-72 3-94   (3 wickets) 95
7-319 8-370 9-375 10-391

First innings – Wall 40–12–70–1; a'Beckett 28–8–47–1; Grimmett 56.2–16–135–5; Hornibrook 41–7–94–1; McCabe 10–4–23–1.
Second innings – Wall 10–3–20–0; a'Beckett 11–4–19–0; Grimmett 17–3–33–1; Hornibrook 11.5–5–14–1; McCabe 2–1–1–0.

Toss won by Australia   UMPIRES W. Bestwick and T. W. Oates
Close of Play First day: Australia (1) 458-3 (Bradman 309, McCabe 12);
Second day: England (1) 212-5 (Hammond 61, Duckworth 0);
Third day: England (1) 242-5 (Hammond 73, Duckworth 15).

Fourth Ashes Test, 1934
Leeds, July 20, 21, 23, 24

Just as at Lord's rain came to damage the wicket and ruin Australia's chance of making an even fight of it, so in the Fourth Test match at Leeds did one of the shortest but heaviest rainstorms seen at a cricket match for years arrive just in time to rob Australia of victory and enable England to draw a game in which they were completely outplayed. Escaping defeat in the luckiest manner possible, the England team accomplished nothing in the match on which they could congratulate themselves. In their unavailing efforts to get together a side which balanced the selectors made further changes from those who had represented England at Manchester. A strained leg compelled Sutcliffe to stand down, Keeton of Nottinghamshire thus getting the opportunity of making his first appearance for his country; G. O. Allen and Clark were left out and Bowes and Mitchell of Derbyshire reintroduced. James Langridge and Nichols attended and it was decided not to include Langridge and to make Nichols – for the third time – twelfth man.

His good fortune in the matter of winning the toss again attended Wyatt and for the third consecutive game England enjoyed the advantage of batting first. Wyatt himself described the wicket as being like a feather-bed, whatever that may have meant. The assumption at the time was that it would be slow and easy. There was nothing in the way it played during the first day to suggest that it was otherwise, yet England, giving one of the worst displays of batting probably ever seen under similar conditions were all dismissed between twenty-five minutes to twelve and twenty-five minutes past five for a paltry total of 200. It can be said that O'Reilly, Grimmett and Chipperfield bowled very well, but nothing they accomplished with the ball was quite sufficient to account for the shocking exhibition of weak and hesitant batting given by the Englishmen. Even Walters, who with 44 made top score, did not, after Wall had been taken off at 30, show anything of the brilliance that characterised many of his strokes at Lord's and Manchester. Keeton made two good cuts and a square drive in scoring 25 out of 43 in fifty minutes and although, after Walters' dismissal at 85, Hammond and Hendren put on 50 in an hour none of the rest, equally with those who had gone before, played in form worthy of the occasion.

Before cricket ended, however, further surprises were in store for the crowd. Bowes and Hammond started the bowling for England and both Ponsford and Brown played them so easily that there seemed no reason to expect any pronounced success for the England attack up to half-past six. Bowes, however, changed ends and, coming on again at 37 from the Pavilion wicket, bowled Brown at 37 and two runs later sent back Oldfield and Woodfull in one over. Stumps were then pulled up, Bowes having sent down ten balls from the Pavilion end and dismissed three batsmen without conceding a run. Australia, therefore, finished the day 161 runs behind with seven men to be disposed of and the situation had thus completely changed. Those, however, were the last crumbs of comfort England were destined to enjoy in this disastrous match. Bradman joined Ponsford the next morning and not until ten minutes to six on Saturday evening did another wicket fall. Giving a great display of batting, the two famous Australian run-getters beat all previous partnership records in Test matches. They carried the score in five and a half hours to 427 before Ponsford, hooking a short ball from Verity, trod on his wicket, knocked the leg bail off and was out. Altogether their stand realised no fewer than 388 runs. They always scored at a good rate but, as usual with Australians, unless the bowling is exceptionally steady, pushed along very quickly after tea when, in an hour, 98 runs were put on. Up to lunchtime they scored 129 in two hours and twenty-five minutes and between lunch and tea 161 in two hours and five minutes.

Ponsford's innings was very good indeed. In the course of the partnership each batsman gave a chance, for Ponsford when 70 should have been caught by Mitchell at cover-point while Bradman at 71 was let off by Hopwood. Ponsford obtained many of his runs by late cuts and turning the ball to leg and all through his innings, which lasted six and a quarter hours and included 19 fours, he hit the ball hard and placed it well when scoring in front of the wicket. Moreover, his defence was rock-like in its steadiness and accuracy. For the greater part of the day Bradman, who unlike Ponsford obtained most of his runs in front of the stumps batted with the utmost certainty but during the last thirty-five minutes when he and McCabe were raising the score to 494 he played in a more light-hearted spirit. Twice he lifted the ball over the ring for six, and hit Hopwood for 15 runs in one over.

Australia, therefore, began the third day in a most comfortable position being 294 runs on with six wickets to fall and altogether Bradman and McCabe added 90 in an hour before McCabe was out. Thanks to some most effective bowling by Bowes Australia's innings was finished off in a hundred minutes, the last six wickets falling on Monday morning for 90 runs. Bradman, sixth out at 550, made his 304 in six hours and fifty-five minutes. Going in third wicket down, he took the leading part in adding 511 runs while as many more wickets fell. Not out on Saturday with 271 he was perhaps lucky in reaching 300 because when 280 he was missed at third slip by Verity. He did not play so well during the fifty minutes he was in on Monday morning as he had done previously but all the same his innings was a masterly affair. He hit the ball very hard and placed his strokes beautifully while until joined by McCabe on Saturday evening he rarely sent the ball into the air. He hit 2 sixes, 43 fours, 1 three, 15 twos and 87 singles.

Bowes was responsible for the Australian innings being wound up so quickly and in the end he came out with what was a really good record of six wickets for 142 runs. Yet on the Saturday when Ponsford and Bradman were scoring so readily Bowes, like the rest of the England bowlers, looked quite innocuous. His analysis was interesting enough to bear dissection. After going on at 37 on Friday he took three wickets for no runs. On Saturday he bowled over twenty-eight overs, did not take a wicket and had 81 runs hit from him while up to the time he dismissed Darling at 551 he took three wickets on Monday morning in nine overs and four balls for 25 runs. Verity was the only other man to get a wicket but his three cost him 113.

England went in again at one o'clock 384 runs behind so that the most they could hope for was a draw. Keeton fell just before lunch at 28 and afterwards Hammond played better than in any other Test match during the season. He was seeing the ball well, hitting it hard and accurately and seemed likely to put together an innings in his best style. With the total up to 70, however, a dreadful disaster occurred, for Hammond, responding to the call of Walters for a foolish run and then checking himself, lost his wicket. From that blow England did not recover. Walters left at 87 but by dint of very hard work and much watchful batting Hendren and Wyatt added 65 in rather less than two hours. During this stand Bradman, trying to stop the ball in the long field with his foot, strained his leg and had to retire. Hendren and Leyland, both entirely on the defensive, stayed together for the last fifty-five minutes and added 36, Hendren having been in for three hours and a quarter when stumps were pulled up. Coupled with the rain which fell on Tuesday this stand saved England but they began the last day with only 188 on the board and still wanting 196 to save the innings defeat. Heavy rain fell in the night and the wicket was very wet, while a further shower caused a delay soon after cricket had been resumed. Then Hendren was out at 190 and when Ames left at 213 the end seemed very near. Just before one o'clock a thunderstorm broke over the ground and, although it lasted only ten minutes, the downpour was so severe that no further cricket was possible. Not until six o'clock, however, was the decision to abandon the match arrived at. Not only the pitch but parts of the outfield and especially that in front of the Pavilion was, even then, far too wet for cricket to be proceeded with.

ENGLAND	First Innings		Second Innings	
C. F. Walters c and b Chipperfield	44	– b O'Reilly		45
W. W. Keeton c Oldfield b O'Reilly	25	– b Grimmett		12
W. R. Hammond b Wall	37	– run out		20
E. H. Hendren b Chipperfield	29	– lbw b O'Reilly		42
*R. E. S. Wyatt st Oldfield b Grimmett	19	– b Grimmett		44
M. Leyland lbw b O'Reilly	16	– not out		49
†L. E. G. Ames c Oldfield b Grimmett	9	– c Brown b Grimmett		8
J. L. Hopwood lbw b O'Reilly	8	– not out		2
H. Verity not out	2			
T. B. Mitchell st Oldfield b Grimmett	9			
W. E. Bowes c Ponsford b Grimmett	0			
L-b 2	2	B 1, l-b 6		7

1-43 2-85 3-135 4-135 5-168 6-170 **200** 1-28 2-70 3-87 4-152 5-190 6-213 (6 wickets) **229**
7-189 8-189 9-200 10-200

First innings – Wall 18–1–57–1; McCabe 4–2–3–0; Grimmett 30.4–11–57–4; O'Reilly 35–16–46–3; Chipperfield 18–6–35–2.
Second innings – Wall 14–5–36–0; McCabe 5–4–5–0; Grimmett 56.5–24–72–3; O'Reilly 51–25–88–2; Chipperfield 9–2–21–0.

AUSTRALIA	First Innings
W. A. Brown b Bowes	15
W. H. Ponsford hit wkt b Verity	181
†W. A. S. Oldfield c Ames b Bowes	0
*W. M. Woodfull b Bowes	0
D. G. Bradman b Bowes	304
S. J. McCabe b Bowes	27
L. S. Darling b Bowes	12
A. G. Chipperfield c Wyatt b Verity	1
C. V. Grimmett run out	15
W. J. O'Reilly not out	11
T. W. Wall lbw b Verity	1
B 8, l-b 9	17

1-37 2-39 3-39 4-427 5-517 6-550 **584**
7-551 8-557 9-574 10-584

First innings – Bowes 50–13–142–6; Hammond 29–5–82–0; Mitchell 23–1–117–0; Verity 46.5–15–113–3; Hopwood 30–7–93–0; Leyland 5–0–20–0.

Toss won by England UMPIRES A. Dolphin and J. Hardstaff, Sr.
Close of Play: First day: Australia (1) 39-3 (Ponsford 22);
Second day: Australia (1) 494-4 (Bradman 271, McCabe 18);
Third day: England (2) 188-4 (Hendren 42, Leyland 22).

Lord Hawke said: 'Pray God no professional will ever captain the England side. I love professionals, every one of them, but we have always had an amateur skipper. If the time comes when we are to have no more amateurs captaining England, well, I don't say England will become exactly like League football, but it will be a thousand pities, and it will not be for the good of the game'. Lord Hawke did not live to see Leonard Hutton, a Yorkshire professional, restore England's post-war cricket fortunes, nor to learn of the Knighthood Hutton received for his services to cricket. In the early years of his long reign as captain of Yorkshire (1883–1909) Lord Hawke was often helped by Louis Hall, a professional who at one time was termed assistant-captain and led Yorkshire throughout the summer of 1885 when Lord Hawke was away. I also wonder what Lord Hawke's reaction would have been to recent suggestions that the present time may be the twilight of the amateur.

Norman Preston, 1960

Fourth Ashes Test, 1938
Leeds, July 22, 23, 25

Australia's success enabled them to retain the Ashes. As a result of the fiasco at Manchester, this was actually the third meeting between the two countries and by general consent it was the most interesting of all the season's Test matches. A fine test of skill had many glorious moments, the cricket was often thrilling to watch, and the decision of the game about quarter past four on the third day confounded all expectations. In contrast to what occurred at Trent Bridge and Lord's, only 695 runs were scored in the match; on each side the captain made top score, Bradman registering yet another three-figure innings.

At no time was the wicket easy for batting and Australia won largely because they possessed bitter spin bowling. For O'Reilly, the match provided a big triumph, for he took five wickets in each innings for altogether 122 runs. Exactly why the pitch, even during the early stages of the game, played so queerly was hard to understand. A likely explanation was that it was kept on the damp side through moisture being drawn to the surface in the humid weather prevailing. At any rate bowlers were able to turn the ball and as the match progressed spin acted more quickly; by Monday the wicket had worn and O'Reilly took full advantage of this state of affairs.

The loss of the services of both Ames and Hutton, owing to injuries, formed a considerable handicap to the Englishmen and as P. A. Gibb, chosen as wicket-keeper in the team for the Manchester Test, also met with an accident on the field, Price, of Middlesex, took his place. The decision to omit Goddard from the England eleven suggested that the selectors, despite a long and careful examination of the wicket before the toss, had no suspicions that the conditions were likely to be more favorable to spin bowlers than to Farnes and Bowes, both of whom appeared in the eleven.

To see England's batsmen struggling for runs after Hammond, for the third successive match, won the toss was at once unexpected and perplexing. In the course of five hours, and despite a splendid effort by Hammond, the innings was over. The Australian bowling had far more accuracy about it than in the two previous Tests and from his first over O'Reilly puzzled the batsmen. Barnett, after offering two chances, was entirely responsible for Hardstaff being run out and although he batted through the two hours up to lunch, during which only 62 runs were scored, he looked strangely uncertain. Not until after the interval did Hammond attempt to change the character of the cricket and then, having hit a no-ball from McCormick for 6, he lost Barnett to a fine one-hand catch at the wicket. Barnett stayed nearly two hours and a half and his stand with Hammond realized 54. With Paynter batting steadily, as many runs came from the next wicket. How much Hammond dominated the cricket can be gathered from the fact that he scored 76 out of 108 and hit 10 fours. Another clever piece of wicket-keeping by B. A. Barnett began a minor collapse for after Paynter, losing his balance, was stumped, Compton, next over, was bowled and, with one added, Price left to a slip catch. Some brave hitting by Wright and Verity brought 41 runs for the eighth wicket but an effort by Farnes to follow the example was quickly stopped by Fingleton, who ran fully 20 yards to hold a skier, and England, after batting five hours, were out of 223.

When Wright, with the first ball be bowled in Australia's innings, got rid of Brown, B. A. Barnett was sent in to play out time with Fingleton and the outcome of this move far exceeded expectations. Barnett, indeed, played a most valuable innings and England bowled for nearly an hour and a half next morning before gaining further reward. The second wicket partnership yielded 59 and Fingleton batted in dogged style for over two hours; Barnett, who made his highest score in Test cricket, was in ten minutes longer. The attack of Farnes and Bowes after lunch was accurate and full of danger; McCabe and Badcock in turn were clean bowled and Australia's first five wickets fell for 145. The light at this time was none too good but Bradman, as in each of the two previous Tests, did not let the occasion pass without placing to his name another three-figure score – his twelfth of the tour. Although a beautiful length leg-break led to Hassett being caught at slip after helping to add 50, Waite stayed long enough to see Australia take an innings lead. Shielding his successive partners, Bradman astutely nursed the bowling and he made every possible run against high-class fielding. His stroke-play and his defence were alike admirable. Bowes, who rarely pitched short and made the ball swerve, had a great moment when he knocked Bradman's middle stump out of the ground. Only two runs were added after the Australian captain was eighth man out – he batted a few minutes less than three hours and hit 9 fours. In dismissing O'Reilly, Hammond made a grand catch, low down with his right hand, after moving quickly across from slip.

Bad light once interrupted this innings and when England went in 19 runs behind an appeal was upheld. Barnett and Edrich survived an awkward fifty minutes prior to close of play and they put 60 runs on the board before being separated next morning. This in fact was the most productive stand of the whole match. For the collapse which afterwards set in no one could have been prepared. O'Reilly, on a worn pitch, and ably supported by Fleetwood-Smith, finished off the innings before lunch-time, England's full ten wickets actually going down for the addition of 74 runs to the overnight score. Successive balls accounted for Hardstaff and Hammond, the latter being finely caught close in at short square-leg, and Compton had the ill-luck to be caught off his wrist. Paynter, after going in third wicket down, made a gallant effort and, not out, batted over an hour, but the sixth, seventh and eighth wickets all fell at 116, Fleetwood-Smith dismissing Verity and Wright with consecutive balls, a feat which O'Reilly performed at the expense of Farnes and Bowes. Except when he changed ends, O'Reilly bowled fifteen overs without a rest and he took five wickets for nine runs apiece. With six men on the leg side close to the bat, and with no-one in the long field, he demoralised the majority of the batsmen. Paynter's innings, in truth, was the one example of resolution and no-one was bold enough to attempt to wrest the initiative from the spin bowlers. England's 123 represented their lowest total against Australia for 17 years.

Left to get 105, Australia had to struggle hard for success. Farnes kept up a splendid attack but misfielding gave Australia valuable runs. Intense excitement came into the cricket when Wright, after going on at 48, quickly sent back Bradman and McCabe. With the first four batsmen in the order all out, Australia had to contend with atrocious light but the batsmen refrained from appealing and, as Hassett began to drive and pull in an easy, confident style, England's chance of turning the tables gradually slipped away. A storm threatened and Hassett, no doubt anxious to settle the match before the rain came, tried to drive a leg-break and skied the ball to point. His brave innings, however, in company with Badcock had carried the total to within 14 of victory and there were five wickets to fall. Rain interrupted the play with nine runs needed but Australia got home without further loss, making the required runs in an hour and fifty minutes. Wright puzzled the batsmen so much that he might have been a match-winner of England had the fourth innings task exceeded 150 runs. On this wicket responsive to spin, he certainly looked more dangerous than any other bowler on his side. The daily attendances were: Friday 23,925; Saturday 36,842; Monday 38,847; making a total of 99,614, of whom 75,614 paid. The receipts for the match amounted to over £14,189.

ENGLAND	First Innings		Second Innings	
W. J. Edrich b O'Reilly	12	– st Barnett b Fleetwood-Smith		28
C. J. Barnett c Barnett b McCormick	30	– c Barnett b McCormick		29
J. Hardstaff, Jr run out	4	– b O'Reilly		11
*W. R. Hammond b O'Reilly	76	– c Brown b O'Reilly		0
E. Paynter st Barnett b Fleetwood-Smith	28	– not out		21
D. C. S. Compton b O'Reilly	14	– c Barnett b O'Reilly		15
†W. F. F. Price c McCabe b O'Reilly	0	– lbw b Fleetwood-Smith		6
H. Verity not out	25	– b Fleetwood-Smith		0
D. V. P. Wright c Fingleton b Fleetwood-Smith	22	– c Waite b Fleetwood-Smith		0
K. Farnes c Fingleton b Fleetwood-Smith	2	– b O'Reilly		7
W. E. Bowes b O'Reilly	3	– lbw b O'Reilly		0
L-b 4, n-b 3	7	L-b 4, w 1, n-b 1		6

1-29 2-34 3-88 4-142 5-171 6-171   **223**   1-60 2-73 3-73 4-73 5-96 6-116   **123**
7-172 8-213 9-215 10-223   7-116 8-116 9-123 10-123

First innings – McCormick 20–6–46–1; Waite 18–7–31–0; O'Reilly 34.1–17–66–5;
Fleetwood-Smith 25–7–73–3; McCabe 1–1–0–0.
Second innings – McCormick 11–4–18–1; Waite 2–0–9–0; O'Reilly 21.5–8–56–5; Fleetwood-Smith 16–4–34–4.

AUSTRALIA	First Innings		Second Innings	
J. H. W. Fingleton b Verity	30	– lbw b Verity		9
W. A. Brown b Wright	22	– lbw b Farnes		9
†B. A. Barnett c Price b Farnes	57	– (7) not out		15
*D. G. Bradman b Bowes	103	– (3) c Verity b Wright		16
S. J. McCabe b Farnes	1	– (4) c Barnett b Wright		15
C. L. Badcock b Bowes	4	– not out		5
A. L. Hassett c Hammond b Wright	13	– (5) c Edrich b Wright		33
M. G. Waite c Price b Farnes	3			
W. J. O'Reilly c Hammond b Farnes	2			
E. L. McCormick b Bowes	0			
L. O. Fleetwood-Smith not out	2			
B 2, l-b 3	5	B 4, n-b 1		5

1-28 2-87 3-128 4-136 5-145 6-195   **242**   1-17 2-32 3-50 4-61 5-91   **(5 wickets) 107**
7-232 8-240 9-240 10-242

First innings – Farnes 26–3–77–4; Bowes 35.4–6–79–3; Wright 15–4–38–2; Verity 19–6–30–1; Edrich 3–0–13–0.
Second innings – Farnes 11.3–4–17–1; Bowes 11–0–35–0; Verity 5–2–24–1; Wright 5–0–26–3.

Toss won by England   UMPIRES F. Chester and E. J. Smith
Close of Play First day: Australia (1) 32-1 (Fingleton 9, Barnett 1);
Second day: England (2) 49-0 (Edrich 25, Barnett 20).

Second Victory Match, 1945
Sheffield, June 23, 25, 26

The finest match of the season, played on a natural wicket at the bomb-scarred Bramall Lane ground, was memorable for a wonderful hundred by Hammond on the opening day when the pitch was at its worst, and the successful bowling of Pope and Pollard, each making his first appearance for England. Hassett put in England on a drying wicket and events moved quickly. In the sixth over Sismey was struck on the chin by a rising ball from Cheetham which touched Hutton's pads and the wound required three stitches. Carmody deputised behind the wicket and performed splendidly. Though Washbrook cut and drove to fine purpose, five England wickets were down for 141, and the two slow bowlers, Pepper and Ellis, were really menacing when Pope joined Hammond. For a time Hammond, who needed all his resource to keep up even his own end, shielded Pope, and there was a rare battle of wits between Hammond and Pepper. Playing back almost the whole while, Hammond delayed his stroke until the last split second and managed to steer the turning ball off his wicket. He never neglected a scoring opportunity and hit two 6s and eight 4s. The stand yielded 107 in ninety minutes, runs coming freely in the latter stages when both men used their height to get to the tossed-up slows.

In the last half-hour on Saturday, Australia made 23 without loss, but on the Monday bowlers met with such success that Hutton with 46 was top scorer while twenty wickets fell for 314 runs. In the heavy northern atmosphere Pope bowled perfectly to his aggressive leg trap, Pollard (three catches), Robertson (one run out) and Wright (one great catch). Pope dismissed the Australian opening pair for 36, but the most damaging blow was a beautiful ball by Pollard which took Hassett's middle stump. Miller offered resistance until he attempted a foolish single when trying to pierce and drive back the closely set leg side. Carmody produced some nice strokes, but Hammond made two sharp chances at slip look ridiculously easy and the remaining Australians were unequal to the occasion, the last five wickets falling for 27.

So England gained a handsome lead of 139, which Hutton and Washbrook augmented with a stand of 56. During their association Miller sent down one remarkable over. Bowling short at a great speed, he rapped Hutton on the left forearm and struck Washbrook on the foot. Washbrook had scarcely recovered from this shock than a short bumper hit him on top of the head, and it was small wonder that he presented Sismey behind the stumps again – with a catch.

At the tea interval the score was 76 for two, and in less than an hour it changed to 122 for seven before stout and well-judged hitting by Griffith and Pollard produced 55, one run less than the best of the day by the England first pair.

The Bramall Lane pitch has a reputation for its staying powers, and when first thing on Tuesday Australia began their task of trying to get 330 in the last innings the conditions for batting were possibly better than at any time in the match. It was a cold morning, and this probably accounted for Hammond dropping Whitington, who was 7 and the score 19. Neither Whitington nor Workman looked comfortable, but both faced the bowling determinedly, even if streaky strokes off Pope and Pollard flew past the slips. The Australian pair made a splendid bid for victory and their stand of 108 was the highest of the match. In all, Workman defied the bowling for three and three-quarter hours. There remained Hassett and Miller, but both were bowled by almost unplayable balls, and Sismey suffered a similar fate, In avenging their defeat at Lord's, England played grand cricket, and the Australians also excelled in bowling and fielding. About 50,000 people were present during the three days, the receipts being £7,311.

England 286 (Hammond 100, Washbrook 63) **and 190; Australia 147** (Pope 5-58) **and 288** (Workman 63, Whitington 61). England won by 41 runs.

Fourth Ashes Test, 1948 – by Leslie Smith
Leeds, July 22, 23, 24, 26, 27

By the astonishing feat of scoring 404 for three wickets on the fifth day of the match when the pitch took spin, Australia won the rubber. Until that fatal last stage England were on top, but a succession of blunders prevented them gaining full reward for good work on the first four days.

The biggest mistake occurred before the game started, for the selectors decided to leave out Young, the slow left-arm bowler who had been invited to Leeds as one of the original party. Consequently England took the field with an unbalanced attack. Having only one slow bowler available, Yardley did not know what to do for the best on the last day, and he was forced to make Compton the spearhead and to employ Hutton, who to that point had bowled no more than 22 overs in the season. Even then England should have won. Evans, behind the wicket, fell a long way below his best form, and three catches were dropped in the field. Australia put together the biggest fourth innings total in a Test Match between the two countries in England; also the aggregate of 1,723 runs was the highest for any match in England.

Handicapped through injuries to Barnes and Tallon, the Australians were forced to make two changes, Harvey and Saggers appearing for the first time against England. The English selectors brought in Hutton, Cranston and Laker for Young, Dollery and Emmett; after being omitted from the original twelve, Emmett was unexpectedly called from Torquay, where he was playing for Gloucestershire in a friendly match, and made twelfth man. The explanation for this surprising move was never officially given, but it was understood that the selectors were worried in case anything unexpected should happen to one of their batsmen.

When Yardley won the toss for the third time in four matches, England gained first use of a perfect pitch. Without Barnes, Bradman did not place a fieldsman close in at forward short leg and the batsmen welcomed their freedom. After their disappointing starts together in the earlier games, Hutton and Washbrook gave England a great send-off with an opening stand of 168, their best partnership in any Test Match. Hutton completely justified his recall to the side and Washbrook successfully eliminated the dangerous high hook stroke which often caused his downfall in earlier Tests. He completed an almost faultless hundred out of 189 and fell in the last over of the day after batting five hours twenty minutes. His second stand with Edrich produced 100. Bedser, sent in to play the last four balls overnight, proved such an efficient stop-gap that the third successive century partnership resulted. For the second day running the

Australians met with no success before lunch, and the third wicket realised 155 before Bedser, who made his highest score in any Test, gave a return catch. Edrich left three runs later after batting five hours ten minutes. This quick fall of wickets revitalised the Australians and the England batting broke down badly. From a total of 423 for two, England were all out 496.

Hassett and Morris opened the Australian innings, but did not shape confidently. Morris left at 13, and next morning Pollard, in his first over, sent back Hassett and Bradman in three balls, making Australia 68 for three. Then 19-year-old Neil Harvey joined Miller, and, delivering a terrific onslaught on the England attack, they rescued Australia from their precarious position. In just over an hour and a half they put on 121 by glorious stroke-play. Loxton carried on the big hitting and, with Harvey, added 105 in ninety-five minutes. Harvey hit 17 fours while making 112 – his second successive Test century. Loxton's terrific driving brought 5 sixes and 9 fours. Yet despite this punishment England held the upper hand, for with eight wickets down Australia were 141 behind. Then occurred a similar experience to that at Lord's, where Australia's tail-end batsmen could not be dislodged. Johnston and an injured Toshack, who batted with the aid of a runner, in turn helped Lindwall with such success that the last two wickets added 103 and England's lead was restricted to 38.

Hutton and Washbrook opened with a century stand for the second time in the match and created a new world record for Test cricket in accomplishing the feat twice. Both left at 129, but England consolidated their position by rapid scoring. Edrich and Compton put on 103 at more than one a minute and, although a slight collapse followed, Evans, with help from Bedser and Laker, punished the bowling. At the close of the fourth day England led by 400 with two wickets left.

To most people Yardley's decision to continue batting for five minutes next day came as a surprise and the reason for it aroused plenty of comment. The main idea was to break up the pitch by the use of the heavy roller. Three runs were added in two overs, and then Yardley declared, leaving Australia to score 404 in 345 minutes. The pitch took spin and the ball lifted and turned sharply. Unfortunately, Laker was erratic in length. Compton, bowling his left-hand off-breaks and googlies, baffled the batsmen several times, but without luck. Evans should have stumped Morris when 32, and Compton only gained reward when he held a return catch from Hassett at 57, but he ought to have dismissed Bradman, Crapp dropping a catch at first slip. In half an hour before lunch Morris and Bradman put on 64, and after the interval, against a succession of full tosses and long hops, runs continued to flow. When 59 Bradman had another escape off Compton, and Yardley, in despair, called for the new ball even though the pitch favoured spin. Evans should have stumped Bradman when 108, and Laker at square leg dropped Morris when 126. Not until 301 had been put on did England break the stand, and by that time the match was as good as won. Morris batted four hours fifty minutes for 182. Miller did not last long, but Harvey made the winning stroke within fifteen minutes of time. No fewer than 66 fours were hit in the innings, 33 by Morris and 29 by Bradman.

The attendance figures of 158,000 created a record for any match in England. Receipts amounted to £34,000.

ENGLAND	First Innings		Second Innings	
L. Hutton b Lindwall	81	– c Bradman b Johnson	57	
C. Washbrook c Lindwall b Johnston	143	– c Harvey b Johnston	65	
W. J. Edrich c Morris b Johnson	111	– lbw b Lindwall	54	
A. V. Bedser c and b Johnson	79	– (9) c Hassett b Miller	17	
D. C. S. Compton c Saggers b Lindwall	23	– (4) c Miller b Johnston	66	
J. F. Crapp b Toshack	5	– (5) b Lindwall	18	
*N. W. D. Yardley b Miller	25	– (6) c Harvey b Johnston	7	
K. Cranston b Loxton	10	– (7) c Saggers b Johnston	0	
†T. G. Evans c Hassett b Loxton	3	– (8) not out	47	
J. C. Laker c Saggers b Loxton	4	– not out	15	
R. Pollard not out	0			
B 2, l-b 8, w 1, n-b 1	12	B 4, l-b 12, n-b 3	19	

1-168 2-268 3-423 4-426 5-447 6-473   496   1-129 2-129 3-232 4-260   (8 wickets, declared) 365
7-486 8-490 9-496 10-496   5-277 6-278 7-293 8-330

First innings – Lindwall 38–10–79–2; Miller 17.1–2–43–1; Johnston 38–12–86–1; Toshack 35–6–112–1;
Loxton 26–4–55–3; Johnson 33–9–89–2; Morris 5–0–20–0.
Second innings – Lindwall 26–6–84–2; Miller 21–5–53–1; Johnston 29–5–95–4; Loxton 10–2–29–0;
Johnson 21–2–85–1.

AUSTRALIA	First Innings		Second Innings	
A. R. Morris c Cranston b Bedser	6	– c Pollard b Yardley	182	
A. L. Hassett c Crapp b Pollard	13	– c and b Compton	17	
*D. G. Bradman b Pollard	33	– not out	173	
K. R. Miller c Edrich b Yardley	58	– lbw b Cranston	12	
R. N. Harvey b Laker	112	– not out	4	
S. J. E. Loxton b Yardley	93			
I. W. G. Johnson c Cranston b Laker	10			
R. R. Lindwall c Crapp b Bedser	77			
†R. A. Saggers st Evans b Laker	5			
W. A. Johnston c Edrich b Bedser	13			
E. R. H. Toshack not out	12			
B 9, l-b 14, n-b 3	26	B 6, l-b 9, n-b 1	16	

1-13 2-65 3-68 4-189 5-294 6-329   458   1-57 2-358 3-396   (3 wickets) 404
7-344 8-355 9-403 10-458

First innings – Bedser 31.2–4–92–3; Pollard 38–6–104–2; Cranston 14–1–51–0; Edrich 3–0–19–0;
Laker 30–8–113–3; Yardley 17–6–38–2; Compton 3–0–15–0.
Second innings – Bedser 21–2–56–0; Pollard 22–6–55–0; Laker 32–11–93–0; Compton 15–3–82–1;
Hutton 4–1–30–0; Yardley 13–1–44–1; Cranston 7.1–0–28–1.

Toss won by England   UMPIRES H. G. Baldwin and F. Chester
Close of Play First day: England (1) 268-2 (Edrich 41, Bedser 0);
Second day: Australia (1) 63-1 (Hassett 13, Bradman 31);
Third day: Australia (1) 457-9 (Lindwall 76, Toshack 12);
Fourth day: England (2) 362-8 (Evans 47, Laker 14).

Third Ashes Test, 1961 – by Norman Preston
Leeds, July 6, 7, 8

This will be remembered as Trueman's Match. Two devastating spells by him caused Australia to collapse. The first occurred immediately after tea on the first day when Australia had reached 183 for two wickets. Then, in the course of six overs, he dismissed five men for 16 runs. His figures were even more remarkable when he came on at 3.40 p.m. on Saturday with Australia 98 for two. At once he conceded a single to O'Neill before he again claimed five wickets, this time in 24 deliveries, for 0. Trueman finished the match with eleven wickets for 88 runs, easily his best in Test cricket.

The game will also be remembered for the controversy over the state of the pitch. In the previous Test the Lord's ridge loaded the dice in favour of the bowlers. This time the batsmen were at the mercy of the bowlers on a whitish-green piebald surface. It had been chemically treated only a few weeks before the contest and never played true although it did not carry the same physical danger to the batsmen as the one at Lord's. The main trouble was that no one could judge how the ball would behave. Sometimes it came through fast and low; at other times it would check in the broken soft places and stand up so that the batsmen had almost completed their strokes before establishing contact. It favoured all types of bowlers and Trueman came out triumphant. Consequently, England inflicted the first defeat of the tour on the Australians and made the series all square with two Tests to play by taking revenge for their defeat at Lord's.

Compared with Lord's, both sides were under new management. Peter May took over the England captaincy from Colin Cowdrey – leader and winner of the toss in nine consecutive matches – and Richie Benaud considered himself fit enough to return to the Australian side so that Neil Harvey was relieved of the captaincy after one successful campaign. Whereas at Lord's it seemed that the loss of Benaud would be a calamity for Australia – and everyone was proved wrong – England entered this match without Statham suffering from a strain. That appeared to be a crippling blow, but not for the first time the selectors sought a player of experience to face Australia and in Leslie Jackson, the 40-year-old Derbyshire opening bowler, they found the man they wanted. England left out D. B. Close from their final twelve and Benaud was presumed to have gained Australia a big advantage when he won the toss, thus breaking England's sequence of twelve successful tosses.

Jackson soon proved he was worthy of his place. He bowled throughout the first hour from the pavilion end during which Lawry and McDonald scored 33 from twenty overs. Jackson also put in another spell of an hour after lunch, but meanwhile England had broken the opening stand ten minutes before the lunch interval when Lawry was leg before to Lock, having offered no proper stroke. He seemed to lose sight of the ball. At the interval Australia had every reason to be satisfied with their score of 77 for one wicket. McDonald had been at the crease for three hours when Lock bowled for the first time at the Kirkstall Lane end and produced a leg-break which left him stranded down the pitch. Meanwhile, Harvey had become firmly settled. Quick on his feet he drove cleanly and anything short was pulled vigorously. O'Neill helped him to put on 50 in less than an hour so that by tea Australia reached 183 for two off 87 overs; Harvey 66, O'Neill 27.

Then came the transformation. Jackson promptly took the new ball at the pavilion end and Harvey square-cut his first delivery for 4. O'Neill faced Trueman and from the Yorkshireman's first ball he was splendidly caught low in the gully by Cowdrey, the stand having yielded 74 in seventy minutes. Nine minutes later, Harvey also left, beautifully caught off Trueman by Lock at backward short-leg. Apart from Davidson no other Australian offered much resistance. Jackson snapped up Burge and MacKay and in successive overs Trueman, bowling with his long run and at his fastest through the air, removed Simpson, Benaud (first ball) and Grout before Allen relieved the tiring Jackson and finished the innings by taking McKenzie's off-stump.

Undoubtedly it was this inspired spell by Trueman on the first day which really decided the match. In ninety minutes after tea England captured the remaining eight Australian wickets for the addition of only 54 runs to the interval score. Friday belonged to the England batsman. Overnight Pullar and Subba Row had made nine together and they took their stand to 54 in eighty-five minutes before Davidson, coming on for the second time at the pavilion end with a shortened run, dismissed the Northamptonshire captain, leg before. There followed the biggest stand of his low-scoring match. Cowdrey was at his best for the only time in this series and he and Pullar added 86 in five minutes under two hours before Pullar played a slow, highly flighted ball from Benaud via his pad on to his stumps. It was the first ball sent down by Benaud in his second spell. Pullar batted three hours and twenty minutes – care being essential on such a difficult pitch.

Whereas most of the Australian batsmen had been at fault in their timing by playing too soon, the England players, until Dexter arrived, effectively used the dead bat. Most of them avoided the drive which was fatal, but May signalled his arrival with a beauty off McKenzie past extra cover. At one period when Davidson and Benaud shared the attack Cowdrey and May did not score for twenty minutes. Still England were 176 for two at tea; Cowdrey 68, May 16.

Australia did not take the new ball until the 94th over and then Davidson promptly induced a return catch from May who had spent eighty-nine minutes over 26 – clear evidence of the troubles which beset the batsmen. Dexter had an uncomfortable time against Davidson and Benaud, but he struggled along for nearly an hour before he lost Cowdrey who had proved safe for four and a quarter hours. His was the innings of a master. Cowdrey hit 11 fours and was trying to sweep a loose ball when it rose and touched his glove. Thereupon Dexter and Barrington carried through the remaining half hour, Barrington giving England the lead by hitting Benaud to the fine-leg boundary.

England resumed on Saturday morning four runs ahead with six wickets standing. They had fought with great tenacity but Dexter, Barrington and Murray rather overdid their caution on this third day. The first half hour yielded only a single against Davidson (leg-cutters) and Benaud. The two ace Australian bowlers sent down eleven successive maiden overs, but for all his patience Dexter was bowled leg-stump, having occupied over two hours for 28. Trueman tried to take the offensive but after one powerful drive, Burge held him in the same over on the boundary. Australia were on top, but Lock launched a severe attack on Benaud while Murray offered the dead bat to Davidson. In seventeen glorious minutes Lock smote Benaud seven times to the boundary, scoring 30 off the Australian captain in three overs. The ball went in all directions but only one four over slip was the outcome of a false stroke. It was impossible to set a field to quieten him.

McKenzie returned and trapped Lock leg-before with his second ball; Murray played on when retreating and after Jackson had twice straight-driven McKenzie fiercely to the boundary, McKenzie ran him out from cover in the next over. Australia had exceeded expectations in taking the last six England wickets in eighty-five minutes for the addition of only 61 to the overnight total. Davidson's analysis during this period was 14-11-9-3 and he finished with five for 63 – similar figures to his performance in the first innings at Lord's where he took five for 42.

England appeared to have missed their chance; their lead was no more than 62 and they had to face the fourth innings. Jackson, at once, brought fresh hope for his fifth ball flattened McDonald's leg stump. Harvey again played superbly. Like Cowdrey, he showed his class by keeping his head down and never committing himself too soon to a stroke. May varied his bowling, trying to find the right combination, but had the mortification of dropping Harvey in the gully off Trueman when the left-hander was 10.

Allen's first ball of the innings at 49 proved a winner. It whipped across for Lawry to edge into Murray's gloves, but Australia progressed satisfactorily when O'Neill joined Harvey. The arrears were cleared without further loss and then at 98 Trueman returned. He began with his full run and his third ball found Harvey playing too soon. Dexter had to wait for the ball to fall into his hands at cover. That was the beginning of the procession already described. The secret of Trueman's success in this spell was that after Harvey left, May advised him to bowl off-cutters off his shorter run to a tight leg-trap. By this method Trueman compelled the batsmen to play at every ball. He bowled Benaud for a pair and in thirty-five minutes to tea the score changed to 109 for eight wickets. Afterwards, Jackson held a return catch from Grout and Cowdrey gained Trueman his sixth wicket by diving to his left and holding Davidson at second slip – another brilliant catch. Trueman's exact analysis from the moment he went on at 98 read 7.5-4-5-6.

Already sixteen wickets had fallen in four and a quarter hours during this amazing day's cricket when just after five o'clock Pullar and Subba Row began the final task of knocking off the 59 runs England needed for victory.

After Australia's downfall, England took no liberties. Davidson upset Subba Row's leg stump at 14, but Pullar and Cowdrey shaped confidently. With forty minutes left before the close England were within 20 of their objective when Cowdrey drove Benaud straight for the only 6 of the match. Cowdrey left with only 14 needed and May, whose inspiring captaincy had done so much, was at the crease when at 6.17 p.m. Pullar off-drove Benaud for the winning hit. During the three days nearly 75,000 people were present and the receipts came to £27,723.

Australia 237 (McDonald 54, Harvey 73, Trueman 5-58) **and 120** (Harvey 53, Trueman 6-30); **England 299** (Cowdrey 93, Pullar 53, Davidson 5-63) **and 62-2.**
England won by eight wickets.

Fourth Ashes Test, 1972 – by W. E. Bowes
Leeds, July 27, 28, 29

England won at three minutes past five on the third day, to take a two-one lead in the series and so retain the Ashes no matter what happened in the Fifth Test at The Oval. A pitch that afforded considerable help to the spin bowlers found batsmen in both teams unable to cope and the Australian cricketers – the less practised against a turning ball – were completely outplayed, as they were on the same ground in 1956 and again in 1961.

Not for a moment would one suggest that conditions had been deliberately engineered to produce such a result, but the fact remained, that they were conditions least likely to help the tourists and one recalled that when the Headingley ground was granted regular Test match status alongside Lord's and The Oval, the Yorkshire club, through their chairman, Mr A. B. Sellers, had to give an assurance that the pitch would be up to Test-match standard. That cannot be claimed for the pitch prepared for this game even allowing for the fact that Underwood is the most skilful bowler in the world when there is help for finger spin. It was without pace, took spin from the first day and grew progressively helpful.

Both teams made three changes. For England, Old and M. J. Smith (Middlesex) were dropped from the party of thirteen chosen and the changes were Fletcher, Underwood and Arnold for M. J. K. Smith, Gifford and Lever, who played at Trent Bridge. Australia had their off-spin bowler, Mallett, for Gleeson, Sheahan for Francis as a batsman, and the slow left-arm bowler and batsman, Inverarity, for the fast-medium bowler-batsman, Colley. They were changes influenced by a quite evident distrust of the pitch which had been flooded by a freak thunderstorm over the weekend. That flood had prevented some use of the heavy roller, and the pitch was obviously damp on the first morning and quite grassless. Australia, on winning the toss, had the lightest of rollers put on the pitch and were no doubt pleased to bat first.

Edwards, after his 170 not out at Nottingham, opened the innings with Stackpole and the latter made an excellent start with a leg-glance and a drive for two boundaries in the first over from Arnold. Snow also made a great start, getting Edwards caught at the wicket when he touched a late out-swinger in the first over. Snow bowled well. Time and again he beat the bat and when he was rested with the score at 31 for one wicket he had sent down seven overs for six runs and one wicket. Arnold, with the score at 32, had Stackpole (21) dropped by Fletcher in the slips. Greig replaced Snow and Arnold was rested after bowling nine overs for 27 runs.

Illingworth came on to bowl and, after he had delivered three overs, Underwood bowled. Spin bowlers on the first morning of a Test match? Illingworth had obviously read the signs aright. Although there was no indication of the havoc to be caused by spin when Australia came in to lunch with a score of 79 for one wicket things began to happen immediately after the interval. Underwood was brought into immediate attack. He shouted for lbw against Stackpole second ball and then, fifth ball, Stackpole played forward and edged a second catch to Knott. Greg Chappell joined his brother and although Snow was used for five overs at the other end it seemed obvious that the spin of Underwood was posing more problems than Snow's speed.

Illingworth took over from Snow and Australia's troubles increased most seriously. Ian Chappell, after he had batted 46 overs, had scored only 26 runs; Greg Chappell seemed to express all the feelings of the tourists when he hit a ball rather uppishly from Underwood towards mid-off which he had intended to go along the ground. He moved down the pitch and gave the spot where the ball had dropped a sledgehammer blow with the bat. He left at 93 when he missed a straight delivery from Underwood and was lbw. In the next over Ian Chappell went out to drive Illingworth and hit a low return catch. The score went to 97 for five when Walters, trying to cut an off-break, was bowled by Illingworth.

Sheahan fell to a spectacular one-handed catch by Illingworth at point off Underwood without scoring and the England captain made a third catch when Marsh tried a huge cross-bat swing at Underwood and skied to mid-on. Sensationally, Australia had slumped to 98 for seven wickets and the crowd of 19,000 almost ironically applauded the 100 in the 62nd over, after three and a half hours. Inverarity and Mallett kept England waiting eighty minutes for the next success and added 47 valuable runs, but Massie and Lillee both failed to score and Australia totalled only 146. In an hour's batting at the end of the day Edrich and Luckhurst made 43 without loss.

On the second day the off-spinner Mallett bowled at Underwood's pace and the left-arm slow Inverarity at Illingworth's pace. They returned some of the spin bowling problems to England. By lunch-time England had lost six wickets for 112 runs. Seven went with the fall of Greig at 128 and only an eighth-wicket stand of 104 by Illingworth and Snow swung the game again in favour of England. Illingworth played a real captain's part by scoring 54 not out in England's total of 252 for nine by Friday evening. In the context of the game Illingworth played superbly. In terms of Test cricket as an exhibition of all that is best in the game it need only be said that his innings occupied four and a half hours. It would be poor watching if this was always the only successful method.

As expected, the Australian second innings disintegrated before the bowling of Underwood. After the initial opening of the fast bowlers (in which Arnold dismissed Edwards for a pair), Underwood took five wickets for 18 runs in 13 overs and ripped through the heart of Australia's batting. It seemed that the game would be over by tea, but fortunately for the crowd of 20,000 Sheahan and Massie were mostly instrumental in continuing the Australian innings until that time, though England needed no more than 20 runs to win. These were made in thirty-eight minutes for the loss of Edrich in Lillee's third over. Underwood, perhaps the world's best bowler on a helpful pitch, snatched 10 wickets for 82 runs in the match. Batting on both sides was flimsy.

The total attendance over the three days was 62,000, and the full receipts for the five days £41,091.

Australia 146 (Stackpole 52) **and 136** (Underwood 6-45);
England 263 (Illingworth 57, Mallett 5-114) **and 21-1**. England won by nine wickets.

Notes by the Editor – Norman Preston, 1973

Freak storms from the Continent swept up over the South Coast a week before the Headingley Test and one of these flooded the Headingley ground at the weekend prior to the match. Consequently, the pitch was a slow turner which angered the Australians. The Pitches Committee of the TCCB cleared George Cawthray, the groundsman of any blame for the condition of the pitch. Fuserium disease which spread while the covers were on during the deluge killed much of the grass before Cawthray and his staff had an opportunity to treat it. It was established that mowing was in no way to blame.

Third Ashes Test, 1975 – by Norman Preston
Leeds, August 14, 15, 16, 18, 19

Abandoned as a draw after vandals had sabotaged the pitch in the early hours of Tuesday – the fifth day. The perpetrators got under the covers at the pavilion end and dug out holes with knives near the popping crease and poured a gallon of crude oil in the region where a good length ball would have pitched.

They made certain that millions of people in England and in Australia would be deprived of the enjoyment of what promised to be a truly great day's cricket. As it happened, rain set in at mid-day and would have washed out the proceedings in any case. There had been a night-guard of one solitary policeman and following this outrage it was obvious that in future much greater vigilance would be necessary to ensure that cricket grounds and particularly pitches, should receive better protection. The captains, Greig and Ian Chappell, looked at other parts of the square but could not find a suitable alternative pitch on which to continue the match, nor could the authorities find any way to arrange another match so late in the season and when most of the Australians were committed to return home immediately after The Oval Test.

During the four days when cricket did take place there were many exciting moments and much splendid play. On three of the four days the gates were closed, but rain at breakfast time on Saturday kept the attendance down that day to 14,000. Full attendance was 75,000 with receipts £54,466.

England 288 (Steele 73, Edrich 62, Greig 51, Gilmour 6-85) **and 291** (Steele 92);
Australia 135 (Edmonds 5-28) **and 220-3** (McCosker 95 not out, Chappell I, 62).
Match abandoned as a draw.

Third Ashes Test, 1981 – by Alan Lee
Leeds, July 16, 17, 18, 20, 21

A match which had initially produced all the wet and tedious traits of recent Leeds Tests finally ended in a way to stretch the bounds of logic and belief. England's victory, achieved under the gaze of a spellbound nation, was the first this century by a team following on, and only the second such result in the history of Test cricket.

The transformation occurred in less than 24 hours, after England had appeared likely to suffer their second four-day defeat of the series. Wherever one looked, there were personal dramas: Brearley, returning as captain like England's saviour; Botham, who was named Man of the Match, brilliant once more in his first game back in the ranks; Willis, whose career has so often heard the distant drums, producing the most staggering bowling of his life when his place again seemed threatened.

Others, too, had good reason to remember this game. It was the first time in nineteen Tests that Willey had been a member of a victorious side, there were wicket-keeping records for both Taylor (all first-class cricket) and Marsh (Tests). Dyson made his maiden century for Australia, and Lillee moved further up the list of bowling immortals. But if the statisticians revelled in such facts, they were, for most of us, submerged in the tension of a climax as near to miraculous as a Test ever can have been. None of this had seemed remotely likely on the opening day when the familiar slate-grey clouds engulfed the chimneys which stretch away from the Kirkstall Lane End. Australia, one up in the series, were unchanged; England made two changes. Woolmer standing down for Brearley and Old returning on his home ground at the expense of Emburey. England thus went in with four seamers and only Willey to provide a measure of spin. It was a selectorial policy which caused considerable discussion. Brearley later confessed he lost sleep on the first night for fear that it had been a mistake. As things transpired, however, it was largely irrelevant.

Australia, having chosen to bat, ended the first day in fine health at 203 for three, the extra hour having reduced lost time to only fifty minutes. Dyson batted diligently for his century, playing chiefly off the back foot, and survived one chance, to Botham in the gully, when 57. Chappell, who supported Dyson staunchly in a stand of 94 for the second wicket, was twice reprieved – by Gower and Botham again – so England, not for the first time this summer, suffered for their ineptitude in the field. The other talking-point of the day concerned Headingley's new electronic scoreboard, which had a mixed reception, being difficult to see from most parts of the ground when the sun began to sink.

It will come as a surprise when, in future years, people look back on a Test of such apparently outrageous drama, to know that the second day was pedestrian in the extreme. Botham, to some degree, salvaged English pride by taking five more wickets, all of them in an after-tea spell costing 35 runs, and finishing with six for 95. Naturally, the assumption was drawn that he is a more effective player without leadership duties. Despite his efforts, Australia extended their score to 401 for nine, thanks to half-centuries from Hughes and Yallop. It was another day of patchy weather and patchy cricket, completed when Gooch and Boycott saw out an over apiece from Lillee and Alderman without mishap.

At this stage, the odds seemed in favour of a draw. An England win was on offer generously, though by no means as extravagantly as 24 hours later when Ladbrokes, from their tent on the ground, posted it at 500 to 1. The reason for their estimate was a truncated day on which England were dismissed for 174 and, following on 227 behind, lost Gooch without addition. Australia's seamers had shown what could be done by bowling straighter and to a fuller length than their counterparts. Other than Botham, who opted for all-out aggression and profited by a swift 50, England at no stage commanded and were occasionally undone by deliveries performing contortions at speed. Botham fell victim to just such a ball from Lillee and the catch by Marsh was his 264th in Tests, beating Knott's record.

The third day ended with unhappy scenes similar to those seen at Lord's, when spectators hurled cushions and abuse at the umpires. On this occasion, Messrs Meyer and Evans had walked to the middle, wearing blazers, at five to six, after a lengthy stoppage for poor light. They consulted their meters and summoned the covers, abandoning play just before the hour. With cruel irony, the light improved instantly, the sun was soon breaking through and the large crowd was incited to wrathful demands for explanations as to why they were not watching the prescribed extra hour. Once more, it seems, confusion in interpretation of the playing regulations was the cause of the ill feeling: they stated only that conditions must be fit for play at the scheduled time of finish and not, as the umpires thought, that play must actually be in motion. Whether it was, in fact, fit at six o'clock is open to doubt, but the TCCB soon adjusted the ruling so that play in future Tests in the series could restart at any stage of the extra hour. This heated diversion seemed likely to achieve nothing more than a stay of sentence for England, a view which appeared amply confirmed by late afternoon on the Monday. England were then 135 for seven, still 92 behind, and the distant objective of avoiding an innings defeat surely their only available prize. Lillee and Alderman had continued where Saturday's disturbances had forced them to leave off, and for all Boycott's skilful resistance, the cause seemed lost. Boycott, who batted three and a half hours, was sixth out to an lbw decision he seemed not to relish, and when Taylor followed quickly, the England players' decision to check out of their hotel seemed a sound move. Three hours later, the registration desks around Leeds were coping with a flood of re-bookings, Botham having destroyed the game's apparently set course with an astonishing, unbeaten 145, ably and forcefully aided by Dilley. Together, they added 117 in 80 minutes for the eighth wicket, only 7 short of an England record against Australia. Both struck the ball so cleanly and vigorously that Hughes's men were temporarily in disarray; when Dilley departed after scoring 56 precious runs, Old arrived to add 67 more with Botham, who still had Willis as a partner at the close, with England 124 ahead.

Botham advanced his unforgettable innings to 149 not out before losing Willis the next morning, but Australia, needing 130, still remained clear favourites. Then, at 56 for one, Willis, having changed ends to bowl with the wind, dismissed Chappell with a rearing delivery and the staggering turnabout was under way. Willis bowled as if inspired. It is not uncommon to see him perform for England as if his very life depended on it, but this was something unique. In all, he took eight wickets for 43, the best of his career, as Australia's last nine wickets tumbled for 55 runs despite a stand of 35 in four overs between Bright and Lillee. Old bowled straight and aggressively and England rose to the need to produce an outstanding show in the field. Yet this was Willis's hour, watched or listened to by a vast invisible audience. At the end, the crowd gathered to wave their Union Jacks and chant patriotically, eight days in advance of the Royal Wedding. Takings were £206,500 and the attendance 52,566.

AUSTRALIA	First Innings		Second Innings	
J. Dyson b Dilley	102	– (2) c Taylor b Willis		34
G. M. Wood lbw b Botham	34	– (1) c Taylor b Botham		10
T. M. Chappell c Taylor b Willey	27	– c Taylor b Willis		8
*K. J. Hughes c and b Botham	89	– c Botham b Willis		0
R. J. Bright b Dilley	7	– (8) b Willis		19
G. N. Yallop c Taylor b Botham	58	– (5) c Gatting b Willis		0
A. R. Border lbw b Botham	8	– (6) b Old		0
†R. W. Marsh b Botham	28	– (7) c Dilley b Willis		4
G. F. Lawson c Taylor b Botham	13	– c Taylor b Willis		1
D. K. Lillee not out	3	– c Gatting b Willis		17
T. M. Alderman not out	0	– not out		0
B 4, l-b 13, w 3, n-b 12	32	L-b 3, w 1, n-b 14		18

1-55 2-149 3-196 4-220   (9 wickets, declared) 401   1-13 2-56 3-58 4-58 5-65 6-68   111
5-332 6-354 7-357 8-396 9-401   7-74 8-75 9-110 10-111

First innings – Willis 30–8–72–0; Old 43–14–91–0; Dilley 27–4–78–2; Botham 39.2–11–95–6; Willey 13–2–31–1; Boycott 3–2–2–0.
Second innings – Botham 7–3–14–1; Dilley 2–0–11–0; Willis 15.1–3–43–8; Old 9–1–21–1; Willey 3–1–4–0.

ENGLAND	First Innings		Second Innings	
G. A. Gooch lbw b Alderman	2	– c Alderman b Lillee		0
G. Boycott b Lawson	12	– lbw b Alderman		46
*J. M. Brearley c Marsh b Alderman	10	– c Alderman b Lillee		14
D. I. Gower c Marsh b Lawson	24	– c Border b Alderman		9
M. W. Gatting lbw b Lillee	15	– lbw b Alderman		1
P. Willey b Lawson	8	– c Dyson b Lillee		33
I. T. Botham c Marsh b Lillee	50	– not out		149
†R. W. Taylor c Marsh b Lillee	5	– c Bright b Alderman		1
G. R. Dilley c and b Lillee	13	– b Alderman		56
C. M. Old c Border b Alderman	0	– b Lawson		29
R. G. D. Willis not out	1	– c Border b Alderman		2
B 6, l-b 11, w 6, n-b 11	34	B 5, l-b 3, w 3, n-b 5		16

1-12 2-40 3-42 4-84 5-87 6-112   174   1-0 2-18 3-37 4-41 5-105 6-133   356
7-148 8-166 9-167 10-174   7-135 8-252 9-319 10-356

First innings – Lillee 18.5–7–49–4; Alderman 19–4–59–3; Lawson 13–3–32–3.
Second innings – Lillee 25–6–94–3; Alderman 35.3–6–135–6; Lawson 23–4–96–1; Bright 4–0–15–0.

Toss won by Australia   UMPIRES D. G. L. Evans and B. J. Meyer
Close of Play First day: Australia (1) 203-3 (Hughes 24, Bright 1);
Second day: England (1) 7-0 (Gooch 2, Boycott 0);
Third day: England (2) 6-1 (Boycott 0, Brearley 4);
Fourth day: England (2) 351-9 (Botham 145, Willis 1).   Man of the Match I. T. Botham

Fourth Ashes Test, 2001 – by Jim Holden
Leeds, 16, 17, 18, 19, 20

Few cricketers play a Test innings that will become an Ashes legend. Mark Butcher joined this elite when he struck an exhilarating 173 not out to ensure single-handedly that there would be no 'greenwash', and show that, for a day at least, McGrath, Gillespie and Warne could be tamed.

Butcher's score matched that of Don Bradman in 1948, when Australia made 404 for three here on the last day to win against the odds. But the immediate comparison was with Ian Botham's 149 not out in 1981, when his hitting transformed not only a match but a whole summer, and a whole sport. Butcher's knock was not as important as that. A fairer parallel would be the fabled 1902 innings of Gilbert Jessop, whose attacking shots and endless verve inspired a remarkable Test victory no one thought possible. As here, it was England's only win of the series.

Butcher's innings, entirely out of character with the rest of a one-sided Ashes contest, was Jessopian in vein: he cut anything short of a length with exquisite power and timing, stepped forward to drive McGrath through the covers, and clipped sweet boundaries off his legs when the bowlers erred in line. The Australians could not contain him and, though it was the only such day of the summer, his innings will never be forgotten. Australia's stand-in captain, Gilchrist, had not thought anything like it possible when he closed his team's second innings on the fourth evening with a lead of 314 runs and 110 overs still to play. Rain had seriously disrupted his game plan, taking maybe two sessions of Australian batting time. But Gilchrist's decision spoke volumes for the tourists' aura of invincibility, and their desire to win the series 5-0. Few in England gave the home side hope of victory either: only once, at Melbourne in 1928-29, had England scored as many in the fourth innings to win. Yet, by conventional cricketing logic, the target was attainable even after bad light and further rain removed 17.3 overs that Sunday evening, revising England's task to 311 from 90 overs.

When openers Atherton and Trescothick fell cheaply on the fifth morning, it seemed that a routine humbling of the English batting would occur. Butcher's early overs were spent evading a wonderful spell from McGrath - but, at 60 for two, restored England captain Hussain hooked Gillespie out of the ground. Many thought this the turning-point, not for the bravura shot itself but for the fact that the ball was lost. Its replacement didn't help the bowlers as much and, on a pitch that was never the minefield predicted, batting became less of an ordeal.

Still, it needed a miraculous performance, and Butcher, whose technique had been modified the previous winter with help from his father, Alan, produced it. He was particularly severe in the overs just after lunch, when it dawned on the capacity crowd that they were witnessing an epic day of cricket. Butcher reached his hundred to a seemingly endless ovation, and when Hussain went, England's sole loss in a session worth 104, their partnership had added 181. McGrath and Warne had one last attempt

June 1939: Hedley Verity, the beautiful action of a bewitching bowler, whose balance, scrupulous length and pensive variety 'all proclaimed the master'.

Roy Kilner, a notable exponent of the game and a man of rare charm, who was self-effacing about his own talents. The donkey seems a key member of the groundstaff.

Percy Holmes, left, and Herbert Sutcliffe after the world record opening stand against Essex at Leyton in 1934. Wisden's rather low-key verdict was that the pair made their runs in 'admirable style'.

Right F. S. Jackson, so much more than a mere cricketer. He was the true allrounder – batsman, bowler, MP, soldier, writer, Governor of Bengal, Knight and the survivor of an assassin's bullet.

Below left (on left) Emmott Robinson, who was said to be the personification of Yorkshire cricket – and 'as Yorkshire as Ilkley Moor or Pudsey.'

Below right Darren Lehmann, always a 'delight to watch' said *Wisden*, who described his swashbuckling style as 'a Compton or a Miller, rather than a Boycott or a Lawry.'

Above Dickie Bird, the most famous of all umpires of whom it was claimed: 'His huge appeal was based on his personal vulnerability. He was a magnet for minor disasters.'

Left Wearing the white rose: Sachin Tendulkar – against Nottinghamshire in the Benson and Hedges Cup at Headingley – is seen in the first bloom of his brilliant career. Aged 19, he became Yorkshire's first overseas player in 1992.

Opposite 15 August 1995: Michael Vaughan, who retired as the most successful captain in England's history – 26 wins from 51 Tests.

G. HIRST.
(YORKSHIRE.)

Left George Hirst, reckoned to be the epitome of Yorkshire cricket – 'he was the happy warrior that every Yorkshire cricketing knight-at-arms would wish to be.'

Below 1 September 1905. Three wise men: George Hirst, Wilfred Rhodes and Schofield Haigh. Rhodes' career, said Neville Cardus, reads 'like a fairytale'; Haigh could produce an off-break that was 'almost unplayable'.

Above 6 May 1948: Johnny Wardle, who *Wisden* reproached for his behaviour by claiming that 'on the field and in the dressing room' it 'left much to be desired.'

Left 1 Jan 1935: Maurice Leyland, described by the master wordsmith R. C. Robertson-Glasgow as 'the salvage-expert among batsmen' – someone who thrived on 'rescue, storm and violent enemies.'

Above Donald Bradman at Leeds, 1934. So successful at Headingley that Yorkshire eventually made him an honorary life member of the club, which in turn made him an honorary Yorkshireman. He scored 963 runs in six Test innings on the ground. Here, he returns to the pavilion after his 304 in 1934.

Left Major Booth: Plum Warner applauded his 'puzzling flight' and his supreme knack of making the ball 'swerve away at the last moment.'

to turn the screw, bowling with economy and menace, but, thanks to the generous declaration, Butcher could afford to be patient.

After tea the outcome was not in doubt. Ramprakash succumbed within sight of the finishing line, leaving Butcher to complete the task. He carved Gillespie for a crackerjack six behind point in an over that brought 19 runs. Finally, he steered Warne away for three and England were home with 20 overs to spare. At their rate of scoring they could have chased 400 and still won, illustrating the extraordinary nature of Butcher's innings, and its entertainment value. He batted five and a quarter hours, faced 227 balls, and hit 23 fours as well as that six. Gilchrist and all the Australian players shook the English hero's hand. Their sportsmanship was welcome, and genuine. Even though they had dominated the first four days and were superior in class and attitude, their smiles were not forced. On the first day, they had opted to bat after winning the toss and scorched to 288 for four. It may not sound much, but rain had delayed the start until 2.15 p.m. Hussain later lambasted his side's lackadaisical approach. Ponting batted with rare panache, his 144 from just 154 halls laced with three sixes and 20 fours, while Martyn had 18 fours when last out for 118 shortly after lunch next day. Simon Katich, Australia's first debutant specialist batsman for over three years, compiled a nervous 15, but a total of 447 looked a good score on a Headingley pitch with a worryingly dry top.

England responded with general competence, all the top-order batsmen starting well but failing to reach 50. Stewart, starting at No. 7 for the first time in 114 Tests, and unhappy at the demotion, responded with a bizarre innings of 76 not out, throwing the bat with daredevil irresponsibility. But his luck held, the follow-on was averted and, after a two-hour interruption either side of tea on Saturday, England reached 309, even making Australia take the second new ball for the first time in the series. McGrath's figures of seven for 76, which took him to 351 Test wickets, were those of a maestro and, in a normal Test, a match-winner. But this was no normal game.

When Ponting flew to 30 in 35 balls, before the light deteriorated, and increased his momentum with wonderful batting next morning, everything pointed to Australia taking the game beyond England's reach. Instead, the weather permitted only 30 runs between lunch and Gilchrist's declaration at 5.35 p.m., as well as limiting the day's play to just 25 overs. It was frustrating for the big crowd, but many would be back on Monday, little realising that Sunday's conditions had provided the stage on which Butcher would storm into Ashes history.

Australia 447 (Ponting 144, Waugh 72, Martyn 118, Gough 5-103)
and 176-4 (Ponting 72); **England 309** (Stewart 76 not out, McGrath 7-76)
and 315-4 (Butcher 173 not out, Hussian 55). England won by six wickets.

Chapter Nine:
Trouble and Strife and
Mess and Muddle

There is a depressing uniformity about the opening paragraphs of the poet Dylan Thomas' letters to friends and acquaintances. Most begin with an apology: for improper conduct; for failing to keep an appointment; for not repaying a loan. Odd though it may seem, I thought about Thomas a lot as I lifted copies of *Wisden* from the 1970s and 1980s off the shelf. For the annual pieces John Callaghan was obliged to file during those decades record repeat behaviour too: civil wars, fissures and family arguments routinely hung over the county back then. They made the cricket seem peripheral, buried beneath the dark inventory of rows and recriminations. Seen as a whole, the dispatches are Yorkshire's equivalent of a misery memoir.

The following phrases give a flavour of it: Callaghan writes that 'a sad summer for Yorkshire spilled over into an angry autumn'; he reflects on 'political intrigue' and 'bitter internal conflict'; he cites a 'serious decline in membership' and reports on 'crisis' meetings. It's easy to slap the label *winter of discontent* on Yorkshire's least successful years, but this would downplay the severity and the scale of the feuding and the damage it caused. At its root was a wrestle for power – predominantly between pro- and anti-Boycott camps – and a club struggling to cope with the loss of the dominance it regarded, blithely and very naively, as its right in the 1960s. To outsiders viewing from afar, the quarrels seemed bewilderingly tangled and petty affairs and established Yorkshire in the minds of onlookers as both intransigent and crassly co-operative in its own malaise. But, as this chapter underlines, the predilection for self-harm was long established.

Read what was said about the 'loss of temper and self-control' in the Yorkshire v Middlesex match in 1925. Read the hoo-ha over the sacking of Johnny Wardle, which led to his removal from the MCC touring team to Australia for 1957-58. And read the condemnation of 'blatant time-wasting' in the successful pursuit of the 1967 Championship, which brought censure for Brian Close and his removal as England captain. Also, some of its most significant figures weren't gently tweezed out of Headingley, but slewed with an axe. 'Let him go,' said Brian Sellers of Illingworth in 1968, 'and take any other bugger who feels the same way.' And two years later he told Close: 'You've had a good innings. I'm going to give you the option of resigning or getting the sack.'

On occasion it is impossible not to nod in agreement with Alan Gibson, who once wrote: 'It is the bugbear of Yorkshiremen that they always feel that they have to behave like Yorkshiremen, or like their fixed belief in what a Yorkshireman should be: tough, ruthless, brave, mean.' Gibson had the benefit of being able to throw stones at this particular glasshouse because he was born in Yorkshire; he was talking from experience.

The evidence to support him is contained within the next 000 pages.

YORKSHIRE V MIDDLESEX
Sheffield, July 5, 7, 8, 1924

This will always be a match of unhappy memories. It led to no end of ill feeling and was one of the chief causes of Middlesex coming to the decision – afterwards revoked – that they would not play Yorkshire in 1925. For some reason the Sheffield crowd, forgetting their old reputation for good sportsmanship, barracked more or less persistently all through the game, making the atmosphere almost unbearable. Under such conditions cricket could not be played in a proper spirit. Some fine work was done by both sides, but no one enjoyed the match.

Notes by the Editor – Sydney Pardon, 1925

I have no wish to dwell at any length on the disagreement between Middlesex and Yorkshire that last season so disturbed the usually cheerful atmosphere of our cricket. For one reason I have only a dim idea of what led Middlesex to say they would not play Yorkshire in 1925. I heard no end of gossip, but scarcely any exact details. Still, one knows the match that mainly caused the trouble was a thoroughly unpleasant one. The Sheffield pubic – false to all their old traditions of good sportsmanship – barracked for three days in most unseemly fashion and Butt, the umpire, felt it his duty to report Waddington to Lord's. Waddington duly apologised for his loss of temper and self-control, and there, so far as he was concerned, the matter ended. The quarrel was healed up, and in the coming season the two counties will meet as before. The trouble in Yorkshire cricket seems to have been confined to a minority of the players – from what I have been told not more than four. In this connection some remarks by Lord Hawke at the Yorkshire annual meeting were very significant indeed. Speaking of individual doings for the county last summer he said that Macaulay ought to have been in the MCC's team to Australia, and that it was entirely his own fault he was not chosen. To that stern condemnation not a word need be added.

PROFESSIONAL CAPTAINS
By C. Stewart Caine, 1928

In the course of the autumn, Yorkshire cricket circles were greatly perturbed by the announcement that, in succession to Major Lupton, Herbert Sutcliffe had been appointed captain of the county team. Objection was taken to this action by two

Yorkshire's decision to break with cherished tradition and sign an overseas player brought some commercial success, checking the worrying decline in membership. Australian fast bowler Craig McDermott, the original choice as Yorkshire's first officially qualified 'outsider', broke down during the winter and required an operation for groin trouble, so, with little room for manoeuvre, the club turned their attentions at the last minute to Sachin Tendulkar. The 19 year-old Indian's appearance on the scene at least silenced all those who, from a distance, accused Yorkshire of being racist, and he proved extremely popular with the public and fellow players. Tendulkar collected his runs with a good deal of style, scoring quickly in the limited overs competitions and being prepared to apply himself diligently in the Championship, but he lacked the experience to dominate ... he managed only one century, which won the match against Durham. He also completed a Sunday League century, but, having arrived too late to influence Yorkshire's Benson & Hedges Cup prospects seriously, he departed unexpectedly early, missing the last four Championship fixtures to play in domestic cricket in India.

Yorkshire in 1992

different parties. Some people urged the undesirability of having a professional captain; others argued that, if the committee thought fit to choose a professional, the post should be given to Wilfred Rhodes rather than to Sutcliffe. Happily the trouble was eventually settled to the satisfaction of all concerned. Sutcliffe declined the honour and, an invitation being extended to Captain Worsley, that gentleman stepped into the breach.

The matter naturally raised the question whether the practice which so generally obtains of giving the captaincy of a county eleven to an amateur, even of moderate attainments, carries with it greater advantages than the appointment of an experienced professional. Personally I think it does. Professionals, it is true, have in the past often captained leading counties – notably Yorkshire and Notts – but the system possesses more or less certain drawbacks. The professional may have difficulty in enforcing discipline. He would naturally hesitate to suggest to his committee that this player or that should be dropped, and so be instrumental in depriving the man in question of some part of his livelihood. Further, feeling that an error of judgement would prejudice his standing with the committee, he might well hesitate to take risks. The amateur is altogether differently placed. If a man is possessed of the qualities of leadership, he can insist upon strict obedience, and silent acquiescence in his orders. His views as to whether a player should be left out are not likely to be determined by any question of that player's earnings, and he can run risks with the knowledge that the worst that can befall him is the possibility he may not be given charge of the side another year.

THE WARDLE CASE

By Norman Preston, 1959

The dismissal of J. H. Wardle by Yorkshire three days after he had been chosen by MCC to go to Australia and the action taken later by MCC in withdrawing their invitation to him became a national topic. It was during the match between Yorkshire and Somerset at Sheffield on July 30 that Mr J. H. Nash, the Yorkshire secretary, announced: 'The Yorkshire Committee have informed J. H. Wardle that they will not be calling on his services after the end of the season.'

Wardle was selected for the match against Lancashire at Old Trafford, August 2, 4 and 5, but while the players were waiting for play to begin, rain having caused a delay, the Yorkshire captain, J. R. Burnet, made the following statement, 'J. H. Wardle has requested that he stand down from the match because of comments he intends to make about his colleagues in a newspaper article to be published while the match is in progress. He has been given permission to stand down and has left the ground.'

The articles duly appeared in the *Daily Mail* and on August 4 Mr R. Aird, secretary of MCC announced, 'The differences between the Yorkshire CCC and J. H. Wardle have up till now been considered a domestic affair, but owing to the press publicity now being given to the matter, the MCC Committee will consider the situation at their next meeting on August 19.'

Meanwhile the Yorkshire CCC Committee met again at Bradford on August 11, when Mr J. H. Nash issued the following statement, 'The Yorkshire County Cricket Club Committee regret the unpleasant publicity given to their decision to dispense with the services of J. H. Wardle after the present season. In past years Wardle has been warned on several occasions that his general behaviour on the field and in the dressing rooms left much to be desired. As no improvement was shown this year, the decision to dispense with his services was made, as it was unanimously considered that it was essential to have discipline and a happy and loyal team before any lasting improvement could be expected in the play of the Yorkshire XI.

Jacques Rudolph got the bird when his throw from the boundary killed a pigeon flying across the outfield.

Yorkshire v Lancashire
Twenty20 Cup, Headingley, 2009

'It is felt that the recent articles published in the *Daily Mail* fully justify the committee's decision. Wardle broke his contract when he wrote these articles without first obtaining permission, and the committee are therefore terminating his engagement forthwith. The committee emphatically reaffirm their high regard for the services of Mr J. R. Burnet and his predecessors in the captaincy, for the loyalty and restraint shown by players in the trying circumstances and for the valued work the former players give so helpfully in acting as cricket coaches.'

The full MCC Committee interviewed Wardle during their meeting at Lord's on August 19, after which Mr Aird announced: 'The committee of MCC have considered certain articles contributed by J. H. Wardle to a national newspaper since the date of his selection for the forthcoming Australian tour. They have also considered a report received from the Yorkshire County Cricket Club, many of the details of which were not available to the selection committee at the time when the team was chosen. The committee considered that the publication by Wardle in the press of the criticisms of his county captain, his county committee and some of his fellow players in the form and at the time that he published them did a grave disservice to the game. They believe that the welfare of cricket as a whole in terms of loyalty and behaviour must over-ride all other considerations. After an interview with Wardle and after very careful consideration of all aspects of the question, the MCC committee have reached the decision that the invitation to him to go with the MCC team to Australia must be withdrawn.'

Wardle received invitations from some counties to join them and on August 13 he informed Nottinghamshire that he was prepared to play for them. Consent of Yorkshire and MCC would have been necessary for the purpose of special registration. A month later Wardle announced that he had finished with county cricket and had signed a two-year contract with Nelson, the Lancashire League club. He had been assisting Rishton, another Lancashire League club, since leaving Yorkshire. Later, Wardle went to Australia to comment on the MCC tour for the *Daily Mail.*

Wardle's benefit in 1957 realised £8,129.

WARWICKSHIRE V YORKSHIRE

Edgbaston, 16, 17, 18 August, 1967

This was a match with tremendous repercussions. The last hour and 40 minutes, in which Warwickshire had to score 142 to win and failed by nine runs, led to allegations of delaying tactics against Yorkshire and to the eventual censuring of their captain, Close. The last phase was in violent contrast to the urgency of the second day when Warwickshire just wrested the lead by four runs. Yorkshire bowled only 24 overs, and, in the last 15 minutes, during which they left the field to the umpires and the batsmen during a shower, sent down two overs, one from Trueman containing two no-balls and three bouncers. Match drawn.

Notes by the Editor – Norman Preston, 1968

Brian Close led England to victory in five of the six Tests and also Yorkshire to the top of the Championship, which they have now won six times in the last nine years. Altogether Yorkshire have won the title outright 30 times, but on this occasion, although their ultimate success was deserved, their deliberate waste of time at Edgbaston in order to prevent Warwickshire winning so that they could take two points, brought upon them and their captain a heap of adverse criticism and the image of cricket was besmirched. That was an exceptional occasion.

Yorkshire in 1967 – by J. M. Kilburn

Yorkshire's behaviour in the field created the sensation of the season. To prevent Warwickshire scoring 142 runs in one hundred minutes in the fourth innings Yorkshire indulged in blatant time-wasting tactics, which brought down the wrath of spectators and the disapproval of the critics. Report of this conduct raised an inquiry by the County Advisory executive committee that resulted in a public censure for the team with full responsibility laid on the Yorkshire captain.

YORKSHIRE IN 1977 – WAR: WHAT IS IT GOOD FOR? PART ONE

By John Callaghan

The disappointment of a sad summer for Yorkshire spilled over into an angry autumn as the selector Don Brennan waged a public campaign to replace Boycott as captain with Cope. Another member of the committee, Mel Ryan, also threatened to resign as a selector unless dramatic changes were made in the running of the team, adding to the air of crisis which hung over a sequence of unsatisfactory results. The matter came to a head at a committee meeting at Headingley on November 9 when it was decided to reappoint Boycott as captain and engage Ray Illingworth, the Leicestershire and former England captain, as team manager from April 1, 1979. After Boycott's triumphant return to Test cricket in 1977 public opinion swung behind him, especially in Yorkshire. This may have influenced the committee, who tried to remove some of the more onerous responsibilities from the captain. Illingworth, who left his native Yorkshire in 1968 over a contract disagreement, said he expected to have a happy relationship with Boycott. Following Boycott's unanimous reappointment, Brennan, who was not at the meeting, announced his resignation from the committee. These actions focussed attention on a situation that had some effect on a season during which the players lacked application in the one-day games, determination in too many Championship matches and inspiration on a general level.

YORKSHIRE IN 1978:
BOYCOTT AND HAMPSHIRE AND THE FLAMES OF SPECULATION

By John Callaghan

Manoeuvring behind the scenes involved a rearguard action by the anti-Boycott lobby, who seized on a welcome run of good results under Hampshire and devalued it by using it as a weapon in the captaincy argument. Thus, by the middle of June, the county was sadly split by the suggestion that the team did better under Hampshire, whose batting also prospered as he deputised for the injured Boycott. The climax came at the end of September when Boycott was dismissed as captain after eight years in command. He was replaced by Hampshire. Joe Lister, the Yorkshire Secretary, when making the announcement, said, 'The committee very much hope that Boycott will continue to extend his invaluable services as a player and have offered him a two years contract to continue as such.' It had been a shattering week for Boycott. He had been passed over as vice-captain of the England team to visit Australia, the honour being given to Bob Willis, and only four days before the Yorkshire decision his mother, with whom he lived, died after a long and painful illness.

Fortunately, the division during the summer had little effect on the playing record although Hampshire was the central figure in an incident at Northampton* when Yorkshire scored only 33 runs in the last 18 overs and threw away a batting point. This match raised ugly issues, with an implied criticism of Boycott's own general rate of progress through his innings. The inevitable committee meeting to investigate the whole business produced nothing positive ... With the findings kept secret, the flames of speculation were well fanned ... As a matter of interest, the results under the two captains were: Boycott: P12; W5; D6; L1: Hampshire P10; W5, D3; L2 – figures which support no particular theory ...

YORKSHIRE IN 1980: AN UNEASY INHERITANCE

By John Callaghan

Another disappointing season for Yorkshire was followed by the resignation of their captain, John Hampshire, who will be replaced in 1981 by Chris Old. Richard Lumb has been appointed vice-captain to cover for Old's possible absence on Test duty. A measure of the confusion that has clouded the county's prospects during several years of political intrigue can be gained from the fact that Lumb made it clear he did not want to become captain. With two former captains, Boycott and Hampshire, remaining in the dressing

---

* Wisden's *account of Northamptonshire v Yorkshire reported the following: Boycott scored 113 in six hours and seven minutes. 'Until he reached 53,' it said, 'Boycott's runs came entirely in twos and singles.' Hampshire and Johnson – the fourth-wicket pair – scored only 11 runs in the final ten overs.*

room, the likelihood of complications is obvious. Old thus comes into an uneasy inheritance. Unfortunately, the appointment of Ray Illingworth as team manger has not solved as many problems as had been expected, partly because no real discipline has been imposed. Too many of the county's promising youngsters have grown up to accept standards that would not have been countenanced in happier times.

YORKSHIRE IN 1981: WHAT FRESH HELL IS THIS?

By John Callaghan

Yorkshire spent another winter locked in bitter internal conflict after further failures on the field created circumstances in which a campaign to have Ray Illingworth sacked as team manager developed. The central issue became the suspension of England batsman Geoff Boycott, who had publicly criticised Illingworth. But there were many other issues floating beneath the surface. These were officially acknowledged when the committee instituted an 'in-depth investigation' into all aspects of the club's affairs*. Boycott and John Hampshire, who asked for his release at the end of the season and joined Derbyshire, were left out of the Sunday League side as a matter of policy, and after a dismal spell the younger members of the side rallied impressively to indicate what might have been with greater application in June and July. There was, too, a good deal of controversy over the captaincy, with Hampshire and David Bairstow standing in for (Chris) Old before the uncapped Neil Hartley was promoted. The picture was confused to say the least … The need for greater self-discipline and a common sense of purpose at all levels was obvious.

YORKSHIRE IN 1982: FACING HARD FACTS

By John Callaghan

The erratic nature of Yorkshire cricket was reflected in the fortunes of their former England seam bowler, Chris Old, who began the summer as club captain only to find himself surplus to requirements in September. The decline in his fortunes resulted from an unhappy start to the programme, particularly in the one-day competitions, with only one victory in nine games – and that against the Minor Counties. In one of the most controversial moves of even Yorkshire's trouble-strewn recent history, Old was replaced [as captain] by the manager, Ray Illingworth, who resumed his playing career at Ilford 15 days after his 50th birthday. Not even Illingworth's experience and tactical skill, however, could compensate for the lack of consistency and, in some cases, application as the side continued to perform some way below expectations. The hard fact that the committee had to face was that in four years of change things had taken a turn for the worse. Not least of the worrying signs concerned a serious decline in membership…

---

* Illingworth was sacked: David Bairstow took over the captaincy. Boycott batted on.

YORKSHIRE IN 1983: FAMINE AND FEAST

By John Callaghan

Yorkshire's satisfaction at winning the John Player Sunday League, their first major trophy for 14 years, was more than counterbalanced by the embarrassment of finishing at the foot of the County Championship table and by the row that followed the sacking at the end of the season of Geoff Boycott. The county's leading batsman was sacrificed to a youth policy which was the committee's answer to their drop from tenth place in the major competition, and the position was further complicated when Bill Athey refused a new contract and left to join Gloucestershire. The pro-Boycott campaigners forced Yorkshire to reconsider their decision, made by 18 committee votes to 7, but despite threats of action by members of the county club, a second committee meeting brought a comparable vote, thus setting the stage for what seemed likely to be a long and bitter winter. Not since 1866 had they won only one Championship (match) and then, anyway, they completed only three fixtures. They also plumped new depths by failing to win a home Championship match, and four consecutive defeats in mid-summer represented their worst run since 1947.

YORKSHIRE IN 1986: EXIT, BOYCOTT

By John Callaghan

The cricket committee voted 4-1 against offering Boycott another year's contract, and when this recommendation was put before the general committee, an amended aimed at extending his career failed by 12-9. Boycott, whose final record with Yorkshire in the Championship was 29,485 runs at an average of 58.27, again headed the county's averages despite missing nine Championship matches with a broken bone in his left wrist. County officials paid due tribute to the 45-year-old opener, while stressing that the committee wanted to give younger talent the chance to develop.

YORKSHIRE IN 1989 – WAR: WHAT IS IT GOOD FOR? PART TWO

By John Callaghan

The general level of Yorkshire's performance throughout the season was so poor that, before the end of the programme, the dressing room sent up a distress signal in the shape of a letter from the captain Phil Carrick, urging the committee to seek outside help. Inevitably, this attempt to break with cherished tradition provoked an angry response from many members and began another round of debate and arguments – the regular winter activity in troubled times. Ultimately, the widespread concern prompted a 'crisis' meeting of the full committee which involved some heated exchanges, notably between members of the cricket committee and Geoff Boycott, who led the criticism of the way the county was being run. The players added to the controversy by making it clear, in a meeting with leading officials, that they took no particular pride in representing Yorkshire and would just as soon offer their talents elsewhere if the money were right. Operating under the shadow of this unpalatable fact, the cricket committee spent seven weeks putting together a blueprint for the future. In the end, though, they came up with very little.

YORKSHIRE IN 2001: THE HUTTON GATES

By David Warner

The club was embroiled in controversies about a frieze depicting Asians in the new Sir Leonard Hutton memorial gates at Headingley, and over an invitation to Surrey president John Major to open the new West Stand, which the former prime minister diplomatically declined. For once, however, it was a season in which actions on the field spoke far louder than words off it.

YORKSHIRE IN 2004: A VOICE FROM PARLIAMENT

By David Warner

Yorkshire gave a trial to Ismail Dawood, a 27-year-old keeper who had done the rounds elsewhere but, at Scarborough on July 21, made history by becoming the first British-born (Dewsbury, indeed) Asian to play Championship cricket for Yorkshire. That built on an earlier breakthrough, when Ajmal Shahzad, a nippy 18-year-old seam bowler from Bradford, played in the Totesport League game against Worcestershire. Shahzad would have had further opportunities if he had not been laid low with a bad back. It therefore came as a surprise when in October Terry Rooney, the Labour MP for Bradford North, accused Yorkshire of 'deep-rooted, embedded racism' during a parliamentary debate on social cohesion. The comments caused outrage at the club: if Rooney's view had ever been accurate, it certainly looked out of date in 2004.

C&G Trophy Semi-final: Hampshire v Yorkshire
Southampton, August 20, 2005

A logistical disaster for Yorkshire may have effectively handed the match to Hampshire, who had been enjoying a few days off. Yorkshire, however, had been playing an enervating Roses match in Manchester, which finished late the previous evening and prevented them from reaching their Southampton hotel until after midnight. And next morning, with the team assembled for an 8.30 a.m. departure to the Rose Bowl, the coach driver was unable to leave for another hour because Health and Safety Regulations made it mandatory for him to have a nine-hour break between stints at the wheel. Finding a long backlog of vehicles on the only road to the ground, the players then had to walk the last mile among 9,000 spectators. Some hitched lifts, captain Craig White jogged and, on arrival, had to ask the umpires to delay the start by 15 minutes. He then lost the toss. Yorkshire were coping with all that when they were 103 for two, but then stumbled as a direct hit from Watson ran out McGrath. White worked hard against tenacious bowling, but their 197 never looked adequate. The early loss of Crawley mattered little to Hampshire after a stand of 147 for the second wicket. Pothas plodded as Ervine raced, his second 50 coming from just 37 balls, and they led Hampshire – who won the match by eight wickets – to their first Lord's final in 13 years. Hampshire won by eight wickets.

YORKSHIRE IN 2006: ADAMS SAYS YES – AND THEN NO

David Warner

It had all started so well. On November 1, Yorkshire trumpeted that Chris Adams, who had just led Sussex to the Championship title, was to become captain and 'director of professional cricket' ... Later that month, Adams drove to Headingley to meet the players, returned the same night to Sussex apparently in good heart, but next morning rang the chief executive, Stewart Regan, to say he had changed his mind and was staying put. He was slammed by Boycott for 'lack of moral fibre'.

YORKSHIRE IN 2008: THE AZEEM RAFIQ AFFAIR

David Warner

Azeem Rafiq, a former captain of England Under-15s born in Pakistan but bred in Barnsley, made a modest contribution on his Yorkshire debut: two overs of off-spin cost 18, yet his appearance would result in countless back-page headlines. Yorkshire beat Nottinghamshire to set up a televised Twenty20 quarter-final at Chester-le-Street, but, in scenes as farcical as they were dramatic, that contest was called off ten minutes before the start – with thousands already in the ground.

A week after Rafiq's debut, the ECB notified Yorkshire that his registration was incomplete. It then came to light on the day of the Durham match that Rafiq did not hold a British passport, so making him an unauthorised overseas player. Following frenzied legal consultations, Durham chief executive David Harker was informed 15 minutes before the gates opened that the game could not take place; his strong protests led to further discussions before the abandonment.

An ECB disciplinary panel cleared Yorkshire of deliberately flouting regulations, but expelled them from the Twenty20 Cup and handed their two points to Nottinghamshire, who qualified for the game against Durham. On appeal, however, the expulsion was rescinded and the result allowed to stand. Crucially, though, Yorkshire were still deducted two points (and ordered to pay £2,000 costs). This denied Yorkshire the chance of qualifying for the multi-million-dollar Champions League, unexpectedly letting Glamorgan into the quarters.

Yorkshire withdrew Rafiq from all cricket, but during August the ECB ruled he could play for the county while his application for British citizenship was processed. He was, however, barred from representative cricket for England Under-19s or the Lions. This restriction was lifted late in the year, and in January 2009 he joined the England Under-19 tour of South Africa. Like Adil Rashid and Ajmal Shahzad, Rafiq worked his way up through the Yorkshire system. After gaining a scholarship, he joined the academy at the start of 2008 – and has now won a three-year contract.

YORKSHIRE IN 2009: HOGGY'S SAD FAREWELL

David Warner

There was little goodwill on either side when Yorkshire parted company with Matthew Hoggard at the end of the season. Hoggard, the sixth most successful bowler in England's history with 248 Test wickets, claimed he had been sacked, but the club insisted he had been released because he had refused to sign 'an extremely competitive' two-year contract with the option of a third year based on performance.

Had Hoggard belonged to an earlier generation of first-class cricketers, he would probably have signed the new contract offered to him in April, when he was already aware that his England days were behind him. Nowadays, however, the financial rewards of representing one's country are so much higher than they used to be that players would no doubt like to feel their earning powers remain just as great when they return to their counties. Another sign of the times was that the news of Hoggard's 'sacking' was revealed by the player himself in the national newspaper in which he had been a regular columnist. Earlier in the summer the imminent closure of Michael Vaughan's playing career was also made public in similar circumstances. Such headline-making disclosures would once have come from the regular cricket correspondent – often earning the wrath of the county concerned – but, increasingly, top players have a foot in both camps.

Hoggard's departure was a reminder that Yorkshire have a long tradition of star players departing in acrimonious circumstances. The difference was that this case was mainly about money, whereas some famous names from the past left for other reasons: Brian Close because the county felt he was against one-day cricket; and Ray Illingworth – who like Hoggard headed south to take up the reins at Leicester – because he wanted the security of a longer contract.

Chapter Ten:
Days in the Sun

It's a peculiarity of the remembrance of things past that the most vivid memories so often originate from what could be classed as small, apparently inconsequential moments: a sound, a scent, a face only half-glimpsed or a place arrived at unexpectedly. In cricket, a whole summer's day can come alive in the mind again at the sight of a scorecard. Whether in print – found among the pages of *Wisden,* of course – or written by hand in faint pencil or smudgy ink, the 'card of the match' conveys to anyone who witnessed it first hand a lot more than the narrative story of runs scored and wickets taken. It also (and very curiously) is capable of re-creating the experience itself: your state of mind, the weather, where you watched the game, who you sat beside and, possibly, even what each of you ate for lunch.

What follows stretches well beyond the furthest tip of living memory. It includes Peate's hat-trick against Kent in 1882, Holmes making an unbeaten triple hundred against Middlesex at Lord's in 1925 and Wardle throwing down the stumps to engineer a spectacular run-out and force a tie against Leicestershire in 1954. But reading them provides both a live connection with a time long before some of us were even thought of, let alone breathing, and the realisation that we share something almost tangible with previous generations. For the emotions cricket's unfolding dramas stir in us are no different from theirs. Thomas Moult's poem *The Names* begins:

> There's music in the names I used to know
> And magic when I heard them long ago.

Moult's 'music' and 'magic' were equally felt by those who came before us, and the line scores and brief, accompanying reports allow us to relate easily to it and to them. I daresay we share the same degree of ever-so-gentle envy, too, insomuch as we regret sights denied us by the unfortunate circumstance of not being born. I am thinking about Brown and Tunnicliffe's 554 against Derbyshire at Chesterfield in 1898; Rhodes bamboozling Nottinghamshire and bowling them out for 13 at Trent Bridge in 1901; Hirst and Jackson taming the Australians at Headingley a year later.

I especially wish I'd seen the heroic Don Wilson stupefy Worcestershire at New Road in 1961 as he batted one-handed for almost half an hour. His left arm was encased in plaster from the elbow to the knuckles because of a fractured thumb. He hit 29, including six fours, in a last-wicket stand of 37 and Yorkshire won by one wicket. In the *Yorkshire Post,* J. M. Kilburn wrote that it was the 'only possible finish that would serve the cause of romance' and likened it to a *once-upon-a-time* fairytale. 'This was fancy beyond the fanciful,' he said. Kilburn was not a writer to exaggerate or indulge in hysterical hype. Take it as read that we missed something particularly special.

Yorkshire v Gloucestershire
Bramall Lane, Sheffield, July 29, 30, 31,1872

Yorkshire v Gloucestershire was a judiciously selected match to play in compliments of Roger Iddison, who had served his Shire so long and so ably in the cricket field; for it was the first match ever played by those counties, and it ensured the first appearance of Mr W. G. Grace on the Country ground at Sheffield, the centre of as ardent, keen, thorough, and numerous a body of admirers of our national game as any county can boast of, and who flocked onto the ground in such numbers that nearly 17,000 were present during Iddison's three days; and although no reliable information could be gathered respecting the actual monetary result, there can be no doubt but that when the subscription lists are sent in and settled the benefit to Iddison will have been one worthy the man, the match, and the county. The thousands that thronged the ground on the Monday went there full of hope of witnessing some big batting by Mr W. G. Grace; how those hopes must have been more than realised. The weather was fine up to noon; then rain fell heavily; but at 1.15 p.m. they commenced and played (barring an interval for dinner) up to 5.10 p.m. when a storm put a stop to further play. The friends of Iddison mustered so strongly that it was computed there were nearly 8,000 at one time on the ground, and those thousands witnessed one of the most extraordinary day's cricket ever played, for when the storm ended the play there had been 208 runs scored and, no wicket down, the score books showing the following unique bit of batting as the result of that two hours and fifty minutes cricket:

Mr W. G. Grace not out	132
Mr T. G. Matthews not out	69
B 2, l-b 5	7
	208

Gloucestershire 294 (W. G. Grace 150, T. G. Matthews Esq 85, Freeman 5-97);
Yorkshire 66 (W. G. Grace 8-33) **and 116** (W. G. Grace 7-46).
Gloucestershire won by an innings and 112 runs.

Gloucestershire v Yorkshire
Cheltenham, August 17, 18, 19, 1876

'A best on record' was made by Mr W. G. Grace in this match; that is to say his 318 not out is the largest score ever hit in a County v County contest. Mr W. G. Grace commenced the innings at 12.30 p.m. on the Thursday; when the innings finished, at ten minutes to four on the Friday, Mr W. G. Grace was the not out man, having made 318 out of the 528 (504 from the bat) runs scored. He was timed to have been about eight hours batting; he ran 524 times between wickets, and the hits he made were seventy-six singles, thirty 2s, twelve 3s, twenty-eight 4s (112 by fourers), three 5s, two 6s and a 7. One critic described this 318 as 'a wonderful innings'; and another as 'played in his very best style with only one chance, and that was when he had made 201.'

Gloucestershire 528 (W. G. Grace 318, W. O. Moberley Esq 103);
Yorkshire 127-7. Match drawn.

Yorkshire v Kent
Bramall Lane, June 12, 13, 1882

There was some extraordinary cricket in this match, which the Yorkshiremen won in a single innings with 20 runs to spare. Kent batted first, and their first wicket (Mr Mackinnon's) went at 20. Then George Hearne joined Lord Harris, and a most determined stand was made. At luncheon both were still in, and the score 91. Resuming after a storm of rain, Hearne was stumped at 98, and ten runs later Lord Harris was easily caught for a faultless innings of 62, which contained only one hit for four. Then the sensational part of the innings occurred, for the remaining seven wickets fell for five runs!

Peate bowled with great success. Mr Wilson went in three wickets down, and carried out his bat for 8! Yorkshire went in at 5.30 p.m., and when stumps were drawn, Hall was not out with 12, and Ulyett out with 63! Ulyett hit at everything, and had made 31 before Hall had scored; and his first 50 were made in half-an-hour. When Hall's innings was completed next morning it was found that he had taken three hours and a half to score 29! Kent went in the second time wanting 59 runs to save the single innings' defeat; but Bates took six wickets at an average cost of two runs, and Peate three for 25, and the Kent eleven were all disposed of for 29. Peate in that innings performed the hat trick, getting rid of Lord Harris, O'Shaughnessy and Lord Throwley with successive balls.

Kent 113 (Lord Harris 62, Peate 7-31) and 39 (Bates 6-12); Yorkshire 172 (Ulyett 63).
Yorkshire won by an innings and 20 runs.

Yorkshire v Australia
Bradford, June 9, 10, 1884

The wicket was in a spongy and treacherous condition, owing to two days' heavy rain, and the bowlers carried off all the honours of a match which the Australians finally won by three wickets. An injury to one of his fingers kept Murdoch out of the match. Bates scored the highest innings, making 24 out of 36 put on while he was in. In the match Palmer took 11 wickets for 54 runs, Peate 10 for 62, Spofforth 9 for 61, and Emmett 6 for 40.

YORKSHIRE	First Innings		Second Innings	
G. Ulyett c Bonnor b Palmer		5	– c Midwinter b Palmer	8
*L. Hall lbw b Spofforth		6	– c Boyle b Palmer	0
G. R. Baker b Palmer		0	– (4) c Bonnor b Palmer	3
E. Lockwood c Blackham b Spofforth		0	– (5) c Giffen b Spofforth	1
W. Bates c Bonnor b Spofforth		24	– (3) c Giffen b Spofforth	8
F. Lee c Spofforth b Palmer		2	– (7) c Bonnor b Palmer	5
I. Grimshaw c McDonnell b Spofforth		2	– (8) b Spofforth	0
R. Peel b Palmer		4	– (6) b Palmer	1
T. Emmett b Spofforth		3	– b Palmer	16
E. Peate b Palmer		3	– not out	12
†J. Hunter not out		5	– c Giffen b Spofforth	7
B 1		1	B 5, l-b 5, n-b 1	11

1-11 2-11 3-11 4-11 5-15 6-26   55   1-2 2-15 3-26 4-27 5-28 6-28   72
7-43 8-47 9-47 10-55   7-28 8-42 9-61 10-72

First innings – Spofforth 19–9–29–5; Palmer 19–8–25–5.
Second innings – Spofforth 23–11–32–4; Palmer 22–11–29–6.

AUSTRALIANS	First Innings		Second Innings	
P. S. McDonnell c Lockwood b Emmett		0	– c and b Peate	4
A. C. Bannerman c Baker b Emmett		8	– lbw b Peate	14
W. E. Midwinter c Lee b Emmett		18	– c Hunter b Peel	17
G. Giffen c Baker b Emmett		2	– b Peate	5
H. J. H. Scott c Ulyett b Peate		1	– c Ulyett b Peate	0
G. J. Bonnor c Peate b Emmett		2	– c Grimshaw b Peate	5
†J. M. Blackham b Peate		3	– c Lockwood b Peate	10
G. E. Palmer c Bates b Peate		5	– not out	7
F. R. Spofforth c Bates b Peate		7	– not out	5
G. Alexander not out		10		
*H. F. Boyle c Baker b Emmett		0		
B 4		4	L-b 1	1

1-5 2-18 3-20 4-28 5-31 6-34   60   1-8 2-33 3-37 4-37 5-37 6-45   (7 wickets) 68
7-34 8-46 9-59 10-60   7-63

First innings – Peate 27–11–29–4; Emmett 27–14–27–6.
Second innings – Peate 27–12–33–6; Emmett 12–6–13–0; Ulyett 2–0–7–0; Peel 12–6–14–1.

Toss won by Yorkshire   UMPIRES L. Greenwood and A. Hill
Close of Play First day: Yorkshire (2) 72 all out

Yorkshire v Nottinghamshire
Bramall Lane, July 23, 24, 1888

Shortly before noon some 8,000 spectators were present. About 11.30 a heavy shower of rain fell on the already soft ground, and though it cleared off about 12 o'clock it was not until 20 minutes later that a start took place in what proved to be a most curious day's cricket. Sherwin beat Hall in the toss, and, acting upon the perfectly justifiable surmise that the wicket would be easier then with the wet freshly upon it, decided to take first innings. Accordingly Gunn and Scotton began the Nottinghamshire batting at 12.20 to the bowling of Peel and Wainwright. The Nottinghamshire batting was of the most feeble character throughout. The score was only three when Scotton was out to a fine left-handed catch at short-slip, and at four Gunn got his leg in front to Peel. Then Barnes and Mr Daft got together, and played carefully for some time. In the first 40 minutes 15 runs were scored, and then Barnes in hitting out was caught at extra cover-point. Mr Beves followed, but just after one o'clock, when the record was 18 for three wickets, a brief storm of rain broke over the ground and stopped play for about ten minutes. On resuming Peel and Wainwright carried all before them. Wainwright with his first ball dismissed Mr Beves, and with his third bowled Attewell. Peel in his first over bowled Mr Daft with a break back. The fourth, fifth and sixth wickets all fell at 18. Brown and Flowers were next together, but a catch at short-slip by Middlebrook soon got rid of Flowers, and, as Briggs was bowled in Peel's next over, the seventh and eighth wickets fell at 22. Afterwards, at 24, Peel bowled Richardson and Sherwin with successive balls and the innings closed at 1.40 p.m. for the smallest total of the season thus far in a first-class match. Peel was heartily cheered.

Subsequently the Nottinghamshire bowlers did extremely well, and as Ulyett was bowled at four, Hall caught at silly point at six, Lee bowled at 14, and Mr Hill caught at cover-point at 16, it did not look as though Yorkshire would make many. However, Peel and Wainwright made a brief stand and added 21 runs before Peel was bowled at 37 for the only double-figure score in either side's first innings. Then once more the bowlers had matters all their own way. At 41 Wainwright was bowled, and at 43 Moorhouse and Preston were smartly stumped, and Middlebrook caught and bowled. Wade was caught from a skier at mid-on at 46, and the innings closed for that score at four o'clock, having lasted an hour and 20 minutes, against an hour and ten minutes that Nottinghamshire had occupied. The wicket, though a trifle easier than in the early part of the day, was still very difficult, and it was generally expected that the 22 runs Nottinghamshire were behind would place them at an immense disadvantage.

At a quarter past four Scotton and Gunn again went in, and Peel and Wainwright again bowled. Gunn was stumped at five, and Barnes came in. Scotton was twice let off, Ellis missing him at the wicket and Peel in the slips, but later the left-hander batted patiently and well. Barnes after a while hit two fours from Peel, but at 24, or just after the arrears had been hit off, Peel bowled him. On Mr Daft coming in a stand was made, and at 33 the first bowling change took place, Middlebrook going on for Peel, while at 38

Wade displaced Wainwright. As the fast bowler was freely hit Peel resumed at 42, and no further change was necessary. Mr Daft was at once caught at point, and Mr Beves joined Scotton. The 50 went up with only three wickets down, but then, as in the first innings, the batting completely broke down. At 53 Wade dismissed Mr Beves and Attewell in one over, while at 55 he got Brown stumped. At 56 Peel bowled Flowers and Briggs, and at 58 he sent back Richardson and Sherwin, the innings closing at 6.15 and stumps being drawn for the day. The day's cricket had been a most remarkable one, the 30 wickets having only earned an aggregate of 128 runs.

On the Tuesday morning rain fell for three hours, and it was not until past three o'clock that the game could be continued. If there had been no more wet, Yorkshire might have found the necessary 37 runs difficult to get, but as it was Ulyett and Hall hit them off in 40 minutes – a somewhat tame finish to an otherwise sensational game.

Nottinghamshire 24 (Peel 8-12) **and 58** (Peel 6-21); **Yorkshire 46** (Richardson 6-12) **and 37 for no wicket**. Yorkshire won by ten wickets.

Gloucestershire v Yorkshire
Clifton, August 16, 17, 18, 1888

This was one of the heaviest scoring matches of the season, 1,053 runs being obtained in the course of three days for the loss of only twenty-nine wickets. Apart from the heavy scoring, it was rendered remarkable by the wonderful achievement on the part of Mr W. G. Grace, who, for the third time in his career, succeeded in making over 100 runs in each innings. The ground was in exceptionally good order, but that the feat also was exceptional is fully proved by the fact that no other cricketer within the last fifty years has ever succeeded in accomplishing it in a first-class match. Mr Grace did it in 1887 at Clifton against Kent, scoring 101 and 103 not out, while so long ago as 1868 he made 130 and 102 not out at Canterbury for South of the Thames against North of the Thames. While no one but Mr Grace has ever scored so well in a big match, the feat has been accomplished in minor engagements by Mr W. Townsend, Mr D. G. Spiro, and Mr F. W. Mande.

Gloucestershire 248 (W. G. Grace 148, Preston 7-82) **and 316** (W. G. Grace 153); **Yorkshire 461** (Hall 129 not out, Moorhouse 86, Wormald 80, Wade 68, Woof 5-87) **and 20 for no wicket**. Match drawn.

Yorkshire v Lancashire
Huddersfield, July 18, 19, 1889

This was one of the most remarkable matches of the season, inasmuch as Yorkshire, having so far lost all their first-class county fixtures, looked to have no chance whatever at the start, and yet at the end of the first day seemed to have the game in hand. Then, in the second stage, they threw away their chances in the most extraordinary manner.

Having won the toss, Mr Hornby went in with Mr Eccles to open the Lancashire batting, and Peel began the bowling, while Lord Hawke, rightly judging that the wicket would prove a bumpy one, put on Ulyett at the other end. As it happened, this pair of bowlers proved fully equal to the task set them, for, in the course of an hour and 40 minutes, they dismissed the eleven for 81 runs. Half the wickets fell for 21 runs. Then Briggs came to the rescue of his county, and rapidly hit up 25. After the interval the home county began their batting to the bowling of Mold and Briggs. Two or three of the batsmen, however, played in a very different style to that adopted by the Lancashire men, and Lee, Lord Hawke, and Moorhouse managed to score 114 out of the 160 runs put together by the side in a little over two hours and a half. Lee hit brilliantly, and made 42 out of 80 while he was batting. His innings was made in 15 hits by eight fours, a three, a two, and five singles. Lord Hawke, who went in at the fall of the fourth wicket at 67, batted with great brilliancy, though he should have been caught at slip when he had scored four. He carried his bat for the highest individual score in the match – 52. In this he made a fine square-leg-hit out of the ground for six, nine fours, three twos and four singles. Lancashire did so badly that before stumps were drawn they had lost four wickets for 22 runs.

Everything pointed to an easy triumph for Yorkshire when the second day commenced, as the visitors, with six wickets to fall, still wanted 57 runs to avert a single-innings defeat. The game, however, underwent a complete and extraordinary change. Mold was got rid of at 27, and Briggs came in. Ward was then missed by Wainwright in the slips from an easy catch, and, as it turned out, the blunder cost Yorkshire the match. Ward batted wretchedly, but he kept in while Briggs made runs in his usual dashing style. The pair nearly hit off the arrears before they were parted, and in all added 51 runs for the sixth wicket. This stand seemed to put heart into the remaining batsmen. Yorkshire were eventually put in to get 75 to win. Mold and Watson were put on to bowl, and the former met with such success, and was backed up by such admirable fielding, that in the course of eight overs he dismissed Wade, Lee, Hall and Ulyett when only nine runs had been scored. Peel made a stand, and though he lost Lord Hawke and Moorhouse at 24, he batted with great pluck and determination, and with Wainwright made a capital attempt to save the game. Unluckily he lost his wicket through slipping down when out of his ground, and was out at 38. Wainwright, after Peel left, hit well, and while he stayed at the wicket the hopes of the Yorkshiremen rose again, but he was at length caught from a miss-hit at 63, when, with two wickets in hand, 12 runs were wanted to win. Eight of these were obtained, but then both Whitehead and Middlebrook were dismissed, and the match ended in a victory for Lancashire.

LANCASHIRE	*First Innings*			*Second Innings*	
J. Eccles c Lee b Ulyett		0	– c Lee b Ulyett		5
*A. N. Hornby lbw b Peel		8	– c Wainwright b Ulyett		1
F. H. Sugg c Lee b Ulyett		1	– c Middlebrook b Ulyett		3
A. Ward b Peel		7	– c Hall b Ulyett		7
F. Ward c Hunter b Ulyett		4	– c Lee b Middlebrook		22
J. Briggs c Wainwright b Ulyett		25	– (7) c Hunter b Middlebrook		41
A. G. Paul b Ulyett		4	– (8) b Peel		16
G. R. Baker b Ulyett		5	– (9) b Peel		29
A. Watson not out		16	– (10) not out		16
A. W. Mold b Peel		4	– (6) c Wade b Ulyett		5
†R. Pilling c Hunter b Ulyett		6	– c Lee b Peel		2
L-b 1		1	B 6		6

1-0 2-8 3-10 4-21 5-21 6-35   81   1-3 2-9 3-22 4-22 5-27 6-78   153
7-54 8-55 9-60 10-81   7-89 8-128 9-143 10-153

First innings – Peel 22–7–30–3; Ulyett 21.2–9–50–7.
Second innings – Peel 29.2–4–55–3; Ulyett 23–9–52–5; Middlebrook 11–2–25–2; Wainwright 5–1–15–0.

YORKSHIRE	*First Innings*			*Second Innings*	
L. Hall b Mold		1	– b Mold		2
S. Wade c Baker b Mold		7	– b Mold		3
F. Lee c Baker b Mold		42	– c Pilling b Mold		0
R. Peel c and b Briggs		14	– run out		18
G. Ulyett b Watson		7	– b Mold		2
*Lord Hawke not out		52	– b Watson		3
R. Moorhouse c Watson b Mold		20	– b Watson		0
E. Wainwright b Mold		0	– c F. Ward b Mold		27
L. Whitehead b Mold		12	– b Mold		5
†D. Hunter lbw b Briggs		3	– not out		7
W. Middlebrook c Pilling b Briggs		0	– c Hornby b Mold		0
B 2		2	B 4		4

1-1 2-26 3-55 4-67 5-81 6-123   160   1-4 2-4 3-7 4-9 5-24 6-24   71
7-125 8-149 9-160 10-160   7-38 8-63 9-71 10-71

First innings – Mold 35–16–76–6; Watson 9–4–24–1; Briggs 26–7–58–3.
Second innings – Mold 25.4–14–35–7; Watson 25–17–32–2.

Toss won by Lancashire   UMPIRES H. Holmes and G. Panter
Close of Play First day: Lancashire (2) 22-4 (F. Ward 4, Mold 0)

Yorkshire v Staffordshire
Bramall Lane, August 4, 5, 1890

An achievement on the part of Wainwright, who succeeded in taking all ten Staffordshire wickets at a cost of only 31 runs, was the feature of the opening day. Six of the batsmen were bowled, three caught, and one was leg before. Yorkshire batted first and a total of

268 was reached. Tinsley played excellent cricket for 96, in which were a six, fifteen fours, two threes, and nine twos, and after nine wickets had fallen, Hunter assisted Peel to put on no fewer than 92 runs before the innings had closed. Ulyett and Peel went in respectively eighth and ninth. Staffordshire were dismissed in an hour and 35 minutes, and next day they were not much more successful. The ten wickets were got down in an hour and 50 minutes for 88.

Yorkshire 268 (Tinsley 96, Brown 6-87); **Staffordshire 67** (Wainwright 10-31) **and 88**. Yorkshire won by an innings and 113 runs.

Lancashire v Yorkshire
Old Trafford, August 7, 8, 1893

The match opened on Bank Holiday, and despite a threatening morning following rain, there were fully 10,000 present at midday, though a heavy storm delayed the game from one o'clock until after luncheon. The crowd subsequently increased until it was estimated that there were over 25,000 present – the actual number that paid at the turnstiles was 22,554. As the wicket was slow and difficult, and not likely to improve, it was felt that Mr Crosfield gained a big advantage for the home county by winning the toss, but the batsmen made very little use of their opportunities. Yorkshire bowled and fielded magnificently, and runs were always difficult to obtain, but a little more hitting and a little less caution would probably have improved the total considerably. To start with, four wickets fell for 22 before the rain stopped play. Ward, who was batting nearly two hours for 19, and Baker infused some life into the proceedings by raising the score to 56, but when the last wicket fell, though the innings had occupied two hours and a quarter, the total was only 64.

The ground was becoming more difficult when Yorkshire went in, but the spectators were certainly not prepared to see them fail as completely as the others had done. They did, however, for Brown, Tunnicliffe and Peel alone made double figures, and the whole side were dismissed by Briggs and Mold in an hour and 50 minutes for 58. Altogether play lasted four hours and 20 minutes, during which time 20 wickets fell for an aggregate of 129 runs.

The even character of the first stage promised a second day of more than ordinary interest. Some showers had fallen, and as the sun came out the pitch was more difficult than ever. Just for a while it seemed possible that Lancashire might do fairly well, for Ward and MacLaren scored freely from Ernest Smith, who was unwisely put on first with Peel, but the professional was out at 18, and his dismissal was rapidly succeeded by others. The turning point was when Wainwright was put on, for from that time the batsmen were outplayed, and the innings terminated for 50 after lasting an hour and a half. Then came the most sensational part of this remarkable match.

Left with but 57 to make, Jackson and Sellers commenced Yorkshire's task just after one o'clock with so much resolution that 24 runs were obtained in 16 minutes, and everything suggested an easy triumph. Then Oakley was put on in place of Mold, and in his first over Jackson was out in the most unfortunate fashion. The ball hit his pad and glanced away, and Oakley appealed for leg before. Jackson ran half way up the pitch, but Sellers, under the impression that Potter had given his colleague out instead of not out, did not move. Sellers, evidently upset by this incident, was bowled at 25; Brown played on at 26, and Wainwright was leg before at 29. Thus a radical change took place in a few minutes. With Smith and Tunnicliffe together, the former hit out vigorously and made the next 12 runs, which appeared to give Yorkshire the advantage once more, but with everything going Smith hit a ball to cover-point, which Crosfield took close to the ground. It was a near thing, and Smith, with a large proportion of the spectators, did not think the catch had been made. The decision proved an important factor in Lancashire's ultimate victory. At luncheon six men were out for 42, while in 25 minutes afterwards the last four were dismissed for an additional nine runs, which left the home side winners. Some little feeling was exhibited over the result, but in such a finish it was only to be expected.

Lancashire 64 and 50 (Peel 6-24); **Yorkshire 58** (Briggs 6-35) **and 51** (Briggs 5-25).
Lancashire won by five runs.

Yorkshire v Sussex
Dewsbury, June 7, 8, 1894

Yorkshire practically won the game on the opening day, when they batted first, on a very treacherous wicket. Hawke and Jackson made 33 before they were separated. Seven wickets were down for 57, both Alfred Shaw and Parris bowling with marked effect, Yorkshire eventually put together a highly creditable total, and Wainwright and Peel then dismissed Sussex in an hour and 20 minutes for 55, the visitors only just escaping a follow-on. Before the drawing of stumps Yorkshire scored 57 for four wickets, and next morning Sussex were set 218 to win. Again the Sussex batsmen were almost powerless against Wainwright and Peel, and the home team gained an easy victory by 166 runs. Wainwright finished the match in a most sensational way, taking the last five wickets in seven balls. He did the hat-trick, and in all obtained 13 wickets at the marvellously small cost of 38 runs.

Yorkshire 133 (Shaw 5-58) **and 139; Sussex 55** (Wainwright 6-18) **and 51**
(Wainwright 7-20). Yorkshire won by 166 runs.

Yorkshire v Somerset
Huddersfield, July 19, 1894

Somerset came fresh from a single innings defeat sustained in the course of one day's cricket at Manchester, and being beaten again in a single innings in one day's cricket by Yorkshire, probably had an experience which had never previously been suffered. The ground was very much in favour of the bowlers. The only successes of batsmen were Lord Hawke, Peel and Hirst. The condition of the turf scarcely accounted for the downfall of 30 wickets in so short a time for 341 runs.

Somerset 74 (Hirst 5-9) **and 94** (Hirst 5-44); **Yorkshire 173** (Lord Hawke 56).
Yorkshire won by an innings and five runs.

Yorkshire v Somerset
Leeds, July 22, 23, 1895

Heavy rain had fallen on the three previous days, and the ground was so soft and difficult that on the opening day twenty-one wickets went down for 176 runs. With the exception of Tunnicliffe the Yorkshiremen failed badly before the bowling of Hedley, who, making his first appearance during the season, dismissed after lunch six batsmen for 9 runs. Somerset, facing a total of 73, were only 27 behind when the third wicket fell; but Peel then bowled magnificently, taking in all nine wickets for 22 runs. Yorkshire on the second day ran up a fine score, the chief honours being borne off by Denton, who was seen to exceptional advantage. Hedley again bowled with great effect, and had a record of fourteen wickets for 70 runs. Peel did even better, taking fifteen wickets in the match for 50, and it was largely due to him that Yorkshire won by 103 runs.

Yorkshire 73 (Hedley 8-18) **and 163** (Denton 60);
Somerset 69 (Peel 9-22) **and 64** (Peel 6-28). Yorkshire won by 103 runs.

Warwickshire v Yorkshire
Edgbaston, May 7, 8, 9, 1896

Yorkshire scored the huge total of 887 and put into the shade all previous records in first-class cricket. By making so many runs Yorkshire robbed themselves of the chance of victory, but, of course, it was a great thing to have accomplished such a memorable performance. As may be supposed the wicket was in almost perfect condition. Yorkshire had the honour of lowering another record, this being the first time in an important match that four separate scores of over a hundred had been obtained in the same innings. Lord Hawke and Peel put on 240 runs during their partnership. Every member of the Warwickshire team, with the exception of Law went on to bowl. Yorkshire's innings occupied the whole of the two first days.

Yorkshire 887 (Peel 210 not out, Lord Hawke 166, Wainwright 126, F. S. Jackson 117, Moorhouse 72); **Warwickshire 203** (Quaife 92 not out, Hirst 8-59) **and 48-0.**
Match drawn.

Yorkshire v Essex
Bradford, June 11, 12, 1896

After the rain, which had interfered so materially with the Surrey match, the ground at Bradford was very difficult, and on the opening day twenty-seven wickets went down for 237 runs. Yorkshire had nothing like their full strength – Jackson, Peel, Moorhouse and Hunter being all away, and except for a fine piece of hitting by Tunnicliffe, the northern batsmen could do nothing with the bowling of the Essex amateur, F. G. Bull. At the start of the Essex second innings, Wainwright proved so destructive that six wickets fell for 20 runs, and there were seven men out for 48 at the close of the day. Yorkshire had only 85 to get to win, but considerable anxiety was felt as to the result. Fortunately for the home side Tunnicliffe again hit in rare form, and Yorkshire in the end won with seven wickets to spare. The credit of the win belonged almost entirely to Tunnicliffe and Wainwright – the former scoring 102 runs for once out, and the latter taking 14 wickets for 77 runs.

Essex 109 (Wainwright 6-43) **and 55** (Wainwright 8-34);
Yorkshire 80 (Kortright 8-44) **and 85-3**. Yorkshire won by seven wickets.

Yorkshire v Derbyshire
Bradford, August 19, 20, 21, 1897

Derbyshire began extremely well, and at one point had 120 on the board with only four men out. Then came an astonishing piece of work by Haigh, who, in two overs, sent back five batsmen without a run being scored off him, dismissing the last three with successive balls and thus performing the hat-trick. The Yorkshiremen could do nothing against Davidson and Walker, and although 31 runs were added for the last wicket, the total only reached 83. Next day when the weather was very showery, Derbyshire again began well, but fell off badly, and on the Saturday, 25 minutes of actual cricket sufficed to give Yorkshire a creditable victory.

Derbyshire 128 (Haigh 6-18) **and 120** (Haigh 5-62, Wainwright 5-39); **Yorkshire 83** (Davidson 6-23) **and 166-5** (Hirst 63 not out). Yorkshire won by five wickets.

Hampshire v Yorkshire
Southampton, May 26, 27, 1898

With all their Army officers away, the Hampshire batting proved lamentably weak on the soft ground which had caked on the top. In the two innings, which in the aggregate realised but 78 runs, Haigh carried off the bowling honours and no one could have turned such an opportunity to better account. Varying his pace skilfully, he got a wonderful break on the ball and had the batsmen completely at his mercy. His record for the match was extraordinary – 14 wickets for 43 runs – and he hit the stumps no fewer than ten times. Between the two collapses of the home side Yorkshire put together the capital score of 157, in making which they were largely assisted by the weakness of the bowling opposed to them.

Hampshire 42 (Haigh 8-21) **and 36** (Haigh 6-22); **Yorkshire 157** (Tunnicliffe 58).
Yorkshire won by an innings and 89 runs.

Yorkshire v Surrey
Bradford, June 6, 7, 8, 1898

In some respects this was one of the most remarkable matches of the season, the extraordinary collapse of the Surrey team in their second innings being by far the worst performance of the southern county all through the summer. No play was possible on the first day, but there was some interesting and even cricket on the Tuesday, Yorkshire scoring 142 for eight wickets, against Surrey's total of 139. Wednesday's play was truly phenomenal. Hirst and Haigh added 155 runs before they were separated, their partnership in all producing 192. Certainly the Surrey bowling, apart from that of Lockwood, was poor, but the performance of the two Yorkshire professionals deserved great praise. Hirst's 130 not out, was his one great batting success last summer. Haigh had never before made so many runs for his county. Wanting 158 to escape an innings defeat, Surrey, had, of course, a thankless task, but a good fight was expected from them. Their batsmen, however, failed utterly before Rhodes and Wainwright, losing nine wickets for 23 and being all out in an hour and a half for 37. Wainwright took the first three wickets and Rhodes the last seven, the latter being splendidly helped by David Hunter at the wicket.

Surrey 139 (Abel 51, Rhodes 6-46); **and 37** (Rhodes 7-24);
Yorkshire 297-9 dec (Hirst 130 not out, Haigh 85).
Yorkshire won by an innings and 121 runs.

Derbyshire v Yorkshire
Chesterfield, August 18, 19, 20, 1898

This game will live long in the memories of those who were fortunate enough to witness it, for Brown and Tunnicliffe, commencing Yorkshire's innings on the Thursday, were not parted for five hours and five minutes, their stand lasting until Friday and producing the unprecedented number of 554. Needless to say this remarkable achievement completely eclipsed all previous records in important cricket, not only for the first, but for any wicket. Tunnicliffe was out first and Brown, having reached his 300, knocked his wicket down. Subsequently the other batsmen threw away their wickets in the most sportsmanlike fashion in order to give their side time to win, and the innings realised

662. Brown gave four chances during the five hours and ten minutes he was batting, and hit 48 fours, six threes and 19 twos. Tunnicliffe was five minutes less making his 243, his figures including 48 fours, three threes and seven twos.

Yorkshire 662 (Brown 300, Tunnicliffe 243); **Derbyshire 118 and 157** (Chatterton 54). Yorkshire won by an innings and 387 runs.

Essex v Yorkshire
Leyton, May 25, 26, 1899

Essex cut a very sorry figure. Indeed, apart from the fine bowling of Walter Mead, there was nothing in the game upon which they could look back with satisfaction. Not one of their batsmen could make headway against Rhodes on a slow wicket. Rhodes gave a very significant suggestion of what sort of a bowler he would be if ever he should be favoured with a wet season by taking 15 wickets for 56 runs.

Yorkshire 172 (Mead 7-37) **and 192** (Mead 7-90); **Essex 59** (Rhodes 9-28) **and 64** (Rhodes 6-28). Yorkshire won by 241 runs.

Surrey v Yorkshire
The Oval, August 10, 11, 12, 1899

This was beyond question the most sensational of all the matches played at The Oval during the season, 1,255 runs being scored for the loss of only 17 wickets. On each side there was an astonishingly successful partnership, Wainwright and Hirst putting on in three hours and a half 340 runs for Yorkshire's fifth wicket, and Abel and Hayward, with nothing but a draw to play for, staying together for six hours and a half, and in that time adding no fewer than 448 runs for Surrey's fourth wicket. Never before we should think in a first-class match have four such individual scores been made at 228, 186, 193, and 273. It may be mentioned that Yorkshire's 704 is the highest total ever hit against Surrey.

Yorkshire 704 (Wainwright 228, Hirst 186, Mr F. Mitchell 87, Tunncliffe 50, Richardson 5-152); **Surrey 551** (Hayward 273, Abel 193). Match drawn.

Yorkshire v Worcestershire
Bradford, May 7 1900

Yorkshire commended their triumphantly successful season in quite a startling way, beating Worcestershire in the course of a single afternoon. Recent rain had considerably affected the ground, and Rhodes and Haigh, bowling unchanged through the two innings, took 18 wickets. Rhodes obtained 11 of them. The game began at 20 minutes past 12 and was all over by six o'clock. Worcestershire's second innings lasted only an hour, the batsmen being almost helpless against Rhodes.

Worcestershire 43 and 51 (Rhodes 7-20); **Yorkshire 99** (Wilson 5-25).
Yorkshire won by an innings and five runs.

Essex v Yorkshire
Leyton, August 15, 16, 1901

The season at Leyton closed with a genuine sensation, a match of very small scores ending just after twelve o'clock on the second day. As rain had fallen heavily overnight, the bowlers were expected to do well, but for what actually happened no one could have been in the least prepared. Essex promptly lost the game, for on winning the toss and going in at a quarter to one – the state of the ground having prevented an earlier start – they were out in as nearly as possible an hour for a total of 30. Four wickets fell for one run, and the only chance of retrieving this disastrous start disappeared when Lucas was run out. Bowling at a great pace, and swerving in an extraordinary way, Hirst was quite unplayable. He took seven wickets – six of them bowled down – and only 12 runs were hit from him. Later in the day in the second innings of Essex he was just as deadly, taking five wickets out of six. In a match in which the bowlers had things so entirely their own way, it was a great feat on Taylor's part to score 44, and apart from a couple of lucky snicks he played very finely.

Essex 30 (Hirst 7-12) **and 41** (Hirst 5-17); **Yorkshire 104** (Mead 6-40).
Yorkshire won by an innings and 33 runs.

Nottinghamshire v Yorkshire
Trent Bridge, June 20, 21, 1901

This match furnished the sensation of the season, the Nottinghamshire eleven finding Rhodes and Haigh unplayable on a sticky wicket, and being got rid of for 13 – the lowest total ever obtained in county cricket, and, with one exception, the lowest on record in first-class matches. One wicket fell for a single run on the Thursday evening and on the following day, when owing to the state of the pitch cricket did not begin till ten minutes to one, the innings was finished off in 54 minutes, the batsmen being absolutely helpless. Counting the few minutes' play overnight, the innings lasted as nearly as possible an hour. A. O. Jones made a leg hit for four, and Carlin a two, the other seven runs being all singles. The innings was so extraordinary in character that it may be of interest to give the fall of the wickets: 1/1, 2/3, 3/3, 4/4, 5/8, 6/8, 7/10, 8/10, 9/12, 10/13.

When Nottinghamshire followed on, A. O. Jones and Iremonger scored 82 in an hour before the first wicket fell, but after that Hirst bowled in form just as wonderful as that of Rhodes and Haigh in the first innings, and soon after six o'clock the match came to an end, Yorkshire winning by an innings and 18 runs. Shrewsbury started playing in the match, but split his hand so badly in fielding a ball at point that he had to retire before play had been in progress an hour, his place in the Nottinghamshire team, thanks to Lord Hawke's courtesy, being taken by Harrison. Denton's batting for Yorkshire was exceptionally good.

Yorkshire 204 (J Gunn 5-49); **Nottinghamshire 13** (Rhodes 6-4) **and 173** (Hirst 6-26). Yorkshire won by an innings and 18 runs.

Yorkshire v Australia
Headingley, June 2, 3, 1902

After being 24 runs behind on the first innings, Yorkshire accomplished a big performance. They clearly owed their victory to Hirst and Jackson, who got the Australians out in about 70 minutes for 23 – with one exception the lowest total ever obtained by a Colonial team in this country. The score was up to 20 with only four men out, but after that there was a dismal collapse, Jackson finishing off the innings by dismissing Hopkins, Kelly, Jones and Howell in five balls. Still finer work was done by Hirst, who got rid of the best batsman, bowling Trumper with one of his deadliest swervers. Noble and Howell bowled splendidly in the last innings, and Yorkshire found it very hard work to get the 48 runs required.

Australia 131 and 23 (Hirst 5-9, Jackson 5-12); **Yorkshire 107** (Howell 6-53) **and 50-5**. Yorkshire won by five wickets.

Leicestershire v Yorkshire
Leicester, May 18, 19, 20, 1905

Some remarkable changes of fortune occurred in the course of the game, the chief feature of which was an innings of 341 by George Hirst – the highest ever played for Yorkshire and the sixth best in first-class cricket. In the face of their opponents' large total, Yorkshire had lost three wickets for 22 when Hirst went in, and he was last out after batting seven hours. Apart from a possible chance at short leg when he was 258, he made scarcely a mistake. Hitting powerfully all round the wicket, he scored 212 by boundary strokes, and among his other figures were a six, seven threes and 20 twos.

LEICESTERSHIRE	*First Innings*		*Second Innings*
*C. E. deTrafford c Grimshaw b Ringrose	58	– c Wilkinson b Rhodes	11
C. J. B. Wood not out	160	– c Grimshaw b Ringrose	24
A. E. Knight c Tunnicliffe b Rhodes	6		
V. F. S. Crawford c Hunter b Ringrose	7	– lbw b Rhodes	12
J. H. King retired hurt	0		
H. Whitehead c Hirst b Ringrose	56	– (3) b Ringrose	12
S. Coe c Hunter b Ringrose	100	– (5) c Myers b Haigh	8
R. T. Crawford c Myers b Ringrose	16	– (6) b Rhodes	1
G. C. Gill st Hunter b Rhodes	0	– (8) b Haigh	1
†A. E. Davis c Tunnicliffe b Rhodes	1	– (7) not out	21
W. W. Odell st Hunter b Rhodes	6	– (9) not out	27
L-b 6, w 1, n-b 2	9	L-b 1, w 2, n-b 1	4

1-73 2-81 3-94 4-210 5-377 6-405   419   1-19 2-41 3-56 4-66 5-70 6-70   (7 wickets) 121
7-407 8-409 9-419   7-72

First innings – Hirst 18–2–70–0; Myers 22–4–82–0; Ringrose 41–10–104–5; Rhodes 41.2–16–82–4;
Haigh 12–0–43–0; Grimshaw 5–2–9–0; Denton 3–0–20–0.
Second innings – Myers 6–0–34–0; Rhodes 23–13–22–3; Ringrose 15–0–53–2; Haigh 11–5–8–2.

YORKSHIRE	*First Innings*	
H. Wilkinson c Davis b Gill	14	
C. H. Grimshaw c Davis b Gill	2	
D. Denton lbw b R. T. Crawford	6	
J. Tunnicliffe c Whitehead b Gill	0	
G. H. Hirst c Whitehead b R. T. Crawford	341	
W. Rhodes c Davis b Gill	11	
S. Haigh c sub b Gill	31	
H. Myers c sub b Coe	57	
*Lord Hawke c and b R. T. Crawford	17	
W. Ringrose c Davis b Gill	8	
†D. Hunter not out	8	
B 10, l-b 7, n-b 3	20	

1-3 2-21 3-22 4-37 5-74 6-218   515
7-401 8-450 9-483 10-515

First innings – Gill 52–11–172–6; R. T. Crawford 47.5–18–117–3; Odell 26–7–61–0; Coe 28–5–100–1;
Whitehead 12–1–29–0; V. F. S. Crawford 2–0–16–0.

Toss won by Leicestershire   UMPIRES J. Carlin and A. Millward
Close of Play First day: Leicestershire (1) 374-4 (Wood 141, Coe 98);
Second day: Yorkshire (1) 276-6 (Hirst 187, Myers 6).

Yorkshire v Leicestershire
Hull, August 1, 2, 1907

On a pitch which placed batsmen at a tremendous disadvantage, Hirst bowled in his
finest form, and by the drawing of stumps on the opening day had practically ensured

the success of his side. Not only did he in the first innings of Leicestershire dispose of eight batsmen for 25 runs, but in the second he obtained the first four wickets which fell at a cost of 11 runs. Moreover in the second innings he performed the hat trick, dismissing Wood and King with the last two balls of one over, and Knight with the first of his next. Next morning, when half-an-hour's cricket finished off the Leicestershire innings, 27 runs were obtained from Hirst, but still his fifteen wickets cost little more than 5 runs apiece. Making the ball go with his arm and coming fast off the pitch he always had the opposing batsmen in difficulties. Odell bowled admirably for Leicestershire. Rothery batted steadily and Bates afforded further proof of his value to the side, going in second wicket down and being seventh man out. Yorkshire won the match by ten wickets.

Leicestershire 60 (Hirst 8-25) **and 54** (Hirst 7-38);
Yorkshire 114 (Odell 8-40) **and 1-0.** Yorkshire won by ten wickets.

Yorkshire v Lancashire
Headingley, May 16, 17, 18, 1910

Rain unfortunately prevented any cricket on the third day, when Yorkshire, with eight wickets to fall, wanted 99 runs to win, and thus a match which held out promise of a most interesting finish had to be abandoned as a draw. So far as it proceeded, the game proved desperately exciting, Lancashire, despite a series of mistakes in the field, securing on what was always a somewhat difficult pitch, a very strong position, and being dislodged from it by George Hirst, who accomplished one of the finest bowling performances of his great career. Almost unplayable, Hirst twice took two wickets with successive balls, hit the stumps eight times, and came out with the wonderful record of nine wickets for 23 runs, his first four wickets being obtained for five runs. Tyldesley batted admirably in Lancashire's first innings, but there were six men out for 144. In Yorkshire's innings, though Rhodes, Watson, Hirst, and Rothery were all missed, the ninth wicket fell at 103. Radcliffe being also let off, the last wicket produced 49 runs.

Lancashire 229 (Hirst 4-55) **and 61** (Hirst 9-23); **Yorkshire 152** (Brearley 5-86)
and 40-2. Match drawn.

Somerset v Yorkshire
Weston-Super-Mare, August 27, 28, 1914

The first match of the Weston-Super-Mare festival was chiefly remarkable for the bowling of Drake. Previous to this match no Yorkshireman had in a first-class engagement taken all ten wickets in an innings. Drake did this when Somerset went in requiring 231 for victory. On the first day he dismissed five men and altogether he claimed 15 wickets at the very small cost of 51 runs. Moreover, Drake was the highest run-getter with 51 and 12 in a small scoring match. He and Booth bowled unchanged throughout the two innings of Somerset, having done the same thing at Bristol earlier in the week – a most exceptional feat.

YORKSHIRE	First Innings		Second Innings	
M. W. Booth c Poyntz b Bridges	1	– (7) b Bridges		9
B. B. Wilson c Saunders b Bridges	20	– b Bridges		9
D. Denton c Chidgey b Hylton-Stewart	52	– c Saunders b Bridges		0
R. Kilner c Hylton-Stewart b Bridges	2	– c Braund b Bridges		4
W. Rhodes c and b Hylton-Stewart	1	– lbw b Robson		25
T. J. D. Birtles lbw b Braund	16	– (9) b Robson		10
A. Drake c Harcombe b Braund	51	– (8) c Hope b Robson		12
P. Holmes b Bridges	7	– (10) not out		3
*G. H. Hirst c Bisgood b Bridges	5	– (6) c Saunders b Robson		10
E. Oldroyd not out	0	– (1) b Hylton-Stewart		23
†A. Dolphin b Braund	0	– b Robson		0
B 5, n-b 2	7	B 4, l-b 2, w 1		7

1-4 2-45 3-54 4-59 5-80 6-114   **162**   1-9 2-9 3-32 4-53 5-69 6-85   **112**
7-132 8-162 9-162 10-162   7-85 8-108 9-112 10-112

First innings – Robson 14–5–45–0; Bridges 17–1–59–5; Hylton-Stewart 9–0–38–2; Braund 8.4–2–13–3.
Second innings – Robson 14–2–38–5; Bridges 14–1–54–4; Braund 4–2–7–0; Hylton-Stewart 2–0–6–1.

SOMERSET	First Innings		Second Innings	
B. L. Bisgood c and b Booth	6	– c Dolphin b Drake		11
L. C. Braund b Drake	1	– (4) b Drake		9
E. Robson c Rhodes b Booth	19	– c Birtles b Drake		3
B. D. Hylton-Stewart b Drake	1	– (5) st Dolphin b Drake		3
W. Hyman b Drake	1	– (6) st Dolphin b Drake		4
*E. S. M. Poyntz b Drake	0	– (7) c Oldroyd b Drake		5
P. P. Hope b Booth	3	– (8) c and b Drake		19
H. W. Saunders b Drake	0	– (9) b Drake		0
J. D. Harcombe not out	5	– (10) b Drake		26
J. J. Bridges c Drake b Booth	7	– (11) not out		1
†H. Chidgey c Holmes b Booth	0	– (2) b Drake		4
B 1	1	B 4, n-b 1		5

1-6 2-14 3-24 4-28 5-28 6-28   **44**   1-13 2-20 3-25 4-28 5-33 6-38   **90**
7-32 8-32 9-44 10-44   7-49 8-52 9-89 10-90

First innings – Booth 8–0–27–5; Drake 7–1–16–5.
Second innings – Booth 9–0–50–0; Drake 8.5–0–35–10.

Toss won by Yorkshire   UMPIRES A. Millward and A. E. Street
Close of Play First day: Yorkshire (2) 59-4 (Rhodes 13, Hirst 5).

Middlesex v Yorkshire
Lord's, June 6, 8, 9, 1925

Brilliantly as they performed on many occasions last summer, the Yorkshiremen excelled themselves in this match, dismissing Middlesex on a good wicket for 118, hitting up 538 for the loss of six batsmen and gaining a glorious victory. The game was rendered especially memorable by the batting of Holmes, who, in putting together an innings of 315 not out, beat the famous 278 by William Ward, which had stood as the record score at Lord's for 105 years. Holmes' batting was superb. On Saturday, when he left off with 121 runs to his credit, he depended mainly upon cuts and skilful strokes on the leg side, but on Monday he drove splendidly on both sides of the wicket, displaying his varied resources as a batsman in a manner that compelled general admiration. Altogether, he was at the wickets for six hours and 50 minutes, giving no chance, making very few faulty strokes and hitting 38 fours, 12 threes and 21 twos.

Middlesex 118 (Robinson 5-52) **and 271** (Hearne 91, Stevens 65);
Yorkshire 538-6 dec (Holmes 315 not out, Leyland 61, Sutcliffe 58).
Yorkshire won by an innings and 149 runs.

Yorkshire v Sussex
Bradford, August 16, 17, 18, 1925

At lunchtime on the third day, Sussex had six wickets in hand and required only 40 runs to win. The result looked inevitable, but by dint of magnificent bowling Macaulay pulled the game out of the fire and gave Yorkshire a victory. In doing this he had these astonishing figures: five overs and three balls, one maiden, eight runs, and five wickets. He took a wicket in each of his first three overs, one in his fifth and the last in his sixth, expending so much nervous energy that, with the match won, he was exhausted.

Yorkshire 119 and 230 (Oldroyd 77, Robinson 54, Browne 7-62);
Sussex 87 (Kilner 5-14) **and 239** (Bowley 105, Macaulay 7-67).
Yorkshire won by 23 runs.

Yorkshire v Australia
Bramall Lane, May 10, 12, 13, 1930

A splendid bowling performance on the part of Grimmett, who took all ten Yorkshire wickets for 37 runs. Grimmett's triumph was the more remarkable as Yorkshire commenced in distinctly promising fashion. Holmes and Sutcliffe put on 59 runs and the score had reached 120 when Sutcliffe, who batted admirably for two hours, was third man out. Then came such devastating work by Grimmett that the seven remaining wickets went down for 35 more runs. From the time he went on at 46, Grimmett bowled with wonderful accuracy and varied his break and flight with delightful ingenuity. He received excellent assistance from Walker who caught one batsman and stumped three. On two previous occasions all ten wickets in an innings had been taken in England by an Australian, Howell performing the feat in 1899 and Mailey in 1921.

Yorkshire 155 (Sutcliffe 67, Grimmett 10-37);
Australia 320 (Woodfull 121, Bradman 78). Match drawn.

Yorkshire v Warwickshire
Headingley, May 16, 18, 1931

Verity seized upon the occasion to accomplish a memorable bowling performance, the young left-hander in the visitors' second innings taking all ten wickets for 36 runs. Only once previously had a Yorkshire bowler enjoyed so exceptional a measure of success, Drake at Weston-Super-Mare in 1914 obtaining all ten wickets in the second innings of Somerset. Up to the time Verity bowled in such deadly form, and by so doing finished off the contest on Monday evening, the match had proceeded on somewhat uneventful lines. Croom and Bates made a stand of 67 for Warwickshire and Parsons drove with power but, Holmes and Sutcliffe settling down in determined fashion, the home side replied with 83 for no wicket. The famous Yorkshire pair stayed together on Monday until the score reached 120 and so registered their 59th three-figure partnership for the county. Oldroyd and Robinson showing the brightest cricket of the match, Warwickshire's total was headed with six wickets in hand. Later on Wood batted freely and Yorkshire gained a lead of 97. Subsequent to the tea interval came the startling bowling of Verity who at one point disposed of four batsmen in one over, getting Smart caught at backward point off the first ball and Foster stumped off the second, while Tate was leg-before to the fifth and Paine taken left handed from a return to the bowler off the sixth.

WARWICKSHIRE	First Innings	Second Innings
*R. E. S. Wyatt b Macaulay	13 – c Holmes b Verity	23
A. J. W. Croom c Wood b Robinson	46 – c Greenwood b Verity	7
L. T. A. Bates c Mitchell b Bowes	54 – c Mitchell b Verity	19
N. Kilner lbw b Macaulay	9 – c Mitchell b Verity	0
J. H. Parsons lbw b Macaulay	48 – c Leyland b Verity	9
W. A. Hill lbw b Bowes	0 – c Wood b Verity	8
†J. A. Smart b Verity	6 – c Mitchell b Verity	0
D. G. Foster b Macaulay	5 – st Wood b Verity	0
C. F. Tate lbw b Verity	8 – lbw b Verity	0
G. A. E. Paine b Verity	6 – c and b Verity	0
J. H. Mayer not out	2 – not out	6
L-b 3, w 1	4	

1-43 2-67 3-100 4-145 5-145 6-176   201   1-16 2-33 3-33 4-51 5-59 6-59   72
7-181 8-186 9-198 10-201   7-59 8-59 9-59 10-72

First innings – Bowes 14–5–25–2; Robinson 20–8–50–1; Macaulay 35–14–61–4; Verity 32.3–11–61–3.
Second innings – Bowes 5–1–7–0; Robinson 4–1–9–0; Verity 18.4–6–36–10; Macaulay 18–11–20–0.

YORKSHIRE	*First Innings*	
P. Holmes b Mayer		58
H. Sutcliffe c Croom b Tate		67
M. Leyland c Kilner b Mayer		2
E. Oldroyd lbw b Mayer		67
A. Mitchell b Wyatt		12
*F. E. Greenwood c Smart b Mayer		30
E. Robinson run out		2
†A. Wood not out		40
G. G. Macaulay b Mayer		0
H. Verity b Mayer		7
W. E. Bowes c Kilner b Paine		0
B 2, l-b 10, n-b 1		13
1-120 2-126 3-139 4-182 5-230 6-239		298
7-267 8-271 9-297 10-298		

First innings – Mayer 30–8–76–6; Foster 17–2–58–0; Wyatt 8–3–12–1; Paine 17.3–3–45–1; Tate 25–6–94–1.

Toss won by Warwickshire   Umpires W. Bestwick and J. H. King.
Close of Play First day: Yorkshire (1) 83-0 (Holmes 47, Sutcliffe 34).

Glamorgan v Yorkshire
Swansea, July 22, 23, 24, 1931

A wonderful bowling performance by Verity was the main factor in a remarkable
Yorkshire victory, the young left-hander actually taking 14 wickets for less than four
runs each and the northern county requiring no more than seven hours to beat
Glamorgan. Nothing could be done on Wednesday until half-past two when
Greenwood, having won the toss, decided to send Glamorgan into bat. Startling success
attended this course, Verity, when tried, getting four wickets in his first two overs for
four runs and seven men being out for 29. Jenkins and Emrys Davies put on 33 but
then Verity finished off the innings. Ryan, at the start of Yorkshire's innings, disposed
of Holmes and Sutcliffe cheaply before there came some confident and powerful
hitting by Leyland who in company with Mitchell, put on 51 in 40 minutes. Ryan,
despite his encouraging start, soon lost his length and at the close Yorkshire with only
three men out, had established a lead of 15. Not a ball could be bowled on Thursday.
The visitors on Friday added 101 in 90 minutes and then declared with eight men out.
Leyland's invaluable display lasted an hour and three-quarters and included ten fours.
Wanting 116 to avert an innings defeat, Glamorgan were dismissed for 91 with an

hour to spare. Verity, when put on at 11, sent down his first four overs for 7 runs and five wickets.

Glamorgan 62 (Verity 6-21) **and 91** (Verity 8-33); **Yorkshire 178-8 dec** (Leyland 77, Ryan 5-86). Yorkshire won by an innings and 25 runs.

Yorkshire v Lancashire
Bradford, May 14, 16, 17, 1932

This was the first match between the counties brought to a definite issue since 1927. On Saturday when the wet state of the ground delayed the start, Paynter gave a great display of driving and pulling which lasted three hours and a half and included five sixes – four off Verity – and 17 fours. He registered his last 50 runs in an hour. Watson helped to put on 67 and Parkinson, making a first appearance, batted in capital form. Yorkshire fielded very keenly and Verity, although on a pitch much too slow for him, severely punished at times by Paynter, took eight wickets for less than 14 runs each.

Heavy rain on Sunday night drenched the ground and might possibly have prevented any cricket on Monday but the application of an absorbent roller allowed of Yorkshire commencing their innings at half-past two. Startling play proved to be in store on the drying pitch, Sibbles bowling in such deadly form that he and Hopwood actually dismissed the Yorkshire eleven in an hour and 50 minutes for 46. Sibbles, often making the ball come very quickly off the ground, sent down 20 overs and four balls for 10 runs and seven wickets. Sutcliffe batted for 80 minutes but after he left – fourth out at 38 – three wickets fell at 42 and the remaining three at 46. In the follow-on – 217 in arrears – Holmes helped to raise the score to 34 and then Sutcliffe and Mitchell played out time and meanwhile brought the total to 81, Sutcliffe showing masterly cricket and Mitchell defending stubbornly.

Next day, however, conditions, if not at all what could have been desired, suggested that Yorkshire might put up a big fight to avert defeat. Sutcliffe was out in the first over and, apart from Leyland, no one offered any real resistance. Leyland hit 43 out of 57 in 45 minutes but so completely did the home batsmen fail to realise expectations that the nine wickets remaining when the last day's cricket began went down in an hour and three-quarters for 86 runs.

Lancashire 263 (Paynter 152, Verity 8-107); **Yorkshire 46** (Sibbles 7-10)
and 167 (Sutcliffe 61, Sibbles 5-58). Lancashire won by an innings and 50 runs.

Essex v Yorkshire
Leyton, June 15, 16, 17, 1932

Holmes and Sutcliffe, Yorkshire's famous opening batsmen, made this match memorable by creating a world's record first-wicket stand of 555. They surpassed an achievement that had stood unequalled for 34 years – that of two other Yorkshiremen, J. T. Brown and John Tunnicliffe, who scored 554 together for the first wicket against Derbyshire at Chesterfield in 1898. The partnership between Holmes and Sutcliffe was the 70th of three-figures in which those two men had participated and their 65th for Yorkshire.

While every credit can be given to the two batsmen for their performance, the fact must not be overlooked that Holmes, almost directly he went in, experienced a great piece of luck. He had indeed scored merely three runs when he was missed behind the wicket, low down on the off side where Sheffield got both hands to the ball but failed to hold it. That fault apart, the batting during the big partnership proved wonderfully sound and confident. Rather unusually, Holmes scored more slowly than his colleague but the pair put a hundred runs on the board in an hour and three-quarters and proceeded to maintain their mastery over the bowling for nearly seven hours and a half. The following times indicate the progress of the batsmen:

100 in an hour and 45 minutes;
200 in three hours 20 minutes;
300 in four hours 35 minutes;
400 in five hours 25 minutes;
500 in six hours 55 minutes;
555 in seven hours 25 minutes.

A curious incident occurred immediately after the new record had been made. Sutcliffe very naturally, since it was obviously Yorkshire's policy to declare as soon as possible, threw away his wicket, playing on with a rather casual stroke, and all the players at once left the field. Then, to everyone's amazement, the total on the scoreboard was altered to read 554. For the moment there seemed reason to fear that the chance of beating the record had been missed but eventually it was discovered that a no-ball had not been counted in the total.

Holmes and Sutcliffe, on a perfect Leyton wicket, made their runs in admirable style. They ran singles skilfully and, if neither man took many risks, runs came at an average rate of scoring. Playing the highest innings of his career, Sutcliffe cut, drove and hit to leg with sound judgment. His straight drives, perfectly timed, were particularly good to watch. Holmes, too, showed a lot of skill when off-driving and cutting but in this innings did not properly reveal his strength on the leg side. He hit 19 fours while Sutcliffe among his figures had a six and 33 fours. The partnership was a magnificent feat in every way and especially of endurance.

The contrast of the Yorkshiremen's batting with that which followed proved truly remarkable. Bowes, with pace off the pitch, and Verity, by cleverly flighted bowling, developed such a mastery that inside two hours Essex were all out for 78. A fourth-wicket stand of 29 between O'Connor and Nichols represented the best of the innings. The last five wickets fell for 19 runs, Verity having the striking figures of five wickets in seven overs for eight runs.

From this pronounced collapse, Essex did not recover, and shortly after one o'clock on Friday Yorkshire emerged from an historic match winners by and innings and 313 runs. In the follow-on, with Essex 477 in arrears, Bowes again made the ball get up awkwardly and, although Crawley brought off some powerful drives, Nichols was the only man who really checked Yorkshire's progress towards victory. By the close of play on Thursday, Essex had five wickets down for 92. Nichols, who had gone in third wicket down at 50, batted with rare pluck and skill and remained to carry out his bat. He withstood the attack for two hours and a half and hit a six and six fours.

Verity, particularly deadly towards the close of the innings, took five wickets for 45 – a performance which gave him a record for the match of ten for 53. Bowes brought his figures for the two innings to nine for 85.

YORKSHIRE — First Innings

P. Holmes not out.	224
H. Sutcliffe b Eastman	313
A. Mitchell	
M. Leyland	
W. Barber	
*A. B. Sellers	
†A. Wood	
A. C. Rhodes	
G. G. Macaulay	
H. Verity	
W. E. Bowes	
B 13, l-b 3, n-b 2	18

1-555   (1 wicket, declared) 555

First innings – Nichols 31–4–105–0; Daer 40–8–106–0; Smith 46–10–128–0; O'Connor 23–5–73–0; Eastman 22.4–2–97–1; Crawley 3–0–7–0; Taylor 4–0–14–0; Bray 1–0–7–0.

ESSEX

	First Innings		Second Innings
L. G. Crawley b Bowes	0	– c Sutcliffe b Bowes	27
D. F. Pope c Rhodes b Bowes.	6	– c Mitchell b Bowes	9
J. O'Connor b Bowes	20	– c Rhodes b Bowes	7
J. A. Cutmore lbw b Bowes.	0	– b Verity	1
M. S. Nichols b Verity	25	– not out	59
L. C. Eastman c Sutcliffe b Macaulay	16	– c Barber b Verity	19
*C. Bray c and b Verity	1	– st Wood b Verity	6
R. M. Taylor c Macaulay b Verity	5	– c Macaulay b Verity	13
†J. R. Sheffield c and b Verity	0	– c Sutcliffe b Verity	5
A. G. Daer c and b Verity.	0	– c Verity b Bowes	0
T. P. B. Smith not out	2	– c Rhodes b Bowes	0
B 3.	3	B 15, l-b 1, n-b 2	18

1-0 2-19 3-19 4-48 5-59 6-60   78   1-38 2-47 3-50 4-50 5-92 6-128   164
7-66 8-72 9-74 10-78   7-148 8-162 9-164 10-164

First innings – Bowes 12–1–38–4; Rhodes 10–5–15–0; Macaulay 7.1–2–14–1; Verity 7–3–8–5.
Second innings – Bowes 23.4–5–47–5; Rhodes 9–5–23–0; Verity 30–12–45–5; Macaulay 16–5–31–0.

Toss won by Yorkshire   Umpires E. F. Field and E. J. Smith
Close of Play First day: Yorkshire (1) 423-0 (Holmes 180, Sutcliffe 231);
Second day: Essex (2) 92-5 (Nichols 19).

Yorkshire v Nottinghamshire
Headingley, July 9, 11, 12, 1932

Verity in this match took – for the second time in his career – all ten wickets in an innings. Prior to lunch on the last day Nottinghamshire scored 38 without loss but on resuming, their ten wickets went down for 29 runs. Verity not only performed the hat-trick in sending back Walker, Harris and Gunn, but got rid of Arthur Staples and Larwood with the last two balls of his next over and then, disposing of Voce and Sam Staples with the third and fourth balls of his following over, brought the innings to a close. This splendid bowling feat Sutcliffe and Holmes followed up by hitting off in about an hour and a half the 139 runs required for victory. Thus, Yorkshire gained a glorious win by ten wickets although, when on Monday afternoon a thunderstorm burst over the ground, they had stood 71 behind with only one wicket to fall.

NOTTINGHAMSHIRE	*First Innings*		*Second Innings*	
W. W. Keeton b Rhodes	9	– c Macaulay b Verity		21
F. W. Shipston b Macaulay	8	– c Wood b Verity		21
W. Walker c Barber b Bowes	36	– c Macaulay b Verity		11
*A. W. Carr c Barber b Verity	0	– c Barber b Verity		0
A. Staples b Macaulay	3	– c Macaulay b Verity		7
C. B. Harris lbw b Leyland	35	– c Holmes b Verity		0
G. V. Gunn b Verity	31	– lbw b Verity		0
†B. Lilley not out	46	– not out		3
H. Larwood b Leyland	48	– c Sutcliffe b Verity		0
W. Voce b Leyland	0	– c Holmes b Verity		0
S. J. Staples b Leyland	0	– st Wood b Verity		0
B 8, l-b 6, w 2, n-b 2	18	B 3, n-b 1		4

1-15 2-35 3-40 4-46 5-67 6-120   234   1-44 2-47 3-51 4-63 5-63 6-63   67
7-159 8-233 9-233 10-234   7-64 8-64 9-67 10-67

First innings – Bowes 31–9–55–1; Rhodes 28–8–49–1; Verity 41–13–64–2; Macaulay 24–10–34–2;
Leyland 8.2–3–14–4.
Second innings – Bowes 5–0–19–0; Macaulay 23–9–34–0; Verity 19.4–16–10–10.

YORKSHIRE	*First Innings*		*Second Innings*
P. Holmes b Larwood	65	– not out	77
H. Sutcliffe c Voce b Larwood	0	– not out	54
A. Mitchell run out	24		
M. Leyland b Voce	5		
W. Barber c and b Larwood	34		
*A. B. Sellers b A. Staples	0		
†A. Wood b Larwood	1		
A. C. Rhodes c A. Staples b Voce	3		
H. Verity b Larwood	12		
G. G. Macaulay not out	8		
W. E. Bowes not out	1		
B 5, l-b 5	10	B 4, l-b 4	8

1-1 2-37 3-122 4-123 5-125   (9 wickets, declared) 163   (no wicket) 139
6-128 7-135 8-152 9-154

First innings - Larwood 22–4–73–5; Voce 22–2–52–2; S. J. Staples 7–2–8–0; A. Staples 11–3–20–1.
Second innings – Larwood 3–0–14–0; Voce 10–0–43–0; S. J. Staples 18.4–5–37–0; A. Staples 6–1–25–0;
Harris 3–0–12–0.

Toss won by Nottinghamshire   UMPIRES H. G. Baldwin and W. Reeves
Close of Play First day: Nottinghamshire (1) 234 all out;
Second day: Yorkshire (1) 163-9 (Macaulay 8, Bowes 1).

Yorkshire v Warwickshire
Scarborough, July 18, 19, 20, 1934

After being dismissed for 45, the lowest score of the season, Warwickshire gained a remarkable victory by one wicket. Rain affected the pitch and though the match did not start until twenty minutes to three, eighteen wickets fell on Wednesday for 126. Sent in by Parsons, Yorkshire began by losing three men for 12 runs and were all out in two and a half hours, but before stumps were drawn Warwickshire had eight wickets down for 25. On going in again Yorkshire made very slow progress and might have been got rid of quite cheaply had not five chances been missed. The pitch was in better condition than at any previous time in the match when Warwickshire went in to get 216. Parsons rose to the occasion and by superb driving he dominated the cricket to such an extent that in less than two hours he made 94 out of 121, hitting three 6s and twelve 4s. Only 12 runs were wanted when he left.

Yorkshire 101 (Turner 51, Paine 8-62) **and 159;**
Warwickshire 45 and 216-9 (Rev. Parsons 94, Kilner 580).
Warwickshire won by one wicket.

Yorkshire v Kent
Bramall Lane, May 23, 25, 1936

A wonderful triumph for Verity, who had a record of 15 wickets for 38 runs. In the Kent second innings he had a hand in dismissing the whole side, for after he caught Fagg he took all the other nine wickets. Kent, who at the time were leaders of the county competition, were completely outplayed from the start. Showers and poor light may have formed some handicap to batsmen on Saturday, but the resistance offered to Verity was dreadfully weak. Although Watt hit a six and three fours off him, Verity secured six wickets for 26 runs. A century by Barber served to show there was nothing seriously wrong with the wicket. By sound strokeplay, Barber hit 158 out of 289 in considerably less than four hours. His chief scoring strokes were 17 fours. By the end of the day Yorkshire led by 78 with only three men out, and when, after heavy weekend rain, the wicket showed signs of becoming difficult, Sellers declared. No one could have been prepared for what followed. Verity made the ball rise and turn either way, and in an hour and a quarter Kent were out for a paltry 39 runs. Half the side fell for 30, and after a few hits by the early batsmen, Sunnucks alone contrived to keep up his wicket. The conditions undoubtedly placed batsmen at a great disadvantage, but Verity showed splendid control of flight, length and pace, and made the batsmen play at every ball. He could scarcely have received better support in the field, where Mitchell often did brilliant things.

Kent 107 (Verity 6-26) **and 39** (Verity 9-12);
Yorkshire 299-7 dec (Barber 158).
Yorkshire won by an innings and 153 runs.

Lancashire v Yorkshire
Old Trafford, July 31, August 2, 3, 1948

Lester equalled the 28-year-old record of P. Holmes by scoring a century in each innings of a Roses game. Altogether the encounter produced five three-figure scores. Lester's first-innings display was rather overshadowed by the brilliance of Hutton, who made 104 out of 184 before a fierce thunderstorm flooded the ground. Lester batted three hours and a quarter for his 125 and hit 18 fours while Greenwood was bowling extremely well. Lancashire lost two wickets for 12, but Washbrook hit a six and 21 fours during three hours and a quarter. Ikin helped to add 244, putting Lancashire on the way to the lead. Lester's second hundred made in 110 minutes was marked by superb driving and vigorous pulls. Yardley preferred that Yorkshire should continue batting rather than declare and the match petered out.

Yorkshire 359 (Lester 125 not out, Hutton 104, Greenwood 6-68)
and 241-5 (Lester 132); **Lancashire 361-5 dec** (Washbrook 156, Ikin 106).
Match drawn.

Lancashire v Yorkshire
Old Trafford, June 4, 6, 7, 1949

Hutton, by scoring a double hundred, equalled the feats of Leyland and Spooner, the only others to accomplish this performance in a Roses match. He batted faultlessly for six hours 50 minutes and his most productive hits were three sixes, a five and 19 fours. Halliday, missed twice, helped in a second-wicket partnership of 163. Following the early loss of Washbrook, Lancashire made indifferent progress against the accurate bowling of Close, Mason and Hutton, eight wickets being down before the follow-on was avoided. Hutton again batted in masterly fashion, and when Yorkshire declared with a lead of 317 his match aggregate was 292 for once out. Yorkshire seemed likely to win when four men were dismissed for 65, but Grieves, dropped four times, thwarted them in a fifth-wicket stand of 69 with Wharton. He hit four sixes and eight fours.

Yorkshire 326-7 dec (Hutton 201, Halliday 69) **and 168-3 dec** (Hutton not out 91);
Lancashire 177 and 227-5 (Wharton 73 not out).
Match drawn.

Yorkshire v MCC
Scarborough, August 31, September 1, 2, 1949

Hutton, who, by scoring 199 in the match, raised his season's aggregate to 3,145 runs. Hutton made his 147 out of 245 in two hours 50 minutes and hit three sixes and 18 fours, all splendid strokes. Close exceeded a thousand runs so completing the double in his first season of county cricket at the age of 18; Coxon and Wardle each took his hundredth wicket, and Cranston on his first appearance of the season played his highest innings in important cricket.

Yorkshire 429-8 dec (Hutton 147, Lowson 58, Wilson 58, Yardley 58)
and 212-3 dec (Lowson 89, Hutton 52); **MCC 430-9 dec** (Cranston 156 not out,
Compton 127) **and 109-5**: Match drawn.

Surrey v Yorkshire
The Oval, July 14, 16, 17, 1951

Hutton completed his century of centuries. After Surrey had broken down when the pitch gave a little help to bowlers, Hutton and Lowson took charge and at the end of the first day their unfinished stand had realised 112. Hutton then wanted 39 runs for his hundred and on Monday 15,000 people turned up. They were not disappointed and Hutton achieved his objective with a stroke worthy of the occasion – a superb drive off

Wait sped past cover-point to the boundary. Altogether the opening partnership produced 197 and Hutton, who batted faultlessly for four hours and 40 minutes, hit 12 fours. Surrey looked in a hopeless position when they batted again 275 behind, but Yorkshire dropped vital catches and finally found themselves wanting 43 in 20 minutes. In a hectic scramble for runs, they paid the penalty for hitting recklessly at every ball, and although they raced to and from the pavilion gate the task was beyond them.

Surrey 156 and 317 (Fishlock 89); **Yorkshire 431-3** (Hutton 151,
Wilson 144 not out, Lowson 84) **and 30-6.** Match drawn.

Yorkshire v MCC
Scarborough, September 1, 3, 4, 1951

Another triumph for Appleyard, who, in his last match of the season, captured the 11 wickets he required to take his aggregate to 200. When eight MCC second-innings wickets were down he needed to take the last two to reach this figure. He succeeded in one over. Appleyard's first-innings analysis was his best in first-class cricket. By aggressive batting, Yorkshire built up a big lead. Seven sixes, three by Wardle off Brown, were hit, and Watson's strokes included 12 fours.

MCC 158 (Appleyard 8-76) **and 273** (May 56); **Yorkshire 333** (Watson 70, Lester 66,
Tattersall 5-122) **and 29-1.** Match drawn.

Lancashire v Yorkshire
Old Trafford, August 2, 4, 5, 1952

Seldom has there been such an exciting finish to a Roses match. With half an hour left, Lancashire were 157 for seven when Trueman and Burgin took the new ball. Trueman dismissed Statham and Tattersall, and ten minutes remained when the last man, Berry, joined Parr. Amid tremendous enthusiasm they defied all efforts to dislodge them, Parr having stayed gallantly for an hour.

Yorkshire 200 (Berry 6-52) **and 163-8 dec** (Close 61); **Lancashire 65** (Burgin 5-20,
Trueman 5-26) **and 166-9.** Match drawn.

Yorkshire v Sussex
Hull, June 2, 3, 5, 1954

The all-round skill of Wardle served Yorkshire well. Going on in the first innings with Sussex 30 for one, Wardle in the next two and a half hours took the remaining nine wickets. Had all chances been held, his figures would have been even better. Lowson, Wilson and Watson batted soundly enough for Yorkshire to finish the first day on terms with eight wickets left, and next day, with Wardle (11 fours) hitting hard and then revelling in a crumbling pitch, they pressed home their advantage. The last morning's cricket consisted of two overs, Wardle finishing with match figures of 16 wickets for 112.

Sussex 154 (Wardle 9-48) **and 178** (Wardle 7-64); **Yorkshire 352-9 dec** (Wilson 75, Wardle 66 not out). Yorkshire won by an innings and 20 runs.

Yorkshire v Leicestershire
Huddersfield, June 16, 17, 18, 1954

A tie, the first in Yorkshire's history. When Wardle bowled the last ball of extra time the issue was completely open. With the scores level, Spencer played the ball down the pitch and went for the run which would have given Leicestershire victory. Instead, Wardle picked up swiftly and threw down the wicket, Spencer being run out.

YORKSHIRE	*First Innings*		*Second Innings*	
L. Hutton c Firth b Munden	60	– c Firth b Spencer	6
F. A. Lowson b Walsh	38	– b Spencer	8
J. V. Wilson c Palmer b Walsh	138	– b Spencer	18
E. I. Lester c Boshier b Palmer	33	– b Spencer	34
W. Watson not out	80	– b Spencer	0
*N. W. D. Yardley		– b Spencer	22
D. B. Close		– c Firth b Palmer	1
J. H. Wardle		– b Spencer	0
†R. Booth		– c Smithson b Spencer	8
F. S. Trueman		– b Spencer	8
R. Appleyard		– not out	1
L-b 1, n-b 1	2	B 4, l-b 1, n-b 2.	7

1-82 2-123 3-183 4-351   (4 wickets, declared) 351   1-13 2-18 3-43 4-43 5-82 6-85   113
7-87 8-97 9-108 10-113

First innings – Spencer 25–3–70–0; Boshier 17–3–51–0; Palmer 12–4–33–1; Walsh 20.5–0–77–2; Jackson 14–3–52–0; Munden 23–4–66–1.
Second innings – Spencer 23–3–63–9; Palmer 12–6–18–1; Jackson 10–2–25–0.

LEICESTERSHIRE	*First Innings*		*Second Innings*
G. Lester b Close	74	– b Trueman	4
M. R. Hallam b Trueman	24	– b Trueman	2
M. Tompkin st Booth b Wardle	149	– c and b Appleyard	6
*C. H. Palmer c Hutton b Wardle	15	– (5) b Wardle	31
V. E. Jackson c Booth b Trueman	1	– (6) c Lester b Trueman	4
G. A. Smithson c and b Close	25	– (4) c Lowson b Trueman	0
V. S. Munden b Appleyard	19	– run out	31
J. E. Walsh b Wardle	0	– c Hutton b Wardle	28
†J. Firth not out	8	– (10) st Booth b Wardle.	3
C. T. Spencer st Booth b Appleyard	0	– (9) run out	8
B. S. Boshier c Watson b Wardle	1	– not out	1
B 8, l-b 4	12	B 6, l-b 11, n-b 1	18

1-58 2-183 3-216 4-223 5-281 6-315   328   1-8 2-15 3-19 4-21 5-29 6-72   136
7-315 8-327 9-327 10-328   7-123 8-123 9-127 10-136

First innings – Trueman 22–1–83–2; Appleyard 31–11–62–2; Yardley 6–1–22–0; Wardle 44.4–18–82–4;
Close 21–3–67–2.
Second innings – Trueman 18–2–44–4; Appleyard 20–8–38–1; Wardle 13–4–36–3.

Toss won by Yorkshire   UMPIRES E. Cooke and H. Elliott
Close of Play First day: Leicestershire (1) 27-0 (Lester 18, Hallam 9);
Second day: Yorkshire (2) 20-2 (Wilson 6, Lester 0).

Yorkshire v Surrey
Leeds, June 18, 20, 21, 1955

This thrilling struggle between the two leading sides in the country drew over 60,000 people and the atmosphere resembled that of a Test match. Surrey struggled hard to preserve their record, but were beaten for the first time in 16 consecutive games. The gates were locked on Saturday when 35,000 saw Surrey fight back after losing their first eight wickets for 119. Lock and Loader, who added 96, each made his highest score. Loader and Bedser completed the recovery with a last wicket stand of 53. Yorkshire found runs hard to get against accurate bowling, but Wilson defended well for nearly three hours and helped to save the follow on. Then Surrey, leading by 102, broke down completely in the last 100 minutes of Monday, losing seven men for 27 in poor light against the fast bowling of Trueman and Cowan. Next day, the last three wickets added 48 and Yorkshire needed 178 to win in three hours ten minutes. Until the last half hour they were behind the clock, but they obtained the runs with eleven minutes to spare. Wilson and Lowson put on 91 for the second wicket and Watson and Sutcliffe 71 for the fourth.

Surrey 268 (Loader 81) **and 75** (Cowan 5-15);
Yorkshire 166 and 178-8 (Lowson 52). Yorkshire won by six wickets.

Worcestershire v Yorkshire
Worcester, July 27, 29, 30, 1957

When the last day commenced with Yorkshire only 56 ahead on first innings with three wickets left, there seemed little to suggest the victory ahead. Success was made possible by the accurate off-spin of Illingworth, who utilised a spot on otherwise placid turf. He took nine wickets for 42 runs, his best performance, and Yorkshire, left to score 67 in an hour, won with seven minutes to spare. The previous day Illingworth showed excellent batting form. Watson, much less enterprising, took more than three and a half hours over 80.

Worcestershire 237 and 172 (Outschoorn 60, Illingworth 9-42);
Yorkshire 343 (Watson 80, Illingworth 58) **and 68-3**.
Yorkshire won by seven wickets.

Sussex v Yorkshire
Hove, August 29, 31, September 1, 1959

Yorkshire made sure of the title in one of the most exciting finishes seen on the ground after being left to get 215 in 105 minutes. With their batsmen playing shots at practically every delivery the winning hit came with seven minutes to spare. Few of the crowd had given Yorkshire much of a chance, but Stott quickly showed the county's intentions. He hit 13 of the 15 obtained in the first over and the 50 appeared in 20 minutes. Within half an hour 77 were scored; 100 came in 43 minutes; 150 in 63 minutes; 200 in 85 minutes and the winning stroke – a deflection to the fine leg boundary by Bolus – was made at 4.23 p.m. Stott batted only 86 minutes for 96.

Sussex	*First Innings*		*Second Innings*
A. S. M. Oakman st Binks b Taylor	33	– (2) b Close	7
L. J. Lenham c Taylor b Trueman	4	– (1) c Stott b Wilson	66
K. G. Suttle c Illingworth b Taylor	5	– st Binks b Wilson	22
E. R. Dexter c and b Taylor	14	– c Birkenshaw b Wilson	33
†J. M. Parks c Bolus b Taylor	6	– c Birkenshaw b Wilson	85
D. V. Smith c Close b Illingworth	49	– (7) c Bolus b Taylor	31
G. H. G. Doggart lbw b Close	5	– (6) c Birkenshaw b Illingworth	10
Nawab of Pataudi b Trueman	52	– c Close b Illingworth	37
N. I. Thomson lbw b Illingworth	21	– b Illingworth	12
A. E. James b Illingworth	4	– not out	0
*R. G. Marlar not out	13	– c Birkenshaw b Illingworth	0
L-b 4	4	B 4, l-b 4	8

1-28 2-40 3-51 4-62 5-63 6-67   210   1-14 2-80 3-99 4-174 5-195 6-247   311
7-157 8-192 9-193 10-210   7-266 8-306 9-311 10-311

First innings – Trueman 19–5–40–2; Close 17–5–54–1; Taylor 22–9–40–4; Illingworth 14.2–3–51–3; Wilson 5–1–21–0.
Second innings – Trueman 24–5–60–0; Close 19–6–51–1; Illingworth 28.3–8–66–4; Taylor 8–5–5–1; Birkenshaw 7–0–43–0; Wilson 24–7–78–4.

YORKSHIRE	First Innings	Second Innings
W. B. Stott c and b Suttle	34	– c Pataudi b Marlar 96
J. B. Bolus hit wkt b Dexter	1	– (7) not out 6
D. E. V. Padgett c Parks b Dexter	0	– (4) c Dexter b Thomson 79
D. B. Close b Dexter	14	– (3) c Parks b Dexter 12
R. Illingworth c Parks b James	122	– (6) not out 5
K. Taylor b Thomson	3	– (2) lbw b Dexter 1
J. Birkenshaw lbw b Marlar	38	
D. Wilson c Oakman b Marlar	55	
*J. R. Burnet c Marlar b Dexter	1	
F. S. Trueman c Pataudi b James	7	– (5) st Parks b Marlar 11
†J. G. Binks not out	1	
B 24, l-b 6, n-b 1	31	B 1, l-b 4, n-b 3 8

1-6 2-6 3-38 4-78 5-81 6-193	307	1-18 2-40 3-181 4-199 5-206 (5 wickets) 218
7-259 8-264 9-305 10-307		

First innings – Thomson 31–7–65–1; Dexter 29–7–63–4; Smith 4–1–14–0; James 24–4–67–2; Marlar 15.4–7–29–2; Suttle 6–1–20–1; Oakman 6–1–18–0; Doggart 1–1–0–0.
Second innings – Thomson 10–0–87–1; Dexter 10.3–0–69–2; James 2–0–15–0; Marlar 6–0–39–2.

Toss won by Sussex   UMPIRES R. S. M. Lay and F. S. Lee
Close of Play First day: Yorkshire (1) 89-5 (Illingworth 24, Birkenshaw 3);
Second day: Sussex (2) 143-3 (Dexter 23, Parks 25).

Surrey v Yorkshire
The Oval, June 18, 20, 21, 1960

The fiery fast bowling of Trueman, who took 14 wickets for 123 and in each innings sent back three men in five balls, was the deciding factor on a firm pitch. In the first innings he disposed of Tindall, Willett and Gibson in five deliveries with the score 93, and in the second repeated the feat at the expense of Barrington, Willett and Gibson when the total stood at 218. Trueman's speed and judicious use of the yorker and bouncer kept all his rivals on tenterhooks. Yorkshire lacked Stott and Taylor through injury, but Padgett and Close made up for the handicap with splendid centuries. Partners in a third-wicket stand of 226, both drove well, Close so powerfully that he hit Lock three times straight into the pavilion – once sending the ball clean through an open window. Close, who batted five and a half hours, hit 22 fours besides four sixes. Surrey, shown the way by Stewart and Parsons, fared much better in their second innings and Lock gained some compensation for the harsh treatment of his left-arm spin bowling by gallantly hitting eight boundaries. Yorkshire were left to make only two runs to win, but only a quarter of an hour of extra time remained when they achieved their victory.

Surrey 123 (Trueman 7-41) **and 312** (Stewart 78, Barrington 62, Trueman 7-82);
Yorkshire 434-4 dec (Close 198, Padgett 117, Illingworth 55 not out) **and 4-1**.
Yorkshire won by nine wickets.

Hampshire v Yorkshire
Portsmouth, May 21, 23, 24, 1960

Magnificent bowling by Trueman, which followed hundreds by Close and Bolus, proved too much for Hampshire. Bolus and Close shared a third-wicket partnership of 151 and Close hit four sixes and eight fours in two hours. Bolus spent much longer over his maiden hundred and altogether he batted five and a half hours for his not out 146 (15 fours). Hampshire played steadily to score 140 for two wickets and then Trueman, taking the new ball, finished the innings with a spell of 10-5-11-6. Following on 208 behind, Hampshire fared even worse. Horton, who played courageously, alone defied Trueman who captured six more wickets for a match analysis of 12 wickets for 62 runs.

Yorkshire 399-7 dec (Bolus 146 not out, Close 102);
Hampshire 191 (Marshall 70, Gray 54, Trueman 6-34)
and 147 (Horton 68 not out, Trueman 6-28).
Yorkshire won by an innings and 61 runs.

Lancashire v Yorkshire
Old Trafford, July 30, August 1, 2, 1960

Lancashire completed their first Roses double since 1893. They achieved victory in a tense finish when Dyson turned the last ball of the match, sent down by Trueman, to the on-boundary. Splendid bowling by Statham and Higgs dismissed Yorkshire for a moderate total on the first day, despite a sound innings by Close. Lancashire took the lead with only one wicket down, due to a second-wicket stand of 121 by Barber and Wharton, but so keenly did Yorkshire bowl and field that Lancashire were denied bonus points. Following a heavy storm just after lunch on the second day, Lancashire lost their last six wickets for 39 runs against Trueman and Ryan, who were able to make the ball fly. Statham again troubled Yorkshire, and only Sharpe and the two Wilsons effectively resisted, so that Lancashire were set to make 78 in two hours. Sustained hostility from Trueman and Ryan made the task far from easy and when Greenhough was bowled by the second ball of Trueman's last over, five runs were still needed. Two singles and two leg byes led to the dramatic climax. During the three days 74,000 spectators saw the match.

YORKSHIRE	First Innings		Second Innings	
W. B. Stott c Marner b Higgs	1	– c Collins b Statham	5
K. Taylor b Higgs	19	– b Higgs	8
D. E. V. Padgett lbw b Greenhough	21	– lbw b Statham	6
D. B. Close b Statham	63	– (5) lbw b Statham	9
P. J. Sharpe lbw b Statham	16	– (6) lbw b Statham	46
R. Illingworth lbw b Statham	7	– (7) c Clayton b Dyson	9
*J. V. Wilson b Statham	13	– (8) c Clayton b Greenhough	20
D. Wilson b Statham	0	– (9) not out	32
F. S. Trueman not out	3	– (10) lbw b Barber.	4
†J. G. Binks b Higgs	4	– (4) b Higgs	1
M. Ryan b Higgs	0	– b Barber	3
B 1, l-b 5, n-b 1	7	L-b 5, n-b 1	6

1-1 2-20 3-64 4-93 5-113 6-146   154
7-146 8-147 9-154 10-154

1-8 2-18 3-19 4-28 5-36 6-63   149
7-89 8-121 9-143 10-149

First innings – Statham 23–7–43–5; Higgs 17.2–6–48–4; Greenhough 15–2–46–1; Dyson 5–2–10–0; Barber 1–1–0–0.
Second innings – Statham 24–13–23–4; Higgs 16–7–35–2; Greenhough 16–6–43–1; Dyson 10–6–12–1; Barber 7.3–0–30–2.

LANCASHIRE	First Innings		Second Innings	
*R. W. Barber c Trueman b D. Wilson	71	– run out	11
G. Pullar c Taylor b Close	11	– b Ryan.	14
A. Wharton c J. V. Wilson b Trueman	83	– c Padgett b Ryan	4
J. Dyson b Trueman	15	– (10) not out	5
K. J. Grieves lbw b Ryan	5	– (4) c Binks b Ryan	27
P. T. Marner run out	4	– (5) b Trueman	0
R. Collins b Trueman	0	– (6) b Ryan	2
†G. Clayton c Close b Trueman	28	– (8) not out	15
T. Greenhough c Sharpe b Ryan	0	– (9) b Trueman	0
J. B. Statham c J. V. Wilson b Ryan	0	– (7) c Binks b Ryan	0
K. Higgs not out	3		
B 4, l-b 1, w 1	6	L-b 3	3

1-26 2-157 3-172 4-187 5-191 6-195   226
7-199 8-199 9-203 10-226

1-16 2-27 3-31 4-32 5-43 6-43   (8 wickets) 81
7-72 8-73

First innings – Trueman 28–5–65–4; Ryan 33–9–69–3; Close 12–3–23–1; D. Wilson 13–7–35–1; Illingworth 16–6–28–0.
Second innings – Trueman 16–4–28–2; Ryan 15–4–50–5.

Toss won by Lancashire   UMPIRES J. S. Buller and J. G. Langridge.
Close of Play First day Lancashire (1) 97-1 (Barber 51, Wharton 35);
Second day: Yorkshire (2) 19-2 (Taylor 7, Binks 1).

Worcestershire v Yorkshire
Worcester, June 3, 5, 6, 1961

Spectators at this casualty-stricken match will long remember the plucky effort of Don Wilson. The end of Yorkshire's unbeaten record in the Championship looked imminent when nine wickets tumbled to a combination of pace and spin with 36 runs still required. Then Wilson, with his left arm in plaster from the elbow to the knuckles because of a fractured thumb, joined Platt with 25 minutes to play. Though the pain quickly prompted him to bat one-handed, Wilson swept Gifford twice for four and when Flavell took the new ball five minutes from the end with 22 runs still needed, he immediately struck three boundaries and a two with one-handed drives. This over also brought four byes. Then Platt took a single off Coldwell and the crowd rose to cheer when Wilson straight drove to the boundary to complete a thrilling finish. He hit 29 in a last-wicket stand of 37. Yorkshire had to fight hard all the time in face of some excellent bowling. They lost half their side for 136 in the first innings, at which point Trueman helped them recover by hitting eight fours while scoring 43 in a stand of 50 with his captain. Later, when left to score 190 for victory, they were 86 for 7 before Illingworth, pressed into service though not fully fit, and Binks added 60 in 55 minutes as a prelude to Wilson's game effort. Worcestershire had their casualties, too. Kenyon went for an X-ray after being struck on the left wrist by a ball from Trueman and Broadbent was reduced to a hobble by a pulled hamstring.

Worcestershire 227 (Headley 61) **and 227; Yorkshire 265-9 dec** (Bolus 54, Horton 5-110) **and 191-9**. Yorkshire won by one wicket.

Yorkshire v Hampshire
Middlesbrough, May 19, 20, 1965

A disaster for Yorkshire who, in their second innings, were dismissed for 23, the lowest total in their history. On the first day 22 wickets fell for 253. Trueman, with a hurricane innings of 55 off 22 balls in 29 minutes, saved Yorkshire from complete collapse. Shackleton, although hit by Trueman for 26 off one over, still took 6-64. Only Marshall did much for Hampshire, who led by four. Before the close, Yorkshire lost two second-innings wickets for seven runs and next morning they were demoralized by the fast bowling of White who, in one spell, took five wickets without cost and altogether claimed 6-10. Hampshire needed only 20 to inflict on Yorkshire the first defeat at Middlesbrough. Yorkshire's previous lowest total was 26 against Surrey at The Oval in 1909.

Yorkshire 121 (Trueman 55, Shackleton 6-64) **and 23** (White 6-10); **Hampshire 125** (Marshall 51) **and 20-0**. Hampshire won by 10 wickets

The Gillette Cup Final: Surrey v Yorkshire
Lord's, September 4, 1965

Yorkshire deservedly became the new holders of the trophy in a surprisingly one-sided match. Despite this, the 25,000 spectators, of whom over 21,000 paid, received six hours of capital entertainment. Yorkshire, spearheaded by an aggressive Boycott, broke most of the competition's records. Boycott made the highest individual score, shared in the biggest partnership with his captain and Yorkshire reached a new total. The previous highest total – 314 for seven by Sussex against Kent in 1963 – was scored off 65 overs as opposed to 60 overs. Yorkshire, sent in, began slowly but gradually. Boycott, well supported by Close, completely mastered Surrey's attack. After an indifferent season and without a first-class century, he cast aside his troubles and played forcing shots all round the wicket. He struck three sixes and 14 fours. Close hit one six and seven fours and Storey, alone of Surrey's bowlers, escaped severe punishment. Surrey's batsmen never got into their stride and the writing was on the wall when Trueman sent back Edrich, Smith and Barrington in four deliveries. Illingworth also captured three wickets in one over and Tindall played an almost lone hand. Boycott was an obvious choice as Man of the Match by the chairman of the England selectors D. J. Insole. Because of a 24-hours downpour, which made part of the outfield waterlogged the previous day, the match had appeared in jeopardy. Heroic work by the ground-staff, reinforced by drying machines from The Oval, enabled the match to begin only an hour and a half late.

YORKSHIRE

G. Boycott c Storey b Barrington	. . . .	146
K. Taylor c Barrington b Sydenham	. . . .	9
*D. B. Close c Edrich b Gibson	. . . .	79
F. S. Trueman b Arnold	. . . .	24
J. H. Hampshire not out	. . . .	38
D. Wilson not out	. . . .	11
D. E. V. Padgett		
P. J. Sharpe		
R. Illingworth		
R. A. Hutton		
†J. G. Binks		
B 3, l-b 4, n-b 3	. . . .	10

1-22 2-214 3-248 4-292   (4 wickets, 60 overs) 317

Arnold 13–3–51–1; Sydenham 13–1–67–1; Gibson 13–1–66–1; Storey 13–2–33–0; Tindall 3–0–36–0; Barrington 5–0–54–1.

SURREY

*M. J. Stewart st Binks b Wilson	. . . .	33
J. H. Edrich c Illingworth b Trueman	. . . .	15
W. A. Smith b Trueman	. . . .	0
K. F. Barrington c Binks b Trueman	. . . .	0
R. A. E. Tindall c Wilson b Close	. . . .	57
S. J. Storey lbw b Illingworth	. . . .	1
M. J. Edwards b Illingworth	. . . .	0
D. Gibson lbw b Illingworth	. . . .	0
†A. Long b Illingworth	. . . .	17
G. G. Arnold not out	. . . .	3
D. A. D. Sydenham b Illingworth	. . . .	8
B 4, l-b 4	. . . .	8

1-27 2-27 3-27 4-75 5-76 6-76   (40.4 overs) 142
7-76 8-130 9-132 10-142

Trueman 9–0–31–3; Hutton 8–3–17–0; Wilson 9–0–45–1; Illingworth 11.4–1–29–5; Close 3–0–12–1.

Toss won by Surrey   UMPIRES J. S. Buller and C. S. Elliott
                                      Man of the Match G. Boycott

Yorkshire v Cambridgeshire
Castleford, May 25, 1967

The match became a desperate improvisation reduced to ten overs for each side after play had been impossible on any of the three days originally allocated. Assembling at Headingley on the new date arranged, the teams found the ground underwater and when they moved to Castleford, some 12 miles away, they met further frustration through a thunderstorm. Honouring the agreement that a result would be obtained whatever the conditions, Cambridgeshire fielded in drenching rain and the cricket verged on the farcical, though some notable catches were held.

Cambridge 43-8, 10 overs; Yorkshire 46-4, 6.4 overs.
Yorkshire won by six wickets.

The Gillette Cup Final: Derbyshire v Yorkshire
Lord's, September 6, 1969

Morgan pinned his hopes on his bowlers, who had seen the side through the previous rounds, but although they proved menacing some loose fielding among many brilliant efforts proved costly. Yorkshire were worried when they discovered that Leadbeater had broken a finger bone in his left hand on the previous day at Hove. It was strapped and he played the vital innings, his 76 earning him the Man of the Match award from Colin

Cowdrey 'by a whisker'. Close was the master tactician and in form with bat and ball for Yorkshire. He kept Derbyshire on a tight rein when he began their task of making 220 to win by asking Nicholson to bowl his 12 overs off the reel and Close himself relieved Old after six overs and conceded only 14 runs in his first ten overs. Derbyshire were handicapped through Page, their most talented hitter, straining a side when fielding and having to bat at number seven instead of three. All tickets were sold, 21,000 people being present on a warm sunny day. Boycott was absent from the Yorkshire team because he also had fractured his left hand in the previous Championship match.

YORKSHIRE

B. Leadbeater c Taylor b Ward	76
J. D. Woodford c Taylor b Eyre	15
*D. B. Close c Page b Ward	37
P. J. Sharpe b Ward	3
D. E. V. Padgett c Buxton b Rumsey	30
J. H. Hampshire c Morgan b Rhodes	2
R. A. Hutton not out	29
†J. G. Binks b Rhodes	4
D. Wilson c Ward b Rumsey	2
C. M. Old not out	3
A. G. Nicholson	
B 3, l-b 13, n-b 2	18

1-39 2-103 3-107 4-154   (8 wickets, 60 overs) 219
5-157 6-177 7-192 8-195

Ward 12–1–31–3; Rhodes 12–2–47–2; Buxton 12–6–24–0; Eyre 12–0–53–1; Rumsey 11–0–33–2; Morgan 1–0–13–0.

DERBYSHIRE

P. J. K. Gibbs b Nicholson	19
D. H. K. Smith b Close	26
*D. C. Morgan run out	5
A. Ward c Close b Hutton	17
I. R. Buxton c Close b Wilson	34
J. F. Harvey b Wilson	3
M. H. Page c Wilson b Close	16
†R. W. Taylor c Leadbeater b Close	2
T. J. P. Eyre not out	14
F. E. Rumsey b Wilson	1
H. J. Rhodes c Hampshire b Old	6
B 1, l-b 4, w 2	7

1-37 2-49 3-54 4-77 5-83 6-112   (54. 4 overs) 150
7-128 8-129 9-136 10-150

Old 9.4–1–25–1; Nicholson 12–5–14–1; Close 11–2–36–3; Wilson 12–0–38–3; Hutton 10–1–30–1.

Toss won by Derbyshire   UMPIRES T. W. Spencer and H. Yarnold
                                           Man of the Match B. Leadbeater

Lancashire v Yorkshire
Old Trafford, May 29, 31, June 1, 1971

With the weather uncertain and the pitch freshened by showers from time to time, the batsmen were always struggling for runs and Engineer with an aggressive 49 was the main scorer in a Lancashire total of 168. In reply Yorkshire began slowly with only 43 from 22 overs after tea on the first day and, trapped on a drying wicket on the Monday, were all out for 79 in the face of excellent bowling by Lever and Hughes. It was Lancashire's turn to struggle on the last morning after a storm had ended play early on the Monday, Hutton followed up his first innings 6-36 with 5-24 and Lancashire were dismissed for 75. Yorkshire were left with roughly three hours to make 165 for victory on a much easier pitch, but with Boycott absent ill they made no attempt to get the runs.

Lancashire 168 (Hutton 6-38) **and 75** (Hutton 5-24);
Yorkshire 79 (Lever 5-27) **and 103-6.**
Match drawn.

Yorkshire v Durham
Harrogate, June 30, 1973

The first defeat of a first-class county by a junior side since the Minor Counties joined the competition in its second year, ten years earlier. It meant that Yorkshire had not won a Gillette Cup match since they won the Cup in 1969. When Boycott won the toss and had choice of batting or bowling it seemed that everything was in their favour. Instead, the Durham opening bowlers, Wilkinson and Alan Old (Rugby international brother of the Yorkshireman) performed so steadily that only 18 runs came in the first nine overs. At this stage Wilkinson bowled Boycott and this success lifted the Durham bowlers and fieldsmen to unexpected heights. They seldom bowled a bad ball and the fielding was superb. In spite of a good innings by Johnson, Yorkshire were bowled out in 58.4 overs for only 135 runs. The Durham captain, Lander, returned the best bowling figures of his career, and was Man of the Match. Nicholson and Chris Old, with the new ball, often beat the bat in their opening spells, but they could not upset the determination and concentration of the batsmen. With plenty of time in hand, Inglis scored 47 runs in good style. Durham coasted to victory.

Yorkshire 135, 58.4 overs, (Lander 5-15). **Durham 138-5, 51.3 overs.**
Durham won by five wickets.

Yorkshire v Middlesex
Bradford, July 10, 12, 13, 1976

Yorkshire recovered from the confusion of 17 for three in the first hour to win a thrilling match by the narrowest margin. Love and Squires led Yorkshire's recovery before Middlesex, without Radley who broke a finger fielding in the slips, fell to Cope's off-spin. Yorkshire struggled to gain a lead of 236. The advantage was always in the balance throughout the last afternoon as Bore and Cope shared the attack on a wicket offering them some encouragement. A late collapse brought the injured Radley to the wicket with his arm in a sling. His brave effort to help in making the vital last five runs was in vain, however, Bairstow stumping him at 235.

Yorkshire 228 (Love 77) **and 214** (Hampshire 59); **Middlesex 206** (Cope 6-60) **and 235** (Featherstone 76, Cope 5-107). Yorkshire won by one run.

Warwickshire v Yorkshire
Edgbaston, May 19, 20, 21, 1982

An extraordinary last-wicket stand of 149 in 140 minutes between Boycott and Stevenson on the second day left Warwickshire in a precarious position. Stevenson's unbeaten 115 made him only the eighth number 11 to score a century in first-class cricket, and the stand was Yorkshire's best ever for the tenth wicket, the previous having stood since 1898. Yorkshire gained a lead of 134, and although Amiss battled in his second innings to reach 74, Warwickshire were only 14 ahead with three wickets remaining at the start of the last day. Boycott saw Yorkshire home to their easy victory.

Warwickshire 158 and 166 (Amiss 75, Old 6-76); **Yorkshire 292** (Stevenson 115 not out, Boycott 79) **and 33-1**. Yorkshire won by nine wickets.

Benson & Hedges Cup Final: Northamptonshire v Yorkshire
Lord's, July 11, 1987

Yorkshire won, having taken the greater number of wickets with the scores tied. Requiring an average of 4.45 runs per over, they had paced their reply almost to perfection, and when the scores were level with one ball remaining, Love, winner of the Gold Award, coolly blocked it.

Winning the toss gave Yorkshire the advantage of any moisture in the pitch on a morning of high summer. Jarvis, in his second over, forced it home when Cook played a sharply rising ball to forward short leg, and he then exposed Bailey's weakness against the ball seaming and lifting outside off stump. Nevertheless Bailey and Larkins were splendidly dismissive of everything within range of their strokeplay until, in the 12th over, Larkins aimed to mid-wicket and instead sent the ball looping high to the long-waiting Carrick at cover. Three overs later, Moxon at slip took a tremendous two-handed catch, diving to his right, to cut short Bailey's promise. There were five boundaries in his 26, cracking shots, and Lamb was emulating him before he slashed at another rising delivery and Bairstow, tumbling to his right, held well a catch off the bottom edge. Now Carrick, from the Nursery End, applied further pressure, obtaining slow turn and benefiting from the irregular bounce. Five overs of tight control gave away just six runs; at lunch his figures were 8-2-18-0 and Northamptonshire after 36 overs were 128 for four.

Thereafter, the pitch lost its sting and Capel and Williams put Northamptonshire on the way to the third-highest total in a Benson & Hedges final with some hard, straight hitting against the second-line seamers and quick running against keen Yorkshire fielding. It was good cricket. When Williams, driving, was caught in the 51st over, they had added 120 in 28 overs. Capel, whose 97 was his highest in the competition, was bowled, swinging, in the penultimate over; his innings of 139 minutes and 110 balls contained 11 fours, many from full, flowing drives.

Moxon and Metcalfe gave Yorkshire an assured start, and if Moxon was initially the more enterprising, Metcalfe was soon leaning into his strokes, the ball too fast over the outfield for fieldsmen. Nick Cook made the breakthrough in the 24th over, confusing Moxon with flight as he advanced and bowling him between bat and pad. Three overs later Metcalfe carelessly hoisted a full toss from Williams to deep mid-wicket; Blakey did the same to a long-hop in the off-spinner's next over. The two slow bowlers checked Yorkshire but, 119 for three at tea after 35 overs, they could afford to await the return of Capel, very wayward, and Walker to step up the rate. In seven overs from them, Love and the bustling Bairstow put on 54.

A diving parry to Geoff Cook at cover by Walker in his follow-through led to Bairstow's run-out, but Carrick, bludgeoning Davis past point for four then short-arm hooking him to the square-leg fence, left his side needing ten from the last two overs to level the scores. Yorkshire were 240 for six when Davis began the last over, and if Bailey's shy from mid-on had run out Sidebottom off the fifth ball, one run would still have been needed. Instead, Love, having hit five boundaries, was not required to score from the 93rd delivery he faced and Yorkshire's many and sporting supporters could come forward into the shadows in front of the pavilion to salute their native sons. The days of darkness were behind them.

NORTHAMPTONSHIRE

*G. Cook c Blakey b Jarvis	1
W. Larkins c Carrick b Hartley	15
R. J. Bailey c Moxon b Fletcher	26
A. J. Lamb c Bairstow b Jarvis	28
D. J. Capel b Hartley	97
R. G. Williams c Bairstow b Jarvis	44
D. J. Wild b Jarvis	6
W. W. Davis not out	10
†D. Ripley not out	6
N. G. B. Cook	
A. Walker	
B 2, l-b 3, w 2, n-b 4	11

1-3 2-31 3-48 4-92 5-212   (7 wickets, 55 overs) 244
6-226 7-232

Jarvis 11–2–43–4; Sidebottom 11–1–40–0; Fletcher 11–1–60–1; Hartley 11–0–66–2; Carrick 11–2–30–0.

YORKSHIRE

M. D. Moxon b N. G. B. Cook	45
A. A. Metcalfe c Davis b Williams	47
R. J. Blakey c Davis b Williams	1
K. Sharp b Williams	24
J. D. Love not out	75
†D. L. Bairstow run out (G. Cook/Ripley)	24
*P. Carrick run out (Bailey/G. Cook)	10
A. Sidebottom not out	2
P. J. Hartley	
P. W. Jarvis	
S. D. Fletcher	
B 1, l-b 4, w 4, n-b 7	16

1-97 2-101 3-103 4-160   (6 wickets, 55 overs) 244
5-223 6-235

Davis 11–1–37–0; Walker 11–0–62–0; Capel 11–0–66–0; N. G. B. Cook 11–1–42–1; Williams 11–0–32–3.

Toss won by Yorkshire   UMPIRES H. D. Bird and K. E. Palmer
Man of the Match J. D. Love

Yorkshire v Lancashire
Headingley, July 27, 28, 29, 20, 2001

Yorkshire's first Championship win over Lancashire in six years preserved their 14-point lead at the top of the table with a game in hand. It was achieved through a phenomenal innings by Lehmann, whose 252 was the highest in Roses history, beating Maurice Leyland's 211 not out in 1930 and Graham Lloyd's 225 in the 1997 non-Championship 'friendly'. In 365 minutes, facing 288 balls, he never offered a chance, and at times toyed with the bowling, periods of relative calm being followed by salvos of audacious shots fired off to all parts of the ground.

Lancashire 373 (Crawley 73, Hegg 76, Schofield 55, Scuderi 56)
and 314 (Crawley 113, Martin 51 not out);
Yorkshire 531 (Lehmann 252, Gough 96, Chapple 5-83) **and 158-3** (Wood 51).
Yorkshire won by seven wickets.

Yorkshire v Glamorgan
Scarborough, August 21, 22, 23, 24, 2001

At 12.13 p.m. on the final day, Byas took the catch that returned the Championship title to Yorkshire after 33 years. He also contributed one of three centuries to his side's impregnable total, but – not for the first time in the season – he had refused to be hurried into his declaration by gloomy weather forecasts, preferring to go by his farmer's instincts. Even so, he cut it fine, for heavy rain was setting in as the jubilant winners left the field. Glamorgan, their injury problems exacerbated when Maynard twisted an ankle during a warm-up session, were picked open by Dawson, who bowled Maher round his legs in his first over and went on to a career-best return. Shortly before the first day's close, Wood retired hurt after ducking into a bouncer from Jones – his helmet grille cut into his cheek, requiring six stitches – but on resuming next morning he pulled his second ball from the same bowler for six: after that, he and fellow-opener White exercised complete control for 63 overs in a 243-run stand. Wood struck 18 fours and two sixes; White, who powered on to 183, hit 25 fours and two sixes. When Glamorgan were six down on the third evening, it was decided to fling open the gates on the final morning, although the 5,000 crowd had to watch a spectacular counter-attack by Jones before acclaiming the new champions. Tearing into Lehmann's bowling, he lashed 46 off 14 balls, hitting six sixes and two fours before slicing to backward point where Byas, having dashed from slip, held the catch that sent the champagne corks popping.

Glamorgan 223 (Dale 59, Dawson 6-82) **and 245**;
Yorkshire 580-9 dec (White 183, Wood 124, Byas 104).
Yorkshire won by an innings and 112 runs

Yorkshire v Nottinghamshire
Scarborough, August 26, 2001

Lehmann's 191, the highest for Yorkshire in a one-day match, helped Yorkshire to their best limited over score. An astonishing array of shots produced his runs off 103 balls, with 20 fours and 11 sixes coming in a 116-minute stay that included an eight-minute stoppage when an ambulance drove on to the field to attend to a spectator. Lehmann's

50 came off 38 balls, his 100 off 67 and his 150 off 86. A full house saw the ball disappear out of the ground three times. Only Surrey's Alistair Brown, with 203 against Hampshire at Guildford in 1997, had hit a higher league score. Lehmann then held a catch and took two wickets as Nottinghamshire fell for 173.

Yorkshire 352-6, 45 overs (Lehmann 191); **Nottinghamshire 173, 43.3 overs** (Bicknell 50). Yorkshire won by 179 runs.

C&G Trophy Final: Somerset v Yorkshire
Lord's, August 31, 2002, by Tim de Lisle

A close encounter between two teams having a nightmare in the Championship was decided by the one man on the field who had not spent months worrying about relegation. When he strode out to bat in a mini-crisis. Matthew Elliott had been a Yorkshire player for two and a half weeks and had not even followed this year's C&G, let alone played in it. After a watchful start, he rediscovered the booming strokeplay that had rung out in the Lord's Test of 1997. He reminded a capacity crowd why the Australian selectors had once preferred him to Matthew Hayden, and played out a trailer for the Ashes by singling out Caddick for rough treatment. Caddick went wicketless for the third time in four Lord's finals, and the only sign of a cutting edge came in a spell of big-hearted swing from his new ball partner, Johnson. Somerset, fielding the eleven that had won the cup the year before, were comfortably beaten, and Yorkshire lifted their first Lord's trophy in 15 years.

Spectators had an interesting day rather than a gripping one. On a low, slow, dusty pitch, runs had to be chiselled out, and most of the bowlers tried cutters and slower balls. The match featured nine men who had played for England in the past two years and it began as a duel between two of them – Trescothick, returning hastily after a broken thumb, and Hoggard. When a Hoggard over went for 20, including four off a free-hit, Trescothick was well on top, even though the big shots left him wincing with pain. But he was lured into a loose drive and his England opening partner, Vaughan, hurled himself to his right at short extra to hold on to a scintillating catch.

Bowler and Cox made sure the momentum wasn't lost, and Somerset chugged along at a curiously steady five an over for the rest of the innings. Although England's new one-day biffer, Blackwell, flopped, Parsons and Dutch hustled them to a total that was maybe 20 above par. Blakey, standing in for the absent Lehmann, had shuffled his bowlers shrewdly, Silverwood hit the bat hard, McGrath was frugal and Hoggard, characteristically, was both the most expensive bowler on either side and the most incisive.

Johnson steamed in from the Pavilion End and removed the dangerous White, playing as a batsman, as well as Wood and the pinch-hitter (or not, in this case) Silverwood. Johnson took his sweater with superb figures of three for 20 from seven overs, but then came Elliott. The difference between him and everybody else was simple: he had the power and precision to beat the deep fielders – 16 times, ten more than the next man (Bowler) on a day of twos and threes. The other batsmen had only to keep him company and look for singles. Vaughan saw this and reverted to his sober mode (56 balls, no fours) before the more combative McGrath completed a fine all-round performance. Elliott's hundred was the first by an overseas player in the final of this competition since Viv Richards in 1979, and he finished with 128 off 125 balls, while his English colleagues managed 108 off 164 between them. In Australia, Elliott had acquired a reputation as an awkward character; at Yorkshire, this meant he fitted in perfectly.

SOMERSET

P. D. Bowler c Blakey b Hoggard	67
M. E. Trescothick c Vaughan b Hoggard	27
*J. Cox lbw b McGrath	34
M. Burns lbw b Hoggard	21
I. D. Blackwell b Sidebottom	12
K. A. Parsons c Sidebottom b Hoggard	41
†R. J. Turner c White b Sidebottom	20
R. L. Johnson b Hoggard	2
K. P. Dutch not out	13
A. R. Caddick not out	0
P. S. Jones	
B 1, l-b 6, w 6, n-b 6	19

1-41 2-122 3-159 4-171 (8 wickets, 50 overs) 256
5-191 6-230 7-233 8-250

Silverwood 8–1–30–0; Hoggard 10–0–65–5; Sidebottom 9–0–49–2; McGrath 9–0–37–1; Dawson 10–0–48–0; Vaughan 4–0–20–0.

YORKSHIRE

C. White c Turner b Johnson	12
M. J. Wood b Johnson	19
C. E. W. Silverwood b Johnson	0
M. T. G. Elliott not out	128
M. P. Vaughan lbw b Jones	31
A. McGrath not out	46
G. M. Fellows	
*†R. J. Blakey	
R. K. J. Dawson	
R. J. Sidebottom	
M. J. Hoggard	
L-b 7, w 15, n-b 2	24

1-19 2-19 3-64 4-157 (4 wickets, 48 overs) 260

Caddick 9–0–53–0; Johnson 10–2–51–3; Parsons 6–0–31–0; Jones 9–0–45–1; Dutch 8–0–43–0; Blackwell 6–0–30–0.

Toss won by Somerset

Umpires J. W. Holder and G. Sharp
Man of the Match M. T. G. Elliott

Leicestershire v Yorkshire
Leicester, May 11, 12, 13, 14, 2005

Leicestershire were sitting comfortably at lunch on the third day, when they declared to set a stiff target of 404. By the close, however, Yorkshire had assumed control, taking heavy toll of some ill-disciplined bowling on a windy afternoon – so much so that they needed only 30 overs on the final day (and 96.1 in all) to complete a remarkable turnaround, and with it their highest successful run-chase in first-class cricket, beating 331 against Middlesex at Lord's in 1910, and indeed their highest-ever fourth innings. McGrath finished unbeaten with a superb 165; England captain Vaughan, making a rare domestic appearance, helped with an attractive 53. Earlier, Yorkshire had been on the ropes. Leicestershire's first innings, dominated by a gritty knock from Ackerman, was hardly massive, but Yorkshire were hustled out for just 151 in reply, with Gibson's six wickets including McGrath first ball. Mongia and Nixon extended the lead, but Leicestershire's bowlers were unable to match their batsmen's efforts. This was the 21st time a team had successfully chased 400 in the Championship, and the 13th instance since 1990.

Leicestershire 278 (Ackerman 85 not out, Maddy 53)
and 276-9 dec (Mongia 70, Nixon 68); **Yorkshire 151** (Dawood 62 not out;
Gibson 6-56) **and 406-4** McGrath 165 not out, Vaughan 53).
Yorkshire won by six wickets

Yorkshire v Durham
Headingley, September 20, 21, 22, 23, 2006

The draw enabled both teams to escape relegation by a whisker. Yorkshire amassed 677, with Lehmann, on his final appearance for them, extending his 80th first-class century (26th for Yorkshire) to his second triple. On the first day, Yorkshire had expressed their gratitude by handing him a silver county cap, but he was saving the best till last. He was out two short of George Hirst's county-best 341 at Leicester in 1905 – and his fourth-wicket stand of 358 with Lumb did set a record, beating the 330 by Matthew Wood and Damien Martyn against Gloucestershire at Headingley in 2003. Lehmann's only chance came at 202, when he was dropped by Benkenstein at backward point, and, when Wiseman finally bowled him, he had batted for 482 minutes, and hit 52 fours and three sixes from 403 balls.

Yorkshire 677-7 dec (Lehmann 339, Lumb 98, McGrath 62, Guy 52 not out);
Durham 518 (Benkenstein 151, Gibson 155, Scott 77, Park 77)
and 181-3 dec (Park 100 not out). Match drawn.

Somerset v Yorkshire
Taunton, June 30, July 1, 2, 3, 2009

Nothing is more demanding for a visiting captain to Taunton, with its notoriously flat pitch, than calculating when to risk a final-day declaration. McGrath got it slightly wrong, but it was not so much to do with his arithmetic as the aggressive brilliance of the Somerset batsmen. Set 476, they carved and clubbed in a style that was always more transfixing than mere slogging. In the end it was a team conquest, and in particularly a daring, dazzling triumph for Trego, whose hundred came from 54 balls. He called it the best innings of his life and surely no one would disagree. It was the second highest successful chase in a Championship match and the biggest since 1925. The finish deserved a larger crowd. One could only sympathise with Hoggard who, despite his eight hard-earned wickets, finished on the losing side after Yorkshire looked poised for their first win in a year.

Yorkshire 438 (Rudolph 191) **and 363-5 dec** (Sayers 152, Lythe 71, Bairstow 66 not out); **Somerset 326** (Trescothick 146, Hoggard 5-82) **and 479-6** (Suppiah 131, Trego 103 not out, Trescothick 96). Somerset won by four wickets.

Honours Board

County Champions
1896, 1898, 1900, 1901, 1902, 1905, 1908, 1912, 1919, 1922, 1923, 1924, 1925, 1931, 1932, 1933, 1935, 1937, 1938, 1939, 1946, 1959, 1960, 1962, 1963, 1966, 1967, 1968, 2001

Joint County Champions
1949

Gillette Cup Winners
1965, 1969

C&G Trophy Winners
2002

Benson & Hedges Cup Winners
1987

John Player League Winners
1983

Note: *Wisden* records but does not recognise the 'unofficial' County Championships which Yorkshire 'won' in 1867 and 1870, or their joint Championship in 1869.

Yorkshire's *Wisden* Cricketers of the Year

1889: R. Peel
1890: L. Hall
1894: F. S Jackson, E. Wainwright
1895: J. T. Brown
1899: W. Rhodes
1901: S. Haigh, G. H. Hirst, T. L. Taylor, J. Tunnicliffe
1902: F. Mitchell
1906: D. Denton
1909: Lord Hawke, J. T. Newstead
1914: M. W. Booth
1920: P. Holmes, H. Sutcliffe
1924: R. Kilner, G. G. Macaulay
1929: M. Leyland
1932: W. E. Bowes, H. Verity
1938: L. Hutton
1939: A. Wood
1940: A. B. Sellers
1948: N. W. D. Yardley
1952: R. Appleyard
1953: F. S. Trueman
1954: J. H. Wardle, W. Watson
1960: R. Illingworth
1961: J. V. Wilson
1963: P. J. Sharpe
1964: D. B. Close
1965: G. Boycott
1969: J. G. Binks
1979: C. M. Old
1993: M. D. Moxon
1999: D. Gough
2001: D. S. Lehmann
2003: M. P. Vaughan
2006: M. J. Hoggard

Yorkshire records

FIRST-CLASS YORKSHIRE RECORDS

Figures correct up to 31/3/11. They include figures from five matches whose first-class status is disputed: the 1878 match v Scotland is considered first class by Yorkshire CCC but not by the ACS; and the four matches v Liverpool and District in 1889, 1891, 1892 and 1893 are considered first-class by the ACS but not by Yorkshire CCC. We have adhered to *Wisden's* guidelines and included them here.

MOST APPEARANCES IN CAREER

W. Rhodes	1898-1930	883
G. H. Hirst.	1891-1929	717
D. Denton	1894-1920	677
H. Sutcliffe	1919-1945	602
M. Leyland	1920-1946	548
D. B. Close.	1949-1970	536
D. Hunter	1888-1909	517
S. Haigh.	1895-1913	513
Lord Hawke	1881-1911	510
R. Illingworth	1951-1983	496

MOST RUNS IN A CAREER

	Career	Runs	Inns	NO	HS	100s	Avge
H. Sutcliffe	1919-1945	38,558	864	96	313	112	50.20
D. Denton	1894-1920	33,282	1,058	61	221	61	33.38
G. Boycott	1962-1986	32,570	674	111	260*	103	57.85
G. H. Hirst	1891-1929	32,017	1,050	128	341	56	34.72
W. Rhodes	1898-1930	31,098	1,196	161	267*	46	30.04
P. Holmes	1913-1933	26,220	699	74	315*	60	41.95
M. Leyland	1920-1946	26,181	720	82	263	62	41.03
L. Hutton	1934-1955	24,807	527	62	280*	85	53.34
D. B. Close	1949-1970	22,650	811	102	198	33	31.94
J. H. Hampshire	1961-1981	21,979	724	89	183*	34	34.61

MOST WICKETS IN A CAREER

	Career	Wkts	Runs	Avge
W. Rhodes	1898-1930	3,597	57,634	16.02
G. H. Hirst	1891-1929	2,476	44,600	18.01
S. Haigh	1895-1913	1,876	29,289	15.61
G. G. Macaulay.	1920-1935	1,774	30,555	17.22
F. S. Trueman	1949-1968	1,745	29,890	17.12
H. Verity	1930-1939	1,558	21,353	13.70
J. H. Wardle	1946-1958	1,539	27,917	18.13
R. Illingworth	1952-1983	1,431	26,806	18.73
W. E. Bowes	1929-1947	1,351	21,227	15.71
R. Peel	1882-1897	1,311	20,638	15.74

HIGHEST INDIVIDUAL SCORES

341	G. H. Hirst	Yorkshire v Leicestershire at Leicester	1905
339	D. S. Lehmann	Yorkshire v Durham at Leeds	2006
315*	P. Holmes	Yorkshire v Middlesex at Lord's	1925
313	H. Sutcliffe	Yorkshire v Essex at Leyton	1932
311	J. T. Brown	Yorkshire v Sussex at Sheffield	1897
302*	P. Holmes	Yorkshire v Hampshire at Portsmouth	1920
300	J. T. Brown	Yorkshire v Derbyshire at Chesterfield	1898
285	P. Holmes	Yorkshire v Nottinghamshire at Nottingham	1929
280*	L. Hutton	Yorkshire v Hampshire at Sheffield	1939
277*	P. Holmes	Yorkshire v Northamptonshire at Harrogate	1921

BEST BOWLING IN AN INNINGS

10-10	H. Verity	Yorkshire v Nottinghamshire at Leeds	1932
10-35	A. Drake	Yorkshire v Somerset at Weston-super-Mare	1914
10-36	H. Verity	Yorkshire v Warwickshire at Leeds	1931
10-47	T. F. Smailes	Yorkshire v Derbyshire at Sheffield	1939
9-12	H. Verity	Yorkshire v Kent at Sheffield	1936

BEST BOWLING IN A MATCH

17-91	H. Verity	Yorkshire v Essex at Leyton	1933
16-35	W. E. Bowes	Yorkshire v Northamptonshire at Kettering	1935
16-38	T. Emmett	Yorkshire v Cambridgeshire at Hunslet	1869
16-112	J. H. Wardle	Yorkshire v Sussex at Hull	1954
15-38	H. Verity	Yorkshire v Kent at Sheffield	1936

HIGHEST WICKET PARTNERSHIPS

First Wicket
555   P. Holmes and H. Sutcliffe, Yorkshire v Essex at Leyton 1932
Second Wicket
346   W. Barber and M. Leyland, Yorkshire v Middlesex at Sheffield 1932
Third Wicket
346   J. J. Sayers and A. McGrath, Yorkshire v Warwickshire at Birmingham 2009
Fourth Wicket
358   D. S. Lehmann and M. J. Lumb, Yorkshire v Durham at Leeds 2006
Fifth Wicket
340   E. Wainwright and G. H. Hirst, Yorkshire v Surrey at The Oval 1899
Sixth Wicket
276   M. Leyland and E. Robinson, Yorkshire v Glamorgan at Swansea 1926
Seventh Wicket
254   W. Rhodes and D. C. F. Burton, Yorkshire v Hampshire at Dewsbury 1919
Eighth Wicket
292   R. Peel and Lord Hawke, Yorkshire v Warwickshire at Birmingham 1896
Ninth Wicket
246   T. T. Bresnan and J. N. Gillespie, Yorkshire v Surrey at The Oval 2007
Tenth Wicket
149   G. Boycott and G. B. Stevenson, Yorkshire v Warwickshire at Birmingham 1982

MOST CATCHES IN A CAREER

		Career	Mts
J. Tunnicliffe	665	1891-1907	472
W. Rhodes	587	1898-1930	883
D. B. Close	564	1949-1970	536
P. J. Sharpe	526	1958-1974	411
J. V. Wilson	521	1946-1962	477

MOST DISMISSALS IN A CAREER

		Career	Mts	Ct	St
D. Hunter	1,190	1888-1909	517	863	327
J. G. Binks	1,044	1955-1969	491	872	172
D. L. Bairstow	1,035	1970-1990	429	905	130
A. Wood	854	1927-1946	408	612	242
A. Dolphin	829	1905-1927	427	570	259

HIGHEST INNINGS TOTALS

For Yorkshire

887	Yorkshire v Warwickshire at Birmingham	1896
704	Yorkshire v Surrey at The Oval	1899
681-5 dec	Yorkshire v Sussex at Sheffield	1897
677-7 dec	Yorkshire v Durham at Leeds	2006
673-8 dec	Yorkshire v Northamptonshire at Leeds	2003

Against Yorkshire

681-7 dec	Leicestershire v Yorkshire at Bradford	1996
630	Somerset v Yorkshire at Leeds	1901
622-8 dec	Essex v Yorkshire at Leeds	2005
601-9 dec	Warwickshire v Yorkshire at Birmingham	2002
597-8 dec	Sussex v Yorkshire at Hove	2007

LOWEST INNINGS TOTALS

For Yorkshire

23	Yorkshire v Hampshire at Middlesbrough	1965
26	Yorkshire v Surrey at The Oval	1909
30	Yorkshire v Kent at Sheffield	1865
31	Yorkshire v Essex at Huddersfield	1935
32	Yorkshire v Nottinghamshire at Sheffield	1876

Against Yorkshire

13	Nottinghamshire v Yorkshire at Nottingham	1901
15#	Northamptonshire v Yorkshire at Northampton	1908
20	Sussex v Yorkshire at Hull	1922
20	Derbyshire v Yorkshire at Sheffield	1939
23	Australians v Yorkshire at Leeds	1902
23#	Derbyshire v Yorkshire at Hull	1921

 # One or more players absent

LARGE MARGIN OF VICTORY

For Yorkshire

Yorkshire (548-4 dec) beat Northamptonshire (58 and 93) at Harrogate 1921 by an innings and 397 runs
Yorkshire (662) beat Derbyshire (118 and 157) at Chesterfield 1898 by an innings and 387 runs
Yorkshire (368 and 280-1 dec) beat Somerset (125 and 134) at Bath 1906 by 389 runs
Yorkshire (194 and 274) beat Hampshire (62 and 36) at Leeds 1904 by 370 runs

Against Yorkshire

Surrey (536) beat Yorkshire (78 and 186) at The Oval 1898 by an innings and 272 runs
Sussex (597-8 dec) beat Yorkshire (247 and 89) at Hove 2007 by an innings and 261 runs
Gloucestershire (291 and 484) beat Yorkshire (247 and 204) at Cheltenham 1994 by 324 runs
Cambridge University (312 and 163) beat Yorkshire (119 and 51) at Cambridge 1906 by 305 runs

TIED MATCHES

Yorkshire (351-4 dec and 113) v Leicestershire (328 and 136) at Huddersfield 1954
Middlesex (102 and 211) v Yorkshire (106-9 dec and 207) at Bradford 1973

FOUR WICKETS IN FOUR BALLS

A. Drake	Yorkshire v Derbyshire at Chesterfield	1914

HAT-TRICKS

A. Hill	Yorkshire v United South of England Eleven at Bradford	1874
A. Hill	Yorkshire v Surrey at The Oval	1880
G. Ulyett	Yorkshire v Lancashire at Sheffield	1883
S. Haigh	Yorkshire v Somerset at Sheffield	1902
H. A. Sedgwick	Yorkshire v Worcestershire at Hull	1906
G. Deyes	Yorkshire v Ireland at Bray	1907
M. W. Booth	Yorkshire v Worcestershire at Bradford	1911
A. Drake	Yorkshire v Essex at Huddersfield	1912
M. W. Booth	Yorkshire v Essex at Leyton	1912
A. Drake	Yorkshire v Derbyshire at Chesterfield	1914
W. Rhodes	Yorkshire v Derbyshire at Derby	1920
A. Waddington	Yorkshire v Northamptonshire at Northampton	1920
G. G. Macaulay	Yorkshire v Warwickshire at Birmingham	1923
E. Robinson	Yorkshire v Sussex at Hull	1928
E. Robinson	Yorkshire v Kent at Gravesend	1930
H. Verity	Yorkshire v Nottinghamshire at Leeds	1932
H. Fisher	Yorkshire v Somerset at Sheffield	1932
G. G. Macaulay	Yorkshire v Glamorgan at Cardiff	1933
E. P. Robinson	Yorkshire v Kent at Leeds	1939
A. Coxon	Yorkshire v Worcestershire at Leeds	1946
F. S. Trueman	Yorkshire v Nottinghamshire at Nottingham	1951
R. Appleyard	Yorkshire v Gloucestershire at Sheffield	1956
D. Wilson	Yorkshire v Nottinghamshire at Middlesbrough	1959
D. Wilson	Yorkshire v Nottinghamshire at Worksop	1966
D. Wilson	Yorkshire v Kent at Harrogate	1966
A. L. Robinson	Yorkshire v Nottinghamshire at Worksop	1974
P. J. Hartley	Yorkshire v Derbyshire at Chesterfield	1995
D. Gough	Yorkshire v Kent at Leeds	1995
C. White	Yorkshire v Gloucestershire at Gloucester	1998
M. J. Hoggard	Yorkshire v Sussex at Hove	2009

MOST HUNDREDS IN A CAREER

H. Sutcliffe	1919-1945	112
G. Boycott	1962-1986	103
L. Hutton	1934-1955	85
M. Leyland	1920-1946	62
D. Denton	1894-1920	61

MOST RUNS IN A SEASON

	Year	Runs	I	NO	HS	100s	Avge
H. Sutcliffe	1932	2,883	41	5	313	12	80.08
L. Hutton	1949	2,640	44	6	269*	9	69.47
L. Hutton	1937	2,448	45	6	271*	8	62.76
H. Sutcliffe	1928	2,418	35	5	228	11	80.60
P. Holmes	1925	2,351	49	9	315*	6	58.77
H. Sutcliffe	1931	2,351	33	8	230	9	94.04

MOST WICKETS IN A SEASON

	Year	Wkts	Runs	Avge
W. Rhodes	1900	240	3,054	12.72
W. Rhodes	1901	233	3,497	15.00
G. H. Hirst	1906	201	3,089	15.36
R. Appleyard	1951	200	2,829	14.14
G. G. Macaulay	1925	200	2,986	14.93

LIST A YORKSHIRE RECORDS

Figures correct up to 31/3/2011. List A records do not include figures from Twenty20 matches.

MOST APPEARANCES IN A CAREER

D. L. Bairstow	1970-1990	403
R. J. Blakey	1986-2004	373
D. Byas	1985-2001	313
P. Carrick	1970-1992	304
C. White	1990-2008	292
A. McGrath	1995-2010	267
G. Boycott	1963-1986	264
M. D. Moxon	1980-1997	237
J. H. Hampshire	1963-1981	234
C. M. Old	1967-1982	221

MOST RUNS IN A CAREER

	Career	Runs	I	NO	HS	100s	Avge
G. Boycott	1963-1986	8,699	255	38	146	7	40.08
D. Byas	1985-2001	7,782	301	35	116*	5	29.25
M. D. Moxon	1980-1997	7,380	229	21	141*	7	35.48
R. J. Blakey	1986-2004	7,361	319	84	130*	3	31.32
A. McGrath	1995-2010	7,118	247	38	148	7	34.05
C. White	1990-2008	6,384	266	39	148	5	28.12
J. H. Hampshire	1963-1981	6,296	223	24	119	7	31.63
A. A. Metcalfe	1982-1995	5,584	189	15	127*	4	32.09
D. S. Lehmann	1997-2006	5,229	126	20	191	8	49.33
D. L. Bairstow	1970-1990	5,180	317	71	103*	1	21.05

MOST WICKETS IN A CAREER

	Career	Wkts	Runs	Avge
C. M. Old	1967-1982	308	5,841	18.96
D. Gough	1990-2008	291	6,796	23.35
G. B. Stevenson	1973-1986	290	6,820	23.51
P. J. Hartley	1985-1997	283	7,476	26.41
A. Sidebottom	1974-1991	260	6,918	26.60
C. White	1990-2007	248	6,120	24.67
P. Carrick	1970-1992	236	7,408	31.38
C. E. W. Silverwood	1993-2004	224	5,212	23.26
P. W. Jarvis	1981-1993	213	4,684	21.99
H. P. Cooper	1971-1980	177	4,184	23.63

HIGHEST INDIVIDUAL SCORES

191	D. S. Lehmann	Yorkshire v Nottinghamshire at Scarborough	2001
160	M. J. Wood	Yorkshire v Devon at Exmouth	2004
148	A. McGrath	Yorkshire v Somerset at Taunton	2006
148	C. White	Yorkshire v Leicestershire at Leicester	1997
146	G. Boycott	Yorkshire v Surrey at Lord's	1965

BEST BOWLING IN AN INNINGS

7-15	R. A. Hutton	Yorkshire v Worcestershire at Leeds..................................	1969
7-27	D. Gough	Yorkshire v Ireland at Leeds	1997
6-14	H. P. Cooper	Yorkshire v Worcestershire at Worcester	1975
6-15	F. S. Trueman	Yorkshire v Somerset at Taunton	1965
6-18	D. Wilson	Yorkshire v Kent at Canterbury	1969

HAT-TRICKS

P. W. Jarvis	Yorkshire v Derbyshire at Derby..	1982
D. Gough	Yorkshire v Ireland at Leeds	1997
D. Gough	Yorkshire v Lancashire at Leeds	1998
C. White	Yorkshire v Kent at Leeds	2000

MOST HUNDREDS IN A CAREER

D. S. Lehmann	1997-2006	8
J. A. Rudolph.........	2007-2010	8
G. Boycott	1963-1986	7
J. H. Hampshire	1963-1981	7
A. McGrath	1995-2010	7
M. D. Moxon	1980-1997	7

Author's note and acknowledgements

There's no option but to repeat myself. In a previous book – called *A Last English Summer* – I quoted what Winston Churchill once said of the Balkans: 'They have more history than they can consume.' I added that the same applied to Yorkshire CCC. I can emphasise the proof of it with one fact. The first, albeit rough, draft of this book ran to more than 150,000 words. The publishers originally asked for 80,000. In the end, through skilful design and the generosity of everyone at A & C Black, we compromised on almost 120,000. We made a decision to concentrate almost exclusively on Yorkshire's matches and players, which omitted most Tests (other than those against Australia). Criteria for inclusion were simply good writing and historical impact; and especially a combination of the two.

Like the rest of us, *Wisden* isn't infallible and so there are pieces that didn't make the cut purely because the writing was dull or stiff. Foremost among them is Yorkshire's victory over the Australians at Sheffield in 1968. Fred Trueman captained the county and regarded beating the tourists as one of the finest moments of his career. Unfortunately – and very bafflingly – the report of roughly 125 words does not mention a single player on either side. The 1901 match against Somerset – one of *Wisden's* matches of the century – is similarly omitted because the report fails to convey the full drama of the game. I hope, however, that almost everything else you'd expect from a book of this type and parameter is found within its pages.

As I know I'm going to be asked this question, I'll answer it now. I think Michael Parkinson's tender and beautifully written tribute to Fred Trueman on page 26 is the best thing in the book.

I am in the profound debt of *Wisden's* Christopher Lane, who asked me to put it together (fittingly at a *Wisden* dinner). I'm also grateful to Alan Bennett, who responded so generously when I asked about the genesis of the 'Nobbut a game' scene in *A Day Out* (see page 3), and to those *Wisden* editors and contributors who have been so supportive in allowing pieces to be reprinted: Trevor Bailey, John Callaghan, Alan Lee, Tim de Lisle, Matthew Engel, Keith Farnsworth, Lord Roy Hattersley, Michael Henderson, Jim Holden, David Hopps, Tony Lewis, Graeme Wright and John Woodcock. A special mention goes to David Warner my proofreader and Derek Hodgson, who know more about Yorkshire cricket than Gibbon ever did about the Roman Empire. William Roberts – from whom I buy so many cricket books – was helpful too.

I thank my agent Grainne Fox and the editorial team at A & C Black for their expertise, advice and unfailing good humour. It's been a pleasure to work with:

Becky Senior, Charlotte Atyeo, James Watson, Jocelyn Lucas, Julian Flanders and Kate Turvey.

Lastly, it is no exaggeration to say that *Wisden on Yorkshire* – like everything else I've worked on – would never have appeared without the patience, tolerance and forbearance of my wife Mandy. How on earth she ever puts up with me is one of the small unfathomable mysteries of the modern world.

Long may I continue to be baffled by it …

Duncan Hamilton, 2011

Index

ALSO AVAILABLE FROM WISDEN

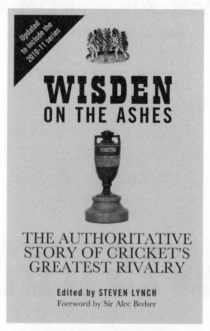

ISBN 978-1-4081-5239-3

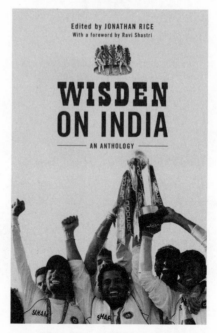

ISBN 978-1-4081-2674-5

ALSO AVAILABLE FROM WISDEN
www.wisden.com

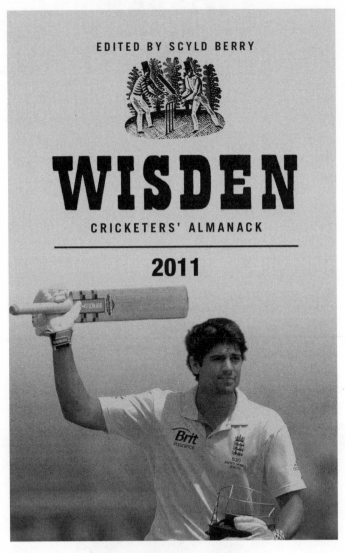

EDITED BY SCYLD BERRY

WISDEN

CRICKETERS' ALMANACK

2011

ISBN 978-1-4081-3130-5

ALSO AVAILABLE FROM WISDEN

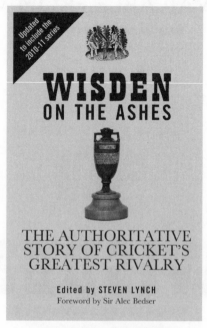

ISBN 978-1-4081-5239-3

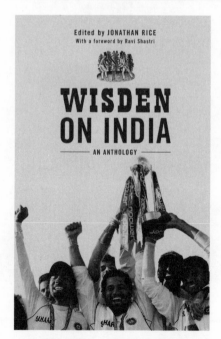

ISBN 978-1-4081-2674-5

ALSO AVAILABLE FROM WISDEN

ISBN 978-1-4081-2756-8

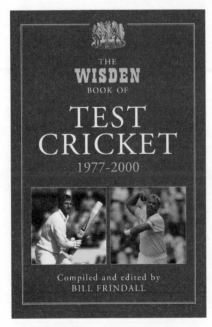

ISBN 978-1-4081-2758-2

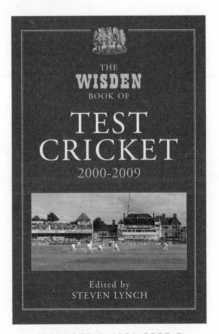

ISBN 978-1-4081-2335-5

ALSO AVAILABLE FROM WISDEN

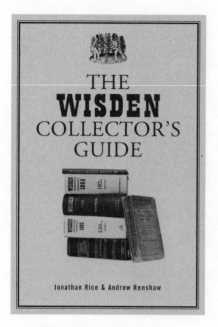

ISBN 978-1-4081-2673-8

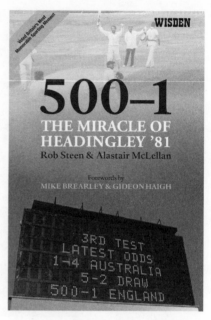

ISBN 978-1-4081-4085-7

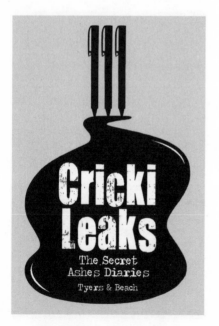

ISBN 978-1-4081-5240-9

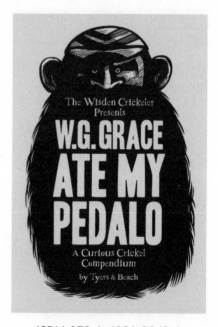

ISBN 978-1-4081-3042-1